Mourning, Spirituality and Change

In her earlier books on well-known writers and artists, Dr Susan Kavaler-Adler (PhD., ABPP) identified healthy mourning for traumas and life changes as an essential aspect of successful analysis. She drew distinctions between a healthy acceptance of mourning as part of development and pathological mourning, which 'fixes' individuals at an unhealthy stage of development.

In *Mourning, Spirituality and Psychic Change* Dr Kavaler-Adler brings such distinctions into the consulting room, exploring how a successful analyst can help patients to utilize mourning for past traumas to move them forward to a lasting change for the better, emotionally, psychically and erotically. She gives an historical perspective on how mourning has been either explicit or implicit in psychoanalytic theory since Freud, and tackles the controversial issue of spirituality in psychoanalysis. Dr Kavaler-Adler explores how psychoanalysis can help people come to terms with difficult issues in a time of great psychic and spiritual disturbance.

Illustrated by richly detailed clinical cases *Mourning, Spirituality and Psychic Change* offers a comprehensive view of psychic transformation, facilitated through psychotherapeutic treatment, which will be of great interest to all psychoanalysts.

Dr Susan Kavaler-Adler, a psychologist-psychoanalyst for twenty-eight years, is the Executive Director of the Object Relations Institute for Psychotherapy and Psychoanalysis. She is the author of more than forty articles, and two books, including *The Creative Mystique* (Routledge, 1996).

Her website is www.kavaler adler.com

Mourning, Spirituality and Psychic Change

A new object relations view of psychoanalysis

Susan Kavaler-Adler, Ph.D., ABPP

Routledge
Taylor & Francis Group

LONDON AND NEW YORK

First published 2003 by Brunner-Routledge

This edition published 2012 by Routledge
2 Park Square, Milton Park, Abingdon, Oxfordshire OX14 4RN
711 Third Avenue, New York, NY 10017

Routledge is an imprint of the Taylor & Francis Group, an informa business

© 2003 Susan Kavaler-Adler

Typeset in Times by Regent Typesetting, London

Paperback cover design by Jim Wilkie

British Library Cataloguing in Publication Data
A catalogue record for this book is available from the British
Library

Library of Congress Cataloging in Publication Data

Kavaler-Adler, Susan.
    Mourning, spirituality, and psychic change: a new object relations
view of psychoanalysis / by Susan Kavaler-Adler.
        p. cm.
    Includes bibliographical references.
        ISBN 1-58391-293-2 (hbk) – ISBN 1-58391-294-0 (pbk.)
    1. Loss (Psychology)–Case studies. 2. Grief therapy–Case studies. 3.
Bereavement–Psychological aspects–Case studies. 4. Psychoanalysis.
I. Title.

RC455.4.L67K393 2003
155.9'37–dc21
                                                2003001041

ISBN 1-58391-293-2 (hbk)
ISBN 1-58391-294-0 (pbk)

Contents

Dedications

This book is dedicated to:

My analysands who have been generous enough to let me use their treatment processes to illustrate the healing of developmental mourning within an object relations psychoanalysis and psychotherapeutic process.

My analysands who have so inspired me to pursue the in-depth study and practice of "developmental mourning."

My analysands for speaking so clearly in their own individual voices in the pages of this book, as the mourning process allowed their articulate self-reflection to emerge.

Dr. Joyce McDougall for her offer to do the foreword for the book.

The candidates at the Object Relations Institute who have inspired me with their thoughts, questions, and comments.

My husband, Saul Adler, for his deep love and generous support in all my endeavors.

My father, Solomon Weiss, who first inspired and applauded my creativity and to my mother, Alice Weiss, who supported it.

Preface

The study of mourning as a life long journey of connecting, internalizing, and letting go of external others, while integrating the symbolic meaning of the relationship with these others in the internal world has pervaded my study of psychoanalytic theory and clinical practice. The profound impact of the mourning process has been with me since my early twenties when I began mourning the death of my father, whom I lost when I was ten years old. Although my own mourning process began with a bereavement, I have come to discover the day in and day out impact of object loss upon all our daily lives.

Therefore, I have found mourning related to separation individuation, object disappointment, and to the mourning of existential grief, guilt, and limits to all, to be avenues to psychic growth and to psychic integration and wholeness. Melanie Klein has been my theoretical mother in the pursuit of the journey and discovery as she was the first to intuit how mourning process was a critical clinical and developmental process, following Sigmund Freud's profound paper on mourning, "Mourning and Melancholia," in 1917.

I have seen how the capacity to engage in and practice this critical clinical and developmental mourning process affects us throughout our lives. Those who mourn continue to grow and those who cannot mourn become stuck in repetitive childhood enactments that sabotage and arrest their lives. I now work in many clinical modalities to help people continue their life-long development through the experience and practice of mourning. This book speaks about the in-depth mourning process in psychoanalytic treatment. However, in addition to psychoanalysis, I practice individual psychotherapy, couples therapy, and group therapy in ways that highlight, embrace, and promote the capacity to mourn. I lead an intensive mourning group and a writing group that tune into and support the full evolution of the mourning and life long growth process.

In all of my work, I have pursued themes of mourning as a developmental growth process and specify the developmental and psychodynamic issues that inhibit such mourning. I have written about blocks to mourning and about the state of developmental arrest seen in a pathological mourning state, which for women artists and writers I have described as a "demon lover complex," (Kavaler-Adler, 1993, 1996, 2000). All my teaching at psychoanalytic institutes, including the continuing teaching and supervision I do at the institute where I am the director, The Object Relations Institute for Psychotherapy and Psychoanalysis, reflects my understanding of mourning as a developmental process. When I teach about psychoanalysis I teach about the interaction of transference interpretation and mourning process. When I teach about the characterological defenses in the personality disorders I teach about how the gradual relinquishing of such defenses allows for the tolerance of "abandonment depression" (Masterson, 1979, 1981) affect states that can lead to the tolerance of the grief of loss within a developmental mourning process.

Foreword

Dr. Joyce McDougall

Mourning, Spirituality and Psychic Change: A New Object Relations View of Psychoanalysis is an adventure into the intricacies, dialectics, and developmental sequences in critical psychic change, observed in vivo in the clinical situation. We frequently hear the patient's voice, facilitating a much needed integration of the various kinds, modes, and levels of mourning that need to be navigated in order to achieve self-integration and to sustain growth in love and creativity.

The capacity to tolerate loss is an important developmental issue and one that Dr. Susan Kavaler-Adler discusses in terms of object relations in both the internal and the external worlds. She demonstrates, with great sensitivity, the extent to which the capacity to feel the grief of object loss is the key object relations dynamic behind progressive changes in psychic structure – whereas the intolerance of such capacity is a primal cause of developmental arrests and of numerous psychopathological blockages in the personality.

In pursuing this theme, Dr. Kavaler-Adler further demonstrates how the grief of object loss is frequently combined with the grief of regret related to hurting a loved one, as well as to compulsive and tenacious patterns of self-sabotage. She also demonstrates the interaction of transference and the facilitation of the mourning process through both the therapist's capacity to "hold" the patient and through interpretation.

Dr. Kavaler-Adler presents two major studies that highlight the analysis of an erotic transference, one with a homosexual woman, and one with a man. She also demonstrates the developmental use of the idealizing transferences and how it can lead to homoerotic, spiritual, sexual, and aggressive modes of experience. Dialogues with well-known object relations theorists add an ongoing texture and background to the clinical vignettes as Dr. Kavaler-Adler employs and illustrates theoretical concepts from Melanie Klein, Ronald Fairbairn, Donald Winnicott, Michael Balint, James Masterson, and Otto Kernberg, as well as Margaret Mahler, Jeffrey Seinfeld, and John Bowlby.

By taking the theme of mourning as a paradigm for the expanding concepts relative to mental health, as promoted by psychotherapy and psychoanalysis, Dr. Kavaler-Adler is able to interweave clinical phenomena that have formerly been restricted to segregated categories. She links the abandonment and depressive mourning of separation–individuation trauma with that of narcissistic injury, of the loss of the primal parents through literal death, and the mourning of bisexuality, as well as that of a grief – in relation to existential guilt and regret – and mourning the attachment to narcissistic parents. She also highlights the mourning required to relinquish the internal envious part-object parents and the loss resulting from spoiling due to one's envious attacks. She then interweaves these various themes and modes of mourning with the grief and guilt of child loss when psychic survival depends on the abandonment of one's own child. The healing process encompasses the conscious experiencing of both grief and guilt in the transference and in the containing environment of the therapeutic relationship. This involves the reparation of both internal and external object relations, including the reuniting of the abandoning mother and her child. Reparation, in its internal object dimensions, leads to the finding and releasing of formerly untapped creative resources, as well as promoting a new and evolving capacity for the mutuality and intimacy of whole object relations – where formerly part-object relations and modes of enactment through projective identification dominated the personality in relation to the external world.

This thought-provoking research will provide inspiring reading for those who are concerned with mental health science as well as those who are fascinated by the mysteries of creativity.

Acknowledgements

I would like to thank Kate Hawes, the Brunner-Routledge editor who selected this book for publication. I thank her also for sending the book for review by objective anonymous readers who were able to comprehend and appreciate the theoretical and clinical contributions of *Mourning, Spirituality and Psychic Change: A New Object Relations View of Psychoanalysis.*

I'd like to thank the entire Brunner-Routledge staff for their efforts in the publication of the book, as well as for their efforts in the publication of my first two books, *The Compulsion to Create: A Psychoanalytic Study of Women Artists* (1993) and *The Creative Mystique: From Red Shows Frenzy to Love and Creativity* (1996).

Finally, I would like to thank all of the people who participated in the April 26, 2003 Object Relations Institute conference where I presented the themes and theory from this book. I especially thank Dr Marvin Hurvich, Dr Albert Brok and Dr Jeffrey Seinfeld.

Chapter 1

Introduction

Traditionally, mourning has only been thought of in terms of the grief of bereavement. Even in "Mourning and Melancholia" (Freud 1917), the object lost was mostly thought of as deceased, although Freud did begin to incorporate the experience of disappointment into his vision of painful personal loss. In this study, however, the mourning process is redefined in developmental terms to reveal a full view of mourning as the key to psychic transformation.

Psychoanalysis began as a psychotherapeutic treatment to help people. In that spirit, its practitioners need to look at the most radical (as in root) source of psychic change, whether the critical factor in making way for it is therapeutic action or therapeutic attunement and reception. The attitude called for, on the part of the clinician committed to advance the process of developmental psychic change (as opposed to arbitrary, novel psychic change) with a patient, is what Freud terms "free floating attention" and what Wilfred Bion (1963) calls the absence of "memory and desire."

Therefore, both therapeutic action and attuned reception are modes of engagement for allowing and promoting the process I call *developmental mourning*. Fully evolved, developmental mourning is the product of affective and cognitive development and the reciprocity between them in the individual. Insight grows through separation–individuation combined with self-reflection. Self-agency and interiority grow through self-integration. These unfolding developmental challenges are intrinsic to the therapeutic process; they advance to its front and center when a patient articulates his experience of the process itself.

Patients' voices can be heard in the pages that follow; they resonate in the clinical narratives – as does the crucial engagement between analyst and analysands. As an object relations theorist committed to a spiral of connection and reconnection as the route to developmental progress, I believe that just such resonance in the rendering of critical dynamics in the clinical situation is vital to psychoanalytic literature. Specifically in the context of this book, it is vital to making theory rich and experience near enough to be accessible and amenable to processing.

Whenever I think of psychotherapeutic work or psychic change, I think of developmental mourning (Kavaler-Adler 1993, 1996). Looking through that lens and addressing the defense, including transference resistances that inhibit the process, clarifies my working vision. For instance, I see character disorders as related to arrests in mourning or as pathological mourning states – states that can manifest in a demon lover complex whereby the bad object predominates, causing developmental arrest – and, although different character disorders feature their own distinct psychic structures, all share the phenomenon of addiction to a bad object, and, by extension, the arrest of psychic connection and the parallel arrest of normal modes of mourning due to cumulative trauma. Trauma related to the disruption of primal bonding and primary internalization in turn disrupts self-integration and separation–individuation; the byproduct is splitting and disassociation circling a bad object constellation.

Illustrative clinical material comprises the bulk of the book. But to construct a scaffold for its assimilation, Chapter 2 articulates a phenomenological theory of developmental mourning. The succeeding chapters examine the roles of mourning in the history of psychoanalytic theory from Sigmund Freud through D.W. Winnicott. Uniting the explicit – as in Freud's "Mourning and Melancholia" (1917) and Melanie Klein's article on 'Mourning and Its Relation to Manic Depressive States' – with the implicit, which is characteristic of object relations thinking about psychic transformation. This sheds a new light on both, and also on the profound need to catapult developmental mourning to the center of the analytic stage.

The extended cases of June, Phillip, and Laura demonstrate that healing along a developmental continuum is possible when the analyst sustains connection long enough for an "abandonment depression" mourning process to take place (Masterson 1981). The method invites readers into the treatment room – to share, for example, June's discovery of a new identity when she comes to terms with her loss of early mother and father objects and with the attendant guilt, rage, and regret.

June's developmental journey continues along a *spiritual* dimension (decisively, in fact, for her ultimate transformation), which introduces spirituality as an emerging axis for the fruition of developmental mourning. That mode of psychic connection is consistently underrepresented (if not, in fact, evaded by professionals in our field, except for Jungian analysts). Accordingly, it is barely touched on in psychoanalytic literature, as was reported by a psychoanalysis panel during the 2000 American Psychological Association Division meeting, which called for a revisioning of psychoanalytic thought to encompass spiritual dynamics.

I have become fascinated by the power of spiritual themes as they surface over the course of treatment. Listening to my patients has taught me that some of them live in the archetypical realms of spiritual energies and entities for quite some time. Moreover, they do so while negotiating the transformations associated first with bringing to consciousness and then with consciously leaving behind a universe of part-object and bad-object relationships. As artists and writers may enter their inspirational domains through relationship with an identifiable muse, analysands may enter theirs through connection with the analyst and the holding environment. The spiritual becomes explicit in the psychoanalytic dialogue, as is seen in the cases of June and Phillip.

Indeed, June's experiences of psychic merger with the analyst catalyze her spiritual odyssey toward a future in which she is free from her past pathological object ties and traumas. She can heal and separate from the analytic object on whom she is at first so dependent, as her natural developmental urge to merge with the object at the beginning of treatment leads to the birth of a new self with the eventual release of aspects of the old and traumatically vulnerable one. It is June's yearning for the idealized object, which she experiences as a direct transmission to God, that engenders her awareness of a potential separate self and its "idiom" (Bollas 1989).

The psychoanalytic object relations approach, unlike a purely spiritual outlook, provides an avenue for the conscious reliving of trauma along with insight into psychic conflict. I invite readers to join me in discovering an integrated vision from a new object relations perspective incorporating spiritual experiences among the connections arising out of the developmental mourning process. Significantly, those connections encompass those of the heart, which, like spirituality, are neglected in the literature, but together with it, are capable of extraordinary synergy. That vision, as elucidated in the theoretical and clinical material that unfolds in these pages, offers the promise of an enriched and particularly hopeful take on the psychoanalytic journey for us all.

Chapter 2

A new metapsychology for clinical phenomenology and psychic health

Where is the human heart in psychoanalysis? Rarely do theorists deal with the heart as a psychic juncture of human experience. Perhaps two exceptions are D.W. Winnicott (1974), when he speaks of the true self, and Harry Guntrip (1976), when he speaks of split off core parts of the self, which he calls hearts. The most recent exception is Michael Eigen, who in *Psychic Deadness* (1996) frequently refers to the hearts of his patients. Indeed, the wounds to the heart that his patients ward off, he suggests, represent a central locus of their psychic identity. As if to underscore the central role of the heart in his book, Eigen offers the following dedication in the book: "To all who strive to make this world a place the heart can live in" (1996: dedication page).

Despite the omission of the heart in psychoanalytic thought, I have found that speaking to analysands in psychoanalysis or to psychotherapy patients, using the language of the heart tends to be immediately communicative, often evoking a resonant response. There is generally a palpable impact when invoking the heart's needs, longings, and its wounds that we all ward off. It is certainly a more direct route to the contact involved in emotional touch than speaking of an id, ego, or superego, or even a libidinal ego or antilibidinal ego personified as an internal saboteur.

Another palpable force that opens patient–therapist communications is the therapist's introduction of the heart's nemesis: the internal bad object constellation, which in the patient is often personified in the form of a demon lover figure. The demon lover figure, when appearing in literary form, is characterized by possessing, attacking, raping, and abandoning anyone dependent on him (Kavaler-Adler 1993, 1996). The demon lover parent, perpetuated in the internal world, generally betrays all trust in love, need, and desire, when reported in fantasies or dreams by psychoanalytic patients. Typically, an individual unconsciously relates to the demon lover personification within through projecting it onto an external other – the demon lover outside.

What distinguishes this demon lover personification and phenomenon? One characteristic is the split off motivational life that the person experiences as compulsion or as possession. Another characteristic of the demon lover personification is its erotic and aggressive instinctual dimensions. Possibly the most significant characteristic, however, in identifying the demon lover is that it functions to obliquely block the heart's functions in channeling love, emotional touch, tenderness and object relations connection. The demon lover lives in those dead and dark places where the heart's sensations and spiritual and emotional longings are frozen out of existence or nullified. He exists as a plug inserted in the black holes and voids of the traumatized psyche (Grotstein 1993). He lives, therefore, in dark and cold occlusions, where the wounds of the heart remain sealed off, foreclosing psychic and potential space – the life of the heart and the energy of love. That is why, when the demon lover is portrayed as a figure of literary myth, as evoked, for example in the poetry and prose of Emily Brontë and Emily Dickinson, he is shown entering the realm of the female cosmos only in the dark hours of the night. For Emily Brontë, he is simply "The Nightwind" (Brontë 1941). For Emily Dickinson, he appears wishing to "peep in parlors shut by day" (Dickinson 1960). The poet searches for the aggressive dark erotic dimensions of the father-god, "the metallic god who drills his welcome in" (Sewall 1974).

A woman may also imagine her demon lover to be the source of secrets about symbolic knowledge. If so, she may then project her own symbolic capacities onto him as an internal object and also onto an external male representative. For example, Emily Dickinson could only write poetry after she had dreamt during the previous night of a phallic king figure arising within her (Cody 1971). Without inspiration from this dark muse, who readily turned to a demon in the harsh light of day, Dickinson felt fallow – sterile of the poetic gifts she so compulsively and readily employed in her relative isolation and seclusion. Armed with her dream muse's phallic power, she could "scan a ghost" and then "grapple" with it for supremacy (Dickinson 1960). For Dickinson, to be possessed by the demon side of the muse–as by the metallic god – also meant being inspired by a phallic form to penetrate the mystery of things, those unnamed things that required symbolic definition. But such nighttime phallic inspiration did not allow Dickinson, nor many other similarly possessed artists, to yield to the feminine part of herself that could potentially suffer the wounds of the heart. By "wounds of the heart" I mean the wounds of love and connection with real objects, the most profound wounds relating back to preoedipal loss and deprivation. For Dickinson, the wounds of preoedipal loss and deprivation disrupted primal bonding and were therefore traumatic. They were wounds of object connection disruption, stemming back to a detached, schizoid mother, who was in a pathological mourning state when her daughter Emily was born. There were also later wounds of negative oedipal disillusionment that stamped her heart with unrequited love, as in Dickinson's unrequited homoerotic infatuation with her school chum, Susan, who was to become Susan Dickinson, her brother's wife (Cody 1971). During her lifetime, Dickinson was unable to heal within the internal world of her psychic structure, those areas of deprivation, which she experienced as psychic wounds. This inability made her extraordinarily vulnerable to narcissistic injury. Stuck in a depressive position of self-protection, she found it impossible to break out of her secluded state. This failure in turn meant the defeat of Dickinson's object relations capacity for love, a capacity that she experienced subjectively as emanating through the spiritual flow and current from the heart. One aftermath of this defeat was that the demon lover within became her predominant love, compelling her to refuse the external other who proposed love and marriage to her, a man she had actually been in love with. I am referring here to her rejection of Judge Otis T. Lord's proposal of marriage. Upon hearing the proposal, Dickinson declared "'No'is the most exciting word in the English language!" and "renunciation is a piercing virtue" (Kavaler-Adler 1990). This piercing virtue was as hard, phallic, and metallic as her demon lover god within. His presence squelched Dickinson's capacity to love a man both real and available, and to receive his love in return, by denying her the opportunity to open her heart to him. The effect of this denial is visible in her poetry, which after her rejection of Judge Lord, whom she adored and was adored by, became overly masculine as her disconnected state was reflected in poetry about a part object god/demon. Such a god/demon – also characteristic of the demon lover theme and character – is psychologically reflective of an internal world with a split off primary object, an object that had been incorporated within her psyche rather than assimilated. This results in an internal world object that is part mother and part father. The persona inside the world of a split off self-part is that of the caricatured masculine object representation it is attached to (related to identifications with the father). However, its psychic structure is that of a primal and maternal figure that has never been integrated into the form of a whole object. It is a part object mother/father that is masculinized, rather than truly masculine. The attachment needs directed at it are characterized by oral hunger and impulse. There is an insatiable craving for maternal supplies and maternal merger.

Simultaneous with Emily Dickinson's obsession with this masculinized primal object we see the devaluation of Dickinson's feminine side in her poetry. Her core true and feminine self became increasingly sealed off and denied. In her poetry she formed a passive reactive view of it as, for example, in the image of a hunted and helpless "doe" (Kavaler-Adler 1993: 236, 239). Her mother's pathological mourning state, brought on by a multitude of unmourned object losses when Emily was an infant, caused Dickinson's feminine potential to became a vestige of an aborted feminine self (Cody 1971). This explains why Dickinson lacked the power of vaginal core receptivity (Kavaler-Adler 1993). Without this feminine power, she failed to develop an adequate sense of agency, and ended up possessed, her moments of transcendence vanishing into the night (Kavaler-Adler 1993). Imprisoned in her unbalanced and caricatured femininity, Dickinson wrote: "I have the power to kill, but not the power to die" (Dickinson 1960). Her own words indicate how the poet had lost touch with her spiritual experience of a primary state of being. Her own words speak of how she had merged with a phallic muse of envisioned inspiration, when she encountered the blocked areas in herself that defended against the reconnecting with her original infant self and its unresolved traumas.

DIALECTIC OF HEART AND DEMON LOVER

Within the context of the dialectic between the heart and the in...
can we approach the phenomenology of mourning? I am defining th...
psychophysical locus for the basic human capacity for love, the human ca...
for love having a spiritual form of energy experienced through yearnings for
another. The "internal demon" I define as a conglomeration of the incorporated
bad objects whose dynamic is derived from a combination of split off instinctual
aspects of the self and primitive object representations, as Thomas Ogden defines
internal objects (1986). These bad objects have not been refined and differentiated
at the symbolic level.

Given this view of pathology, I would like to propose a somewhat new metapsychology of psychic health, in which it is seen as an avenue that opens up
through the mourning process. By metapsychology I refer to basic organizing
theoretical assumptions regarding mental functioning at different levels of abstraction, with some more clinical-experiential and others more abstract and conceptual.
As in my earlier work on developmental mourning, I expand on Melanie Klein's
phenomenology of the mourning process, envisioning an open system of psychic
health capacity.

One way that I have described this open psychic system is in terms of a capacity
for multiple forms of psychic dialectic, including what I've defined as "love–
creativity dialectic" (Kavaler-Adler 1996). Such dialectic involves a capacity to
have a back and forth flow between the internal object relations that transform into
creative process and the love connections of interpersonal relations. This organic
flow consists of the interaction of psychic motivation and psychic agency with the
two spheres of object relations experience – internal and external.

I would also like to propose a phenomenology of the mourning of love objects,
in which we do not have to rely on the metapsychology of the death instinct as
defined by Klein to locate the origin of the pain of object loss. I am responding here
to Klein's suggestion that the death instinct is the source of all anxiety and defense:
in as much as there is a force within each of us that not only counteracts mourning
but opposes reparation of object relations within the self and its internal world. I
believe in negative internal object constellations imbued with instinctual aggression, not in a death instinct. I distinguish such internal constellations from a
death force, because it can be modified by mourning that unblocks healthy developmental processes. I employ the theory of Ronald Fairbairn to refute Klein's conception of an ever active death instinct or death drive. I also employ my own theory of "developmental mourning" as a resolution to trauma to counter the idea of
a death instinct. The idea of a death instinct opposes an understanding of aggressive and erotic drives that are always experienced through object connections and
their internalized forms, and which become malignant in compulsive repetition
only when mourning is prohibited by psychic defense structures following early
trauma. Klein herself never spoke of an instinct without an object constellation
attached to it, as represented in the psychic fantasies discovered in her clinical

ork. However, when she went into flights of metapsychology, she betrayed such vivid understanding.

When mourning is blocked, reenactment of early pathological character syndromes results along with internal states of emptiness. Typically, analysts speak about mourning in the context of whether it occurs or not. They therefore rarely view mourning as a phenomenology of psychic process and psychic health, although Klein did clinical and theoretical work that began to outline this direction of thought. I would like to attempt to define the phenomenology of mourning and see if it can be depicted separately from Klein's "death instinct" metapsychology, while retaining Klein's clinical understanding of grief. Grief, when spoken of in the developmental and clinical context to which I refer, does not only pertain to object loss in relation to death, separation, and disappointment. It also refers to the pain involved in the mourning that expresses itself in the pain of regrets over our own hostile aggression towards loved objects, a mourning process that causes its own form of object loss. The mourning of regrets also involves the mourning of self-loss due to self-sabotage, and the development of compassion and concern for the self, as opposed to being compulsively driven towards self-blame and self-betrayal. I wish to emphasize that this notion represents my own extension of Kleinian theory, since Klein would probably too rigidly compartmentalize the concern about the self, viewing it as existing within the psychic state of the paranoid-schizoid position. Indeed, Klein schematically draws a contrast between an obsessive protection of the self in the paranoid-schizoid position and concern for the love object in the depressive position. Such a schema does not deal with concern and compassion for the self. I add to Klein's protection of the self or concern for the object the qualitative distinction between self-compassion in a depressive position mentality, and a paranoid mode of self-protection. Concern for the self within a depressive position state of mind involves a compassionate empathy for the self, not just a defensive attitude of self-protection against others seen as hostile threats. The paranoid mode, as opposed to the capacity for concern in the depressive mode, involves an internal persecutory object, which, because it is projected outward, is then perceived as emanating from an external enemy.

Guilt itself may contain developmental forms, including a persecutory self-attack in the paranoid-schizoid position and a sorrowful pain of regret in the depressive position. We may add to this phenomenology the metapsychological hypothesis that hostile aggression can also represent an attempt to ward off consciousness of persecutory aggression within. This internal, protosymbolic aggression is defensively reacted to. It is not conceptualized. It creates a dissociated state of guilt (experienced first as self-hate), which differs from the pain of regret experienced as grief by someone in the depressive position. Although object loss can be the result of warded off guilt, manifesting as persecutory aggression, I would say that object loss, which is not yet felt consciously and mourned, can also create a sense of pathological guilt (in contrast to depressive position guilt or existential guilt). This was noted by Fairbairn (1952), in speaking of the moral defense of the child, who masochistically blames himself rather than hold the parent accountable for behavior that is harmful, so as to protect the image of the parent and thus to protect the child's own sense of safety. Nevertheless, neither persecutory guilt, which in the paranoid position described by Klein is experienced as an attack from without, nor pathological guilt, experienced, according to Klein, as an attack from within in that same position, nor the potentially compassionate state experience in what Klein described as the depressive position of pining for the object in a mode of empathic regret, need be attributed to an abstract force comprised of "death instinct" energy. The redundancy of the death instinct theory can be maintained even if a split off aggression is involved in the dynamics of the paranoid position.

Redefining Klein's view of developmental and clinical dynamics without the death instinct, I would summarize the essential human anguish in Klein's phenomenology as the pain and conflict related to the depressive position experience of concern for the other. I refer to the other outside the self, as well as to the other experienced through memory and desire as existing within the self. This core human anguish affects both self and object representations because in the depressive position it is subjectively felt. On a pure visceral level it can feel like a wound or block in the flow of love to and from the human heart. Stripping away all of the multitudinous defenses and dynamics of Klein's internal world, we are left with one primary psychic stance that both paranoid and manic strategies are defending against (in the depressive position, manic defenses ward off guilt and loss). That position is being vulnerably open to loving and needing. It is only in this position that we can love – and in Klein, only our love continually modifies hate. It is also only in this position that undifferentiated and split off objects become assimilated into the central part of the psyche (Bion's psychic digestion from beta to alpha) through new symbolic forms. Such symbolic forms have representation in the cognitive and conceptual sphere of secondary process thought or in an internal world comprised of differentiated images.

The symbolic level achieved through object digestion involves the internalizing and representing of a true other as an object in the internal world or secondary process of the psyche. An external object must be symbolized in order to be assimilated into this internal world of representational images and verbal and conceptual forms, such as in the verbal conceptualization or imagination of our parents. In Bion's (1963) terms, psychic object digestion transforms beta elements into alpha, with alpha elements being constructed in symbolic and representational terms. Undigested beta elements remain unassimilated visceral intrusions, promoting the interpersonal pressures of projective identification, as opposed to intrapsychic projection, and tending to be personified at the border of psychic and somatic reality.

Thus a demon lover personification, which establishes a possessive hold on the woman's psyche, in the form of a split off part of the self merged with an object representation, can be transformed into a more pure symbolic representational form. Ogden (1986) and Fairbairn (1952) refer to the "bad object" as a dynamic presence that can be transformed into symbolic representations and then be integrated into a central self-structure. Such a transformation requires the experiencing of that which was formerly visceral, sensory, somatic or behavioral in a new symbolic form. For this experience to occur, openness to mourning within a position of psychic vulnerability and interpersonal dependence is necessary.

Then the symbolic representation, now an introject rather than an internal object, can be integrated within a central self-structure (Fairbairn 1952). This central self-area would be the resource for secondary process thought and internal world representations that are neither split off and dissociated, nor repressed. I would view preconscious modes of operation mentioned by Lawrence Kubie (1958) as being psychically housed in this central self-area. The preconscious becomes the area of linking free associations, parts of self, as well as self and object connections in the internal world and affect-laden cognitive connections. Bion's notion of linking areas of the mind and self and other coordinates within the mind seems relevant here. Integration of formerly split off self-parts (protosymbolic rather than symbolic) requires the conscious experiencing of that which was formerly visceral, sensory, somatic, or behavioral in form. For integration to occur, an open acceptance of a position of psychic vulnerability and interpersonal dependence is necessary. This stands in psychic contrast to a state of narcissistic self-sufficiency, whether enacted through manic defense or grandiose delusion. In this position of need and love, of psychic vulnerability and interpersonal dependence, a mourning process can transpire, in which experience is transformed into representation through the grieving of loss and regret. If the person experiences the sadness of object longing, loss, and regret, this creates an open avenue for new modes of object contact with current others in his or her life. This in turn allows for the creation of more mature, intimate, spontaneous and sustained forms of interpersonal connection.

The position of loving and needing is not a position that we can perpetually maintain. People can approach it to the degree that they are open to suffering the wounding of the heart. This involves both tolerating the pain of narcissistic injury (paranoid-schizoid position), and the hurt of sabotaging potential love relations. Loss of love due to sabotage of self or other creates consequences of object loss, which can be subjectively felt as the poignant and differentiated pain of regret. The capacity to suffer consequent regret is not a masochistic mode of suffering – based on clinging incessantly to an idealized object – nor is it the suffering of a Victorian superego morality. It is a form of organic suffering that consists of the deep grief of sadness, which engenders a capacity to relinquish and let go. It is mournful suffering, or the enduring of what is, rather than the cherishing of suffering for its own sake.[1] Such real suffering is expressed through tears of grief, which can never find an outlet through an hysterical tantrum exorcism or masochistic ventilation of complaint, as both are controlled by the ego and represent enactments or reenactments. When the self is sealed off by splitting or closed off by repression, it is impossible for such authentic grief to evolve. Margaret Mahler (1975) locates the early source of authentic grief in the "low-keyedness" shown by the 2-year-old toddler, who is exposed to the developmental vicissitudes of separation.

To re-establish a position of loving and needing we must be able to surrender, not just to the overtures of love, but to the rupturing of our boundaries (Miller 1986). One can choose to let in an "other" who might ravish, but not rape. An example of someone who succumbed to such ravishment is the dancer Suzanne Farrell, who experienced choreographer George Balanchine as her masculine muse, not her demon lover (Kavaler-Adler 1996). She never turned Balanchine into a demon in her mind, unlike Camille Claudel with Auguste Rodin. Farrell didn't have the psychic imprint of early maternal trauma that Claudel had.

Farrell merged with Balanchine's creativity, employing him as her male muse, as he used her as his female muse. But when Balanchine wished to possess her through marrying her, even when he was twice her age, with a terrible track record of marrying and divorcing a string of prima ballerinas, Farrell was able to say "no." Subsequently she survived the consequences of separating from her muse. When she married another man, a dancer in the same company, closer to her own age, she was forced to leave Balanchine's company. Even though she was acclaimed as one of the finest dancers of her time, American dance companies blacklisted her. It took her a year of poverty to find a job with a well-known Belgian dance company. Despite this treatment, Farrell never turned her muse into a demon, as opposed to the sculptress Camille Claudel.

Immediately after Claudel and Rodin broke up their personal liaison, Claudel demonized him. For the rest of her life, she refused to accept any gestures of help or concern from him. Rather, Claudel displaced her hatred for her mother onto her former lover, reenacting within her unconscious the cycle of possession and abandonment enlisted in the fantasy of her demon lover as perpetual perpetrator and persecutor. After alcoholism, suicide attempts, and continual murderous assaults on her own artistic products via the ritualistic smashing of her sculptures, Claudel spent her last thirty years confined in a mental asylum, where she refused to sculpt. Although Claudel blamed Rodin for all her misfortunes, and hallucinated that his protegés were stealing her sculptures, it was not he, but her mother who prevented her from leaving the mental asylum.

In contrast, Suzanne Farrell preserved her love and admiration for George Balanchine and for his creative work, despite their personal and professional rift. She even returned to work with him once reparations appeared possible. Ravished (penetrated) and not raped by his mental creations, she remained in love with dancing in Balanchine's ballets, and after her retirement from dancing following hip replacement surgery, she has continued to teach his dances to a new generation of dancers. As this example shows, in contrast to the demon lover who in the woman's internal world emerges as a rapist, a male muse both ravishes and empowers the woman in her internal world, as he inspires her. Consequently, the woman is inspired in her external achievements.

Taking in the muse and surrendering to the muse within involves being open to the existential awareness of how it is possible to hurt a loved one. Jerome Miller (1989) speaks of the capacity to surrender to suffering as necessary if we are to gain entry into the moral order. This capacity, he sees, in broad lifelong terms, not merely occurring only in a specific stage of life. He believes in lifelong growth through a positive and spiritual form of suffering. He speaks of an existential morality. I see this as similar to Melanie Klein, who believed one could automatically enter a state of grief upon gaining the conscious knowledge of our own self-agency in hurting the one we love (Klein 1957). This capacity, I believe, is what Winnicott also meant by "the capacity for concern," which was seen as developing out of an external psychic holding environment that is made internal through internalization. Once the holding environment is internal a psyche can "hold" grief (Winnicott 1974).

Given the very human horror at facing what we have up to now avoided (Miller 1989), our many modes of evading knowledge of our secret transgressions are more than understandable. This makes it quite painful when we attempt to face our acts of omission as well as commission in hurting a love object (or love "other"). Klein's paranoid system, as well as her manic defense, describes the mechanisms of avoidance. However, when Klein postulates a death instinct, she conjures up an abstract force that negates the moral nature of the subjective pain in human beings, even as she approaches that pain with the phenomenology of the depressive position. Consequently, she undermines, in my view, the power of her own theory by adding a heavy theoretical overlay that can be redundant, if not nullifying, of the human anguish involved in the consciousness of our own agency in the anxiety we experience.

When she invokes the death instinct, Klein takes the "I" out of human consciousness and leaves us with the "It." We become objectified even by ourselves, losing our subjectivity and with it our sense of agency and choice. Klein's metapsychology of the death instinct, in contrast to her clinical theory of mourning and the psychic journey from the paranoid to the depressive position of mind, returns the human psyche to the possessive demon lover.

What does the demon lover personify? He may personify split off sadomasochistic modes of aggression, which are highly eroticized and exciting in terms of intensity. A demon lover obsession or complex often relates to a person who is avoiding self-confrontation or self-awareness. Such a person operates through splitting and dissociation, or through repression – resulting in simultaneous obsession and avoidance in relation to highly charged aspects of the self. In this masculine personification (comprised of split off self-parts and an object representation), a protosymbolic visceral form may be the impinging force within the person. Klein fails to account for the demon personification as a repository of the "unthought known" traumas of the past. The term "unthought known," which was coined by D.W. Winnicott, has been used by Christopher Bollas (1989). In using this term, Winnicott is referring to a traumatic experience that has been split off from consciousness due to its overwhelming nature, so that it is known, but not consciously thought. That is, he is not referring to a drive instinct that is repressed, but to a real trauma the person experiences as too overwhelming to bear to repress. So the entire trauma is dissociated and split off. Only when individuals have enough support from a "holding environment" in treatment can they tolerate consciously reliving and reexperiencing the trauma, thereby bringing the experience to a symbolic level of thought.

Indeed, if they were to become known, this could permit a symbolic muse demon form to exist as a symbolic container (manifested in the transference in psychoanalytic treatment).

This "unthought known" could be trauma related to parental abuse, which has been too intolerable in childhood, and which thus becomes dissociated and sealed off from emotional connection. However, defensive and retaliatory aggression needs to be experienced consciously to move beyond the position of victim. Once the trauma is accessible in symbolic form the person's own aggression can be faced in relation to the internalized demonic parent object, which in its displaced forms is often fantasized as a demon lover. Once the demon lover constellation, which consists of a part self and part object, can be symbolized the subject can become a full human being, by facing one's own personal aggression as well as in erotic desire. This involves facing the demon lover personification within so as to symbolize it, rather than being possessed by it. Specifically, anyone, woman or man, must own how she/he may have become the traumatizing object through primitive incorporative (oral) identifications within the internal world. Through commission or omission, the internal world self and other fused psychic structure enacts its compulsion in the manifest interpersonal world. We continue to repeat the unthought known traumas of our past. When we confront this repetition through insight into omission and commission in love relationships, our self-confrontation can open us all to personal meaning. Such self-confrontation can open us to feeling the links between past trauma and the compulsive repetitions, which impose past attachment tragedies on current strivings to love and be loved. We discover our betrayals towards and from the one(s) we love through feeling it on a grief-stricken affect level. Thus, through experiencing the pain of regret, based on disillusionment with oneself, and the pain of loss related to disillusionment with the other, we open the door to consciousness.

This is the mourning process. Our lives can take shape through the poignant absence of love as it punctuates love experience, and as it punctuates the flow or arrest in her own capacity to love. As former child victims, we must own how we may have a part in repeating our trauma through identification with our abusers. We must face our compulsive commission or omission of repeating the "unthought known" traumas of the past, often in sadomasochistic enactments. Such self-confrontation opens anyone, woman or man, to personal meaning. Grief stricken affect serves to highlight both the trauma and the reactive betrayals of the victim towards the new objects with whom she reenacts her drama. Thus the door to consciousness opens through experiencing the pain of regret.

THE PAIN OF REGRET

The pain of regret is an emotion that is subjectively experienced as an emotion either emanating from the heart or expressing a connection to another through one's heart! The pain itself can feel like a wound in the heart to the degree that it is experienced somatically. Mourning is of the heart. That is, it comes from love connections in the heart that bring self-realization along with object loss. Grief experience in mourning allows us to reconnect, on a spiritual level, with those who we want and need to love, but who have been lost to us because of too much unconscious or dissociated hate (in addition to actual literal loss of contact). Klein's subjective theory of the yearning for the capacity for reparation is all related to self and other connection. Repairing connection transforms us at times through viscerally alive, heartfelt feeling. Through the heart connection we consolidate the central self, developing a true self that is connected to the world that is capable of emotional connection. If such heart connection were not profound and essential, the kind of repeated visualizations I practice in my monthly mourning regrets group would not bring the acutely felt responses that are voiced in those groups. Those able to locate their hearts through feeling connections, as opposed to through mere physiological awareness, can speak of their conflicts with those they love quite articulately. They employ descriptions of the heart as the congealing point of love, which when blocked in feeling signifies blocks in love for others. The stomach is often felt as anger raging, wanting to throw up the other as one throws up food. The visceral locale of the heart provides an active metaphorical and figurative language for discussing problems in both loving and creating.

However, wounds to the heart can come from narcissistic injury as well as from object loss. When this occurs, we may retreat from object relations and object attachment in general. Distrust and fear can become prominent, especially when we interpret loss and injury as rejection. When we do we can create a fear of humiliation in addition to the fear of loss.

PSYCHIC STRUCTURE

If we approach these phenomena through the lens of psychic structure we can view Fairbairn's theory, which is so focused on psychic structure, as a reinforcement of Klein's phenomenology, without resorting to her metapsychology of death instinct. Yet it is also possible to go beyond Fairbairn's profound emphasis on trauma and real object relations incorporations to the realm of intrapsychic fantasy, as explicated by Melanie Klein and the Kleinians with such fervor. Then we can see motivational dynamics in objects differing from the passive Freudian object of hallucinated desire. Objects of motivational force and yearning may click in with an innate grammar of the mind (Ogden 1986), as well as with an instinctual base of eroticism and aggression. Jungian archetypes might be proposed as one aspect of the mind's innate predisposition to certain psychic fantasy forms. Past lives, as intuited and remembered psychic phenomena, might also be proposed.

PSYCHIC FUNCTIONING, PSYCHIC MOTIVATION, AND PSYCHIC CHANGE

Our real experience is never enough to make up our psychic reality. That is, this outward experience does not fully correspond to our psychic fantasies. In the process of creating these fantasies, we somehow color our original external experience. But the terror we feel upon facing our internal combinations of psychic fantasy and actual internalized experiential imprints[2] can be a major source for coloring the internal domain. This is manifested in protosymbolic forms that can transform into psychic fantasy only through mourning and self-integration. By "protosymbolic" I mean visceral or sensory presymbolic experiences that act on the organism, but have no represented form in the secondary process (Freud) or the internal world (Klein). No death instinct energy need be proposed for metapsychology, when Klein's treatise on guilt and Freud's treatise on frustration can account for all forms of hostile or destructive aggression.

Guilt, as defined phenomenologically by Klein, along with the motive of frustration, as propounded by Freud, can account for much psychic conflict and psychic pathology, whereas shame, self-loss, and traumatic psychic voids can account for much in developmental arrest. The idea of something as abstract as death instinct energy does not seem to add to our understanding of these phenomena. Klein (1957) implies that we experience guilt subjectively, through psychic fantasy, both consciously and unconsciously. The pain of regret that accompanies guilt at the depressive level of concern can be traumatic in dimension – that is, experienced as existential pain. We may see such pain simply in terms of learned superego rule systems that cause suffering by internal repression and retaliation for instinctual wishes and for object longings. The pain of regret, however, can be seen to extend further into an existential awareness of hurting another, which may also be applicable to the hurting of one's self, or to the pain of regret due to self-sabotage. This hurting of the other or of the represented self within our own internal world is as instinctual as love itself, for Klein. For example, Klein speaks of the baby yearning and pining for the mother, while simultaneously feeling concern for the mother, upon the psychic entrance into the depressive position. Such an intuitive capacity for concern has, moreover, its own erotic and sexual dimensions. This can be seen in analogy with unconscious gratification felt from an abusive assault, an assault that Fairbairn would probably define as an antilibidinal phenomenon, when it is derived from early parenting and is rearticulated in an internal split off world. I prefer to refer to a libidinal attack on a vulnerable or dependent self that exists within the psyche, which has its unconscious form of both masochistic and sadistic gratification, due to the drive discharge in submission and the identification with the aggressor. Once entering the psychic capacity for the depressive position, the issue for all of us is no longer self-attack and unconscious gratification, but is rather the existential pain of regret, which refers to the intense grief of hurting the other whom we love.

Klein would view the parents' role in child development as that of receiving offers of reparation from the child. If they can do this, the child can then develop a capacity to consciously face regret, and thus to develop concern, as the acute pain of regret can lead to concern. However, as Winnicott (1965) suggests, the primary parent must not only receive reparation from the child, but also, through this, the parent models the experience of concern. This contrasts with Klein's emphasis on innate phenomena rather the internalizations. According to Winnicott it is the role of the mother that is critical. If she is not "good enough" the child's development is severely affected. Without a "good enough" mother, and the internalization of her care and responsiveness to the child's true self, the child's potential capacity for concern can convert into a regressed state of persecutory guilt. The child can grow up with a paranoid-schizoid position masochism, in which any potential sense of responsibility or self-agency is defensively turned into a sense of being "bad." Klein would emphasize the gravity of the subjective anguish involved in the depressive pain that leads to concern through the experience of conscious loss of the love object and the loss of the object's love. However, for the person to tolerate such psychically transforming anguish, my clinical experience leads me to agree with Winnicott that with the holding environment of an object relations psychoanalytic treatment is critical to allow the pain of regret to become a tolerable grief experience.

But is it not still necessary for an original holding environment to be well established between infant and mother, and later between toddler and mother, and then child and mother, for the child to develop the capacity for concern at all? Is not such development as instinctually based as Klein's view of a six-month-old infant entering a depressive position mentality suggests? Even if I were to accept this six-month timetable, which I don't, I would certainly be skeptical about Klein's belief that we instinctively develop concern for an "other," without our differentiating the nature of that other, or the capacity for concern of the original other–the mother. I don't agree with the six-month timetable because virtually all reported clinical experience points to the 2-year-old separation era as the stage of the depressive position affects and of the depressive position conscious need state. It may be more that we must first experience our capacities in the presence of a good enough benign other if we are to realize these capacities, which are partly instinctual and partly object related, as is suggested by Winnicott (1965). Once experienced with the other both interpersonal relations and internal self-relations are effected. A compassionate mother provides a model for us to realize any innate potential for concern. One development of such a capacity is based on our internalizing her being in the position of receiving concern, an identification with the mother showing concern, and her mode of demonstrating it. An analyst can provide this model at a later stage of development and throughout adulthood.

REGRET, CONCERN, AND GUILT WITHOUT A DEATH INSTINCT

The pain of regret is a subjective and conscious phenomenon combined with the capacity for concern. It can define psychic health as evolving through a metapsychology based on the phenomenal experience of mourning.

Klein's death instinct, in contrast, is an abstract force. This abstract force exists as an axiom within her metapsychology. Even though it is without a conclusive phenomenological and clinical base, Klein nevertheless sees the death instinct as the motivation behind hostile aggression. Her death instinct differs from other instincts, such as Freud's erotic and aggressive instincts, in that we may define them in visceral and body-based terms. Klein's death instinct is too abstract. She has it appear at our birth – and then we are supposed project it out, causing us inevitably to fear that it will bounce back at us in retaliation.

Such an abstract force is not necessary to explain the spoiling process in the paranoid-schizoid position, nor the manic defense consisting of loss and guilt in the depressive position. In fact, it merely confuses the issue. When we evade a poignant guilt, whether it involves hurting the one we love, or wounding ourselves, the anguish we suffer to avoid conscious responsibility is enough to explain unconscious depressive position despair, when we feel all love and love objects are lost. Envy, whether due to developmental arrest and its sense of lack, or due to aggressive drive impulse, or both, is enough to explain any paranoid-schizoid position spoiling and devaluation defense operation. Envy, like anguish, is not an abstract force. Comprised of organic (oral and oedipal erotic) need elements, envy is body based. It is a psychic form of voracious hunger (Kavaler-Adler 1998). When the body's somatic hunger is dissociated, hunger is insatiable. Only body-based hunger is limited by the body's organic needs. Envy, a psychic conversion of somatic hunger has no limits, and its insatiability is a profound part of its malignancy, especially when unconscious.

LIMITATIONS OF MELANIE KLEIN'S METAPSYCHOLOGICAL THEORY OF THE DEATH INSTINCT

Why did Klein emphasize the death instinct? The explanation could be fairly simple. Perhaps, wanting Freud's approval, Klein adopted the term "death instinct," while actually implying something different from Freud's use of the term. Freud's meaning of the "death instinct" related to a movement towards a conflict-free, nirvana-like state, or tensionless state. Rather, the theory as she states it reflects a belief in a hostile aggression that has murderous violence within it, and whose violent impulse generates terror of retaliation from an omnipotent and envied enemy.

Unlike Freud also, Klein does not deal with the erotic part of this aggression as such, assigning eroticism in the abstract to the loving impulse of the child towards an all-good-breast-mother. I believe this omission reflects a shortcoming in Klein's ideas. Here is where she might really use Freud in terms of his theory of aggression in dual instincts, rather than rely on his theory of a death instinct. Nevertheless, we can find space in Klein's overall phenomenology to contain this erotic dimension. The erotic dimension can interact with the impulse of hostile aggression and its manifestation as destructive or spoiling envy, forming sadomasochistic dynamics. Also it counteracts hostile modes of aggression as erotic impulses combine with tenderness within love. Klein explicitly dealt with this modifying effect of love, but neither differentiated it from eroticism, nor combined it with eroticism.

We may see this interaction of eroticism with aggression quite vividly in clinical work, as we also see the counterbalance of the two. In one of my own cases it became quite clear to me that whenever I interpreted my patient's aggression by itself, she would retaliate by adapting a cold manner. She would then project this coldness onto me. For example, when I interpreted that she wished to attack me ruthlessly, without guilt, she could not contain or hold the guilt my interpretation induced. She responded in an icy voice with retaliatory accusations. When, however, I spoke of the anxiety behind the aggressive attack, not just in terms of feared retaliation in the paranoid position, nor as feared pain and loss of the object in the depressive position, but rather as a fear that she could not contain her erotic feelings for me (as both a breast mother and an oedipal father in the transference), she was able to hold, and therefore to own, the guilt of her aggressive assault. This allowed her to take responsibility for her assaultive aggression. Consequently, she could symbolize the agony of the assault in her internal world and central self-consciousness. By my including her erotic fear in the interpretation, the patient did not have to be overwhelmed with the feeling of being bad or evil, as she would be if I just focused in my remarks on her sadism or attack.

Kleinian theorists generally do look at the anxiety that lies behind aggression, but if they operate out of a metapsychology of the death instinct, it deters them from seeing the analysand's anxiety as potentially caused by powerful erotic cravings. More specifically, psychoanalysts shaped by Klein's ideas of the death instinct would typically not account for powerful erotic cravings for both a primal omnipotent mother and for a differentiated oedipal father. Obviously, they would not then focus on or even acknowledge the fusion of these cravings and yearnings in the preoedipal character, where they are often personified as a demon lover figure in psychic fantasy. Sometimes this occurs when specific body-based transference fantasies in the patient are present, as in the case just reported.

To speak of being overwhelmed by an abstract death instinct drive does not add much to our understanding of the clinical conflict around a core anxiety and its fantasized object related fears! Most people tend to be overwhelmed by the terror of giving up control and facing our regrets and losses squarely. Faced with this prospect, most often the formation of a split off internal demon lover personification is preferable, particularly for those with early psychic imprints from object loss and parental deprivation or abuse. Extreme sensitivity to narcissistic wounding is one manifestation of such imprints, and these wounds get projected and personified in terms of who provokes them. Only in a state of the deepest meditation on life's many forms of existential wounding could Dickinson have written: "To scan a ghost is faint / But grappling conquers it" poem #281 (Dickinson in Johnson 1960:129).

However, this woman poet had to write poetry day in and day out to keep up such courage in the face of despair. She could not stay fully open to mourning and thus to love and need. So she resorted to identification with a masculine mode of psychic experience as a defense. Part of her then became the "metallic god who drilled his welcome in," even as part of her still remained an arrested female self. She described this arrested female self, in one poem, as a doe, a doe that flees from an assault by murderous masculine forces (Cody 1971). Dickinson's doe therefore is not an image of femininity that encompasses the feminine power of receptivity and heartfelt vulnerability, nor does Dickinson's female possess the vaginal power of receptivity and its organic expansion of interiority.

EXISTENTIAL MORALITY IN ANALYSIS (KARMA)

Despite her view of the death instinct as an abstract force, Klein's theory of the depressive position allows for the articulation of an existential morality in psychoanalysis. I agree with Joyce McDougall (1995) that Freud's assigning the death instinct as causation for the repetition compulsion is unnecessary if not totally fallacious. The repetition compulsion can be explained in terms of demonic object incorporations and the compulsion to repeat all that is not consciously felt and mourned from a point of self-agency within the psyche. It can be explained as an attempt to do over and repair. It can be explained as a stage of object addiction. On a structural level, it can be explained as part of the primal self getting sealed off with its primal objects.

Formerly (in Freud's day) attempts to remain outside a rigid and self-righteous Victorian morality caused Freud and many of his followers to assume that psychoanalysis should be "neutral" in terms of moral judgments. Analysts championed this view, believing it allowed them to act as more benign superegos. This stance, involving a code of professional ethics, has been seen by many analysts as a way of modifying rigid superego structures with patients.

Yet perhaps it is easier for us to say today that there is no relationship without judgment, and judgment always involves some form of ethics and morality. Klein's focus was always on the preoedipal areas of primal psychic conflict, which predate the cognitively structured superego of Freud, as Freud's superego emerges only through resolution of oedipal level conflict. At the more primary psychic level that Klein addresses, I see her posing moral dilemmas in development as conflicting strivings to allow one's love to supersede hate. Klein's thinking is about the struggle involved in the painful awareness of our compassion when having hurt the one we love, even if the hurt is inevitable. Entrance into the depressive position allows for the conscious owning and symbolization of an instinctive morality, one in which we seek to heal splits between ourselves and others, which also is the route to healing splits within the self. The healing of splits in the self that has created rifts with any outside other is the beginning of viewing what was previously solely a fantasy object – and therefore internal – as truly "other." Winnicott (1974) would probably speak of "object survival" here, or allowing the other to be experienced as external reality, when our own omnipotent gesture and our own psychic fantasy omniscience cannot control it.

For Klein, however, the first experiencing of the object as "other" has moral implications. We do not merely attach to the other and then discover that the other can survive. But we do inevitably feel a sense of remorse for the attack on the other, and it is this pain of regret or element of remorse, which begins to bring us into the human order, as defined by the existence of a primal reality of concern. Again, the natural depressive position capacity to feel such remorse for hurting the other – the one loves and needs – is assumed by Klein, but not by Winnicott. From Winnicott's perspective, as well as from the perspective of most object relations theorists, who emphasize the early preoedipal environment, the capacity for remorse would depend on whether remorse is experienced first through the attitude of the early mother and later on through all parenting figures. However, I think the idea of the exclusive impact of the parent's behavior on the child's capacity for remorse is open to question, and Klein's emphasis on an innate capacity for remorse and concern, which has its developmental flowering and evolution as the depressive position mentality evolves, merits serious consideration. I have treated adult borderline patients, who despite enormous parental inadequacy, neglect, and abuse, emerge as profoundly sensitive caretaking adults when they are caring for others dependent on them and are not themselves in a position of vulnerability to dependence on the other. It is not clear in these cases that there were any consistent adult models of concern in their childhood that compensated for the incompetence of the primal parents.

This remorse can be for avoidance or omission, or the crime of commission in active attack. Jerome Miller's observation is pertinent here: "One must be willing to suffer to enter the moral order" (1989: 192). One cannot feel remorse and face the "unthought known" elements of our past behaviors, acknowledging the unnamed "ghosts" of our moral crimes, without conscious suffering of the metaphorical wound of the heart with which we feel empathy for the hurt we create in the other. What I am describing is not just guilt. It is an empathic concern for the one we love and wish to be loved by. In relation to avoidance of an existential, and perhaps instinctual, morality, Miller also remarks: "We come to create the very destiny that we seek to avoid." This is another view of the repetition compulsion, one stated from the perspective of a subjective self.

EXISTENTIAL GUILT AND REGRET

The writer Henry James lends a provocative punch to the whole subject of human avoidance being the essence of moral turpitude in his famous tale: "The Beast in the Jungle" (James 1903). In this story, the protagonist awaits some tragic fate, as one would wait for a profound attack of destiny or disaster, as one would wait silently and surreptitiously for an attack sprung by a beast in the jungle. Ironically, this male example of humankind discovers that the horrifying beast he has awaited in terror throughout his entire life is his own internal beast expressed silently in the evasion of love. The beast is his own sin of omission in failing to love a woman who had devoted her whole life to being with him, even as he remained in a state of self-aggrandized expectancy. After her death the anti-hero realizes that this woman had lived a meaningful life whereas he had led a sterile one. She has had a full life precisely because she had loved him. But he, so preoccupied with the fetish of his own fate, had missed the beast, the beast of evasion. His life leaves him in a psychic void because he failed to commit to this woman who had remained so devoted to him until her death, the woman who had sacrificed her life to wait with him for his "beast" to spring. The beast metaphor becomes an ironic psychic assault on the male protagonist's sense of things. Until his female friend's death, this man always rationalized his failure to love and commit by saying it was due to his fate of awaiting the dreaded beast to attack, awaiting his dramatic life crisis that never came. After the death of his female friend, the protagonist finally realizes the real nature of his failure, realizing he not only failed to commit to this woman, but more profoundly, had also failed to love her. This failure was in itself the horrible beast he had so feared. As the male protagonist's life draws to a close, he realizes that the beast had sprung at him because of an absence, an absence of his own capacity to love, an absence of his own ability to commit to life through committing to love. His avoidance had been his beast.

Through this realization by his protagonist, Henry James artistically portrays what Jerome Miller concludes, that our remaining human and possessing morality depends on facing the horror of our own avoidances, rather than becoming conscious of unconscious instincts that are detached from a sense of our own agency. This distinction too is the essence of Klein's view of human evolution as passing from a paranoid-schizoid position of consciousness to that of a depressive position consciousness.

EXISTENTIAL MORALITY EVOLVING THROUGH MOURNING PROCESS IN TREATMENT

The clinical situation in which the analyst attends to the mourning process, allowing a natural developmental course to unfold, offers an opportunity to clearly observe this process. As I have stated previously (1985, 1995), two patients vividly displayed the transformation in psychic positions from the paranoid to the depressive position in changing free associations to the same nightmares over time. Each patient had associations to figures in dreams as monsters that induced in them a state of annihilation anxiety and terror. Later in treatment, after much developmental mourning, they each could hold and tolerate guilt. Consequently, instinctual persecutory objects could change to aspects of aggression within the conscious control of self-agency. Otherwise, these would remain out of control impulses, not yet refined into secondary process feelings, and so continuing to be projected and split off as outside monster objects. When split off impulses are joined with object representations of monsters, areas of resistance develop that can manifest in inter-personal terms as avoidance of human compassion. The lack of self-integration and of the self's capacity for agency are critical.

Quite spontaneously, each patient remembered and associated to an earlier nightmare. Naturally, and without any prompting, they each revised their earlier associations to these nightmares. One of these two patients asked at this juncture: "Remember that monster in the nightmare in which my father and I appeared." When I said nothing, she continued: "I said that monster was my mother. Now I see it differently. The monster is me! It's my own greed and insatiable hunger." This insight represented her reowning of split off aggression, as opposed to a defensive protection of the parent as in Fairbairn's moral defense. The other female patient similarly exclaimed, at a later point in the analysis, when she spontaneously recalled the earlier nightmare: "Before I saw that food coming alive in the dream as dangerous animals that could get out of control and eat me. Now I see them as my own hunger, my wanting more and more."

What is required to face our own avoidances as a means to finding our own sense of power and self-agency upon potential entrance into the depressive position? This process of self-surrender involves the psychic ability to "let go," as opposed to the assertion of any active act of will. We surrender to a capacity to suffer wounds and to suffer the rupturing of our boundaries (Miller 1989) by another, as in the ravishment of psychic and sexual penetration. To face our "truth" in this way, there must be a subjective capacity to psychically and emotionally suffer psychic truth – the truth of what is. To surrender to suffering what is psychically real we must have a self, a self that is separate and developed enough to have a sense of agency. To tolerate this surrender, we must develop a sense of self-agency through the internalization of ego functions of frustration tolerance and affect tolerance based on primal interactions. If primal interactions do not forge this capacity to tolerate surrender, we must then develop it through the interactions within a therapeutic holding environment.

THE INTERACTION BETWEEN DEVELOPMENTAL MOURNING AND INTERNALIZATION

Developmental mourning opens the avenue for us to internalize these ego func-tions and capacities, undeveloped during infancy because of a lack of empathic responsiveness from our parents. At the same time, new internalizations within an object relations holding environment in therapeutic treatment enable patients to develop the tolerance of mournful suffering so that developmental mourning can occur. In the treatment of adult patients who have suffered early deprivation of primal good enough internalizations, interaction between internalization and mourning occurs. Therefore, it is often difficult to say which came first, the chicken or the egg, internalization or mourning.

Developmental mourning, as I have defined it (1993, 1996), plays a critical role here. Through the experience of mourning in the presence of a skilled and trained other, one can leave a paranoid state, in which one's own split off eroticized aggression appears as a monster from without. One can enter the realm of self-agency and self-empowerment. Sometimes, as Thomas Ogden (1986) notes; analysts themselves must go through an internal change to modify the paranoid transference of the patient. This can permit the patient to find an entrance to the depressive position capacity to own the agency of his or her own aggression. Without owning aggression, we cannot surrender to a position of loving and needing, which is the critical position for object connection and contact and for the assimilation of object experience in the central self-core. Without the owning of one's aggression, self-agency cannot develop, and therefore symbolic understanding cannot enter awareness and be psychically processed. Self-agency is needed before we can symbolize. Both the capacity to face the pain of regret in mourning and the capacity to surrender to the grief-laden suffering of object loss are essential for self-agency to consolidate, although identifications are significant as well, forged through internalization.

June, a woman I treated, who had left a marriage in her native country to come to live in the United States, had to face the pain of regret over leaving a child behind to make a new life for herself. She suffered terrible grief over the guilt related to this abandonment. In the past, she had run from this guilt, but had been acting it out unconsciously by extreme self-sabotaging behavior. When she was finally able to face her guilt consciously in treatment, and to feel the depressive pain of grief related to having hurt someone who she might have grown to love, she was able to give love more freely to those close to her in her current life. Furthermore, she could begin to share her secret sense of shame with others, and to thus experience a sense of choice about allowing others to know her, a freedom she had never known before. She also began to find her voice in public situations, whereas previously she felt forced to remain silent. Before she had been alone internally and was psychically pursued by internal attacks from an antilibidinal ego (Fairbairn 1952) or a persecutory object. We may also describe them respectively as the internal narcissistic mother of envy and the internal borderline mother of regression and abandonment. However, such a transition from disowned aggression in the paranoid stance, where we experience ourselves as victims of the monsters outside, to that of feeling our own hungers and desires, allowing us to move beyond compulsion to free motivation (Kavaler-Adler 1993), depends on object relations internalizations. If Klein neglected this aspect of psychic development, Winnicott's primary emphasis on good enough mother internalization for self and psychic development covers the theoretical gap.

Such good object internalization is missing in Fairbairn's theory, in which only bad object incorporations are present. Bad object incorporations are split off from the self, or the "central ego's" core. Nevertheless, Fairbairn's ideas of psychic structure seem to allow me, if not invite me, to offer the following elaboration that could account for such internalization.

I believe that an extensive phenomenology of a mourning position, as distinct from an overall depressive position, is a position of loving and needing. The mourning position is a psychic position of suffering mournful affect. The theories of both Winnicott and Fairbairn can be used to fully fortify Klein's phenomenology related to this depressive position extended to a position of mourning and conscious regrets. I do not believe that Klein's own metapsychology of a death instinct, and of an object that preexists within an innate drive, can adequately support the clinical theory of psychic positions and phenomenology that she defines. Therefore, I wish to elaborate on Ronald Fairbairn's "endopsychic structure," and to illustrate how we may use it to account for a developmental view of good object internalization. My elaborated view of Fairbairn's psychic structure can account for the internalization of Winnicott's good enough mother, while also providing analysts with a paradigm for resolving pathological mourning.

Chapter 3

A phenomenological theory of developmental mourning

WEDDING FAIRBAIRN'S PSYCHIC STRUCTURE AND KLEIN'S PHENOMENOLOGY

Whereas Fairbairn proposed a differentiated psychic structure, that of Klein remained amorphous (Greenberg and Mitchell, 1983), and some would say chaotic. Although chaos may at times authentically be reflective of an inner psychic life in process, a theory of psychic phenomenology requires something more. Such a theory needs to bridge the gaps between individuals and to point out common internal threads that effect behavior, while also identifying behavior that transforms simple reenactment into meaningful experience. A theory of psychic structure must accompany clinical observation and psychic phenomenology. We may clinically observe such psychic structure as, for example, in defense maneuvers. I find Fairbairn most helpful here. But I suggest that we expand his metapsychology of real trauma by substituting Klein's phenomenology of real guilt (existential guilt, guilt due to hurting the other in reality, not just fantasy), for the spurious guilt depicted in Fairbairn's description of moral defense. In Fairbairn's moral defense, the child who blames himself for being bad and provoking the abuse or neglect of an inadequate or "bad object" real parent continues throughout his life to enact a defensive self-blame in order to ward off awareness of his parents' true nature. In this way, the child protects his/her self from the tremendous sense of vulnerability that awareness engenders. Such self-blame is not guilt in the sense that Klein used the term. Klein spoke of our inner pain created by realizing our own actual aggression against another, an "other" who we always associated unconsciously with the primal mother, the one we need and love within the internal world. Klein opens doors to human morality, and to the visceral feeling of human morality in the heart, where we experience it as grief.

With this in mind, I find Fairbairn's psychic structure theory helpful in the following way. Our surrenders to suffering the heart's wounding and its related sense of object loss, manifesting as the pain of regret, is what allows the sealed off and split off closed system to unseal. Generally, those who need to assimilate dissociated or split off self-areas require a compassionate other to accompany them during this process. Understanding from this compassionate other can enable the person to surrender to grieving, and thus to the unsealing and integration of the split off self-parts. Usually, this person who can be compassionate on a constant basis is a psychoanalytic psychotherapist. A resonant empathy within an environment of emotional safety may be necessary to permit grief, self-integration, and symbolic assimilation to occur in the context of an overall developmental mourning process. Surrendering to suffering, wounding, object loss, and the pain of regret clears the way for contact with new external objects. If a person possesses limited or constricted psychic capacity for such psychic suffering, this prolongs and fortifies certain pathological predispositions. Attachment to internal and primal bad objects becomes entrenched, along with the operation of projective identification as the dissociated attempt to rid oneself of the bad object scenario.

Although Fairbairn does not speak of projective identification, and only of a sealed world of object relations that is split off from the central ego, and thus split off from external world relationships, projective identification from within this sealed off world is inevitable. A person with a sealed off bad object situation dominating in her psyche will unconsciously pressure anyone in her external world to play a part reflecting the sealed off bad object as the external object. This scenario follows from a closed (static) internal bad object system, in which the person enacts pressures on others through projective identification.

Although the schizoid character, as described by Fairbairn, may seem to operate exclusively through intellectual avenues sealed off from experience in the outer world because his central self is divided and eviscerated of all affect connections and object attachments, this is not entirely true. Rather, the sealed off worlds left within, with their perpetual reenactment of self and bad objects from infancy, exert a pressure on the outside world. And although he does not manifest it as dramatically as does the paranoid patient whose projective identification is obvious, the schizoid also projects into his/her own internal world a sealed off (split off) internal state, a state characterized by emptiness and devastation. Along with projective identification and introjective identification, the schizoid character, as well as any character incapable of mourning, retains a merger of libidinal ego and exciting bad object, as well as of antilibidinal egos and rejecting objects, fused together as one. Albeit unconscious, this fusion results in a continual libidinal gratification from sadomasochistic relations.

How can Fairbairn's model enhance rather than detract from Klein's theory, specifically in relation to her phenomenology of a vulnerable position of a being open to loving and needing, as part of what can be called a "mourning position?" The answer, I believe, lies in locating a psychic position of loving and needing, in which object desires and yearnings can be felt along with openness to feeling object loss (the mourning position?) in Fairbairn's central self (central ego). In such healthy cases, unlike in the pathological cases described by Fairbairn, the self is open to contact and connection with a true "other" (an external object, with its own subjective self-core). We must be careful to distinguish this vulnerable and psychically penetrable self from Fairbairn's (1952) "libidinal ego," which we may describe as being in a constant state of over-stimulated longing and excitement, as it attempts to attain a response to its true self by the "exciting object." The libidinal ego is perennially in a state of need and longing. The libidinal ego cannot love because it is sealed off in an addictive symbiosis with the exciting object that never truly responds. Although the consciousness of the exciting object's unavailability is cut off from the libidinal ego's "knowledge," the rejection exists. The libidinal ego is split off due to the rejecting object's abuse or abandonment of the libidinal ego. Fairbairn's libidinal ego is always lusting after an unavailable "exciting object," one that tantalizes, but doesn't respond with adequate object contact or real responsive love for the libidinal ego as a unique self. The libidinal ego remains, therefore, a split off "pure pleasure ego," as depicted by Masterson (1976), addicted to an exciting object. This pure pleasure ego can remain dominant in the person's psyche if one has not experienced adequate internalization of a good enough holding object from early mothering (in the borderline character particularly, subject to addictions). Similarly, the grandiose self-area can remain dominant in the narcissistic character.

The libidinal ego endlessly repeats the Greek tragedy of pouring its love (or really "need") into a "vacuum," in Fairbairn's terms (1952). A person's libidinal ego splits off when he/she experiences the childhood trauma of being prevented from becoming his true and developing self (Winnicott 1974). The split off trauma then repeats itself through the internal world psychic structure, a reverberating compulsion to repeat that mimics the internalized blueprint of trauma suffered, but not yet felt, from infancy and childhood (the unthought known).

As a sealed off psychic structure the libidinal ego can never be loved. Rather, the libidinal ego (Seinfeld 1993) is continually excited and traumatically frustrated. Consequently, a closed system of unrequited love develops within the internal world. Any available "other" in the external world remains unappetizing to the libidinal ego, which constantly "yearns" for the original primal object, despite its "badness," and perhaps particularly for the erotic parts of the object's demonic aggression. This primal and eroticized intensity when personified is the exciting object's demonic tantalization. This tantalization operates in combination with the exciting object's unavailability as a truly responsive object. Such constant unavailability continually reinforces the traumatized nature of the libidinal ego, keeping it in a tortured and tantalized state, walled off from self and external other contact.

OVERLAP OF FAIRBAIRN AND KLEIN IN THEIR CONCEPTS OF PSYCHIC STRUCTURE

Klein's persecutory object is visible in Fairbairn's half-fused constellation of antilibidinal ego and rejecting object. Both are part objects! We may see Klein's idealized object in the libidinal object's view of the exciting object. Klein's good object can potentially be part of Fairbairn's model if seen as the central ego's attachment to a responsive external object once its split off schizoid parts are integrated within the central ego area. In this way, the true "I" of the person can emerge. This result can hypothetically occur if an available external object is present, in the person of the psychoanalytic psychotherapist. To integrate and assimilate the split off libidinal ego into the central ego (or central self), the patient must enter a state of emotional surrender to the analyst. The trust required for such surrender only develops over time. First analysands need to understand their neurotic defenses in order that these do not obstruct the path to emotional surrender. The presence in neurotic patients of an internal good enough object will facilitate their trust of the analyst in his or her containing and interpreting capacities. In such cases, the prognosis is for a growing capacity for emotional surrender to become a more sustained evolution over time than for patients with character disorders. For those with more primitive defenses, who are in a state of more vulnerability due to a borderline level of preoedipal trauma, the surrender may seem to occur at the beginning of treatment. This is when the pain is too great for the patient to contain, and the need to release the pain and open to contact from another is urgent. However, in such patients, backlash reactions of extreme distancing, compulsive clinging and manipulation, and overall avoidance will also present on a continuing basis. The analyst must understand and articulate to the patient such distancing and its varying forms of dissociation to promote the patient's capacity for awareness and agency during the process of emotional surrender. James Masterson (1976) writes about the "abandonment depression," which constitutes one description of the surrender process in the borderline patient. The surrender to the analyst's containing presence and to the analyst's reliable ego functions in the face of the patient's internal chaos permits affects of mourning to emerge, along with a cognitive recognition of what is being mourned so that symbolization can occur. During the mourning process, the patient expresses rage, loss, and, ultimately, grief. Consequently, the libidinal ego, as a split off "heart" of the self integrates with its central core-self (or Fairbairn's central ego). Klein like Fairbairn would look towards self-integration, integration of the split off parts, as the road to mental health, part of which is the willingness to accept awareness of psychic reality. Facing internal psychic reality reduces distortions of external reality. The inside psychic change effects the outside relationships.

Although Klein speaks of repression and of making the unconscious conscious, some of her clinical cases illustrate primitive character structures in which Fairbairn's "vertical splitting" – a term also used by Kohut (1971) – and its self-dissociation are most in evidence. How does Klein's theory of self-integration, if viewed through the lens of Fairbairn's endopsychic structure, affect the internal world in its relation to the external world as described by Fairbairn? Do Fairbairn and Klein differ in their view of inside and outside? If so, is it possible to make their perspectives more complementary?

INSIDE/OUTSIDE AND INTERIORITY

For Fairbairn, "inside and outside" are in opposition. For Klein, inside and outside operate in parallel. What kind of dialectic can we then create between Klein and Fairbairn in this matter? If we establish that there is a dialectic, we need to understand how this dialectic affects our thinking about the individual's capacity for interiority. For example, how does a dialectic between inside and outside enhance our capacity to mourn and surrender to the affects and cognitions of grief? Genuine grief that is increasingly experienced from a psychic as well as a sensory and visual space within can expand our awareness of interiority. Symbolic linguistics and visual images are present within the psychic space, whereas on the sensory level, a body-based protosymbolism exists. Our awareness of interiority is consequently expanded as mourning opens psychic space in the central self (Fairbairn 1952). The case of June will reveal this growth in internal space that allows for a self-view that incorporates a vision of interiority.

When I speak of inside and outside as in opposition in Fairbairn's theory I mean that Fairbairn focuses on an internal world that is mainly sealed off in a closed system, with the relationships in this world repeating themselves endlessly and monotonously. They are perpetually mirroring and mimicking their own past. They are primal relationships that are so inadequate and "bad" for the nurturance of object relations that they remain transfixed in time. In other words, the child self encased in Fairbairn's original libidinal ego has not gained enough for the primal attachment needs to be experienced with others who are separate from the original primal object. Consequently, the mothering object is continually projected outward or introjected within the psyche. Others become projection screens, and this is not limited to states of desire or need. Nor is it limited to states of libidinal frustration, as Freud once characterized such projection.

The outside for Fairbairn is a world apart, where true "others," external objects such as psychotherapists, wait for the patient to contact them. The central ego in Fairbairn is the only part of the endopsychic system (or "self") open to the outside world and to new "others" who exist outside the sealed off world of object relations repetitions within, beyond Winnicott's "omnipotent gesture" (1974). In Fairbairn's schizoid, the central ego, eviscerated of emotional life, exists as an intellectual shell, contacting the "others" in the outside world only indirectly through a functional but dissociated intellect. Fairbairn's central ego (a functioning and cerebral ego) is devoid of internal contact with emotional need and love, the desire for attachment, and the object-related craving (and later yearning) for connection we are each born with. Inside the emotional heart of the self, which Fairbairn locates in the libidinal ego core, there exists, he implies, a potential for true self feelings, although a person cannot realize this potential in the form of a subjective sense of motivation from within until he integrates the split off libidinal ego (or self). I would add that in order to gain subjective motivation, one also needs to acquire a sense of self-agency through the internalization of another's empathic responsiveness.

Guntrip has called Fairbairn's libidinal ego a split off "heart" of the self. In addition, he proposes the existence of a "regressed ego" that overshadows the libidinal ego self with a second split off heart (Guntrip 1976). Guntrip speaks of Fairbairn's split off libidinal ego as an active and hungry oral ego, and his own contribution, the "regressed ego", as a passive, withdrawing part of the self that is highlighted in the schizoid character. Theorists such as Jay Greenberg and Steven Mitchell (1983) and Jeffrey Seinfeld (1990) believe that an additional split off part is unnecessary. I concur with them on this point. So rather than referring to an integrating regressed ego, I prefer to focus on integrating the split off libidinal core, or heart of the self. The self's heart is a potential true self, which can only evolve through a new relationship with outside others.

By calling the libidinal ego a dependent self, Seinfeld (1990) makes a play for a more experiential language of self and object than Freudian instinct theory, which uses the term libido. The dependent self longs for the other. It clings to the parental object it depends on, existing in a state of endless yearning. This dependent self is sealed off within the internal world. It perpetually lusts for the split off "exciting object," which is the part of the internalized original parent. Frustrated needs for object attachment are focused on the exciting object and its pure instinct desire. But attachment to the exciting object precludes an adequate dependent attachment. Since the part-object parent excites and perennially disappoints, it serves as a tyrannical oppressor that, as the "rejecting object," perpetually exists in a sealed off state. The rejecting object itself represents an incorporation of the experience of the parent as an abandoning or disappointing object. Moreover, the rejecting object exists in relation to the split off part self, called the "antilibidinal ego" by Fairbairn. The antilibidinal ego identifies with the rejecting object and with it constitutes the "internal saboteur" of Fairbairn. This "internal saboteur" can be felt by the person as self-assaultive and often as a hypercritical and hostile force within. As an incorporation of the experience of the parent as an abandoning or disappointing object, the antilibidinal ego identifies with the rejecting object and continually repeats the parent's aggression in a traumatic mode of repetition compulsion. Together, and yet split off from one another as well, the libidinal and antilibidinal egos play out their hypnotic dance of repetition with their semi-fused persecutors represented by the exciting and rejecting objects. Fairbairn, as indicated, called the rejecting object and its hooked in antilibidinal ego the "internal saboteur." In the libidinal ego all hope is dashed repeatedly by the antilibidinal ego's experience of parental rejection. However, because these two self-states within the libidinal and antilibidinal egos are dissociated, the libidinal ego continues to naively hope to win the object, even when the antilibidinal ego, identified with the rejecting object part of the object keeps abusing and rejecting its counterpart, the libidinal ego. Dissociated from the experience of the antilibidinal ego, the libidinal ego keeps hoping to win love and nurturance from the exciting object, which unbeknown to it keeps transforming into the rejecting object. Meanwhile, the "exciting object" continues its dance of tantalization.

PSYCHIC CHANGE AND INSIDE/OUTSIDE

The only avenue to psychic change in Fairbairn's theory lies in the libidinal ego joining the central ego through risking involvement with the outside world. The therapist can play the role of this key external object, representing the whole outside world that awaits if the libidinal ego can leave its addiction to the internal exciting object and can connect first to the therapist, and then to others in the outside world. Possibly these outside others can provide a better or more benign mode of relationship than that still enacted and reenacted with the early primal parent within the internal world. If not benign, the external relationship will at least be a novel one in contrast to the old object of monotone repetition.

From this description we can see that for Fairbairn the inside world is static and unchanging, a world of suffocation and addiction, although touched by excitement within the libidinal ego area. This static closed system regenerates anxiety, rejection, loss, narcissistic injury, and annihilation terror. In contrast, the outside world of Fairbairn might be seen as a world of potential aliveness, spontaneity, and fullness (as in Winnicott's true self-experience), although Fairbairn never explicitly states this. I would see the outside world, outside the sealed off closed system of split and part object relations, as a world of rich and unknown possibilities – the outside world is the world of potential whole object relations and whole self development.

Fairbairn nearly assumes that external objects are better than those split part primal objects housed inside. In this manner, inside and outside are opposed to one another. However, Fairbairn neglects to deal with the projective identification processes of the sealed off libidinal and antilibidinal egos. Such projective identification exerts pressure on all outside others, others who are present with the person who has split off (dissociated) parts. There is pressure on the outside others to engage in the sealed off internal world enactment provoked in the past. Fairbairn deals only with external objects as free agents that offer potential salvation, not as those vulnerable to the pressures of projective identification.

In contrast, Melanie Klein's internal and external worlds are, as indicated, parallel worlds. They are mirroring universes. To be inside with our internal objects is not to be sealed off in isolation. In Melanie Klein's internal world, the person loves, hates, fights, and lusts with all her passions. She destroys and repairs her internal objects. She takes on her parents in hostile or benign intercourse. She sucks or tears up the breast mother, while remaining within her comforting presence. The preoedipal object relations of the past may exist within this internal world, but they are dynamic and interactive with others in the external world. Through psychic mechanisms of both projective identification and introjective identification, the two worlds interact and exchange with one another perhaps. When we make love to our internal object, assault it or attempt to make reparations to it, the same relational operations transpire in relation to others in the external world. The initiation of motivation as well as compulsion originates from within.

The inside does not seal off, and therefore does not only house compulsive monotony as in Fairbairn's inside.

To be inside in Klein, then, does not mean to be imprisoned in "bad object" relations as it does in Fairbairn. For Klein, good and bad exist inside as they also do outside. Consequently, traveling from one realm to another, from inside to outside, does not involve opening up life and emotional touch, or true "contact." Inside and outside, contact exists, intermingled with psychic fantasy.

DEVELOPMENTAL MOURNING AND SELF-EVOLUTION THROUGH EXPANDING INTERIORITY

At this point, we may be able to answer the following questions. How can a theory of mourning phenomenology benefit from either or both theories? Can a theory of mourning phenomenology be independent of an either/or metapsychology, as represented by Klein's death instinct theory or Fairbairn's "real experience" (as opposed to a dialectic of real experience and psychic fantasy, described by Winnicott (1974) as essential to psychic health)? Such internal metapsychology significantly differs from a dialectic of real experience and psychic functioning, which Winnicott (1974) – for one – has described as essential to psychic health. How can we approach a description of interior life with a theory of mourning phenomenology, particularly interior life as it is felt subjectively from within? As our awareness of interior life expands with the mourning process we find a subjective and phenomenal state of "interiority" that is continually found and refound in the clinical situation.

For any one person to succeed at mourning, it is often necessary for that person to be emotionally touched by another outside the self. An example of this can be seen in the successful mourning of Charlotte Brontë (Kavaler-Adler 1993), which required that the author be emotionally touched by the professor for whom she later yearned and grieved. Once a person is emotionally touched in this manner, past object relations that have been incorporated, but not assimilated and digested in the psyche, can be transformed into symbolic forms through the grief affect experience within mourning. Cognitive memories of lost but incorporated objects can be relinked or reconnected to each other and to dissociated affect states related to these incorporated objects.

Mourning composed of memory, symbolization, and the affect experience of grief, can transform formerly split off incorporations into new integrated whole object forms. It is within the experience of conscious and grieved object loss that blocked symbolic capacities become unblocked. Unblocking may follow the release of a formerly dissociated and projected primitive aggression or the conscious reconnecting with repressed aggression (Kavaler-Adler 1993). The unblocking process may involve expressing rage prior to genuinely experiencing grief. As blocked symbolic capacities emerge into conscious and preconscious experience, free associative functions begin to operate with observing ego reflection. Representations can then form in the central self that serve as symbolic containers for formerly split off self parts, comprised of self and other object relations constellations (Stern 1985).

Interpersonal communication and mental associations generally stimulate such mourning. In this respect, we may see the inside world of Fairbairn as an interior sealed off world that opens to the world through the mourning process, transforming the personality's internal psychic object relations. Through the unsealing of the split off elements of the internal world, the central self expands. Only then can we open to the prospect of being emotionally touched by the outside other. Such reception of outside contact forms an emotional connection and also reinforces the capacity for the cognitive working through of the mourning process, which ultimately allows for the resolution of addictive and tenacious repetition compulsions. Through an opening to the emotional connection with an external other, the split off and sealed off dissociated object constellations can unseal from their formerly isolated state. Thus, object relations become present in current time and space and are alive with the kind of spontaneity found in Winnicott's true self and Freud's free association process. An incorporated object, formerly in a narcissistic form of an "image object" (Kavaler-Adler 1996), now comes alive with a potential for emotional contact. Our narcissistic preoccupation with merely mirroring the self (promoting grandiose self structures) can lessen through the new external object connections that form as the mourning process is promoted through varying stages of development ("developmental mourning"). Consequently we become truly interested in others. We become aware of their subjectivity as we expand our own interiority.

Within Fairbairn's theory, emotional touch would seem not to be enough for object relations and mourning. However, Fairbairn in his later papers (1952) implies that the central ego might house healthy or good enough objects without being sealed off from contact with the external world, differing from the libidinal and antilibidinal egos. Then emotional touch from the outside can make an impact (in the central self or ego area). Fairbairn never elaborated on this aspect of his theory. As summarized by Greenberg and Mitchell (1983), Fairbairn's theory mainly focused on pathology in the internal world, which he depicted in terms of the sealed off libidinal and antilibidinal egos. This observation raises the question: "Can a sealed off libidinal ego mourn?" I would say this is impossible, because a part object has no subjectivity or agency. Also, there is no emotional connection between the libidinal ego and outside external others, due to its split off, sealed off nature. Emotional connection between the split off part and the outside other would be necessary for the development of the psychic motivation for mourning. Such emotional connection, as opposed to sadomasochistic reactions, would also be needed to allow for the emotional contact that transforms excitement and despair into object related longings. Unlike Klein's view of a depressive position self-state in which the person dissolves blocks and defensive maneuvers to claim a vital heart of self and to allow for a vulnerability to loving and needing, in Fairbairn's metapsychology, the libidinal ego can merely yearn for an unavailable "exciting object," whose rejection is imminent, but dissociated. Consequently, the libidinal ego has no opening to emotional touch.

What would interiority be like in Fairbairn's central ego, if his/her emotional life and needs for object connection were not entirely split off? Could interiority be a source of meaningful grief and positive psychic suffering that is used to transform the personality? When suffering constitutes the existential experience of what is, mourning allows the psychic structure to remain open to current object relations within the interpersonal relations and thus to new internalizations. The changing of the old psychic structure is related to the psychic suffering[1] of yearnings for old modes of object connections, stemming back to the primal connections of infancy. The person must relinquish these old connections to renew object connection with external others in the present. Facing suffering involves confronting the loss of defensive control and facing the relinquishing of old and habitual object relations and their internal world imprints. When a person experiences powerful grief suffering, the letting go occurs, and basic attachment longings free up for new and current relations, both within the internal world of the central self and with external objects. In the process, the person owns her aggressive and erotic impulses and discovers representations of them in the central self-area, rather than keeping them split off in dissociation or repression. The integration of drive impulses and object relations attachment enables the person to experience a subjective sense of aliveness, which lends a feeling of interiority to psychic experience and identity. The central ego (self) area is enlivened.

Perhaps here is where we need to join Melanie Klein's internal world to that of Fairbairn, conjecturing that some amalgam might be possible. If Fairbairn were to have an alive internal world, located in the central ego, where an alive heart of the libidinal self would reside and connect with an external other in current reality,[2] this could be the nexus between Klein's dynamic internal world and Fairbairn's internal world. This amalgam could, like Klein's internal world, be a world where inside and outside interact, although in the psyche Klein theorized they can also merely mirror one another through mechanisms of projective identification and introjective identification. However, here, in this amalgam of Klein and Fairbairn's models, the emphasis would be on internalization as a mechanism to refresh the internal self and stimulate the condition for love, self-expression, and mourning. Projective identification and introjective identification could be mechanisms reserved for the split off ego parts.

Klein never emphasizes internalization. Rather she focuses on innate psychic fantasy relations, which, when played out within, affect how we view and interact with the external world. However, in Klein's later theory, particularly in her treatise "Envy and Gratitude," not published until 1957, Klein does open the door to a theory of internalization. In her dialectic between envy and gratitude, she suggests that loving connections growing through internalizations from without can modify the seemingly endless spoiling processes of envy, as gratitude is expressed to an external other and love modifies hate. This notion does not negate Klein's overall emphasis on modifying hate through making conscious unconscious psychic fantasies of it, which express themselves in the interpersonal attitude of envy. But in "Envy and Gratitude" she opens herself to the idea that internalization from outside objects may be a route to building the self. This is a notion that Winnicott later develops extensively, as in all his papers in *The Maturational Processes and the Facilitating Environment*, such as "The Capacity to Be Alone" (1965). Moreover, in "Mourning and Its Relation to Manic Depressive States" (1940), Klein speaks of an external object – Mrs. A's son – as profoundly impacting on his mother's internal world, arousing the internal objects of her past by association and emotional linking. In addition, his psychic presence allows the mother who survives his death to begin a psychic interaction between mourning for the external objects of the present reality and the past reality from childhood. The impact of outside and inside, past and present, is engendered in the process – not just cycles of projection and introjection.

Klein's movement towards a theory of internalizing both good and bad objects, but especially good objects – the good breast – as we take the loved one inside at the moment of expressing gratitude, has powerful implications for her theory of mourning as a clinical and developmental process. In addition, her theory of internalization has implications for my extension of the concept of internalization into a theory of mourning process that exists throughout the life cycle. I have spoken of such a theory in *The Compulsion to Create* (1993). Klein moves towards Fairbairn's theory of real experience and trauma shaping the psyche (here Klein, Fairbairn, and the other British object relations theorists are in line with Freud's "shadow of the object falling on the ego"), while still returning to the fullness of interior space as a home for instinctual personifications in the form of psychic fantasy objects and object relations. Her weakness is in formulating all these loose internal relations into a single psychic structure, and here Fairbairn is helpful.

For Fairbairn, the central ego and its external object provide an area for alive internalization, whereas the split off libidinal and antilibidinal egos show the area of psychic conflict created by early internalizations, which we can easily see as invested with instinct and fantasy. The person does not feel conflict as "conflict" until the two split off selves are integrated into the central self. The conflict is enacted as a split, as occurs with in borderline patients. As contact is made with the outside world, it makes possible movement from split off libidinal self-parts, with heartfelt longings, into the self's central open system.

THE KLEIN–FAIRBAIRN INTERACTION

Here is where Klein's theory of mourning and Fairbairn's theory of psychic structure most obviously interact. For Klein's focus on mourning as clinical process allows us to comprehend how Fairbairn's closed off internal system, with its split off libidinal and antilibidinal ego constellations, opens up to the outside world, expanding beyond projective identification with outside objects. Klein's focus on mourning extends beyond Fairbairn's exorcism to a sustained connection with outside objects, who are emotionally and psychically encountered for the first time, rather than recycled through the projections and introjections of a closed internal system. When the process of mourning is done in the presence of an empathic other – at best a steady therapeutic presence who offers empathic understanding, confirmation, and reflection of the ideation of the lost object constellations that surface through the affect experience of grief and loss – this allows for the opening of psychic space so that emotional contact with new outside objects can take place. This results in internalizations of novel interpersonal experiences. This is how Klein's theory provides an affect process underpinning for Fairbairn's psychic structure theory.

Conversely, Fairbairn's psychic structure theory offers a system of thought about psychic structure organization and the organization of psychic structure change that permits us to picture the results of Klein's clinical and developmental mourning process. Fairbairn has spoken of the need for the split off egos to surrender their internal addictive clinging to the bad objects that enact old traumas in a dissociated and split off psyche. Otherwise, they cannot open to new attachments (and internalizations) to outside others who are currently present in their lives. However, one resists surrender by tenaciously holding onto the primary mother, who has so vividly become incorporated in the sealed off area of the psyche (as exciting and rejecting part objects). The person will not let go of the original object because of the power of aggressive and erotic drives empowering that age-old archaic connection.

She holds onto it because of profound infant needs for security that she has come to associate with that original object since the beginning of her life. In addition, she holds on to it because of the fear of retraumatization when encountering new others, others who exist outside of the area of control of the closed off internal system (in Winnicott's language, "outside one's omnipotent gesture"). Yet, once the person takes the risk and depends on the new object for new object attachment, this affects the entire internal closed off system, as the central ego area of Fairbairn's psyche expands through new internalizations. And even though mourning promotes this process, the process in turn encourages renewed modes of mourning and its progressive developmental consequences. For with an opening to outside object connection comes the subjective feeling of being emotionally touched or encountered from the outside. If this sense of emotional touch reaches the split off heart of the self in the libidinal ego, then a new affect life is born, which allows the person to process grief affects and their related cognitive links to memory traces of objects during varying phases of developmental mourning.

Fairbairn (1952) speaks of the fantasy of exorcism as the route to freeing the libidinal ego of its imprisoning bad object, and its anti-life force in the antilibidinal ego (the "internal saboteur"). Exorcism, however, is not a psychic operation that lasts! Such fantasized exorcism simply results in projective cycles, as described by Klein. There must be emotional contact between the patient's rage and grief and the analyst's empathy if the closed off part of the psyche is to open to new attachments and psychic growth through new and healthier internalizations. The process also involves a new consciousness of past traumas that the person formerly felt compelled to repeat, when still in the closed internal self-system.

THE CONTRIBUTIONS OF JAMES MASTERSON AND D.W. WINNICOTT

Masterson's (1976, 1981) conception of an affective "abandonment depression" carrying on a process of "separation" works well here. "Abandonment depression" is experienced through an anguished emptiness, often visualized as a huge void in the self (Dickinson's "abyss," see Kavaler-Adler 1993). When mourning and its grieving affect experience begin to heal, this profound psychic sense of absence is a process that extends beyond any fantasized exorcism. It is an avenue to connection with the subjectivity of an "other," that, when internalized as psychic structure, can repair early maternal bonding which has been traumatically disrupted. Rage and grief, within the developmental mourning process, can open affective routes for object connection when the presence of a psychotherapist allows such affect, as well as the needs for connection it signals, to emerge from within the void. Just as the person needs emotional responses from outside others for emotional contact to happen, so too in object relations psychotherapy and analysis, the patient needs the analyst to provide a holding environment for the abandonment depression mourning process to occur. Analysts do this by offering the patient an empathic mode of listening and safety. They offer their analysands (patients) a symbolic understanding of their rage and aggressive attacks, which often accompany grief experience. In this manner, the analyst becomes a good enough object in Winnicott's sense of an object that does not (to a good enough degree) retaliate or emotionally abandon the patient. Such a holding environment, with the analyst as an external object who also stimulates in the patient object attachment longings, sexual desires, and aggressive modes of reacting to an outside other, results in the patient's experiencing a frustration that will renew her awareness of past trauma, as well as bringing to the forefront of her consciousness intense psychic conflict.

Psychic change and growth come when the individual experiences trauma and conflict in tolerable doses through the modifying presence of the analyst, who helps give words to this experience of both trauma and conflict. However, change ultimately does not just come through consciousness of that formerly unconscious and split off, but also through the core affect experience of loss, which if tolerated, allows for the opening of the primal psychic place of object attachment within the libidinal ego or dependent self. The tolerance of the grief related to object loss (and related self-loss) constitutes the most painful developmental suffering of the individual (along with its aggressive constellations) and so engenders the possibility for true and lasting psychic change. Loss is ubiquitous in psychic change and growth, although it is frequently unacknowledged or even not felt by the person involved in the change.

Robin Morgan (1986) quotes scientists on thermodynamic theory who maintain that every expenditure of energy is accompanied by some loss. Similarly, all psychic change, growth, and expenditures of psychic energy are paid for by some loss, which the person must mourn. Otherwise, some deterioration in psychic growth and psychic integration occurs. If we do not consciously experience the suffering evoked by object loss, the closed off part of the self remains unreached, and consequently, the self does not integrate split off and repressed parts, which are unavailable as long as the loss is being defended against. Thus the self does not transform developmentally. This idea is based on the premise that object loss that is experienced, but not consciously known within the central self area of the psyche, blocks our capacity to face psychic conflict. Such "unthought known" experience also blocks surrendering or relinquishing of old modes of relationship that persist in the psyche following trauma. The "unthought known" blocks surrender to awareness of a full range of frustration and trauma, which overstimulates the psyche and promotes psychic conflict.

With the analyst's presence, and with his/her symbolic articulation of the process, with his containing mode of affect modulation, and his/her help in integrating cognitive functions, the patient in psychotherapy is often able to bear the pain of mourning. Without the analyst's presence it can be unbearable to tolerate such pain. Instead of mourning, a multitude of defensive modes of splitting and cutting off responses result. The analyst provides a constant empathic, supportive, and symbolic mode of response, offering the patient verbal explanations for her affect experience and her self and object connections (linking functions), encouraging the patient to conceptualize and integrate the memories that are connected with the pain of grief. In turn, when the analyst provides the patient with a safe environment, the patient is able to progressively internalize the therapeutic presence and response. These internalized transactions between patient and analyst create microstructures and secondary functions along with symbolic capacities and representations that are transformative.

A NEW METAPSYCHOLOGY OF PSYCHIC DIALECTIC: WILFRED BION AND RONALD FAIRBAIRN

Relying on these functions of the analyst, the patient assimilates new object experience and digests the old forms though symbolic understanding. Wilfred Bion (1984) has spoken of such psychic digestion, so critical to self-integration, in terms of unmetabolized alpha elements that are transformed into symbolic beta elements through the containing function of the analyst (as through the original containing function of an infant's mother). We psychically digest and process any mode of external object relationship, including our own regrets about the role we play in losing the love or presence of a love object. Such mourning process allows us to symbolize. In Fairbairn's psychic structure terms, incorporations of undigested and unsymbolized objects, which I will call incorporations, act upon us like demons and demon lovers (split off aggressive and eroticized self and other constellations). They can only be transformed into the realm of symbolized representations within a conscious central personality (or central ego) through the process of mourning. Mourning process involves a dialectic within the psyche between subjective self experience and the affect related to the impact of object experience that we must remember and mourn. Simultaneously, we must permit an external dialectic between the patient's eruptions of rage and grief, and the analyst's help in bringing the patient to awareness of both memory and psychic fantasy related to these affect eruptions. We need less of a dialectic with the external other, or analyst, when the eruption of affect already is linked in the patient's association and memory with self and object representations from past experience. Through mourning process a developmental evolution of self-integration occurs. This is why I use the term "developmental mourning."

We mourn losses related to the object we love and hate, and toward whom we have regrets. If we can tolerate both the love and hate of ambivalence (Klein's definition of the depressive position capacity), the psyche can process loss and the guilt of regret, thereby modifying a too primitive or punitive superego structure. Through mourning we can amalgamate memory and current perception of the object into a symbolic internalization that integrates, rather than divides, internal and external reality. Such integration in turn promotes awareness of interiority and intersubjectivity. For Fairbairn, this would increase the spatial dimensions of the container in the central self and modify split off incorporations that remain viscerally alive with reenactive dynamics. These reenactive dynamics can be related to the experience of a demonic force. Such "demon" experience (Fairbairn 1952) is a form of incorporated object connection which, due to its sadomasochistic nature, cannot yet be symbolized and understood. This sadomasochism, incessantly repeated in the psyche, presses to be reenacted in behavior. It is filled with raw and primitive affect experience, and with manic erotic intensities (impulses) that lack gender differentiation or the differentiation of an object's sense of agency. The eroticized aspect, when in this manic and undifferentiated form, extends the demonic intrusions experienced on a visceral level into the mode of a demon lover personification.

If we define the inner heart of the self as a core of spiritual and emotional longings – longings which are associated with the capacity to love another and to nurture object connection with another – we may view the closing off of the heart of the self and its longings as having severe psychic structure consequences. These consequences have been seen by Fairbairn, who portrays them in terms of a closed off psychic system, with its split off egos, and its sealing off from affect contact with others outside the self system. In essence, Fairbairn was describing a state of pathological mourning or blocked mourning, where the heart and its longings for an external other are blocked, because the internal sealed off primal other is clung to on a profound psychic level. Consequently, the integrating of that split off heart of self as referred to by Guntrip (by Fairbairn as the libidinal ego, and by Winnicott as the "true self") has powerful consequences for renewed psychic development. With new and better external relations and internalizations, psychic image representations of both old and new objects become increasingly possible. Grief affect and mournful perception, in which the distinct idiosyncratic nature of the other is perceived, fuel and oil the formation of symbolism and the internal "taking in" of external forms to create symbols. The experience of grief is in turn facilitated by the analyst's words and thoughts, which differentiate thoughts, feelings, experiences, and the symbolic representations of all these factors.

This facilitation by the analyst also means that protosymbolic experience is converted into symbolic experience, as I have shown in the case of Lois, in *The Creative Mystique* (1996). The visceral and sensory experiences of objects that lack representations in the internal world or secondary process (Fairbairn's central ego) are connected to symbolic forms. Lois's fantasies and hallucinations of snails floating in her mouth and in the decor around her were transformed in her psyche into the symbolic form of a rapist, a form of demon lover figure. Lois actually experienced her demon lover in the form of the man who raped her, although there was also a blueprint for the demon lover in her internal world, as indicated by her dream life. Often the demon lover is created totally from within as in the case of Emily Dickinson (Kavaler-Adler 1993).

Through the mourning process in her object relations therapy, Lois came to realize that she had displaced and projected the image of her visceral experience of her mouth on her rapist's penis into the symbol of the snail, rather than facing the raw horror of a memory of the actual event. Yet she was unaware of the symbolic translation as long as she operated on a presymbolic level, with protosymbolic enactments of part object experience (the part objects of mouth and penis without their context), and merely reacted to the world and her body as if they were full of snails. The transformation from the protosymbolic sensation and visceral enactment occurred through the emotional touch and connection between her and myself as her analyst (Kavaler-Adler 1996). We reached symbolic realization through the being together, helping to unblock and open Lois's rage, grief, and loss. This affect experience, caused by the communion of analyst and patient, constitutes "developmental mourning" process (Kavaler-Adler 1993, 1996). The analysand articulates this mourning in the sphere of being with and "going on being" (Winnicott 1974). This sphere of being together holds and contains the patient's enraged and grief-stricken anguish of grieving. Some theorists, such as Ogden (1986), might conceptualize this area of analyst and patient in communion within the empathic atmosphere of the holding environment (Winnicott 1974) or "therapeutic object relationship" (Grunes 1984) as an intersubjective area. But it is both intersubjective and interpenetrating, thus enlarging a psychic capacity for what I call "interiority." In Bion's terms, it becomes containing when the analyst can transfer the protosymbolic experience of the "being together" during mourning into symbolic interpretations, which during mourning are process focused rather than contact focused. The analyst's verbal naming of emotions and self states within the analysand results in symbolic formulations that the analysand can take in and assimilate into a cognitive self view, a view that allows the analysand to see herself/himself in process.

In Fairbairn's terms, the central ego (central self) is expanded as symbolization grows through the unblocking of the sealed off psyche. This occurs with the rage and grief of mourning. New symbolic understanding is achieved on a cognitive level, as mourning opens psychic space for the analyst's interpretations and internalizations. As Lois began to open to needing me as the available external object, she could mourn and internalize a better object experience. Simultaneously, she could modify the rage that served as both drive discharge and Fairbairn's form of bad object exorcism. As her rage was modified, Lois could turn to grief within the continuing therapeutic object relationship in treatment (Fairbairn's turn to an external object). Thus, the libidinal heart, or the child self, was able to reenter the world through entering the central ego and experiencing its mournful suffering (as opposed to masochistic suffering). A sense of being newly alive and of healing self-injury could follow. Once integrated into a central self, self-agency becomes possible, as affects, needs and hunger are owned. Interpersonal communication follows. Rage can then be contained in the service of this communication and of this ongoing connection. This would be seen in the case of Lois, where the core self rejoins the central ego-self. Splits were healed, as Lois could truly relive the traumas that led to an injured sensation within the heart of the self, while simultaneously owning her rage and self-agency.

The affective experience of grief and remorse reflects mourning process, as does the naming of object experience that the patient remembers along with the affect experience in the containing presence of the other. Transference is not bypassed, but processed. I am (and other analysts) not just the external object who enables the patient to connect his interior to a responsive other outside. I am also the symbolized demon rapist and the longed for early holding mother, both idealized and demonic, existing in different areas of the patient's psyche. The patient can idealize or repress and/or dissociate an image of me, just as she can idealize or repress and/or dissociate an image of me as demonic. When dissociation predominates, due to early trauma, this conjures up in the patient the subjective experience of alternating self-states. At one point, the dissociated part comes into focus, and the formerly conscious part splits off into a state of dissociation in the background of psychic awareness, as in Kernberg's description of the borderline (1975). The analysand's mourning process can entail naming of all my envisioned and projected parts, as seen through the primary object transference, and this extends to the naming of the relationship itself. Each of the analysand's self-parts is named in its connection to my parts, as object. I have a functional use as an object for complementary self-parts, both as a transference object and as an emotionally felt external "other," effecting in Lois's case her receptivity to contact and connection.

DEVELOPMENTAL PERSPECTIVE

Fairbairn and Klein's theories reinforce and commingle with one another, as Winnicott's internalization and object survival theories also interact with them. All these theorists combined offer a developmental perspective! What seemed diverse perspectives of Klein and Fairbairn, in relation to outside and inside, can be made to exist coherently together.

Mourning process converts a pathological mourning state, where inside and outside are opposed, in Fairbairn, into an area of potential interaction. Meanwhile, Fairbairn's psychic structure explanation of pathological relations from infancy remains intact. The mirroring of inside and outside in Klein is expanded more fully into an interactive penetration of inside and outside through mourning. This inter-penetration refers to outside contact, or emotional touch from a real other (as opposed to a fantasy other), who exists outside of the closed internal system within, which continues to play out its drama based on a blueprint of past enact-ments. The one who can touch the psyche from the outside is an individual who has not succumbed to being used by the projective identifications of the patient, an individual who is not locked into the patient's closed system of object relations (bad or inadequate object relations from the past). This can occur as a transforma-tional experience that modifies the closed system, with its compulsive enactments. I was able to be this kind of transitional other for Lois. When she opened to gratitude and thus to internalization of a good other, as Melanie Klein wrote in "Envy and Gratitude" (1957), she formed new and more permeable psychic struc-ture. She could then allow me to penetrate her psychologically, to emotionally touch her from the outside, and so help her create within herself an avenue for her to understand symbolic interpretations and reflections of her self-process. This creative interaction enhanced her cognitive grasp of her emotional journey through mourning.

The following cases of mourning within psychoanalytic psychotherapeutic treatment illustrate the theory just espoused. Each analysand expressed the mean-ing of her/his own mourning experience as it took place in the psychotherapeutic situation.

LOVE–CREATIVITY DIALECTIC

My own theory of love–creativity dialectic is a modern integration and extension of Klein, Fairbairn and Winnicott, along with my own clinically informed insights. I have spoken about this theory as a theory of psychic health in *The Creative Mystique* (1996). My basic premise is that successful self-integration ultimately manifests as a continuing capacity for psychic dialectic. This capacity for psychic dialectic allows for the navigation of psychic conflict throughout critical develop-mental phases as internalized good-enough object connection allows for self integration, which in part is related to the ability to be conscious of loss and to mourn major losses throughout life. My belief in the primary role of psychic dialectic in development relates back to the work of Sheldon Bach (1985), who speaks of narcissistic states as being evidenced by failing in psychic dialectic. He explained narcissistic states, in part, as a cognitive phenomenon, one which developmental arrest has blocked or derailed healthy psychic dialectic. Characteristic of narcissistic pathology is the foreclosing of inner life, in as much as one can either be all in one's own perspective or all in the other person's perspective, but cannot freely go back and forth in one's mind between a subjective perspective and an outside perspective. This creates problems in empathy, compassion, and/or in self-reliance and self-centering.

Psychic dialectic is not just about maintaining a fluid and conscious transition between subjectivity and other objectivity. It is about the fluid transition (Winnicott's transitional stage and transitional space being clinically relevant here) between all aspects of duality in one's psychic nature, between masculine and feminine self-aspects, between thinking and feeling, heart and stomach affects, between affect and impulse. I extend the dialect of the psyche and its personality to the terrain of innate psychic potential for both love and creativity, seeing the capacity to express this dual and yet differentiated potential as a need to do so. I believe that a baseline definition of psychic health is quite simple. We need to be able to love and create, without using interpersonal relations as a defense against creativity (self expression and self identity definition) and without using creativity as a defense against love and its expression in intimacy (Kavaler-Adler 1993). Those of us who can both love and create, achieve developmental increments in intimacy and creative self-expression, and to the extent that we can do so, we can evolve towards psychic health.

We need to express our needs for connection and for identity in this dialectic of love and creativity. We need to flow back and forth between the internal world from which we draw creative self-expression to the interpersonal world where we express and give love, and therefore where we nurture our internal worlds through internalizing new object relations connections. If there is a psychic impasse, or even a partial impasse in the form of a delay between connecting with our internal world (creativity) and connecting with others (love), then we are diminished in our innate potential and are diminished in psychic health. This always is a manifestation of impairments in self-integration, whether due to psychic conflict (between unconscious psychic fantasy and conscious desire and impulse), or due to developmental arrest and its splitting (and dissociative) processes (as described by Fairbairn and Klein). Perhaps women bring a free flow between two sides of the brain (corpus callosum) making them more capable physiologically of fluidity in the dialectic. I see both male and female, however, as needing the flow between love and creativity, and to the extent that defenses wall off part of the psyche and obstruct the dialectic, my clinical and scholastic studies having shown that pathology results. I have demonstrated this most distinctly in my studies of women artists with preoedipal trauma (Kavaler-Adler 1996, 1993).

When obstructed by pathological mourning, in the sense Fairbairn speaks of how one clings to old regressive self and object constellations, varying somatic and mental symptoms result. The demon lover complex also is an object relations symptom of this blocked pathological mourning state. In this complex, internal object ties are split off and sealed off from contact with the central self and the external interpersonal world. This manifests as split off impulses pressing us from within and seeking exorcism through pathological forms of projective identification (the borderline putting out the "bad self" and yet retaining its impulses) a form of failed exorcism. The personification of split off impulses, affects, and part objects creates the sense of inner demons. When eroticized these personified self part aggressive impulses, combined with primitive part object imprints (precursors of symbolic representations), which can enact impulses that have been internalized during psychically disruptive real object relations, can create the experience of being possessed by a demon lover.

TIME AS AN OBJECT

Two kinds of time exist in relation to the love–creativity dialectic: organic time versus a linear time. Linear time limits can create intense time pressures, as well as creating a diminishment in psychic space. We need both organic and linear time, but if the flow between these two modes of time is disrupted, the blocks create time into pressures that can be felt as personified and persecutory. True self-spontaneity, and creative process free association occur most vividly when one can feel held by organic time and allow linear time to exist non-intrusively in the background of one's mind.

When suspended in organic time, those on the verge of creativity experience the sense of being held in infancy by the symbiotic mother, who is now felt as a current muse. If linear time intrudes into the foreground of experience, rather than staying in the background, psychic blocking results, symptomatic of the clinging to old objects and object constellations. Then pathological mourning forestalls psychic dialectic. When one can let go through mourning, which requires sustained love connections, either internal or external, one can let go of linear time. This allows our internal persecutory personas to simultaneously let go of us. Then we can allow organic time to be in the foreground, contributing to the feeling of flow at these times – the limits of linear time. Whether we merge with a psychic muse or with another person in a state of intimacy, we are in a connection that sustains the flow of time. The maternal psychic image that exists unconsciously in relation to organic time is felt as a holding in eternity in the "eternal now." The psychic fantasy (Klein) of the holding mother becomes our Winnicottian transitional object. This is why artists and writers often personify the creative process itself as mother. This fantasy mother, derived in part from the internalization of the symbiotic phase (Mahler *et al.* 1975) mother of infancy, can be experienced as a muse by the artist (male or female). However, for the female artist (Kavaler-Adler, 1993, 1996), the muse is often a maternal object of need (breast) dressed up in the father's whole cloth personality – existing as a mother within father – similar to Melanie Klein's description of the father in mother as a universal psychic fantasy (more consciously undifferentiated in the borderline or narcissistic character).

SPACE AS OBJECT, CONTAINER AND ENVIRONMENT

The "demon lover" is a spatial phenomenon within the psyche, as well as a temporal one that interacts with time as an internal object, i.e. interacts with the holding mother. The demon lover exists in the dark occlusions between connection – where connection with the mother has been disrupted, early on in life, leaving its psychic imprint. The depressive position of Klein evolves from experiencing the muse connection as it transforms split off demon lover aggression into the subjective pain of ambivalence, loss and regret. By assimilating the dark internal voids bit by bit, caused by aggression within the gaps of bonding, and by tolerating the pain of the emptiness and the hostile aggression, bit by bit, which pervades the spaces in between connection with the internal mother (now muse), one can convert internal darkness into light, as psychotherapy patients often show in dreams. This is a psychic journey towards love that is akin to a spiritual journey towards the light. From a spiritual perspective, this can be seen as light evidencing a new bonding with God, which may or may not reflect a pattern of bonding with the early mother of infancy. Not to assimilate the darkness is to gradually be possessed by it and by the personified drama of abandonment and/or intrusion by the demon lover. As eroticism combines with emptiness and aggression, the muse turns to a persecutory demon lover figure, such as Emily Dickinson's "metallic god who drills his welcome in," or Dickinson's god who lets loose one thunderbolt that "scalps my naked soul." However, when enough good object internalization takes place, the capacity for love can modify or override the split off manic erotic form of aggression. Then the depressive ownership of aggression as the pain of hate with love can be felt, owned and psychically processed.

In Wilfred Bion's terms, psychic beta elements can be transformed into alpha elements. Then protosymbolic enactments of mind, body, and action can be psychically processed into words and symbolic meanings. Such meaning reflects the fundamental desire for the object and its disappointments. Meaning reflects the struggles and the fears in relation to the object, the wishes to control it, and the relinquishing of the psychic control over the object in order to find love. It is in this state of love that psychic flow and psychic space opens. Through this processing that allows love healthier psychic structure forms, structure based on symbolic representations of objects ("introjects"), rather than psychic phenomena reacting to split off intruding demon objects. These newly forming symbolic representations can be housed within the new psychic space that opens. The new psychic structure forms a sense of self that has continuity over time, despite conflicting areas of self-experience.

Chapter 4

Mourning as explicit and implicit in psychoanalytic theory

Sigmund Freud, Melanie Klein, and Ronald Fairbairn

In "Mourning and Melancholia," Freud remarks: "The shadow of the object fell on the ego" (1917). This now famous observation opened the door for the development of object relations theory. For here, Freud implies that basic human character forms through psychic structure, which has been internalized by our relationship with a parent, with whom we both interact and identify. The object, then, is no longer merely the object of an instinctual drive aim, but a live, ever-powerful parental figure always present in our internal world and its psychic operations.

I believe it was no accident that Freud first addressed the object-related nature of psychic structure in the context of discussing mourning as a psychological process. In bringing together object relations, the internalization of the object to build psychic structure, and the need for the healthy mourning of object loss, Freud combined three major elements of object relations theory. His intuitive grasp of this seems to have come directly from clinical work, whereas other intuitions of his may not have. Bringing together these three elements of object relations theory in "Mourning and Melancholia" was a critical inroad for psychoanalysis because it is the successful mourning of object loss, which in itself requires sustained maternal relatedness through all the preoedipal stages of self formation that allows relationships to be internalized symbolically as opposed to being incorporated in psychically indigestible forms. It is in this context that for the first time in Freud's writings, he implies that it is through primary human relationships, which cannot exist in a vacuum without the negotiation of separation and loss consequent to these relationships, that psychic development and psychic change and transformation take place. In "Mourning and Melancholia," Freud acknowledges the profound impact of the parental object on the human character. He makes a preliminary attempt to differentiate the undigested parent object, who exists as a haunting presence in the mind of the "melancholic," from the actual external other (object), who is lost to the individual. Although he does not address the need for a psychic digestion of this external other, which transforms the external personality into an internal object capable of existing at a symbolic level as an introject, he implies the notion of an indigestible object – referring to the displaced form of that object located within the melancholic's psyche. The melancholic attacks himself to indirectly attack the lost object, while also protecting the idealized image of that lost object from any direct attack.

The article leaves the reader with two possible views of Freud's melancholic's dilemma. The first view is that the lost object remains as a preoccupation in the mind – a preoccupation based more on hate than on love for the object – because of the actual nature of the object, i.e. related to the objective bad qualities of a parent or lover. Such a preoccupation, reactive to hate for a real object, would be symptomatic of the lost object's psychic indigestibility, and, consequently, of its failure to have allowed sufficient psychic nourishment in relationship to become a benign symbolic representation, referred to as an introject, within a preconscious internal world. This results in the visceral and mental phenomenon of the lost object feeling like an indigestible intruder in the psychophysical system, due to its split off and dissociated presence in the internal world. The second view, by contrast, is more consonant with Freud's drive theory than his object relations theory as newly expressed in "Mourning and Melancholia." This second view is that the preoccupation with hate for the lost object is due to drive-induced fantasy formations relatively independent of the object's realistic nature. Freud's drive theory bias probably would have led him towards the notion of pathological symptomatology (such as the mental preoccupation or obsession) being induced by instinctual impulses and energies beyond the actual nature of the parental object. Yet his newly sprouting interest in object relations in "Mourning and Melancholia" might have tipped his theory toward the other explanation, in which he would consider the profound impact of the actual parent.

Once Freud stepped into the arena of the impact of the lost real object, he began, figuratively speaking, a dance with Ronald Fairbairn, who was later to attribute the displaced hate of the melancholic to an actual bad-object situation. In "Mourning and Melancholia," Freud describes the melancholic as in a state of self-deriding preoccupation, a form of obsession that weighs heavily upon him, disguising itself, when existential guilt and grief are absent as are depressive despair or guilt. The melancholic invokes a "moral defense" (Fairbairn 1952) that wards off the loss of the good image of both the object and the feared loss of the object itself. Melancholics can turn hate as a retaliatory instinct on the self, but the paralyzed capacity to grow past this retaliation, extends beyond instinct to the hate for an object that is perhaps truly inadequate or "bad," but is certainly not a "good enough" object (Winnicott 1974). Such an object is unsymbolized due to its over-whelming and traumatic nature. This "bad object" does not provide enough love within the psyche to allow grief affect to be released and associated memories to be processed, as occurs during a normal mourning state. However, in this discussion, Freud's focus is on the drive instinct, manifested as hate, which causes an uncontrolled attack that must be turned backward upon the self. He is not concerned, as Fairbairn was later, with the actual nature of the lost and incorporated object. If the object is felt as bad within the internal world, according to Freud it is because of the person's own hate (which could make ambivalence intolerable). In addition, in "Mourning and Melancholia," Freud does not deal with healthy psychic internalization, that is, the internalization of the other in a psychically digested form, resulting in the creation of psychic functions and capacities. This omission was later corrected by the British Kleinians, and other object relations theorists: starting with Klein herself and including Wilfred Bion, Hannah Segal, and Michael Balint. Freud, then, did not foresee how the patient's painful release of object cathexis could open psychic space. This was true even when he could formulate a normal mourning process in evidence by a growing ability to face the reality of loss, and could formulate a slow and anguished relinquishing of an object attached with adhesive libido to the psyche.

The British theorists who followed Freud's first understanding of mourning as psychic process began to realize that new internalizations contribute to more mature symbolic structures that can replace or modify those formerly constructed from the modes of relationship with the lost object. These later theorists grasped that mourning process not only permits new object connections in external inter-personal reality, but also opens psychic space for new psychic internalizations beyond those provided by the object lost. These new psychic internalizations contribute to more mature symbolic structures, replacing those formerly con-structed from the modes of relationship with the lost object. Whether these old modes of relating were primarily pathological or not, the chance to relinquish them and to modify the impact of their early blueprint, is our only hope for psychic change, which is based on the transformation, as well as modification of psychic structure.

In sum, despite his omissions, Freud's thinking allowed others, from Klein to myself, to find a way to such conclusions. Indeed, when the mourning process is understood in the broader dimensions Klein described, we may perceive it as an essential developmental process. Mourning contains the initial affective and object-connected elements for psychic change. Psychic change occurs as the undigested object becomes digested and symbolized. Such a process leads to the release the person's potential self and innate developmental strivings. Klein was the first analyst to write about mourning as a critical clinical and developmental process. She had an intuitive vision that enabled her to see beyond grief over object loss and object disappointment to a whole range of affect states, including the most hostile and aggressive. Klein related the affect state of whole or part object attachments – in psychic fantasy experienced as internal objects we often contact through free association – back to the infant's primal object. This key insight led to a greater understanding of the dialectic of current object attachment, related fantasy forma-tions, and to primal object attachments, which Klein suggests, are the origin of the mind's fluid and creative form. Grief, as part of a psychic mourning process, creates links between the old and the new object ties, because during grief the patient identifies primal objects, related affects, and current external and fantasy objects. Without denying the immensity of Klein's intuitive leap of faith into mourning and self-surrender as a road to critical psychic transformation, we still need to understand that Freud's genius catalyzed and galvanized Klein's thinking. How could we know if she even could have written "Mourning and Its Relation to Manic Depressive States" if Freud had not conceived "Mourning and Melancholia" in 1917?

MOURNING AND MELANCHOLIA

In "Mourning and Melancholia," Freud speaks of two different psychic (or self) states, referred to in relation to the healthy mourner and the psychically arrested melancholic. One state is characteristic of the person who is capable of tolerating the pain of loss and all the processing of grief experience in mourning, and the other, which he labeled the "melancholic," lacks this very same capacity. The melancholic, Freud describes, seems to be stuck in a paralyzed state of pathological mourning. This involves a combination of self-contempt, self-devaluation, and self-attack serving as a perpetual defense against the reality of loss. This defense of aggression turned against the self also wards off consciousness of the melancholic's hatred towards a person whom one has lost and perhaps, as a result, is compelled to idealize. This is a way of preserving the sense of having had something good, even when the actual experience with the lost object may have been one of deprivation and disappointment.

There is not enough love towards the lost object in the psyche of the melancholic to neutralize his own hate. Therefore the lost object cannot be transformed into a good enough object, since good object symbolization in the psyche requires being linked to the lost object by loving feelings, or from a significant degree of love that exists within sadness of grief. Consequently, to protect the image of the person lost, the patient must ward off consciousness of the real hateful nature of the object. The psychic situation is all the more profound if the lost other is one of the two primal parents or if the unconscious associatively links this lost other with these primal parents. (This linking and displacement process is later described by Melanie Klein in "Mourning and Its Relation to Manic Depressive States" 1940.)

Freud's hypothetical mourner, in contrast with the personified view of the melancholic, would appear to actively suffer the psychic pain of facing the reality of losing a loved other, since Freud speaks of the mourner's necessary task of gradually and painfully disengaging his/her "libido" from the lost love object. Although Freud never explicitly discusses it, we may easily deduce that such active mourning, with its poignant grief affect, permits the loss of the other to provide existential meaning. Yet we must remember that his emphasis, stemming back to his view of drive and instinct as constituting the foundation of his theory, was on psychic release as opposed to symbolic meaning. Here too, Klein and her followers, such as Hannah Segal, filled in the blanks in Freud's theory. But once again, this would have been impossible without Freud's creative thinking. Freud's mourner is caught in a conflict between holding onto the lost other – which requires denying the reality of the loss – and letting go, which means facing the affect level anguish of painfully withdrawing emotional need and attachment from the one who is no longer there. Freud steers away from any description of an alive visceral and body-based emotional anguish (an anguish that awakens the psychic processing of hate as well as love) in his remarks on such a conflicted mourner. Rather, he resorts to a description of the severing of an "adhesive" libido or what we might also call a sticky libido. But whereas Freud refers to the withdrawal of the libido from the lost external other as a painful process, he offers no visual, visceral, or subjectively felt body metaphor from which we may derive an experiential sense of this concrete libido. Because of its alienation from subjective experience, his notion of the libido remains an abstraction.

When Freud discusses the melancholic, however, he begins to enter the realm of the subjective and simultaneously the realm of what later became object relations theory. Freud tells the reader about the melancholic who keeps attacking himself with self-hating criticism. Such attacks, he suggests, are particularly related to the melancholic's unconscious accusations toward the lost object. Whereas this suggestion implies that the melancholic has a heightened ambivalence towards the lost other, Freud does not indicate whether this is due to frustration and disappointment caused by life itself or to the melancholic's own limitations in loving. Rather, he goes on to question why the melancholic is so pronounced, vocal, and vociferous about condemning himself for his inadequacies and his own perceived inadequacies in loving. He asks whether someone who sees himself as defective, as implied by his manifest self-accusations, would not actually be too ashamed to so vocally express his self-hate before others. Would not the melancholic, on the contrary, silence himself to hide his shame? Addressing this conundrum, as he has outlined it, Freud concludes that the melancholic's manifest complaints against himself are actually divorced from the subjective experience stored in the melancholic's unconscious. The melancholic's complaints against the self, Freud therefore concludes, are at the level of psychic truth actually displaced complaints against the other, the other who has been lost. In railing against himself, the melancholic actually protects in his conscious mind the other's image. However, because all his aggression is turned inward, the melancholic becomes unable to mourn the loss of the departed other. This formulation allows us room to conclude that self-contempt and self-attack defend against experiencing both the loss of the other and the knowledge derived from facing one's hate. The aggressive assault against the self, Freud suggests, comes from a sadistic part of the person. This part of the person might also appear contemptuous and arrogant, I would presume, in its hostile self-attack. This arrogant part of the self appears to falsely presume itself to be self-sufficient and lends an attitude to the personality of being above or apart from the vulnerable and needing part of the core self, which is attached to the lost other. This illustrates one permutation of what Klein later described as a manic defense against grief, guilt, and loss in the depressive position.

Viewing Freud's essay through a Kleinian perspective, I would say that when the melancholic defends against need and love, he/she employs both self-contempt and self-attack. Although the melancholic person may be directing this self-attack against an incorporated other, as Freud suggests, the self-attack is defending against loss of this other as well as against hate of this other. Furthermore, the melancholic is defending against a basic need for the other, and perhaps against object need in general, as would be in keeping with Klein's manic defense stance. This defended and aggressive state prevents the mourning process from unfolding. The attack is turned against the self, and thus against one's ego as well as against one's libido, and its true object is only unconsciously known.

Although Freud speaks of releasing the libido in mourning in "Mourning and Melancholia" and not specifically of the ego, he is recognizing the ego as a psychic structure at this time, in 1917, for it is he who in the same essay speaks of "the shadow of the object falling on the ego." Given this formulation, the melancholic's attack on the ego then can quite rightly be an attack on an object lost in the external world and incorporated within the ego's structural form. When the melancholic attacks the object within its own ego, the libidinal desires that could be seen by contemporary theorists as intricately linked with a core infant self (going back to Klein), are repressed into unconsciousness. Given the acceptance of this explanation, it is quite comprehensible why the melancholic consciously experiences no subjective hate, rage, or anger. Such a schema precludes the possibility of love occurring, for it can only emerge after the conscious experience of a tolerable degree of hate. Without navigating past hate to love, the person cannot truly mourn. The pathological defense against mourning experienced as self-attack is promoted by unmetabolized hate, a hate perhaps felt as an abstract aggressive "internal saboteur" (Fairbairn 1952), that is, neither symbolized through being directed at an object, nor differentiated at the level of feelings and thoughts. (This compulsive, reflexive, and out of control "internal saboteur," which I have also called a negative "internal editor," in relation to my work with writers, can also be characterized in terms of Bion's beta elements. Lacking psychic digestion through the symbolic apparatus of the ego the "thoughtless" self-attack is perpetual and unrelenting, evading all modes of self-reflection and observing ego judgment.)

In formulating this schema, Freud enters object relations theory territory when he views the lost object, not only as external and departed, but also as an internal object under indirect attack. Manifestly, it is a Freudian ego that contains the imprint of the lost object as that object registers itself within an "internal world," a term later introduced by Klein. However, in describing his melancholic, Freud also speaks of a split ego, which is formed when one part of the ego (or self) attacks another part that has come to serve as a displaced target for aggression against a lost external object. The part of the ego attacked contains the repressed libido or libidinal component, and thus seems to have led to Ronald Fairbairn's naming his libido a libidinal ego, as opposed to an id. However, Fairbairn's libidinal ego can be personified as a child self, whereas Freud's repressed libidinal component, residing in the ego, and attacked by the split off, arrogant part of the ego, still has the instinctual power of Freud's id, with its impulse and drive. Therefore, if the libido of Freud is released through conscious symbolism and psychic fantasy, it becomes a powerful force of its own. This differs from Ronald Fairbairn's theory (1952), in which the libido merely becomes a healed internal child that must reunite fully with a central ego to be whole. In "Mourning and Melancholia" this split ego is Freud's chief illustration of how the "shadow of the object" can fall upon the ego. Fairbairn's view of this would be that the parent's mode of attack is inherited by the ego and then is repeated by the ego in the form of an "antilibidinal ego" attacking the libidinal ego or self. Fairbairn's libidinal ego or self is not distinguished from an internal, but split off child self, assumed to be formerly arrested in development. For Freud, however, the hate towards the parent is primary and is based on instinctual drive, not just on reactivity to the parent's actual behavior. So when this hate is turned against the self, the thrust of the instinct interacts with the parent's inherited mode of aggression, even if Freud would agree with Fairbairn that such internal parental aggression is compelled by identification.

We may now proceed a step further into object relations theory. We can consider whether the melancholic observed by Freud is protecting the lost object by attacking a vulnerable part of the ego (whether we see this vulnerable part as a libidinal id as Freud would see it, or as a child self – "libidinal ego" – as Fairbairn might see it). We may see such protection of the lost object as a displacement of the primal mother object onto the lost love object. This is in line with both Freud's concept of displacement and Klein's view of all objects being experienced as displacements from the primary object in the darkness of the unconscious (Klein 1940). Thus, if the melancholic is protecting the lost love object by attacking his own ego, he may be protecting the primary love object from whom the lost love object is a displacement, i.e. the mother. This protection of mother can be seen as an idealization of mother and as an idealizing defense for two reasons. First, the melancholic is motivated to idealize the lost object simply because it is lost. Even if it is not literally dead, for the melancholic it is dead as an internal object. Accordingly, the melancholic broods on his sense of abandonment through self-abusive attacks. The actuality of death imposes on the melancholic a reverence towards the lost object that might invoke in him a prohibition against conscious hate. More specifically, the melancholic may then displace hate initially targeted at the lost other onto the self. Loss of another, not through death, but through separation or abandonment, might also seem to the melancholic to demand a defensive idealization. Such a scenario could promote a partly fictitious reverence for anyone lost to the melancholic's own sense of control. The absent object is also lost to any attempts to offer reparation for former aggression toward the object, as well as lost as an object that could receive reparation for current hostilities felt towards the other. Idealization defends the melancholic's psyche against awareness of such aggression whether predominantly instinctually based, or predominantly based on retaliation for traumas and frustrations promoted by the former relationship with the object.

Second, the melancholic is motivated to establish a defensive idealization after object loss because this protects the image of the object still felt to be an essential other for both identification and dependence. At the level of the primal object (mother–father), we may view the denial of hate towards the object as the type of security operation described by Fairbairn as the compulsion to be "Satan in the world ruled by God, as opposed to being god [a good child] in a world ruled by the Devil" (Fairbairn's moral defense). In this second scenario of idealization after loss, the ideal image is projected onto a parent who may have been incorporated early on (in the preoedipal years) as a bad object. But even if the parent is not split off and dissociated in the infant's mind as a bad object, and may indeed have been technically "good enough" (Winnicott 1974), the lost parent or parent displacement object needs to be protected from the spoiling operation of the melancholic's own devaluing aggression. In either scenario, the mourner is paralyzed in the mourning process. Unconsciously, he may feel the developmental urge to mourn in order to heal and integrate the psyche after loss, while, simultaneously, the urge itself is arrested and in the process may be fused with aggression. Nevertheless, the urge to heal through mourning represents our psychic motivation towards internalization of the good in the object along with our loving enhancement of that goodness. Only in this way can the person form a symbolic representation of the lost object. Without this symbolic representation, the person experiences visceral intrusions and/or disassociations to be prompting a splitting process that maintains a perpetual discontinuity. This can be felt by the individual as a compulsive cutting off behavior that disconnects psychic links with internal self-parts and external others, so that all object relations, internal and external, get disrupted on a continuing basis. Borderline patients clearly demonstrate this cutting off mode of disconnection on a moment-to-moment basis (see Bion concepts on "attacks on linking" in *Attention and Interpretation* 1988).

In sum, we may see from the previous discussion that Freud's melancholic leads to what Fairbairn later called the "bad object" addiction, which is based on a compulsion to both cling to and control the primal parent object, especially if that parent is realistically a bad object. Much is fleshed out in Fairbairn's theory that is left vague in Freud's, particularly in relation to the hate for the object that is being turned inward, based on any real transgressions of the object. In Fairbairn's theory, the hate towards the object is motivated by actual exploitation or deprivation by the parental object, while the motivation for hate in Freud's melancholia is left open to speculation. In Fairbairn, the hated lost other has truly been responsible for traumatizing the self through neglect, abandonment, or abuse. There is just cause for the motivation to hate, not just some need for release from an innate pressure, promoted by instinctual aggression. Yet Freud seems to imply, as well as Fairbairn, that when hate is turned against the self, the self is split, at least in the moment of the impulse to attack, thus creating sealed off areas of the same original self that now operate reactively to one another. In Fairbairn, this splitting is more than in a moment of impulse. It is a profound psychic phenomenon that effects psychic structure and promotes prolonged modes of dissociation within the psyche. The part of the self attacking the other part – (antilibidinal ego attacking the libidinal ego, related to Freud's superego attacking an id) – cooperates in such a dissociated form that a perpetual state of reenactment of the traumatizing behavior of the parent is both perpetual and inevitable. Once the lost other is internalized, the self-attack perpetuates itself, repeating the behavior of the parent to hold on to that parent, and to deny the loss. The self-attack perpetuates the visceral sense of the other living within the self. The recriminations directed against the self, as observed by Freud in "Mourning and Melancholia," therefore also constitute unconscious or dissociated attacks against this lost object. Conscious hate is not felt, but retaliatory impulses are expressed in a dissociated and split off form against the libidinal self (libidinal ego). It is the retaliatory impulses incited towards the object, which are responsible for traumatizing the self through neglect, abandonment, or abuse, that are turned against the self. This creates sealed off areas of the same original self, which operate reactively to one another, but in such a dissociated form that a perpetual state of reenactment of early trauma or failed object relationship is inevitable. As we incorporate, rather than psychically digest, lost others, within an internal world that is sealed off and split off from the external world and also cut off from an internal world (within a central ego core) where symbolic introjects reside (derived from digested objects), we are compelled to attack these split off incorporations. In doing so we may be repeating internally our parents attack on us, as Fairbairn suggests, reenacting a drama that has not been broken down by ego consciousness into symbolic (alpha) forms. The complaints and recriminations directed against the self in these attacks therefore also consti- tute unconscious attacks against the parent whose loss we find ourselves unable to deal with.

The result is a state of pathological mourning because developmental mourning cannot proceed until the person possesses enough true affect love[1] to allow the rage, grief, and sadness characteristic of developmental mourning. These feelings can only surface if we rediscover the heart-aching psychic longing for the lost parent, despite our hate for that parent experienced as an incorporated internal object. We must be careful to note, however, that it is not only aggression turned inward that arrests the love and longing which comprise an affective base for mourning (in the forms of bereavement, reparation, and developmental process). In addition, the nature of the object, combined with its psychic arousal and psychic distortion during the time of early incorporation, arrests mourning and so prevents a primitive incorporation from being transformed into a higher level symbolic internalization. To be internalized in the form of healthy psychic structure, the object must be digestible into the symbolic form of an object representation. This object representation is an entity that can be differentiated from other object representations, from self-representations and from "image objects" (Kavaler- Adler 1996), which are distorted and idealized incorporations from the other that the self seeks identification with at the expense of psychic contact and connection. This object representation can therefore be truly interactive with fundamental self- parts of the entire personality.

For example, a symbolized and differentiated object representation can interact with the self-motivating agency of the personality. Such an interaction differs from one in which an object remains in the gross form of an incorporated alien, only capable, without any sense of self agency, of a monotonous imprinting, as in Konrad Lorenz's animal instinct manifesting as imprinting behavior from genera- tion to generation (1974). The incorporated alien is only capable of imprinting, resulting solely in visceral reactions that promote a subjective sense of being perpetually haunted and possessed by an internal demon, rather than a sense of being engaged in an interaction that allows and promotes a feeling of self-agency. The imprinting of a gross incorporated object, which is generally aversive in its nature as in Fairbairn's "bad object" (also related to Bion's beta elements, felt as alien to the central and conscious self) solely results in visceral reactivity. The combination of incorporated trauma in early object relations and the splitting off of one's own aggression onto the incorporated object creates the sense of a demon that possesses, haunts, tantalizes and tortures. At the milder level of experience, the haunting can take the form of a neurotic obsession. But in a more severe form, such as evidenced by the phenomenal experience within the psyche of a personi-fied demon, we also need to account for the erotic component of this alchemy, in which our subjective experience reflects the poetry of possession by a demon lover (Kavaler-Adler 1993). Fairbairn never accounted for this erotic component. Even Freud, at the time of writing "Mourning and Melancholia" (1917) was so preoccupied with issues of aggression that he failed to connect the aggressive assault on the self that he describes in the melancholic with psychic eroticism.

When we apply passionate hate, perhaps the type described by Winnicott in his famous paper "Hate in the Counter Transference" (1975), to the witch's brew of an erotic bad object within, a demon lover is created which remains in a sealed off area of the self, where it simultaneously is craved and repulsed by the libidinal ego self (Fairbairn) or by the id (Freud). A secret love, generally of an infantile or childlike nature, is also present here, a love that can bind the pathologically arrested melancholic in his or her addiction to such an internal object. This love is titanic simply because it extends back to the original and primal love an infant enters the world with, a love the infant is compelled to offer to the available mother or father. Such a love is filled with need, but also with longing for emotional contact and object connection. Fairbairn, not Freud, emphasizes such a point when he speaks of all humans from birth being object seeking, seeking of connection from the core of their basic psychic structures. Also, for Fairbairn, when love turns to rage, it is caused not merely by frustration in relation to being born and adjusting to reality as one grows, but most often by overwhelming trauma. Primal trauma overwhelms the psyche when our need to be loved for our true nature is neglected or rejected by the mother and then by other significant others. Even with its omissions, Freud's early work on trauma opened the way for Fairbairn's exclusive focus on it.

MOURNING AND ITS RELATION TO MANIC DEPRESSIVE STATES

In "Mourning and Its Relation to Manic Depressive States"(1940), Klein uses her own subjective emotional process to understand the profound nexus among the capacity to love, the capacity to mourn, and the capacity for psychic character transformation. Although thinly disguised as the case of Mrs. A, Klein describes her personal suffering at the critical moment following the death of her elder son, Hans, in a skiing accident, when he was in his young adult years. During this time of great personal grief, she tunes into the nuances of her own psychic operations, blessing us with the gifts of her theoretical offerings derived from her introspective experience.

Klein takes us inside her psychic life, discovering an "internal world" with psychic fantasy (or "fantasy") scenarios that speak to us in colorful language in contrast to the mechanistic language Freud employed in outlining his drive theory. In my reading of Klein (1940), this seminal female theorist views these psychic fantasies as intertwining the libidinal force within us with our internal objects, or as providing psychic space for a dialectic of self-yearnings and dynamic visceral and visual images of the other. The other exists inside of us, according to Klein (1940), represented by the psychic molds of internalization and instinctual impulse that consolidate to construct psychic fantasies (or "fantasies"). Consequently, for Klein impulse is transformed into the subjective affect melodies of whatever might be described as the human spirit. (I believe Jungian archetypes could easily be seen as part of this amalgamation and alchemy.) Through these scenarios, in which self-yearnings engage internal objects, we can discover diverse modes of crying and of object connection. Klein (1940), and later her former analysand John Bowlby (1963), introduced the notion of an aggression that need not serve as a defensive barrier against mourning, but rather which when felt in the conscious subjectivity of relationship to another, may become a stepping stone to a mode of mourning that evolved on the affective, as well as the cognitive level. Such consciously perceived aggression has developmental consequences in terms of promoting self-integration, as well as enabling the emergence to consciousness of unconscious murderous impulses, and unconscious object needs. Following Klein's commentary in her 1940 paper on mourning, we find that psychic necessity will cause us to experience mourning in the form of grief and bereavement for someone loved and lost in our current life. We experience this through the veil of several more primal internal objects, derived from the earliest years of life. As Klein demonstrates so succinctly, our free association can restore links between these deeply imprinted unconscious figures, enabling us to consciously reunite them. In this way, in-depth mourning for our current loss opens the way to the source of our feelings of loss and, consequently, to positive mournful suffering for this original loss.

In "Mourning and Its Relation to Manic Depressive States," Klein also described how manic triumph and manic defense can shield us from the grievous loss of another. Mentally clinging to that other creates an existential dilemma involving our own mortality ("To be or not to be"): whether it is nobler in the mind to die with our love object or to psychically survive it and mourn it. To choose the latter alternative, Klein suggests, means facing life with a conscious awareness of our own mortality. For our survival, we need to choose to let the other die, even though this other was so intrinsic to the shaping, binding, and cohering of our own soul. But if we choose this path, we also experience how close to death we are ourselves. Ultimately, we are in this process giving up omnipotent control over the other, choosing to face our existential helplessness by allowing the other to die, as John Steiner, the modern British Kleinian, speaks of it (Steiner 1993). His seemingly poetic view of allowing our object, now an internal object incorporation, to die, can be seen as the conscious confrontation and acceptance of our loss, accepting the reality of death, separation, and all forms of loss through accepting one poignant loss during the mourning process. In addition, through Klein we discover that revenge, when it is not conscious and symbolic, arrests our innate human capacity to suffer what is, namely, "the slings and arrows of outrageous fortune," and to suffer as well the loss to us caused by consciousness of our mortality, a suffering that enables us to escape anomie (Kavaler-Adler 1990).

In contrast to Freud's melancholic, the aggression of Mrs. A – Klein's alter-ego – fails to emotionally paralyze her. Rather, she remains in touch with her conscious hostility towards her lost love. Initially, she experiences this hostility through displacements back to her brother and mother, which she recalls in a dream fragment. Although shock over her son's death has disrupted Klein's dream life, she rapidly employs free association to restore it. In this dream, Mrs. A visualizes a mother and son: "She saw two people, a mother and son. The mother was wearing a black dress. The dreamer knew that this boy had died, or was going to die. No sorrow entered into her feelings, but there was a trace of hostility towards the two people" (1975: 356).

In analyzing the dream later, she senses a conscious hostility towards these dream characters and begins to associate, which causes her to travel back in her life. She now remembers the mother and son in the dream as her brother's schoolmate and his mother. The boy she recalls was a rival of her brother. In a memory she associates to the dream image, the schoolmate behaves contemptuously and arrogantly towards Mrs. A's mother and brother. Mrs. A (Klein) gives a defensive meaning to the rage she feels within the dream, by allying herself, in her associations, with her own mother and brother. She detests the contemptuous schoolmate of her brother's in her dream, but she finds herself unable to keep her peace of mind in relation to her own family in the dream, her mother and brother, who appear within the dream. She realizes that she has displaced her hate from her own mother and brother onto the schoolmate rival and his mother, and that this is not an adequate defense to keep her peace of mind. She begins to experience the envy behind her hate that is put into the brother's schoolmate through projective identification, but which is still unconsciously with her. Her associations lead to envy of her brother, which is more uncomfortable for her to feel than the reaction formation defense of wishing to defend him against his friend and rival. She also is led through her associations to realizing the envy of her mother behind her envy of her brother. In a critical and urgent self-analysis of this dream following her own son's death, Klein is forced to realize that the hostile rivals in the dream also represent herself. She too had exuded an air of contempt towards her brother and mother, which extended forward in time and psychic space, to her own son, who she came to associatively link with this brother who died during her early twenties. This new consciousness of her aggression permits Klein to recognize within herself a manic stance of contempt, control, and triumph. This stance, she is able to realize, permits her to feel herself as superior in status to her dead son. Such a realization frees her to understand the possible implications of her arrogant attitude towards him. Now she comprehends that seeing herself this way simply because she still lives while he is dead walls her off from the conscious pain of her loss and the recognition of her own mortality.

Klein's ability to face her own defensive attitude allows her to navigate beyond being walled off from an existential vulnerability. Relinquishing her manic defense, she moves into a psychic position of loving and needing the lost love object, in this case, her son. However, her psyche still links him to her deceased brother. But Klein's growing consciousness of these links allows her to face a grief that extends backwards, beyond her present loss to the earlier losses of primal love objects. From this personal experience, Klein concludes that mourning always involves our facing a complex array of haunting and disparate, yet linked, love objects residing in fantasy and memory states within our internal world. Moreover, she concludes that it is her innate, but temporarily sealed off, loving capacity that permits her to face her aggression so that she is not walled off by her defenses against it. In facing it, she freely moves past hostility in its manic mode of narcissistic expression to a state of love for the lost other, which in turn creates within her conscious grief and remorse. In the mourning process she comes into contact not only with the grief of loss but also the pain of regret. The conscious experience of the psychic pain of regret, concerning her own murderous and hostile impulses towards those she loved but was also envious of, reflects the depressive position fantasy and affect experience of remorse. She feels the pain of regret for having defensively placed herself above her son, in her own mind, after she became aware of his deceased state. She realizes that this manic stance not only can express a hostile rivalry with her son that repeated her unconscious rivalry with her brother and mother, but that the manic stance was also a way of defending herself against a wish to join her son in death. This wish was expressed within her dream. It would, if carried into reality, result in her own annihilation.

In another dream Mrs. A has following her son's death, her son appears, and she begins to follow him into the land of death. But because she is facing her manic stance, and the rage and loss behind it, she can also face the dream through an association process. In this dream, Klein experiences a transforming moment, in which she changes her wish to join her son in death into an opportunity to separate from him in order to go on living. If we use the terminology of Steiner (1993), we may say that Klein here demonstrates that she was capable of the deepest letting go within mourning, in that she could let go of her lost object, her son – that is, let him die. She could accomplish this task, despite her heart-breaking anguish at his tragic death at such a young age.

Klein herself seemed aware of the intimate link between her letting go and her capacity to survive a conscious awareness of her own hostile impulses, a feat Freud's melancholic could not accomplish. Klein's conscious accounting for her own aggression is seemingly not experienced by Freud's successful mourner. Rather, he experiences loss as a progressive relinquishing of the pain-laden attachment of an adhesive libido. In other words, for him loss is primarily related to need and attachment, and consequently, Freud does not allude to the mourner's aggression. But Freud's melancholic was overwhelmed with aggression. Because this aggression remained unconscious, however, it was displaced onto the self. Such repression paralyzed the melancholic's psyche and prevented mourning from proceeding. From this discussion we see how Freud and Klein differ in their understanding of the normal mourner.

MODES OF MOURNING

"Mourning and Its Relation to Manic Depressive States" (1940) is an exegesis on the affective phenomenology of mourning. Not only does Klein locate links between objects in the internal world through her own mourning, but she discovers that affects are complex, and we can progress from one affect to another in an existential as well as a visceral sequence. In bringing us beyond the splitting of the paranoid-schizoid position to the integration process of the depressive position, where the internal affect states of grief, guilt and loss can be tolerated, the mourning process also indicates a developmental direction. For Klein, hostility, as indicated, is related to a repressed self and object experience, which can be transformed in the subjective experiencing of loss. Although Klein does not employ the term "self," her theory, as illustrated in dreams and cases, indicates that any impulse is tied to an object in psychic fantasy that is an ongoing subject of love and hate. This object of Klein is not an object that just serves as a target for impulse aim and discharge, as in Freud's early theory of drive tension and discharge. The object relationships experienced within the full affect range of the mourning process allow for a psychic metamorphosis that is an all-encompassing process. This mourning process, as first described by Klein in the case of Mrs. A, in "Mourning and Its Relation to Manic Depressive States," involves the rediscovery of the unconscious routes to primary object experience. This mourning process leads to the new discovery of the sources of conscious rage towards the lost object, in regard to the object being linked back to the primal objects in the psyche.

In facing our aggression we open the way to the experience of grief. This process is I believe sequential. Specially, it follows a psychically developmental form. One way of experiencing the progression is in terms of modes of crying. As Klein describes Mrs. A's experience in mourning her recently lost son, she notes that at first Mrs. A's crying brought her no relief. At this time Mrs. A was dreaming but had not yet experienced her dreams at the level at which her psychic shock was taking place, in relation to her son's death. Not only her unconscious (as in instinctual fantasy), but her entire internal world in its implied, but not articulated, subjective sense of self, seems at this juncture, temporarily sealed off. When the deep internal and core self is sealed off, often due to blocked aggression (either repressed or dissociated), tears bring no relief. Crying at this point is more like a mode of ventilation. It does not elicit relief if internal object connection is blocked, or if the tears emerge from a place above the deeper core of sadness within the psychic area of object yearning. Real crying, crying from this deep inner core, is critical as it is impossible to revive love when crying does not allow connection through the sad grief-laden affect of connection with the lost object. True mourning – with its symbolic representation of object forms – cannot occur without this object connection through grief affect. Often, this more "surface" crying is seen in a sealed off self and appears masochistic (demanding without letting go) and narcissistic (from an isolated inner core). Such tears may have a different quality than those experienced with grief, where the sadness in the tears is palpable. Without a love connection, we cannot feel sadness, and without sadness we cannot consciously experience and then symbolically identify the revival of the intensity of past love and longing.

When Mrs. A moves through the initial shock of her encounter with her son's death, she begins to open to some contact with friends. This contact in turn seems to allow in her a progressive unsealing of the core self and its internal world. It is now that crying begins to bring relief.

The crying of patients with masochistic and narcissistic characters often appears to be a venting without true grief as it lacks the free interaction of grief with regret and remorse. Love in any analytic sense seems to be lost, and narcissistic pre-occupations prevail. In such cases, the patient remains unconsciously (but sometimes consciously) in a state of awe and terror, even horror, at the prospect of crying. To those with so much sealed off pain from early trauma, crying may signify the prospect of drowning in an ocean of tears, of crying forever, with an unending "bleeding heart" (paraphrase of a remark by a member of my mourning regrets group). In this way, through the fear of drowning, the mind works at an unconscious level to repress the urgent need to yield and surrender. Sometimes, the inhibition of crying is evident as a pseudomasculine psychic structure, which like Fairbairn's antilibidinal ego serves as a perpetual "internal saboteur" (1952). This often develops when early education is repressive and humiliating, particularly in relation to the need to cry (see Harry Guntrip's poignant examples of squashed emotion and squashed crying in *Schizoid Phenomena, Object Relations and The Self*, 1976).

Such psychodynamics can result in disease, somatic symptoms, and in psychic demon lover possession (as expressed by many artists in their work). Of course, this does not mean that blocked grief is the only cause of profound disease. The cause would seem always multiply determined, and it often has innate genetic factors involved. In Edith Sitwell's poem, "Still Falls the Rain" (Kavaler-Adler 1993), the poet seemingly describes a pathological mourning state in which we may see endless rain as symbolizing an endless rain of tears that have never been allowed to be cried. The poem expresses that these uncried tears haunt the poet, hinting at the unexplored oceans of grief within. The endless uncried tears, when incipient and inchoate in the psyche, can easily be projected outward onto the world as an external precipitation.

The subject of tears cried and uncried is a critical clinical subject. There may actually be many forms and qualities of tears that psychologists have yet to identify. A visceral and phenomenal differentiation of crying is significant to understanding our clinical work in terms of what I have called "developmental mourning" and its arrest. Klein's report of Mrs. A illustrates the inhibition of control being released in the mourning process, as Mrs. A's manic stance yields and Mrs. A surrenders control, and thus surrenders to true grief, in which tears finally bring relief. When hostility is unconscious, as in contrast to the process described in the case of Mrs. A, the split off aggression can appear in the internal world as merged with a bad object representation, which is experienced in personified form as a demon lover. When the aggression is split off from primal trauma, the demon lover can become a psychosomatic "unthought known" (Bollas 1989; Winnicott 1982), dissociated from the affectively alive self of agency. The person may also externalize the demon lover through modes of projective identification. These modes then impact on all those with whom he emotionally engages in the moment, let alone on those who upon whom the person is dependent. This demon lover object in the internal world, experienced often as a visceral personification, is bereft of contact and connection, tenderness and touch, and possesses no conscious sense of aggressive agency. Klein's awareness of her own hostility as she describes herself in the case of Mrs. A denies the possibility of the creation of such a split off demon object at this point in her experience. Splitting off aggression through projection and projective identification, rather than reclaiming it from repression as Mrs. A did in Klein's seminal paper, is a paranoid position experience (as in Klein's paranoid-schizoid position) that precedes the manic stance of contempt and triumph in the depressive position, as depicted by Klein in her phenomenology.

FAIRBAIRN'S THEORY IN RELATION TO THE PSYCHIC PHENOMENON OF MOURNING

Fairbairn, like Klein, believed in an internal world with internal objects, but the nature of his internal objects differed significantly from hers. In emphasizing the role of trauma in psychopathology, as opposed to that of instinctual drive and its expression through psychic fantasy, Fairbairn theorized about internal objects which he saw as created by real parents who impact on a child by gross overstimulation through neglect and abuse. Yet despite their differences, Fairbairn and Klein focused on internal objects from the earliest infant and preoedipal stages of life (the era of Balint's *Basic Fault*), as opposed to the notion of internal objects as higher level differentiated representations that could be part of a Freudian secondary process. Both Klein's and Fairbairn's internal objects are primary process modes of phenomena. As such, they can exacerbate a primal split in the psyche, creating dissociative phenomena rather than repressed thoughts or impulses. These internal objects are gross and prone to visceral and sensory modes of protosymbolic incorporation.

Fairbairn's internal objects are not merely repressed and unconscious. They are sealed off in a closed internal self-system, split off from the core self in touch with the external world. Such internal objects exist in relation to split off self-parts, explicitly called by Fairbairn "libidinal egos" and "antilibidinal egos," in deference to Freud's use of the term "ego," as opposed to the term "self."

These internal objects enact their drama upon the psyche via the mode of demons, called "bad objects" by Fairbairn, produced by early trauma, when the traumatizing parents are incorporated in a gross, undigested psychic form. They are highly assaultive or abandoning, and therefore Fairbairn gives them the rather colloquial label of "bad objects." Indeed, in his early papers he actually calls them "devils" (1952).

My own view of Fairbairn's theory is to some extent consonant with the views of Greenberg and Mitchell (1983). As they do, I view Fairbairn's theory as describing pathology, not health, because his schema of "endopsychic" (Fairbairn's term for intrapsychic) structure includes only perpetual attachments to bad objects, or objects causing the reenactment of core preoedipal pathology (see *The Creative Mystique* 1996 for a description of psychic health). In Fairbairn's internal world, there are no good internal objects and no internal objects refined into secondary process conceptual and symbolic representations. (If he had described them, he would have had to place them in his central ego, but, as indicated, he never does this, focusing rather on major split off parts of the psyche relegated to the sealed off closed system in the libidinal and antilibidinal ego areas.) Without the presence of good internal objects (and only the existence of dissociated bad objects and their inadequate self parts), there are no adequate avenues to relations with the outside world and with external others in that world. Consequently, Fairbairn's internal world, I believe, clinically reflects that of those in a frozen psychic state of pathological mourning, as opposed to the internal world of those who have a capacity to mourn old objects and so move on to new and present relationships.

Fairbairn's split off child selves act as fixed psychic structures yearning for unreachable object connections. Their imprisonment under the antilibidinal ego personas keeps the child self from accessing them. Such exciting and rejecting objects are structures initially incorporated from early primal and indigestible parental objects. These initial parental objects are too overwhelming or traumatic to be symbolized in the differentiated forms of "introjects." They cannot love the child selves, nor can they love one another. In their personified forms within the split off and sealed off psyche, these original parental objects can cause the more grossly schizoid child persona to pour all its love and need into a psychic vacuum. Fairbairn also wrote about children tormented by what I call demon lover type parents. Such parents excite the child in his/her craving for object love, but then reject the child's actual emotional connection with repeated traumatic frequency. The demon lover parent is the seductive parent who seduces and abandons or the parent who tantalizes with his mere presence, and yet remains unavailable for responsive connection at an emotional level.

Fairbairn in this sense viewed everyone as the victim of inadequate parenting.

Thus, he viewed all of us as relatively schizoid in that we each have a split off early experience with our early parents, when this experience is too frustrating and depriving. Fairbairn does not distinguish between repression and pathological modes of splitting, than those derived from a primal split in the self. Nor does he distinguish between those who can internalize a whole object and those who, because they cannot internalize a whole object, exist in a state of perpetual object loss. Consequently, Fairbairn can slide too readily from the hysteric to the schizoid, without distinguishing between a hysteric with neurotic psychic structure, symbolized internal objects, and neurotic defenses based on repression, and a primitive hysteroid character, who has a more prominent schizoid dimension. Neither does Fairbairn differentiate oedipal and preoedipal levels of development, causing him to reduce the wish to sleep with one's parent to a primal need for self-connection (1952). As such, he ignores the role of higher level oedipal conflicts related to incestuous wishes and castration fears.

Despite these problems, Fairbairn offers a delineated psychic structure theory, whereas Klein is most diffuse in her description of the location and geometry of internal object structure. But what she does provide instead of a structural theory is a phenomenology of emotional process and affect through her grasping the developmental meaning in the mourning process. When Klein fills in her lack of psychic structure theory with Freud's psychic structures, her writing is at its most confusing. The problem mainly stems from the fact that Freud's psychic structures operate at a higher psychic level than those shown in most of Klein's clinical cases. Therefore, Klein promotes confusion for her readers when filling in the lack of psychic structure in her theory with Freud's neurotic-based structures of id, ego, and superego. By contrast, Fairbairn presents us with an alternate model of psychic structure that is most suitable to those arrested at the preoedipal stages of development.

However, Fairbairn's psychic structure, as indicated, excludes any internal world of good self and object relations. Thus, it excludes the possibility of internalizing, as part of core and progressive self-structure and good external relations, stemming back to our relations with our primary parents. In Fairbairn's model, therefore, everyone is addicted to their early bad objects (parents) because they were so bad that each of us has no room for growth into new relations with healthier external objects, either during childhood or adulthood. For Fairbairn, the psyche remains arrested in a static state of reenactment, operating from an internal world, which has barricaded itself against current external object relations, or what is today commonly called interpersonal relations. In Fairbairn's schizoid type, external relations operate primarily on an intellectual level, split off from the body and from what we commonly call our internal life and internal feelings. All emotional life and human needs for psychic connection to others operate in a sealed off state, behind a barrier that can be called a schizoid barrier (Ogden 1986). Because Fairbairn himself seems to have had a schizoid personality (Sutherland 1989), as did most of his Scottish patients, he may have tended to conceptualize most pathology in terms of schizoid dynamics. This conceptualization could only give lip service to what had formerly been called hysterical and obsessive phenomena, viewing them merely as surface defense styles that in his experience hid the deeper, schizoid, nature of his patients.

Fairbairn also did not deal with the projective identification that Klein defined as pressuring others in the external environment from within the internal world. Therefore, his schizoids are cold, distant, and intellectual, not only at the level of overt character description, but also in their entire emotional impact on others. Klein would certainly differ with this notion. She might point out how the sealed off world of a schizoid character, with its split off psychic constellations of primitive self and other enactments, pressures all outside others, despite their being overtly removed from such a person through split off psychic constellations of primitive self and other enactments. Even if we feel, for example, like falling asleep when in the room with them, in our sleep we dream their impoverished and demonic internal world creatures. For Fairbairn, these creatures exist in a static internal world system, split off from emotional contact with others. The static drama in this closed internal system does not affect others in the outer world. But here Fairbairn neglects the role of projective identification, which exerts a pull toward the involvement of external others, pressing them to join in the reenactment of the internal closed system.

In deference to Fairbairn, Klein hyphenated her paranoid position, rewording it as the "paranoid-schizoid" position. She also, however, wrote explicitly of how they differed theoretically, as noted by Grosskurth (1986) in her biography of Klein. Klein, for example, never reduced psychic fantasy, derived from internal life, to being a real replica of external relations. For her, the id existed, as did the body. Accordingly, she held to her notion of primal impulses as deriving from within through body-based instinct dimensions. Although she may have neglected real relations too much, her theory of instinctual life extended beyond pathology and beyond pathological mourning.

FAIRBAIRN'S THEORY AS A THEORY OF PATHOLOGICAL MOURNING

In discussing the state of pathological mourning, I want to address Fairbairn's concept of bad object addiction. The traumatized child, in Fairbairn's view, clings to the primary parents despite their horrific abuse and psychic neglect. This clinging shows that the child has entered a state of pathological mourning because of being unable to mourn the loss of the original parent and then let go of them to move on to other external relations. To move on the child would require the reception of enough parental love so as to tolerate the feelings of loss as well as those of object longing and connection. The child would also need to preserve a good enough internal imprint from the original parents to develop symbolic representations of them and symbolic capacities for processing differentiated object relations. However, Fairbairn's traumatized subjects lack all these capacities!

Rather, major parts of themselves are ensconced in imprisoning relations with internally incorporated objects. These internal objects are neither digested nor assimilated into symbols that would permit us to consciously face the early experience that we carry within us, so as to differentiate past from present. Instead we remain captive to the bad objects that are psychic incorporations and concretizations of past, early, and dissociated experience. It can feel like being possessed by demons. Consequently, the reflexive reenactment in response to these internal object pressures does not diminish. In Fairbairn's static closed system of object addictions, there has been no progressive movement from Bion's beta to alpha (1989), or from gross psychosomatic phenomena and dissociated self and other part objects, into symbolic introjects with differentiated internalizations. We may in fact see this closed system as an arrest in Bion's sphere of beta elements, which exist as gross psychosomatic phenomena and dissociated self and other part objects. Love is not sufficiently felt in this static closed system, unless the object is totally idealized. Consequently, there is no possibility of any real interactions with the object in the external world. An idealized object is a mental creation that cannot be related to in reality. In this psychic situation, one's needs are overwhelmingly implosive and explosive, causing impulsive and compulsive behavior to predominate over any relaxed or in-touch state of being. The psychic space for the processing of emotional experience and interpersonal experience into psychic experience is inadequate. Transitional space (Winnicott 1974) too would seem to be lacking in the area between self and other. Thus, the person cannot feel loss or surrender the object. The child self, split off in the adult mind, is often reenacted in sensory and psychosomatic forms and projective and introjective defense modes. This child self still clings to the original and primal traumatizing parent (incorporated as a "bad object").

Fairbairn first observed this internal object situation in external terms when he worked in a British clinic with severely traumatized children in foster care. He observed children, who placed in foster care with more benign parents than their abusive primal parents, would continually try to escape from their foster homes, to return to their original home from which they only recently had been rescued. According to Fairbairn's observations, these children seemed to make no realistic differentiation between their primary abusive parents and their foster parents. No matter the extent of the abuse they had been rescued from, the children wanted to return to their original "mommy." Psychically, the primal mommy was the only mommy! The less the original mommy was able to nurture the child's developmental needs, the less that child had adequate internal assets to move on to other relationships and to negotiate interactions with more separate and differentiated parents. Such children, Fairbairn observed, experienced their foster parents as alien, no matter how objectively "good" these new parents were in reality. The developmentally arrested child could not make the new connection. In such a child's internal world, the primal and overriding connection continued to reside with the old mommy.

These observations of Fairbairn concerning abused and traumatized children placed in foster care allow me to conclude that to the degree that loss and mourning for the original parent is incomplete, the parent cannot be internalized in a healthy symbolic form as a differentiated object represented within the internal world. Rather, the grossly incorporated parent becomes incorporated within the psyche, thereby enacting its intrusive and visceral drama as a split off and friction producing part of the self (as Fairbairn's internal saboteurs and antilibidinal egos). Extending Fairbairn's observations to my own, I see that the arrest in the psychic capacity for mourning can also be understood in terms of a lack of self and other vitality or of a free dialectic between self and objects parts within the psychic structure. A sadomasochistic enactment of the traumatizing object assaulting the split off child self substitutes for a free motivational dialectic. Mourning, and its resulting symbolic differentiations, is prevented from occurring precisely because for that to happen a dialectic of self and other within the psyche (internal world within a central ego) is needed. This dialectic is needed in order for grief affect (sadness, loss, guilt, and longing) to combine with symbolic object representations of the lost object. But due to the lack of internalization and symbolization of an emotionally (or libidinally) available self-experience, no self and object dialectic occurs within the central ego.

Only with mutual interaction between child and parent can the child experience love and the gradual disillusionments of wished for unconditional love in a tolerable affect range for full development to take place. And only when it is supported by such a base can the psyche then promote symbolic understanding of experience as a healthy self-experience. But when during the early relating with the primal mother, the child is radically deprived of emotional response and availability, he or she can never form such symbolic understanding, and the sadomasochistic reenactment of abuse and neglect is perpetually promoted. This outcome we often see in dissociated forms reminiscent of Fairbairn's split off dramas, which are sealed off in an endopsychic domain within. Without mutuality of self and other, the child's developing sense of self-agency is blocked. Consequently, aggression becomes an endless monotone of sadomasochistic repetition rather than a neutralized fuel for agency and interaction.

In such a situation, the consciousness of our own aggression is intolerable. Such a scenario contrasts with the psychic apprehension of aggression as a hostility within self-agency, as understood by Klein's Mrs. A (1940). Unlike what occurred in Mrs. A's case, here aggression cannot be refined by an interpenetrating mixture with love, thereby producing a subjective feeling of loss, particularly of loss of a love object. Rather, hostile aggression repeatedly reincites itself.

It is in this sense that Ronald Fairbairn's object relations theory is a theory of pathological mourning. For according to Fairbairn, we may become attached in an addictive way to an internal bad object and to its original mode of bad object relationship. When this is eroticized, as it generally is (although Fairbairn neglected to deal with this element of eroticization), those addicted to their bad object become psychically possessed by a demon lover. They are drawn magnetically towards the demon lover, resulting in their being repeatedly hurt, deeply wounded, and traumatized through tantalization and abandonment. Such abandonment is always part of the demon lover complex scenarios. With borderline and narcissistic characters, in contrast to Fairbairn's schizoid personalities, the pressures of projective identification emanating from a closed off system are acted out dramatically in external relations in the world.

Chapter 5

Mourning as implicit and explicit in psychoanalytic theory:

John Bowlby, Michael Balint, and D.W. Winnicott

MOURNING IN THE THEORY OF JOHN BOWLBY

British analyst John Bowlby was a contemporary of Klein, who was also his analyst. His extensive research with animals and children led to an increasing awareness of the significance of mourning as a primary aspect of human psychic development. His ideas on the topic of human psychic development dovetailed with Fairbairn's notions. He found the need for the other to be with us from birth. Bowlby, however, spoke of attachment theory, whereas Fairbairn spoke of longings for the other from birth as a profound need for connection. In viewing the human psyche as primarily motivated by a sense of self that is always in relation to an object, both Fairbairn and Bowlby complemented Klein. But, unlike Klein, they believed that the other we yearn for from the moment of birth is the real parental other rather than, as she proposed, a fantasy object created in the earliest stage of life.

Since Bowlby believed in attachment as fundamental to psychic and developmental growth, for him, the ability to tolerate object loss through the capacity to mourn becomes a primary criterion for the continuance of human growth, which can occur through separation from the primal womb and the primal self and mother dyad. Consequently, the inability to tolerate such loss, Bowlby suggests, and I agree with him, constitutes the most critical factor in the development of pathology and psychic arrest. Thus pathological mourning, in which the mind and body continually cling to a lost or long-departed object, becomes the chief factor in psychopathology and psychic disturbance.

In his article, "Pathological Mourning and Childhood Mourning," Bowlby (1963) clearly defines his distinct emphasis on understanding the need to mourn and the consequences of the failure in the capacity to mourn. But although his focus differs from Klein's, his ideas still significantly relate to Kleinian theory. Like Klein, he sees mourning as a fundamental part of development. In addition, Bowlby, like Klein, differs from all those who believe that mourning consists solely of sadness and grief, a view stemming back to Freud's "Mourning and Melancholia." Instead, what Bowlby and Klein both emphasize is the role of aggression in healthy mourning. That is, they do not view aggression towards the lost or temporarily missed object as a sign of pathological mourning. When the aggression is conscious and linked to the lost object, rather than displaced onto others, repressed, dissociated or turned against the self, Bowlby sees it as a link in the affect chain of mourning experience. However, unlike Klein who views this aggression as a hostile attack on the object, motivated by paranoia, sadism, and the manic defense attitude of triumph over the object, Bowlby suggests that this aggression is a healthy reaction to the loss of the object. He believes that anger is the mourner's reproach and protest against the other for leaving. For Klein, in contrast, the hostile nature of the aggression requires reparation towards the object, and unless such reparation is successfully made and received, the mourner is left with unresolved and usually unconscious or split off guilt that can block the processing of grief. Klein's assumption of hostile sadism characterizing the nature of the aggression lends an additional aspect to her mourner's affect process. Rather than processing grief, Klein believes that the mourner must also process guilt. Thus, Klein's view of mourning, as a depressive position phenomena, creates a theory about the psychic processing of loss related to grief. For Klein, the processing of grief is always intricately involved with the processing of guilt over hostile impulses toward the lost object, and those linked at a more primal level in the unconscious with the lost object.

In contrast, Bowlby contends that the mourner's aggression – whether it be that of a child who is temporarily left by a parent, or that of an adult who has lost a love-object through death – need not arouse guilt as long as the aggression is received by the object as healthy anger, a natural protest reaction against loss. If the mourner expresses such aggression in the form of a reproach towards the temporarily or permanently departed object, Bowlby suggests, it actually represents–in the context of our consciousness of attachment needs – a sign of both object relatedness and developmental achievement. Only when repressed does this aggression become a block to mourning and provoke symptoms of pathology related to pathological mourning. If guilt is aroused within the mourner in reaction to his/her own aggression, it would probably be due, Bowlby believes, to the rejection of the mourner's aggression by others, including the one who might have returned after having been away. Therefore, from Bowlby's perspective, guilt in such a situation would be a neurotic phenomenon, not an existential phenomenon, as in Klein's theory.

For Klein, an element of self-agency always provokes the degree of the loss, for even if the object is lost through death, which is beyond the control of the mourner, the loss of love suffered is partly the result of a destructive fantasy attack upon the lost object. The mourner must first feel conscious guilt about these fantasies before being able to grieve. Only through this process can the mourner renew his or her love for the object and so experience true object-related loss and grief sadness rather than anger.

For Bowlby, as suggested, we do not have to view anger following loss as hostile sadism, but rather as a cry of protest, a reflection of need, love and longing. An empathic response by a parent to a child to this protest, coupled with an understanding that there is pain in the anger motivated by the loss itself, helps the anger to subside quickly. Love is restored, which in turn, allows for the capacity to feel loss and to develop a growing facility for mourning throughout life's many disruptions of attachment.

MOURNING IN THE THEORY OF MICHAEL BALINT

Michael Balint was one of the British object relations theorists who struggled with finding an avenue connecting all those suffering from core psychic disturbance at the level of preoedipal trauma. Balint outlines his main thesis in his book, *The Basic Fault* (1979). Here, he followed Sandor Ferenczi's experiments with gratifying patients, and engaging with them in a "mutual analysis," in which all limits and therapeutic environment structure are sacrificed. After having been in analysis with Ferenczi, Balint inherited Ferenczi's practice, after the older man died. So Balint set forth to treat Ferenczi's severely disturbed patients. However, he began to see how Ferenczi's penetrating insights into a sealed off interior life could never be sustained beyond momentary contact as long as his experimental method disregarded the psychoanalytic framework of treatment, with its limits and structure. Still, Balint remained inspired by Ferenczi's willingness to venture into the dark areas of preoedipal experience. Freud had generally avoided these areas in his absorption with neurotics at the oedipal level of psychic conflict – although he discovered the preoedipal conflicts, described in his paper "Female Sexuality" (1931). But, Balint found himself captivated by the preverbal aspects of his patients' experience, surmising that those traumatized at a primal, or preverbal, level, could not successfully employ verbal interpretations from their analyst. In fact, in *The Basic Fault*, he blames the Kleinians for their primarily verbal and interpretive approach, claiming that some patients swallow interpretations and throw them up, rather than comprehending them at a symbolic level that can lead to insight and connection. In the same book, he also faults Winnicott for his "management" approach with "false self" patients. This agenda of behavioral caretaking, Balint contends, detracts analysts from employing the structure within the frame of therapeutic sessions that enable the analytic work to lead to psychic reparation.

In *The Basic Fault,* Balint states his well-known axiom that people need another person akin to the absolute way that they require oxygen:

> 'We inhale the air, take out of it what we need, and after putting into it what we do not want to have, we exhale it, and we do not care at all whether the air likes it or not. It has to be there for us in adequate quantity and quality; and as long as it is there, the relationship between us and it cannot be observed, or only with very great difficulty; if, however, anything interferes with our supply of air, impressive and noisy symptoms develop in the same way as with the dissatisfied infant, or with the unsatisfied patient in the first phase of the new beginning. (Balint 1979: 136)

This instinctive need operates no matter how primitive that "other" is, not even if the other takes the form of an inanimate environment. Assuming that primal self-trauma occurs because of disrupted contact with this undifferentiated other, Balint concludes that regression in the adult patient to the primal disruption (the "basic fault" level) is necessary to heal the psyche. He also assumes that the analyst needs to serve the function of becoming the needed object. The analyst does this by co-existing with the patient in the way needed at the level of regression to the basic fault. Becoming the needed object may involve a harmonious "interpenetrating mix-up," in which analyst and analysand are joined by whatever kind of emotional mode of "being together" is necessary to allow the preoedipally traumatized adult to contact the disrupted inner self, which has been until now sealed off from contact and connection. Healing occurs through this "being together;" and, it may involve nonverbal experience of varying kinds, including touching between analyst and patient. During at least one session, for example, Balint held the thumb of a patient as a way of attempting to contact the patient's internal experience at a body level. He was, through this behavior, trying to find an avenue free of split off cognitive mentation (Khan 1974).

However, unlike Ferenczi, Balint does not neglect attending to limits in the treatment relationship, in the treatment frame, and in the patient's life, in regard to promoting changes in the patient's original psychic structure. Therefore, he distinguishes between "benign regression" and "malignant regression," pointing out that limits in treatment, imposed by the analyst, are essential to allow the patient to open up to the pain of early trauma contained within them for a benign regression to take place. Not to set such limits can lead to malignant regressions, in which the patient demands more and more from the analyst, in an insatiable way, as a defensive maneuver to avoid experiencing the painful reality within them. By entering the same primitive psychic frontier as Ferenczi, his own analyst, Balint attempts to salvage the best of Ferenczi's pioneering efforts, while simultaneously learning from Ferenczi's mistakes. The result was that Balint acquired a disciplined technique, which also permitted meaningful contact at the preverbal level, before the patient could symbolize his internal experience (especially when related to trauma). As I understand Balint's writings in *The Basic Fault*, when contact is made at a preverbal level prior to any understanding of the patient's internal state that can be expressed in words by the patient, and prior to any understanding that could be received in words as interpretations from the analyst, the avenue of contact made in a protosymbolic form – as in holding the thumb of the patient, or allowing the patient to turn a somersault – can lead to an internal experience within the patient in the presence of the analyst. This internal experience can allow the patient to tolerate increasing degrees of internal experience, including that of early trauma, so that trauma can be ultimately understood and conceptualized at a symbolic level.

Balint has also attempted to communicate with the psychoanalytic community at large when concerning the topic of regression. The whole notion of regression, he asserts, came into disrepute after Freud encountered escalating demands from patients who indulged in a malignant form of regression. Balint defines malignant regression as a psychic state in which the patient craves to get something from the analyst to fill up, heal, repair, or feed the insatiably hungry self. The analyst's submission to any request from the patient who is in this state leads to a proliferation of escalating demands towards the analyst. We may observe this kind of malignant regression in the starved, impulsive, and unrelenting pressure on the analyst to meet the patient's demands. But beyond the behavioral level, Balint implies that the patient with "basic fault" preverbal trauma has a traumatized, sealed off self-core. Only "in the moment," alive, affect contact with the analyst can truly nurture and heal this sealed off self. Such an interaction counterpoises object connection with instinctual gratification.

Although classical analysts speak of abstaining from promoting their analysands' instinctual gratification, they do not deal with ego and object relations gratification through connection. This latter mode of gratification, Balint suggests, promotes benign regression in the basic fault patient. The gratification of needs for contact and connection, as opposed to the gratification of instinctual desire in the form of libidinal release, is what Balint finds critical to healing primal trauma.

Drawing my own conclusions from *The Basic Fault*, I offer the following interpretation of Balint's ideas. As long as the traumatized area of the self remains sealed off (split off psychically through dissociation), the patient will remain in a state of emotional starvation. The patient will then desperately try to get something from the analyst to fix the internal situation. But nothing can help the patient as long as the primary level of contact is blockaded. If the blockage continues, the patient will act out his or her despair towards and against the analyst in escalating demands, a pattern of behavior that has been compared to pouring liquid into a leaking container (Grunes 1984). Balint knew that experiences like this with severely disturbed patients had given the whole concept of regression a bad name. Thus, in order to speak to the need for psychic regression in basic fault patients, while also addressing the objections of the psychoanalytic community, Balint distinguishes between "malignant regression" and "benign regression."

Benign regression is a state in which the patient focuses on his or her own internal experience. In malignant regression, the patient compulsively focuses on getting something from the analyst or is obsessed with changing or controlling the analyst, either by demand, or, I would add to the view of Balint, through the psychic pressures of projective identification. In dealing with benign regression, the analyst follows the patient's cues in order to facilitate an internal experience in the patient, which has until the present time been warded off. As contact is made between analyst and patient at a preverbal level, at a level of emotional experience prior to separation, the analyst and patient flow together in a merger of experience that Balint calls a harmonious mode of "interpenetrating mix-up." However, for this to occur – for the patient to contact an area in the internal self that has been perpetually sealed off – the analyst must set limits to structure the session and the therapeutic environment. Through the analyst's use of limits in the treatment, a malignant regression can be transformed into a benign regression.

Balint himself gives such an example. A patient repeatedly requests an extra analytic session after failing to do any analytic work in the session already provided for him. Each time Balint accedes to the patient's request for an extra session, the additional session is vacuous and empty of any meaningful contact or analytic work. This result makes psychological sense, given that the patient's request at the end of the scheduled session really is an expression of his yearning for the object, a yearning he evaded throughout the session time. It is only when the patient feels the limit of the session at the end of the analytic hour that his hunger for the analyst (object), come into his conscious awareness. Each time Balint grants the extra session, the external limit and its corresponding internal trauma, are again bypassed – for acceding to the patient's request preserves the sealed off area of object hunger. Given such indulgent conditions, the patient cannot feel the pressure of the limit – as an aide to bringing his or her needs into conscious awareness. The evasion of contact and reenactment of pathological structure functioning are instead repeated with the potential for endless repetition.

When Balint sensed what was happening, he differentiated himself from Ferenczi by consciously and respectfully refusing the patient's request for an extra session. He denied the patient's request, explaining that he based his decision on the lack of analytic work in the extra session and his interpretation that the request reflected the patient's belief that the analyst was omnipotent, capable of providing all that the patient needed, despite the infantile nature of the need. After the analyst's refusal to grant another session, the patient had to go home, conscious of his internal sealed off state of emotional isolation, "unmedicated" by any soothing and placating offering of extra time. It is now at this juncture that the patient begins to have an emotional experience formerly unavailable to him. Balint learns of this development when the patient telephones him on the weekend. Bereft of his extra session, the patient for the first time grows tearful. The tears result from his experiencing the conscious pain of longing for the object and suffering the conscious pain of his internal isolation. In this example, Balint demonstrates how setting a conscious limit allows the analyst to create the conditions in which a malignant regression may become a benign regression.

How does the process of mourning enter the picture? Toward the end of *The Basic Fault*, Balint, to a limited degree, explicitly connects his clinical theory with the mourning process. He speaks of the analyst as witness to the patient's mourning. For healing preverbal trauma, he implies that a mourning process must occur. Attempting to fill in the blanks in Balint's statement about witnessing mourning, I might say that his benign regression involves contact between the presence of the analyst and the patient's sealed off core self-area, which has been dissociated and split off from the self's ego operation in the world (Fairbairn 1952). This contact should automatically open up the patient's experience of loss and rage in response to feelings of the disruption of "going on being" (Winnicott 1974), which occurred during earliest infancy when the fused self and other experience is felt by the infant to be traumatically interrupted. The grief within this form of "developmental mourning" (Kavaler-Adler 1996, 2000) is for the lost primal object and for the lost state of early mother–infant fusion or symbiosis, which has also been called a state of dual unity by Margaret Little, a follower of Winnicott. Its emergence at this time does not negate that mourning takes place at many different levels of experience.

Although Balint does not theorize about the interaction of the mourning process and the internalization process, he implies its existence. More specifically, Balint's mode of being with his patient implies not only a here and now experience of contact that can initiate healing, but also operates as a means to internalization and the building of psychic structure. I would add that in order for this psychic structure not to be simply imposed on a persisting pathological structure, psychic space must be opened through mourning. Balint himself speaks about mourning for the basic fault patient, whose failings in mothering have promoted primal loss, and he speaks of the analyst as a witness to it.

THE MOURNING PROCESS IN THE THEORY OF D.W. WINNICOTT

D.W. Winnicott was a student of Melanie Klein, who greatly influenced Winnicott's thinking. His genius took a different path than hers, as his passionate intellect focused assiduously on the effects of the real mother on psychological development, whereas Klein's most neglected area of theory was its relation to the real parents, as opposed to the effect of mother and father as psychic fantasies.

In differentiating himself from Klein, while still profoundly influenced by her, Winnicott responded to her theories on aggression and guilt with his own view of a mother–infant matrix that he suggested could provide containment for developmental process. He never explicitly dealt with the mourning process, as did Klein. Yet his discussions of early development, and of the reliving of trauma within the holding environment of the treatment situation are best understood in interaction with a critical mourning process in treatment.

Winnicott's theory on "object survival" (1971) is his most explicit clinical theory that relates to the developmental function of mourning. Here, Winnicott speaks poetically of the need for the expression of aggression accompanied by the murderous fantasy of killing off the object, in both the infant in relation to the mother and the false self patient (character disorders) in relation to the analyst. He does not distinguish between infants with separation, or transitional stage trauma (his term for a time of separation) and normal infants. When he speaks about adult patients with preoedipal character pathology, however, which he refers to as false-self pathology, he is on solid ground in his clinical observations of these phenomena.

Winnicott observed a patient with primitive affect needs exhibiting such affect within the treatment situation before entering a higher level of symbolic understanding. Although he does not employ the concept of the "death instinct," Winnicott seems to believe that innate factors, as well as real trauma, contribute to the patient's general need to express a form of primitive rage-filled hostile aggression in a contained "holding environment," an environment promoted by the presence of a new mode of object relations psychotherapist. This kind of expression of aggression, Winnicott's essays imply, is a protosymbolic enactment of a psychic fantasy that can come to be symbolized through the experience. According to Winnicott, the psychic fantasy takes the form of saying, "Hullo object! I destroyed you. I love you. You have value for me because of your survival of my destruction of you. While I am loving you, I am all the time destroying you in unconscious fantasy" (1971: 90). Much depends on whether the therapist can survive the patient's murderous aggression, in the sense of not retaliating (including not making symbolic interpretations that cannot be received at a symbolic level) and not emotionally abandoning the patient.

As I have written in clinical articles such as "Object Relations Process in the Treatment of the Preoedipal Character" (1993), and "Opening Up Blocked Mourning in the Preoedipal Character" (1995), such a concept of object survival can be expanded. In Winnicott's terms, however, the main point is that the therapist needs to be able to sit through an aggressive assault, propelled by intense archaic affect, without being compelled to strike back either through interpretation or behavior, at the time of the assault. Also, the therapist needs to be connected enough to this core of good object internalization to be able to sustain a sense of emotional connection to the patient, despite the patient's rageful tantrum that disconnects from relatedness. In this way, the therapist can be receptive to the patient's overtures for emotional contact, once the assault has reached its denouement. Anything less than this can be experienced as abandonment by the patient, particularly with the preoedipally traumatized patient, where annihilation anxiety is a constant threat – as Winnicott spoke about in writing about "unthinkable anxieties," in which the reexperiencing of object loss annihilates any sense of self.

Winnicott believed that once a patient experienced his therapist/analyst survive in this way, he could feel the gratitude of love because the mothering object has survived. Thus, Winnicott describes the psychic fantasy of the patient in the midst of primitive rage, in terms of a paradox: "I love you all the while I am killing you."

If the analyst survives the murderous impulses of the analysand, it would always be to a relative degree, as in Winnicott's "good enough" mother. One survives to a good enough degree, and this allows a natural developmental process to unfold in the analysand, rather than retraumatization. With good enough object survival, the analysand's archaic aggression can gradually be transformed into a symbolic level of psychic fantasy. Once reaching the symbolic level, the analysand is enacting the impulses to kill through a psychic fantasy that contains the impulse, rather than through the archaic rage affect. Such transformation is gradual and depends on the safe or containing environment provided, both by the analyst and by the analytic space and boundaries. The transformation to the symbolic level involves the analysand entering a state of mind where free association is possible, as well as the conscious constructing of psychic fantasy. A clear illustration of this is explicated in "Opening Up Blocked Mourning in the Preoedipal Character" (Kavaler-Adler

1995) In this article, I discuss the survival of my patient's rageful attack on me as the externalized bad object immediately leads to a newly unblocked level of symbolic functioning in which the patient could free associate to a dream for the first time. Consequently this patient could comprehend the symbolic messages in analytic interpretations for the first time. Such symbolic comprehension then leads immediately to the inner experience that allows a profound and critical developmental mourning process to begin.

Winnicott divides the mother of the presymbolic (or protosymbolic) patient into two, as object mother and environment mother. The patient's primitive aggressive attack can be targeted for the object mother (bad mother) and the environment mother then serves unconsciously as the holding mother (early idealized mother in Klein) who contains the experience and survives it. Developmental mourning then, as it follows such an attack, becomes the mournful grief related to yearnings for the lost holding mother of childhood experience or of idealized fantasy. This can only happen when the analyst plays the role of the transitional environment mother in external form. Such a role is particularly important when the original mother had not formerly survived the analysand's childhood aggression. Often the real and original mother was abusive, psychically absent, or neglectful. If this occurs to a traumatic degree, there would be a split off bad mother, as described by Fairbairn (1952), or what Winnicott calls an "intrusive mother" in the psyche (Ogden 1986). A lack of adequate contact and connection with the child's developmental needs during the separation era (called the "transitional stage" by Winnicott) results in a compulsion to express the murderous attack, related both to trauma and frustration of drives, in action rather than in a reported psychic fantasy.

In Winnicott's terms, the patient kills the object who arouses overwhelming instinctual hunger (as in Fairbairn's "exciting object"), but is received into the symbolic arms of the environment mother. When thus received, the real external presence of the other, the analyst, can first be truly perceived, rather than continuing to be distorted through the projections of the internal object mother onto the analyst. Winnicott assumes that symbolic functions have been arrested in the development of those with preoedipal arrests that he refers to as false self patients. Therefore he believes that the analyst's containing of verbally enacted aggression is necessary to allow the development of symbolic capacity. The analyst must hold within himself his own retaliatory impulses, as well as the words and affect of the patient who uses words as concrete weapons, similar to knives and guns. When the patient moves to the symbolic level, and truly becomes an analysand, she/he can begin to conceptualize the wish to kill the analyst. Then he/she can conceptualize the loving gratitude for the analyst's allowing the expression of such a wish without being really killed off, or without being emotionally killed off in terms of losing warmth or relatedness in relation to the analysand.

Otto Kernberg disputes Winnicott's thesis that symbolic functions have not yet been developed in such patients (1985). Kernberg believes that the symbolic functions are developed but blocked in such patients due to primitive "oral rage." Whether Kernberg's or Winnicott's view is more accurate, the expression of rage in a containing therapeutic environment does seem to allow the use of symbolic capacity.

In the case of "Opening Up Blocked Mourning in the Preoedipal Character," one sees the clear dynamics of object survival and the initiation of both symbolization and developmental mourning (Kavaler-Adler 1995). After my survival of this female patient's aggression, the patient could for the first time open up the pain of deep grief in relation to the loss of her mother, who died when she was nine. The pain opened up when I interpreted the transference in this woman's first dream following her aggressive assault. This was the first dream that she could associate to her free association capacity, which had opened up after her rage was expressed and unblocked. I said, "You feel like you are giving and giving to me and I am taking and taking from you, but unconsciously it is the opposite. At an unconscious level you feel you are taking and taking and taking from me (as reflected in the dream), and using me up just like you felt you used up your mother and killed her!" This interpretation led to an intense grief stricken sobbing in which my narcissistic patient exclaimed: I did it! I did it! In her subjective view, she had killed her mother, because she thought she had not loved her mother as much as her mother loved her, and in fact that she had expressed hate for her mother by wishing she was a younger mother. As this patient sobbed out her profound grief, and opened an ocean of mournful sadness, her pain and longing were both palpable for me.

I don't believe that my patient and I could have gotten to this point of mourning in treatment without my patient going through her primitive rage tantrums, as Winnicott suggests in "The Use of an Object and Relating through Identifications" (1971). This patient did not only reach a level of symbolic capacity through her rage towards me in the treatment, which later could be understood more clearly as transference. She also reached a level of psychic dialectic that allowed for the processing of grief affect into mourning process, linking cognitive representations of objects with affect. My patient's memory of her mother was reengaged through this process, as she navigated through her guilt and loss, with psychic fantasies of her mother within her mourning experience. Her mother came back to life as a symbolic image and as an awakened memory, rather than being someone she could only seek in my concrete presence, trying to pressure me into literally touching her and soothing her. Once she grieved, my patient could allow a new form of symbolic holding, not only in the midst of an aggressive assault, but while sleeping peacefully and allowing an unconscious infant part of her to emerge between us. After her deep mournful grief, she could say, "It doesn't hurt so much now when I think of my mother." Also she could tell me at this point that she could now think of the mother she remembered in her dream without acute pain. Thus she opened to a new relationship in the present with me, her analyst, without sealing off so quickly again. Following her mourning, my patient slept peacefully during one session. Significantly, I could feel a very different kind of experience when in the room with her. I could hear music like that of a lullaby. I felt her gentleness and my own, and I felt baby feelings in my lips and fingers, which I have never felt before or since.

This is a case illustration of Winnicott's clinical theory of object survival and how it is intimately related to the opening of psychic space and psychic symbolic capacity, which in turn allow the development of an inner dialectic for the processing of affect connections to internal objects through mourning. A new-found capacity to experience grief affect in all its intensity results, rather than merely repeating the cathartic exorcism of paranoid or narcissistic rage, which has no consequence in psychic change or transformation, and merely reinforces a closed system.

The capacity for concern

Another aspect of Winnicott's theory, called "the capacity for concern" (1963), touches on a capacity for mourning as a developmental and clinical process. In his paper on "The Development of the Capacity for Concern," Winnicott addresses the issue of moral development through a developmental progression in which guilt becomes tolerable for the first time, and implicitly draws on Klein's conceptual-ization of "the depressive position." He establishes a clinical approach to helping a patient contain guilt so that a capacity for human concern forms in the psyche, where formerly there was only an infantile "ruthlessness," in which an infant necessarily uses the mother as a part object fantasized to be there for gratification of infantile impulses and demand, or a "subjective object," an object perceived by the fantasy of the infant as being there exclusively to provide support for its needs and developmental functions (Winnicott 1974). The transitional stage bridging the gap from Winnicott's infantile "pre-ruth" mentality to that of conscious ruthless-ness, or to ruth and concern, is that of a period of "held guilt." According to Winnicott, the developmental ability to tolerate guilt by containing it is developed in a dyadic relation to an environmental mother, who lives in the present for the adult patient through the presence of the analyst. Just as Winnicott writes of a transitional stage function of the therapist-mother, or "environmental mother," in allowing a patient to begin to tolerate states of solitude in "The Capacity to be Alone," he writes of the transitional stage function of the therapist as an environ-ment mother, in his (1963) paper, "The Development of the Capacity for Concern." In this paper he implies that the unaware and amoral state of ruthlessness trans-forms to concern, as guilt can be held and felt as a growing conscience, rather than being so overwhelming that it automatically triggers demonic aggression and retaliatory reactions (retaliations).

In "The Capacity to be Alone" (1965), Winnicott speaks of the developmental need of a child to be with the mother, who is present, but yet absent in the sense of not expressing any needs of her own. Thus, the child can begin to internalize an experience of having the mother there, while the child is into his own needs and his own capacities to play and create. This is not a fusional state of primary infant "dual unity" with mother, but a transitional state in which mother is a transitional object, who, like a teddybear, is at that point "present," but not making any demand on her child. As the mother's non-intrusive presence is felt subliminally, and is internalized without any conscious interaction, the child builds in the psychic structure of a mother who is benign, loving and containing. Thus, the child can be alone without mother, without suffering the tortures of "unthinkable anxiety." He/she can now be alone and yet have the other internalized within, so that solitude is not emotional isolation, or as Winnicott says in "On Communicating and Not Communicating," (1982, 1963) one can be isolated without being "insulated." In "The Development of the Capacity for Concern," the mother plays another transitional stage function. She is present so that guilt can be held and not enacted as aggression. When Winnicott describes this role in terms of a therapist working with a false self patient, he speaks of the therapist helping the patient to point out something positive about himself. He advocates this as a means of repairing the patient's equilibrium, when the patient is being confronted with his aggressive side. With this therapeutic technique, the patient need not leave the session thinking he is bad, which at the level of preoedipal pathology could easily become all "bad" due to primitive splitting.

How does Winnicott's writing about this transitional stage process of "held guilt" lead to a capacity for concern, and how does this relate to a developmental mourning process? It appears that the ability of anyone to have an experience of "held guilt" is a prerequisite to feeling grief in the sense of remorse, and therefore in the sense of Klein's depressive position mourning. One can only mourn regrets about hurting the object one loves when guilt can be contained and not denied, nor projected as blame onto another.

D.W. Winnicott's "transitional object"

Another aspect of Winnicott's theory pertains not just to the transitional stage already discussed, but to the transitional object. Whether the transitional object be a child's teddybear or blanket, or whether it be a therapist providing a presence to allow the development of the capacity for solitude and concern, the question can be asked as to whether the transitional object needs to be internalized in order for the developmental movement to attachment of a whole and separate object to take place. Evidence for this successful journey through transitional object use to relationship with a whole object can be seen when loss and mourning for the whole and separate object can be tolerated.

Prior to this, there must be enough good enough contact with the primary mother of infancy, at the stage of "dual unity" (a term used by Winnicott to speak of infant symbiosis) for an infant to separate enough from the concrete mother to have a transitional object and to enjoy the capacity to play with it. Playing with the transitional object can allow for some independence from the early object that may be experienced as omnipotent in states of fusion.

Although some analysts have proposed that the transitional object itself need not be mourned for development to continue, the transitional stage has not been successfully bypassed and the transitional object has not been successfully used for a critical developmental function, if the relinquishment of the transitional object does not lead to a full object attachment, in which the object's subjectivity can be experienced, including its needs. Once such an attachment is formed, and the unique identity of the object as an "other" is psychically connected to and internalized, the loss of the object will necessarily induce grief and mourning as a psychic and emotional response. If this does not happen, whole object relations have not been achieved, and then those first used as a perpetuated transitional object experience will be objects of addiction rather than of attachment. The hungry instinctual cravings for part object that is the target of addiction can be transferred to an alternate target of addiction when disappointment occurs. The differentiated nature of the object upon whom these hungers are attached is bypassed.

When there truly is whole object attachment, there is an internalization of the object that builds the core of self feeling and of object constancy at the same time. In fact, it is because of the perceived otherness of the object that symbolic internalization of a differentiated other takes place. This differs from the case of the transitional object that remains an external event (with Winnicott's 1953 unanswered question for the child as to whether he/she found or created the object). The otherness of the object leads to a sense of poignant loss when that unique object is no longer present or available. Once a separate object with its own subjectivity is felt, and psychically experienced at the level of internalization within the internal world – (within the central self of Fairbairn, not in a split off and sealed off part, which undigested incorporated objects exist) – the experience of both concern and grief over object loss become psychic necessities that are most clearly articulated through a mourning process. This mourning process has its own ongoing developmental role, because consciousness of grief and longing for the lost other will transform the symbolic internalization of the other into a resource for visualized memory that serves as links back to actual experiences with the loved and lost object.

Chapter 6

The case of June, Part 1:

Finding a new identity through the mourning of traumatic loss and guilt, primal rage, and poignant regret

June entered treatment in her mid-thirties, when she was suffering from severe anxiety, with compulsive and addictive behaviors that seemed to trap and control her. She was attractive, but had a dejected look on her face, except for when she felt inspired by ideas and visions that she associated with me and who I represented to her. As soon as she would stop a complex of compulsive actions, such as eating, shopping, or raging at her boyfriends, she would feel an internal emptiness and numbness. She was not yet aware of the underlying depression and its infant sources, but she wanted to feel, to feel better, and to find meaning in her life by exploring and examining who she was. Another presenting symptom was that of overwhelming guilt and its accompanying fantasy of being a criminal. This symptom related to the way she had left her first husband, her son, and her entire family in Australia.

June was desirous of starting a better life in America, and she tried not to look back, because the pain of doing so was too great. She detached from her emotions to cut off the emotional links to her childhood and early adult life relationships. She wasn't sure why she had chosen to remain in the United States after staying for a year to earn money; however, she knew instinctively that there was no turning back. June felt her psychic survival depended on staying in New York and finding her true internal direction in life. Up until the time she left her homeland, June had been constantly driven by hopes that were profoundly disappointed and by compulsive and addictive behaviors that were felt subjectively to rule over her like driving demons.

Finding her way in New York was very difficult, and June was fortunate to be able to rely on her superior intellectual capacities as she entered school in New York, while also working as a nurse to earn money. She entered an undergraduate psychology program in a public university, and became fascinated with the psychological studies. She began to think she might find answers to questions not yet clearly articulated about herself and about how lost she felt, and about how alienated she felt now that she had cut off from her country and family. June knew that she had felt lost for a long time, and that she had felt numb for a long time, despite her active life in her former country.

June decided to enter treatment with me after hearing a lecture I gave in one of her university psychology classes. I believe that she projected onto me her own passion, which had been split off from her central self and was originally projected into her mother. She gained access to her own passion by taking in my rhythms, my voice, and the content of my words and thoughts. She was particularly taken with poetic phrases I employed to discuss my books on women artists, writers, and poets. Although she had seen a psychotherapist on a once a week basis, she wanted a deeper engagement than she had felt with this somewhat inexperienced therapist. When I was introduced as a psychoanalyst and spoke in my lecture about object relations theory, she became intensely curious about what object relations thinking and psychoanalysis were all about. The combination of this curiosity and the severe level of her daily suffering made her quite willing to enter a psychoanalytic process, which consisted of several sessions a week on the couch, with me sitting behind her in the traditional way for psychoanalytic work.

As far as a diagnosis is concerned, June obviously had early and accumulated trauma related to parental pathology that undermined her autonomy and her entire separation and individuation process. She defended herself with the splitting, dissociation, projective and introjective mechanisms characteristic of an upper level borderline character. Sometimes she also showed the weakness of reality testing and ego autonomy of this kind of character. Nevertheless, June also had profound capacities for internal experience that developed over time in treatment, and she began to symbolize such experiences as she mourned her early losses.

In addition, June evidenced the kind of idealizing and twinship transferences of someone with the narcissistic features of a self-disorder as it has been defined by Heinz Kohut (1971). Her early narcissistic vulnerability and split off grandiose self were reflective of James Masterson's writings on the closet narcissist (1985). To encounter June is to come across a rich and vivid personality, but one that needed to emerge from behind the pathological constrictions of borderline and narcissistic defenses and ego weaknesses.

Through her treatment, three years of which is written about in these two chapters, June emerged like a butterfly from a cocoon as her self-integration process took place through critical developmental mourning. Both her internal and external life developed in full, but there could not have been any psychoanalytic process to bring this about if she had not had the holding environment on a consistent and intensive basis necessary to tolerate the primitive affect states of a grief and mourning process that reached back repeatedly to infancy and toddlerhood. June's capacity to cry was extremely necessary and significant. Eventually, she could reconnect with her deeper self without crying, but for several years she needed to sob deeply on the couch each time she compulsively cut off from herself, and needed to find herself again. June's capacity to connect to herself and to sustain connection over time was promoted by new and healthy internalizations of relatedness and attunement in treatment.

June's newly evolving capacity for connection during the course of treatment allowed her to marry, to earn a new professional degree in graduate studies in psychology, to pursue a career in psychology, to develop a spiritual life where once there had been an inner emptiness, to reunite with her son who had entered his adolescence, to reconnect with her family, to begin to teach and write in her chosen field of psychology, to pursue public speaking. It also allowed her to reunite with a split off vulnerable tenderness and repressed sexuality that encouraged an increasing intimacy in her personal life.

June presented homicidal and suicidal ideation at the beginning of her treatment. She experienced insatiable emotional hunger combined with a sense of empty numbness, and a persistent internal attack from a split off punitive part of her that she would eventually come to connect with a conscious sense of guilt. June focused primarily on me in the beginning of her treatment, looking at me as a guiding light for her own development. She was fearful of focusing on herself, because she was confronted with a dark interior world, and a painful and tumultuous affect life when she did open to express herself. Although her tendency to focus on me was a defense, her view of me also served as a powerful motivation for her engagement with the treatment process. Because of her idealized view of me, she wanted to become like me as a means to finding herself. When she sensed in me a passion for the internal experience of psychic life (fantasies, imaginings, visual forms of affect states and desires), she was sensing her own potential passion, potential vision, and potential internal life. She chose to work with me on an intensive basis. She began with two sessions a week, then three, and by the third year of treatment attended five sessions a week, which she continued for three years. Due to scheduling problems however, she attended two double sessions a week, and one single session. She spoke of wishing she could have eight sessions. For June, the opportunity for an object relations therapy and analysis was a salvation. She articulates this in many ways, often poetically and with a sense of gratitude. She found an opportunity to face her grief.

In the beginning June's grief felt enormous to her, and she carried an onerous burden of guilt. She felt like a criminal whenever she thought of her past and of the family and particularly of the child she had left behind. Even when she acknowledged the loving and compassionate parts of herself, she would still speak of the criminal part pulling her backward. I think of June's internal state as being haunted – an anguished state that coexisted with her enormous hope for change. June viewed me with respect, envy, admiration, and idealization. For her, I was a muse. She spoke of me as an inspiration for her, and assigned to me what she spoke of as a mystic vision of the internal world. Once she assigned me such a quality, she wanted what I had, my vision, as she saw it. She ultimately gained her own vision by increasingly sustained connection to her internal life.

"What will happen to me?" she cried from a prone position on my psychoanalytic couch. Having left Australia many years ago, June was haunted by memories of her life there, which included her father, mother, brother, ex-husband, and her son, who was 2 years old when she left. She condemned herself through the harassment of a punitive superego, acting like a harsh antilibidinal ego structure, largely constructed from her father's relentless assaults of cynical and verbal contempt. How could she have been so numb, so detached, so indifferent, she asked herself, as to have "felt nothing" when she left her family and decided to stay here in America, after a year's visit? This question had haunted her for many years, but she only verbalized and articulated it when she felt I was with her and was listening to her. The symbolic message of an articulated question can reverberate in the mind until it either annihilates or reveals the self. Like the unfolding of a Henry James tale, the symbolic message of a once articulated question can become a personified force, with a weight and shrill cry of its own, ever reverberating in the mind until it explodes into the alternate consequence of self-annihilation or self-revelation.

Although entering treatment in a state of mind that might be classified within terms of Melanie Klein's (1940) paranoid-schizoid position or Heinz Kohut's (1971) idealizing transference, June was to experience Klein's depressive position repeatedly in analysis. Her existential despair was to turn to existential grief. She would sob in the sessions (total body crying on the couch). Split off self-parts felt to June like demonic entities shaking her down as she lay on the couch. In one session with June, I quoted Shakespeare's Hamlet speaking to Horatio. I did this to mirror some of her own descriptions of how it felt at that time to lie on the couch and encounter her internal world. She felt I understood her when I spoke Hamlet's words to her: "There are more things in heaven and earth, Horatio, than are dreamt of in your philosophy!" (*Hamlet* I, v: 166). June joined in by describing how many people in her life felt to her like they were inside of her operating like voracious psychic vampires whom she could never successfully feed, nor satisfy. Gradually, she would acknowledge her projective identifications that enmeshed her with others, and she would begin to consciously understand her emotional starvation and her obsessive-compulsive and addictive behaviors. June talked about feeling possessed by compulsions to shop without limits, to eat without limits, and even to read without limits, although the reading paid off in constructive ways towards her education, while the other activities only made her hate herself. Engaged in compulsive activities that felt out of her control, June was distracted from her feelings of numbness and from what she would later describe as the *hard stone in her once frozen heart*. She wanted to escape from an emptiness within that she described at first as like a hollow pipe extending from her stomach to her throat. She often related her psychic experience in visceral terms.

Despite her existence in manic activity and frantic escape, with her keen intelligence, June had completed a nursing degree in Australia, and this had enabled her to work as a nurse in the United States while pursuing undergraduate and graduate studies in psychology. She also had acquired along the way several boyfriends, and at the time of entering treatment she was living with a man who would become her husband. She was, however, quite alienated from her family, and she felt alone and isolated. June feared that she would "never have deep friendships" and that she would fail to have significant "meaning in my life." She saw me in the beginning as her potential rescuer from this tragic fate. After hearing me speak at her school on the topic of creative compulsion, she defined me as the "master therapist" who could unlock her frozen heart. June's unconscious sense of self transforms from frozen snow to loose and free-swirling oceans of water in her later dreams. However, the frozen unconscious was also her formerly frozen heart, and her formerly frozen internal mother as incorporated in her frozen rage states, which often were reactive to June's moves toward separation.

June's belief in me fostered her belief in herself as her idealization of me led to a twinship transference (Kohut 1971). In this transference state, June experienced herself as living through a view of me that was idealized, in that at that time June lacked an awareness of my less desirable qualities. She told me initially: "At the center of you there is something good, something divine. You have a large soul." She then imagines a good center in herself opening in resonance with my soul. Rage and tears, and the experiencing of pain behind a "killer rage" led the way. In her state of twinship she said: "I feel you, like I hear the way you hear, see the way you see." This was a wish to be her own idealized self, but her conscious sense of herself was just the opposite. At first she had defined herself as a numb person, and then as one possessed by a killer rage.

Each time June acknowledged her feelings of hate, and her murderous impulses towards those who represented the guilt laden responsibilities of her early life, she relaxed a little, and her internal "potential space" opened (Ogden 1986). June had dreams of large apartments and houses to be bought and resided in, which represented her opening up within her internal world. Such internal space had been foreclosed by split off and unconscious hatred. Acknowledging the hatred freed June. Yet, she would use the term "criminal part" to speak of the personification of her hate and sadism, which she recalled particularly in relation to others' accusations towards her of being indifferent. She accounted for each memory of a guilty act, such as using the colored pens of a classmate in school without permission. In her unconscious this act could be as horrible to her as the neglect of her child, who she left in the care of her mother when she came to America.

MOURNING, SEPARATION TRAUMA, AND PSYCHIC STRUCTURE

Developmental mourning is a self-integration process in which various splits and divisions in psychic self-structure can be healed as separation from the parents evolves. This healing occurs as connections are enhanced between various aspects of the self, so that self-states and self-parts can evolve into the levels of separation and individuation. For patients who have had serious developmental arrests in the evolution of a separate self due to separation trauma during the critical separation–individuation phase of rapprochement, at the age of 18 to 36 months (Mahler *et al.* 1975) as well as earlier and further on during development, the mourning process necessary for healing and integrating the self is particularly intense and painful. The pathological state of the self that is both fused with the mother and divided from itself has been labeled an "abandonment depression" by James F. Masterson

(1981) in his work on developmental arrests due to separation trauma in borderline and narcissistic patients. Behind Masterson's work is that of the British object relations theorist Ronald Fairbairn (1952), who described psychic structure in its pathological state of primal division and primal sealing off from healthy and new object relations in the external world of interpersonal relations.

June's mourning process, within an intensive object relations analysis, illustrates primal separation trauma. Throughout her three years of treatment, June progressed from a more symbiotic psychic structure, in which she sought fusion with me as an idealized symbiotic mother in the transference, to increasing levels of differentiated self-expression as a separate and individuated self evolved. As Masterson has described, each step forward developmentally is followed by a backlash into modes of defense that can appear as attempts to re-fuse with the primal symbiotic mother object. The primal symbiotic mother is an object that is internal but that is enacted with the transferential other through attempts at reunion and merger. Alternate modes of defense are withdrawal from contact with the external other and rage at the other, who is experienced as withdrawing the minute the other (transference object) is no longer perceived as cooperating with a merger experience. Also, narcissistic modes of grandiosity and manic defense can be part of this withdrawal from the external other, experienced in relationship with the analyst. All these modes of defense are ways of attempting to ward off the agony of a primal rage and terror that comes with a disrupted and traumatic separation during childhood. The primal rage and terror must be felt consciously as the patient moves from a former state of numbness and symbiotic illusion into a more separate state. If the rage and terror can be contained in the treatment situation, the connection with the analyst can allow for the transformation of symbiotic cravings and yearnings into the grief and sadness of developmental grief and disillusionment. Then genuine object love is experienced, which allows rage to be felt and transformed into object-loss sadness. Consequently, object longings in the form of love connections can open a new and separate form of object relationship in the external world. The interpersonal and therapeutic connection with the analyst serves as a vehicle for this new and more separate mode of relatedness (Balint 1979; Grunes 1984). June, like other analysands, developed her creative capacities as she created and recreated this new mode of in vivo relationship.

June moved through the intense affect states of abandonment depression, with an initial idealizing transference that served a developmental function. The idealizing transference allows a primal symbiotic illusion to express itself, an illusion of recreating an early infant state, in which the self and other are experienced as merged and also as omnipotent. Through this illusion, June allowed her dissociated longings for individuated self-expression to be experienced through my voice. At first, my speech, views, and articulation of June's developmental dilemmas became for her, her own self-expression. Then, through identification and internalization, her psychological development naturally evolved towards finding her own voice. She found her own increasingly vivid ways of expressing her own experience. This is all seen in the transference with the analyst. Genuine object connection grew out of this idealizing transference, and therefore I only interpreted its defensive aspects. In this way its developmental aspects were allowed to flourish. June experienced repeated backlash reactions leading to a collapsing sense of self and a return to an old and helpless self, following each step forward into separation, with the self's individuation being expressed in words. June expressed her individuation as "coming out" or into the world, or as being "out there." She also repeatedly expressed the related primal terror. Early on, she said that she would be terrified of putting herself "out there" as she saw me doing, because she was afraid of being destroyed: "I feel that if I was out there like you, people would want to destroy me." Later, she had less fear that she would be killed by others if she risked being out there, or if she had different opinions. The threatening others can be conceptualized as a symbolic alien other, which represented on internal envious mother figure, one who resented any movement toward independence on June's part.

Through my understanding of the dynamics and knowledge of June's history I concluded that June's childhood mother was reflexively engaged in this unconscious tug of war over June's success. June's internal mother compelled June, as her first child, to be either an idealized extension of herself or the bad child who contained her split-off dark side, with all its unacknowledged and unassimilated aggression. When in the state of her mother's bad self, June felt heavy, gloomy, dirty, dull, numb, and serious. In June's mind, this was a contrast to who I was – her transferential mother. To get out of this state, while still enmeshed in psychic symbiosis with the childhood mother who had become a fused symbiotic internal object, June could move toward achievements in the world, such as making good grades at school. Through this outward achievement, June could gratify her mother's narcissistic wishes, given the frustration of her mother's own arrested state, because she felt a constant pressure to achieve.

There was another message from June's mother as well. Any achievement also threatened to evoke June's mother's dissociated envy, and June would experience this threat in projections of her internal envious mother onto others. Any step on June's part toward having her own voice, her own opinions, and her own accomplishments was followed by terror, grief, loss, a collapsing of self confidence, and paranoia about being assaulted or killed. This created her backlash reactions of somatic visceral aspects. She would feel choked, suffocated, repulsed, and would become nauseous from choking back a vomiting anger and a sense of poison within her. Alternately, June could return to the visceral sense of an empty pipe within her, or to deadness and numbness. As her affect life came alive, however, through the separation and mourning process, she also had backlash reactions of boiling hot rage, as if she were on fire, and eventually she would face other affects of object loss, affects of grief, disillusionment, and sadness. Despite these painful backlashes, however, June's developmental strivings to be out there in the world persisted and flourished into a culminating triumph throughout her treatment. As she became increasingly aware of formerly dissociated affect states, she began to acknowledge her envy, greed, hunger and insatiable cravings. Instead of just being a victim of the projected internal mother, she became an agent of her own envious and murderous wishes as she hungered to have what I, as the other, had. As long as I represented an idealized extension of her self, she could feel enlivened and restored by my success in the world, for she was to me as her mother was to her. But she, too, like her internal mother, had wishes for being the center of things herself, and so although she could momentarily be thrilled as a part of me relishing my accomplishments, her own dissociated envy and lust for fame, power, and destruction would also erupt. So at one time she could feel sincere admiration for me, such as after seeing me present some of my work before an audience, related to her interest in psychology: "Your presentation was just marvelous! There is something in you developing. It's just going to get better. I guess I feel warm inside now." And: "I don't know how it happened, but I feel excited." At other times she would feel envy: "I envy your vision. I want it for myself." June's vicarious experience of my success in being out in the world was obviously intense and extremely visceral, which suggests the early level of its psychic origins, as in her feeling hot and excited in her body when expressing her response to my presentation. Her envy, therefore, could be just as intense and visceral, and this could in part explain why when she projected envy onto others they often had the powerful and sensual form of a vampire, since the projection contained a highly visceral oral erotic hunger, from primal infant development.

As June progressed from wanting to be a part of me and wanting to be merged with me as her idealized object (and self-extension), she began to want a higher form of identification. With some progress in separation she could say: "I want to be like a musician who takes in from you, and then uses it for myself. I want to become myself, but I can take in and learn from you." She began to feel that she could take me in as a model and psychically digest me, rather than remaining a part of me. As she moved in this direction, June still felt elated after a presentation of mine, but then experienced a feeling of loneliness afterward, when she suddenly is overwhelmed by the awareness of being a separate being. As self and object images separate out in her internal world, which she experienced consciously through remembering a dream, she became developmentally and psychically separate, and so being a part of me no longer worked for her.

Then June's anxiety about the conflict of wanting to be out there, and yet fearing exposure and hate from others, returned to her in a new way. As her observing ego develops through mourning, allowing her to reflect on her own anxiety, June said: "I'm so happy for you when you're out there and I see your joy and excitement. But I'm not there yet. Will I get there?"

Despite her hesitation and fear, and her concern about her own capacities, June began to feel desire for, rather than dread of, taking risks to be out in the world, through her own performances, presentations and successes. But on the way, in her developmental journey, June felt both states of paralysis and states of conscious envy. In a state of helplessness and paralysis, thrown back on the inadequate self that feels like it lacks agency without the support of a mother (she spoke of grandiose pride on top of a helpless inadequate part) she cried with grief over her despair. She had risked being out there and then collapsed. I interpreted the bind she was in due to the separation trauma she carries with her and she was deeply relieved. I said: "You feel helpless because you're in a psychological bind in your mind. You fear being out there because you're so afraid of being hated, resented, and envied, but you simultaneously fear staying in the cocoon or shell that you felt you lived in originally because you no longer could stand to feel empty, detached, and numb. Withdrawing now makes you feel isolated and alone."

Another way June attempted to deal with this bind was to try to raise herself up from this helpless state by a defensive manic triumph in relation to me, as if triumphing over me (as a transitional mother and model) would raise her up. She told me in one session in her second year of treatment: "I'm going to have a large apartment and a concierge, and you'll be in this little office." She laughed with conscious contempt at this mental triumph and said: "I want diamonds and pearls now." By the time she was able to say this to me she did not need me to interpret it. She interpreted it herself: "I can't believe that I can be so open about my envy and contempt now." In this session she progressed from an urgent wish for a bigger apartment to a feeling of missing me and wanting to continue our journey into her internal world, wishing for the riches within. The symbolic gifts from her relationship with me became more important in the transition of the session, and she relinquished the immediacy of the wish for a concrete achievement of attaining a new and bigger apartment. But overall she was becoming increasingly conscious of her wish to shine in her own right. She articulated this in the third year of treatment: "I no longer want to be fused with you. I want to have my own voice now." Such a wish expressed her developmental progression from wanting to be an extension of the idealized me (a state of psychic symbiosis in which she lived happily in a vicarious relation to me), to a later state of a differentiated self-identity, individuation and connection, and separation and relatedness.

INTERNAL PARENTS AND PSYCHIC STRUCTURE

Although Ronald Fairbairn's model of psychic structure explains June's psychic change, such a description is in part related to the separation–individuation issues described by Masterson. Both Fairbairn and Masterson considered the splits in psychic structure they observed through dissociated self-states in terms of the internalization of traumatizing parents, and both dealt with dynamic internal objects as part of psychic structure. Masterson focused on intense bad object parts of the parents specifically in terms of the traumatizing abuse of parents in relation to developmental needs for separation. Parents who were operating out of their own developmentally arrested psyches, whose early trauma had caused them to develop borderline, narcissistic, and schizoid character disorders, could not allow their children to separate. Thus, as soon as the developmental needs for separation and autonomy (as defined in Mahler's separation–individuation process) were expressed by the child as an 18- to 36-months-old toddler, the mother began to be abusive, or self-allusive through illness. Such a mother operated out of her own dissociated (split off) states to hold her child back, rather than supporting her toddler's developmental growth. This pattern began in these early years and would continue throughout the child's growth, as long as the child remained dependent on the mother. In this view of parental pathology in relation to separation trauma, the father is seen as either compensating for the mother's resistance to her child's separation or as compounding the problem this set up in the child's mind. Often the father is seen to compound the pathological effect, since the mother has married a man who has similar developmental problems to her own. When he does so, he is internalized as a dynamic internal object of pathogenic effect, in addition to the mother, because his noxious qualities do not allow for a benign object internalization in the form of a symbolic representation of a parental object. Other times the father is a healthier alternative, but becomes a part object and the object of addiction, because the basic self-integration process has been arrested.

In June's case, there are two incidents related to her mother that suggest the overall developmental pattern of resistance to separation. When accompanied by June's reports of her mother's behavior and attributes, the reflexive assault of a dynamic internal object becomes meaningful as a repeated separation trauma and its malevolent splitting processes. June's report of her father's attitude and behavior is also consonant with this reflexive internal assault being built into her intrapsychic structure.

In the first incident, which occurred when June was still in her preschool years, she went to a neighbor's apartment one day. She came home in a happy state and showed her mother a candy the neighbor had given her. Her mother threw the candy into the fireplace with an explosion of rage and accusatory words toward June. June felt she did something terribly wrong, but didn't understand what. In analysis, June came to realize that her mother must have been reacting to her "betrayal" by visiting others, rather than staying home with her mother. In tones of her own evolving object-related anger, following periods of rage affect surfacing, June declared: "My mother played outside with me every day. I could never have friends." June never had friends when she entered school either, because she never had learned how to make friends.

The second incident occurred when June was an adolescent, engaging in normal teenage behavior. The compounding of sexual growth and separation urges together seems to have doubly threatened her mother, who this time struck out directly at June. One time when June returned home from a disco, her mother shocked her, and perhaps erotically aroused her, by slapping her hard across her face. The echo of this slap would reverberate forever, and it had echoes in the past as well as in her mother's history.

When the parent's history has been particularly traumatic, the intense affect experience required for consciously processing the trauma is intolerable, especially without psychotherapy. June's mother, who was not Jewish, lived in a German occupied country during World War II, before her family moved to Australia. One memory that the mother shared with June was of watching Nazi soldiers smash a little girl against a wall, killing her. How much June's mother unconsciously relived this horror in her own aggression is hard to know. We can speculate, however, that this observation of a little girl being killed could have become part of the mother's own rages that then assaulted June, and could have been part of her slapping June.

In her treatment sessions June would often want to either slap me, or be slapped, and she would speak of these impulses and fantasies of slapping as smashing. Sometimes she wanted to "trash the room," but she was able to be conscious of these impulses over time and could articulate them. She might want to be slapped, out of guilt for her unforgivable "crimes," particularly crimes of neglect related to her own child. June also might wish to smash me out of frustration if she wished to separate from me, or if she couldn't connect with me as a separate other, or if she felt I wasn't understanding her. There could also be an erotic element in June's wish to slap or be slapped. She was reliving and reenacting the harsh, punitive and arousing part of her relationship with her mother.

June may also have been reliving the horrors of her mother's past that resided as "disquieting muses" (Plath 1961) in her mother's dissociated psyche. The poet, Sylvia Plath, used the phrase "disquieting muses" to describe a dissociated part of her mother's self that resided within her own mind. In one of her poems, Plath speaks of the ghosts inside her mother's mind, ghosts that haunted her through her mother's haunted state. She and her mother were psychically joined, due to the lack of an adequate separation. Without an alive father to promote separation, since her father died young, Plath became psychically enmeshed in a profoundly guilt inducing sadomasochistic symbiosis with her mother, which led repeatedly to suicidal despair, and to yearnings to join her dead father as her rescuer (Bennet 1990; Kavaler-Adler 1996). Plath's mother's frustration and grief stayed frozen in the form of psychic ghosts as she tried to be cheerful for her children after her husband died. The facade of cheeriness became an oppressive force in itself as did June's mother's sugary sweetness. "It's all false," June declared at times, echoing Plath's (1961) words about self-annihilation through the engulfing sugar sweetness of the mother. Plath's "disquieting muses" were like internal psychic ghosts that could operate through projection and projective identification to create external demon lovers, as in the example of Plath's relations with her poet husband, Ted Hughes. Only the anguish of a belated separation could save such a daughter as Sylvia Plath or June, but in order to separate June needed to face the ghosts of her own dark side that harbored her mother's ghosts as well. One day June declared: "Before I came to America, my mother possessed me!" Her internalization of her mother and her mother's "disquieting muses" were part of June's own demon lover theme, as she languished in a state of pathological mourning until she entered object relations psychoanalytic treatment.

June's father became the compounding other half. June's father became internalized as an enemy, a condemning judge, a contemptuous critic and a demeaning perpetrator of humiliation. His chief attitudes, according to June were derision and contempt. She felt demeaned and kept this inside herself as a shameful part of her self-concept. She felt her father took her libido and killed it. Her father's comments seared her visceral insides and assaulted her feminine and sexual being. His negativity and despair poisoned her heart. His silent cold rage engulfed her. His sustained depression (his abandonment depression in a dissociated and frozen form) was complicated by his alcoholism. This demoralized June as she was subject to her father's indifference or to his attack. She felt annihilated by him.

As a teenager June played volleyball, which was her one successful approach to having friends, to being out there, and to being both liked and good at something. It was the first time she felt she belonged to a group, and was the first time she felt attractive to boys, but her father ruined this new feeling. He attended one volleyball game and told her afterward: "You looked frightened. You'll never make it." She also had memories of her father's rage when she attempted to dress in an attractive way. Unlike the father who supports his daughter's developmental growth, particularly in regard to feminine and creative growth, June's father continually assaulted that growth (Kavaler-Adler 1988). He told June to take off a sexy dress and her makeup, and he personally cut her hair so that she couldn't have the stylish Jane Fonda cut that was popular at that time. June saw her father as a man who was too weak to be with anybody but a woman who was "castrated," someone passive and asexual.

PSYCHIC STRUCTURE

Given June's report of her parents, her reliving of her life with them in her current life, and June's pattern of connection and backlash disruption of object connection, I believe June's psychic structure at the point of entering treatment reflected a closed initial object system similar to Fairbairn's (1952) split-off libidinal and antilibidinal ego structures (part self and part object). As I described in my opening chapters, Fairbairn's model of endopsychic structure consists of two main split off self-structures, which he calls libidinal and antilibidinal egos. Seinfeld (1990) refers to these as dependent and antidependent self-structures, and Masterson (1976) refers to these as good and bad self-structures in relation to the subjective affect state involved. These self-structures are split off from the central ego that is in contact with the outside world of external objects, and they are sealed off from contact with the outside world. They repeatedly reenact their age-old infant and toddler drama in a closed internal system with the two part objects. Through projective identifications, these part structures pressure others in the external world to hook into the closed psychic system and to reenact its drama in a reflexive manner. The part-object components, derived from the internalized parents, are that of the "exciting object," which is joined to the tantalized and helpless libidinal self, and the "rejecting object," which is joined to the antilibidinal ego and is more aggressive. Both mother and father elements can be merged into each self and object structure, with the alive aspects of both mother and father becoming part of the exciting object, and the abusive aspects becoming part of the rejecting object. The role of psychic fantasy in enhancing the internalized experiences of the parents becomes a prominent feature of June's psyche when it is viewed in terms of her phenomenological changes from the Kleinian paranoid-schizoid position to the depressive position.

When Masterson speaks of Fairbairn's libidinal ego and its exciting object, he refers to it as a pure pleasure ego (split off from the more Freudian central ego). The term "pure pleasure ego" replaces the Freudian term "id," and is believed to develop through experience in the world, as opposed to through innate drive or psychic fantasy. Masterson refers to the exciting object as the "good mother" of symbiosis and of "reunion." It becomes the target of merger fantasy projections. Masterson speaks of the antilibidinal ego as a "bad self," because when this part of the dissociated ego is conscious one feels bad, with affects of rage, hate, primal pain, and grief. Devalued self-experience predominates. Masterson refers to the rejecting object as the bad object, a visceral object component that feels bad in the sense of being attacking, abusing, humiliating, indifferent, and cold. It is composed of conglomerates of the parent's hostile aggression, as experienced by the child, and is housed in the child's psyche as he or she enters into a developmentally arrested state of adulthood.

Both Masterson's and Fairbairn's psychic structure can be seen to exist in June's internal world. Her mother's assaults against separation are part of what composes the rejecting object along with the mother's envious attacks in general, with the addition of the father's contemptuous, demeaning, hostile and ridiculing attitude. June's antilibidinal ego then acts like a profoundly primitive superego when fused and contaminated by the two bad object parent components of the rejecting object. The antilibidinal ego is attached to this aversive (or bad) part self and aversive part object structure (the antilibidinal ego and rejecting object combined), and therefore is in opposition to the alternate self state of the libidinal ego and its tantalizing exciting object. The exciting object is composed of June's parents' pleasure giving and object hunger gratifying aspects, for both parents were experienced in part as seductive. Her father is the simpler and perhaps the more caricatured persona in her memories. He was seen as handsome, musical, somewhat romantic, and often seductive. Following many phases of abandonment depression mourning, June remembers her father as seductive, but also punitive, poisonous, and full of hostile contempt. On a visceral level she said she experienced his retaliating punch after each seduction as a "scorpion bite." Due to the traumatizing effect of her father's behavior, she turned on herself with contempt and venomous self-rejection, acting out an antilibidinal attitude. This antilibidinal attitude can be compared to Freud's (1917) reproach against the lost object turned inward against the self, and to Fairbairn's (1952) moral defense, used to protect the image of the truly abusive parent, upon whom one is dependent.

Only through her mourning process in treatment did June develop a sense of compassion and empathy toward herself, modifying a primitive superego mode of self-assault. Children always identify with their parents for defensive as well as developmental reasons. As long as June identified with her father's contempt and turned it against herself, she defended herself against the agonizing pain of remembering her father's moment's of derision and pointed attack. When she began the anguish of remembering, June began to let go of a lifelong attitude of contempt. June melted into compassion, allowing her, with my support, to tolerate the remembering.

The other source coloring the exciting object and its libidinal ego came from June's mother. Her mother would "seduce" her into telling her secrets, and when she did so her mother would punish her. June felt betrayed. In the split-off libidinal ego experience (Fairbairn 1952), June would remember only the pleasure of her mother's seductions, splitting off the aggression at first. The mother's "lightness" might also be consciously reexperienced through projections onto me in the transference. Through the reowning of projections, June also experienced the pure pleasure ego (Masterson 1976) as her mother's excitement and joy. This part of her mother revealed itself in the transference (hugs and kisses with her mother), when June saw me as "genuinely happy and enjoying [yourself]," or being warm, spontaneous and fun, or nurturing, like a good mother. She also experienced me as light, full of joy: "You must have experienced such states of joy!" And she also saw me as affectionate, carefree, telling the tale of life's possibilities and promises.

In the early part of her analysis, June felt herself, by contrast to me, to be "heavy and depressed," serving as the depleted half of this light mother of vision, hope, love, and fairy tales. She was an antilibidinal self, joined with her mother as an exciting object, as opposed to the joining of a libidinal self and exciting object. Yet at other times the exciting part-object mother, projected in the transference onto me, aroused in June an insatiable feeling similar to that of Fairbairn's tantalized libidinal ego. June had said to me during an early session: "When you speak I find myself thinking of eating a steak." Another time she said: "I ate a hotdog before I came here and I felt like I could have eaten eight hotdogs." The eight hotdogs then became eight therapy sessions she wished to have with me rather than her usual five.

June experienced her hunger for me not only in terms of food, but also as an intellectual, emotional and spiritual hunger. When reading books that I had written, June said she felt as if I were writing in her mind, and she even said she could sense my smell as she read these books, which she had decided to study as part of her psychological studies. Also, my voice would enter her as an internalized good mother, explaining psychological happenings to her, especially when she felt such shifting self-states as the sudden switch from good and joyful feelings to horrifying, pain igniting, and despairing thoughts, such as "everything ends anyway." In this sense, I became an internalized benign person within June's central ego functioning, but I was simultaneously a seductive good mother exciting her with my voice, smell and persona. June used me also as a good object, however, separate from the bad and exciting object. In this manner, she countered the words of her father's despair, such as the intrusive thought that "everything ends any-way," or the suicidal thought of "lying on the couch and stabbing myself with a knife," or of "taking an overdose and dying." For my voice sounded to her like a "melody." The ego-enhancing cognitive message was accompanied by my visceral aspect as an object she hungered to take in and digest.

When June couldn't digest the interactions between us or the interpretations and confrontations I articulated, June tried to swallow me whole, in some primitive mode of incorporative identification, and then she felt like vomiting, returning to a psychological bulimia that in her teen years had been enacted, before she put distance between herself and her mother by coming to the United States. As I became the exciting and rejecting object in her mind, I aroused a sense of aversive repulsion in her antilibidinal ego (or self). When June was becoming increasingly attached to me and was regressing deeper into the transference, she said: "I'm afraid of my feelings for you. When I feel this hunger for you, I'm afraid that only this will be important. I'm afraid nothing else will matter." She particularly felt this when she wanted to possess me exclusively, and was jealous of any others I had relationships with. She was conscious of wanting to knock her rivals off, whether they be my male colleagues or my other patients.

June introjected her own fantasy of me as the tantalizing object and she became engulfed by it. Thus, I as the exciting object necessarily became a rejecting, or more succinctly, "aversive" or "bad" object, due to her projective and introjective defense processes. June swallowed me in an incorporative introjection and then projected me out again as a devouring vampire. But in the background holding environment transference, I was always the more benign mother aspect.

The father aspect of the exciting and rejecting objects was generally perceived as existing in certain male teachers that June encountered in her studies in psychology. Whenever she would experience the internal switch, however, from a libidinal state of desire, in which she would feel allured by the tantalizing exciting object, to that alternate and oscillating state of being possessed by the haunting rejecting object, she would then experience the drama of the demon lover within (Kavaler-Adler 1996, 2000). This was the drama of an inspiring muse god who turns sadistic and often murderous. Her contrasting and often polarized views of the object related to switches in her own self-states. Out of such switches evolve the projective and introjective cycles of Klein, and the ongoing borderline character psychic mechanism of projective identification. Klein (1946) describes projective and introjective processes and discusses the split off parts of the self.

June experienced, through the deep affect mode of primal mourning, that she could bring together the self-experience of opposite affect states. Such opposite affect states can be described in Kernberg's (1975) terms of contrasting pleasurable and unpleasant self, object, and affect units, which become interpreted by the subject as good versus bad self-states, felt to be provoked by good versus bad objects. Only by going back and forth, with a conscious connection to these formerly dissociated states, could June begin to form a psychic and developmental dialectic between the affect highs of joy, pleasure, and euphoria and the lows of despair, suicidal depletion, homicidal revenge, paranoid devaluation, and humiliation. When June first came to treatment, she felt only numb and detached. Her subjective report of her interior state was one of an empty pipe being lodged in her guts, extending from her stomach to her throat. Her constant state of emotional and psychic starvation was prominent as feelings of self-depletion made her see herself as "dead." At best she would see herself as gloomy, dirty, and sad, which later brought up associations to her mother's dirty laundry at home and wearing dirty clothes to school. The other side of her, which later came up as "flying" (the more grandiose aspect, which was polarized with the inadequate and helpless victimized self), had not yet become conscious.

This alternate grandiose side of June was affectively more alive than her depressive side, which contained her numbness and associated views of herself as inadequate. This grandiose side had been dissociated all of her adult life. She was compelled to project this dissociated grandiose and vitally alive part of her onto me. Consequently she exhibited the initial idealizing transference, described here, prior to later modes of negative, benign mother, and erotic transferences. Only when June felt the dissociated grandiose part of her more consciously, with each entry into the dark shadow world of her antilibidinal ego constellation, did she create a dialectic between both sides that allowed for a feeling of heart and soul connection, from which an ever-flowing stream of love could be contacted. The antilibidinal ego (Fairbairn 1952) can also be referred to as Bion's "destructive superego" (O'Shaughnessy 1999) or Klein's punitive superego. However, Klein does not account for the parents' input into this structure as Fairbairn does. Nevertheless, she does understand the drive aspect that Fairbairn minimized.

When June realized that the shifts of oscillating self-states within her operated despite outside events, and were not only triggered by outside events, she was amazed and full of gratitude as she would be increasingly over time. She would remark: "I can't believe nothing's going on on the outside!" Later she would say: "Outside I'm accomplishing things and things are great, but inside I feel like shit. The shift took place during the night. Nothing happened. I was feeling good, the best ever, for several days. Then all of a sudden, in the middle of the night it shifted." But as she tolerated the shifts with a new consciousness, bringing the alternate and shifting self-states into her sessions, June suffered the pain and grief of what was happening inside her. This allowed her to create dialectics that made her feel more and more whole, and she began to return to her own sense of power and her own voice. She began to visualize the changes as powerful opposite parts of her coming together. Round and rectangular shapes emerged in her mind, which she interpreted through her own associations as images of her new psychic wholeness. She also dreamed of four women dancing in a rectangle, which her associations indicated to be different aspects of her feminine personality traits coming together in a new harmony. More and more, as her self became whole, June visualized her psychic experiences and her internal world. This was what she wanted when she came into treatment – to have perspective on her internal world, which she spoke of as having vision. Her greatest source of envy toward me consisted of her wishes to have what I had in the sense of what she perceived as my vision and my "dervish" (all-encompassing dance) perspective on the internal world.

The psychic phenomenon of vision comes up in the work of Virginia Woolf, who experienced life as a contrasting chiaroscuro adventure in a factual world versus the world experienced through vision (Kelley von Buren 1971). Kenneth Wright's (1991) treatise on vision and separation states that only with vision can we truly separate, because only with vision do we progress past the concrete components of "touching and doing" to emerge into a less concrete and more symbolic state of being, which allows for the transcendence of separation. June began to visualize a major drama in her internal world as she synthesized her reading in psychology and her own visceral and psychic experience. She came to appreciate Klein's psychoanalytic theory most of all, as she declared, "I'm reading Klein in a different way. She really is speaking about Creation, the creation of the internal world."

And how does this internal world, with its blueprint models of psychic structure become the dynamic world of drama that June experienced? Certainly Edith Jacobson's (1964) symbolic representations in the mind could not suffice to explain it, nor Mahler's internal representational blueprints, nor any other American ego psychologist who attempted to tame the British object relations theories that tangled with primitive psychic structures. We have to turn to British theory to find explanations. This is what Thomas Ogden (1986, 1997) has done. Ogden contributes his critical understanding of the dynamic of internal objects, which cannot be explained by pure representational forms. He addresses the visceral phenomenon seen in Fairbairn's internal "devils" (1952) and "bad objects," and Klein's haunting phenomenon of the "persecutory object" or "persecutory breast," the breast with hypervigilant eyes. He also addresses Harry Guntrip's internal man with a periscope, peeking out from inside the shut-off interior of the schizoid personality and to Guntrip's "vacuum cleaner" sucking self, which was one of June's phenomenal feelings of self in the beginning of treatment. Ogden's explanation for the dynamic quality of an internal object is that part of the self splits off from the core self (or in Fairbairn's words, from the central ego) and becomes attached to or fused with an object representation, so that the dynamic quality is provided by the visceral self part, even though in its intermingling with the object we experience ourselves as haunted by the presence of an internal object. Both the libidinal ego and antilibidinal ego can be seen as these split-off self parts, and they are merged with the object representation of part objects, which are conceptualized by Fairbairn as exciting and rejecting objects, or in his earlier writings as internal saboteurs.

EVOLUTIONS BEYOND SEPARATION DYNAMICS IN MOURNING

Masterson and Fairbairn have given a critical perspective on pathology and resolution of developmental trauma. The mourning process both builds on their findings and extends them. Although June's core pathology at the outset of treatment can be seen in terms of an arrested separation process, there are aspects of this separation process that need to be further defined from the patient's perspective. Also, there are dynamics of regression and psychic evolution that extend beyond this separation process, the latter still falling under the heading of developmental mourning, although they pertain to psychodynamic experience through the experience of psychic conflict.

Further, there are offshoots of the separation–individuation process that extend into the moral realm and the spiritual realm. The moral realm can be most vividly revealed through the language of Klein's "depressive position," and can be spoken of as an existential phenomenology that bypasses a victim or superego morality, particularly transcending a neurotic superego morality. The spiritual realm needs to be spoken of most specifically through the words of the analysand. To theorize the spirituality too much would be to risk turning it into religion. However, the existential morality and spirituality that extend from the primary symbiosis interacting with a separation–individuation process, (whether accomplished in childhood or later in adult psychotherapy) are joined together in a view of Klein's depressive position. Those, which might be reductionistically referred to only as merger fantasies by some, have a reality and aliveness that extends beyond an initial idealizing transference. Spirituality first emerges through merger wishes that may arise as an outgrowth of an original spiritual potential and as a connection with the heart as it comes fully alive out of a frozen state. The evolving self then journeys into areas of intuition once psychic reparation is made to one's internal objects.

REGRESSION TO INFANCY

Klein was the first theorist following Freud to venture into preoedipal areas of psychic fantasy and of experience with the real parental objects, as in when she spoke of the real parent being able to receive reparation or not. She focused on the preoedipal areas that Sigmund Freud only brushed upon, and through her the school of object relations theory developed in England. Klein focused on attunement to a full range of psychic fantasy in patients who ranged from psychotic and schizoid to borderline and neurotic. She entered the realm of infancy again and again in her case reports and theoretical treatises. Although June can be seen as arrested in a primal bind and conflict related to toddler stage separation trauma, the earlier infant spoke through her, not only in fantasy and dreams, but also in the psychoanalytic transference. The infant spoke with and through June as a fear of being too insatiable, a terror of using me up as the transferential mother. She spoke of "taking and taking" and yet not being able to receive, a breast fantasy that haunted her deeply. Similarly, June spoke of getting and getting and yet never being satisfied. And she spoke of a primal infant guilt about demanding too much, about being too much for me, her analyst to tolerate. "I need you inside of me," she said, but she felt this wish revealed a ferocious and voracious insatiability that she was afraid would drive me and others away. In her paranoid fears, we would all hate her for getting, and yet never being satisfied. She pictured herself ending up all alone, in a state of despair.

SUBJECTIVE EXPERIENCE OF THE VISCERAL AND AFFECT PROCESS WITHIN DEVELOPMENTAL MOURNING

June conveyed the vivid visceral level in which she experienced the intense affect journey of her abandonment depression mourning process. When June first entered treatment she described herself as numb and empty, and she used the word dead. She mentioned the empty pipe inside of her. Along with this empty pipe came a compulsion to eat and shop, and various kinds of manic activities that involved doing and undoing. Only in treatment did she became aware of the insatiable hunger that operated behind these compulsions, which reflected a state of emotional starvation viscerally felt as emptiness within. June also came to feel as well the sealed off aspect of her internal world, operating with the kind of closed system that Fairbairn speaks about. The sealing off of the internal world and her sense of body emptiness were two connected psychic events. To the extent that June stayed locked in with her primal internal objects (which had exciting and rejecting aspects tied in with split off libidinal and antilibidinal self parts), experiencing people in her current life (external objects) through the lens of these internal objects and self parts, and provoking others into enacting the roles of her internal objects and self parts through projective identification (Kernberg 1975), she would remain in a dead and depleted state of psychic deprivation or emotional starvation. With a sealed off internal world June was doomed to remain insatiable.

However, there was much more going on. She had an opening to contact through a yearning for connection with me. She partly perceived me through the lens of her internal objects as an "exciting object" with its idealizing transference motif, and she felt passion with me that she responded to, despite her inner deadness. I was also a good enough object, to paraphrase Winnicott, whom she could talk to. June was eager to confess her guilt and find acceptance for her "bad self," as she defined it, for the "criminal" part of her. She had no awareness in the beginning that behind her guilt lay a primal rage that related back to separation trauma and to a profoundly inhibited separation process, with its intolerable sense of frustration. She dreamed of going into oceans, but she had no idea at the beginning that she was journeying into the ocean of her unconscious through treatment, and as she opened herself to the abandonment depression rage and grief, she also opened the door to areas of repression, allowing her dream life and her psychic fantasies to emerge. Increasingly, she yearned for an interiority that came with a sense of being in her body. This came naturally with the abandonment depression mourning, and an inward sense of a life that she would eventually refer to as being in an "ocean cave." She became more and more fascinated with the subject of the unconscious as her own unconscious awoke into consciousness and her internal world of primal objects came to life.

But first there was the rage! The empty pipe became a raging fortress of flames. She felt fire in her guts and a boiling explosion of rage in her belly. In certain sessions she would feel cold in the beginning. Then, as she began to explore her guilt-ridden thoughts and her painful sense of being tortured by demands from her family and from colleagues at work, her body would begin to heat up. Since June was incapable of setting boundaries with those making demands at this early time, all those making demands on her were experienced as emotional "vampires," as she would project her own insatiable "vacuum cleaner" sucking hunger onto them. Facing all this consciously allowed her to define her victimized state, and to understand her own agency in it. As she connected with her formerly sealed off internal self, her visceral coldness turned to the opposite extreme of heat.

This visceral heat was to take many forms throughout her treatment. June would feel the heating up of sexuality and lust, with tingling feelings opening the sensations of kissing in her mouth and lovemaking in her body. Then later she could feel the spiritual heat flaring up within her, reminding me of Emily Dickinson's phrase "a soul at its white heat" (1960: 243). But in the beginning, it was the heat and fire of rage, which later would differentiate into object related hate. As she developed a full range of feeling states, coming out of a numb body that formerly somatized all her affects, through sensations of vomiting and choking, the visceral awareness heightened. This expanded June's sensitivity to the rage behind separation, loss, and humiliation.

June never ceased feeling states of rage, where once there had only been depression, numbness and detachment. At first it felt overwhelming, but with the containment of it in our treatment sessions, she began to feel she herself could contain it more and more. Sometimes the rage felt like a bomb inside of her, and sometimes like a fire or boiler. In Dickinson's poem (1960: 443) about the compulsive attention to detail in daily practical matters that contained an internal bomb and prevented it from exploding either in suicidal or homicidal directions, we can see the abandonment depression affect states described by Masterson. The abandonment depression rage is referred to by Dickinson through the metaphor of a literal bomb: "I got a bomb, and I hold it in my bosom." June's rage was similar to this in the beginning of her treatment. It was diffuse and visceral, sometimes turning to the somatic and becoming nausea. Later, however, she felt she had anger she could contain and communicate in words, even if at first it would feel to her like a "killer rage." June began to learn increasingly of the grief and loss that lay behind her rage, and of her impulses to smash, slap, and pinch that often went with it. This change drastically affected her outside life. She had fewer explosions of rage at home with her husband, who commented on this. By the third year of treatment she came in and reported that she felt full of anger, a more modified form of aggression. This she was able to contain. She could analyze it and then understand it, rather than acting it out. She refrained increasingly from acting the anger out, either in the active form she used to act it out with her husband, or in the passive silent cold form she would act it out with others, particularly her mother and brother (who had moved to America and were connected to her again).

The modification of the aggression came with the mourning process as her deep layers of sadness emerged from a formerly sealed off place. Initially it was thoughts of her father's contempt and of her mother's guilt-provoking demands on her that caused her to withdraw or become mechanical as a way of avoiding her rage. The grief she then experienced opened up longings for her mother and father, which had formerly been diverted into concrete objects such as food and clothes. The rage then began to take on a new meaning in terms of object loss (the loss of the good mother) and in terms of the pain of her own guilt as she saw her compulsion to push her family away. The rage June felt from the demands of others or the indifference of others could all be related to the initial object loss of her mother, who internally held onto her in a regressive symbiosis. It also related to her father who had emotionally abandoned her and who was still doing so in her internal fantasy world, which always would get projected.

THE HEART AND THE WOUND

Related to June's rage, June experienced visceral sensations of stabbing pains in her heart or her hip. She felt a core sense of a profound internal wounding that she had carried within her all her life. When June felt stabbing pains in her heart, she associated it with both myself and her mother. As the visceral sense of stabbing transformed into emotional pain, and then emotional longing her mind free associated to fearing that her mother was dying. This reaction came just after June had taken another step forward in her separation process, in her third year of treatment, coming out into the world and being acknowledged for professional accomplishments, such as giving presentations as a psychiatric nurse in a hospital. I interpreted her separation trauma reaction as her expectation that her mother would die if she separates from her and finds her own direction and her own voice in the world. June was stabbing herself in the heart because she believed she was stabbing her mother in her heart: "I'll become more successful in my career, and my poor mother will be left behind with nothing, after giving everything to me," and believed she was killing her by separating. To her internal mother, separation was a betrayal. This internal mother reacted by stabbing her with guilt and she in turn wished to stab the internal mother, who pulled her back into a regressive symbiosis, and attacked her if she moved forward into her own individuation and autonomy.

Yet, June's guilt extended beyond a defensive reaction to her rage, and beyond her wish to kill and stab her mother. There was a sense of primal longing for a mother behind her guilt, and a differentiated longing for her mother as she existed in the present as an external other. Feelings of grief and sadness had led to this more differentiated longing for her mother, and her pain became a pain of regret. Even though it was neurotic and defensive guilt that made June feel her autonomy was a crime, it was an existential guilt that made her feel she was responsible for pulling away from her mother throughout her adult life and even now in the present (during her third year of treatment), when she was truly independent and could choose to have a relationship with her mother. So she stabbed herself in her heart!

As June focused on the visceral pain in her psychoanalytic sessions, the stabbing transformed into the emotional pain of fearing that her mother would die before she could speak to her, before she could learn how to communicate with her, before she could learn how to say: "I miss you." June sobbed as she felt the anguish of longing for her mother, longing to forgive and surrender after so many years of withholding herself and being mechanical with her mother. And even more grievously, the visceral stabbing pain opened up into a longing to be able to say things to her father as well, to reach him before his death, to have a father, to say "I miss you." June cried with a new form of grief, as she proceeded past the rage she had come to express and toward the father of her past. She had felt her rage and her hurt, and now she could miss the potential father she might have in the future.

June felt there was a virus in her heart, like she had been poisoned by the hate of another after she had felt good, again going into a backlash of pain after reaching a point of accomplishment and good feeling. As her grieving, however, extended beyond object loss to a positive sense of her newfound vulnerability, June interpreted the virus in her heart as the vulnerability to the impact of the other, the opening to the feelings of the other that she had blocked out her whole life. She said, "The stone in my heart has dissolved." She was now able to experience a psychic position of loving and needing, which Melanie Klein implied was a position of psychic health. This is an undefended state that we can all reach at moments, if we can surrender to its vulnerability.

On some days June felt her lungs opening up in a session, and following this she was able to speak in a relaxed and spontaneous way in her classes. She was amazed that she could speak freely, without self-consciousness, with a feeling of being inside of her body, and with a freedom from her former hypervigilant watchfulness of herself, as she surrendered to the sadness within, and through this opened to authentic and present interpersonal contact, and to the new healthy psychic internalizations that would come from such contact. June's lungs opened in sessions, expressing the somatic symbolism of this "coming out" process, entering a state of continuing identity in the world, with an individuated voice and a true and spontaneous self. Interestingly, I had a visceral counter-transference, as my lungs too had felt expanded in the session in which she felt her lungs open. Sometimes I would share such a resonance with her, because it helped her feel that I was in tune with her as natural developmental evolutions came about. I consider the sharing of such visceral counter-transference events in a totally different category from sharing personal self-disclosures in treatment. This sharing of my resonant reaction could be seen as falling under the category of what James Masterson has called the developmental function of "communicative matching." This function takes place between therapist and patient, as between mother and toddler, when the developmentally arrested patient is progressing in the separation process, after the separation trauma has been faced repeatedly in the painful affects of the abandonment depression. Masterson speaks of the therapist providing a developmental function that the mother of the patient was unable to provide in infancy and childhood.

In contrast to my sharing of this visceral resonance as a way of providing developmental attunement, there was another visceral and affective counter-transference event. In a session in which June reported a dream of her internal self and other images separating out, which is a novel developmental phenomenon described in Mahler *et al.* (1975), I noticed that my feelings at that time did not match those of June. June reported: "I dreamed that my body and my mother's body separated from one another," at a time when she was in a major internal turmoil, and she didn't know why. When I spoke to her about her guilt she became more and more distraught. At other times it was helpful to speak to her about her horrors and crimes as she saw them. Only when she reported her dream did I realize her need for my validation of the internal developmental transformation that was taking place, placing the interpretation of the developmental event before the psychodynamic conflict related to her guilt. A guilt interpretation was only helpful in this context when it could be joined with her backlash reaction to a new step in intrapsychic separation. Since there was no external event that June was aware of creating such internal upheaval her reporting of a dream was critical. Yet, interestingly, it also made me aware of my conscious objective mode of counter-transference affect. June assimilated the information about the developmental change as self and mother images becoming representational in her mind as two separate bodies, she was relinquishing her sense of having a merger between her body and mine. This was very upsetting for June, but once I interpreted it, she was much relieved, and she began to feel a sense of joy, flow, visualization and creativity open within her.

In contrast to other times, when I had felt similar feelings to those she felt and described, now that she had gone through critical steps of separation through the deep grief affects of the mourning process, I felt quite differently. Instead of a flow of joy at the end of the session in which she felt such joy, I felt depressed. I was feeling quite separate from her and I thought this was related to her body and mine, as the symbolic transference mother separated out in her mind. I shared this connection with her and she said, "That's too bad. These feelings are so wonderful. I'm sorry you're not feeling them."

VISCERAL EXPERIENCE OF CRYING AND SOBBING, AND THE WOUND METAPHOR

Another visceral event that took place during the abandonment depression and the grief and mourning process was June's experience of the wound inside of her. She said: "I had the image of a wound inside of me. It was sealed before I met you." She related very strongly to an article on "woundology," describing how people hold on to their psychic wounds and become fixated in a victimized place, where they identify with their wounds. June said that in contrast to this, she had found that by sharing the wound with me it opened up and transformed. She felt this wound in her chest, near her heart, and when it opened up she felt the heat of lava and bubbles, of heat energy opening, as if she were a volcano opening and pouring out its internal elements. The visceral sensations in June's heart opened her up to the pain behind the rage stabbing her in her heart. As she navigated through this pain, she felt a deep grief sadness that is the essence and core of the developmental mourning process. In navigating through this process June found a new self emerging where once she only had her old, fused, and undifferentiated self. June experienced vividly the depth of the abandonment depression, the separation process, and the developmental mourning process: "It felt like I hit rock bottom last time. It felt like something cracked inside of me as I cried and now I'm walking around with pain in my heart. I'm realizing I sort of killed off everybody in a way. I had this denial that I needed anyone. I used to put the hunger into concrete things, like food and shopping. I really want to call my mother and talk to her now."

Her object hunger opened as she faced the pain of her regret and pain of losses created from her own action. This object hunger awareness must naturally lead to grief: "I'm an insatiable hungry baby, wanting more and more. It's hard to feel consciously that place in the center of my heart, where the insatiable hunger is. I feel the stabbing there. I felt some virus got on there, into my heart. But maybe that's because my heart is not as frozen as before. I didn't feel it before. Why now? It's like something reached into my heart and I felt I had to slow down or else I'd get a heart attack. I really hope my mother will be alive. I'm afraid she'll die soon [*she's sobbing as she speaks*]. It feels like I'm feeling the pain because something is going on with my mother and I have to reach her before it's too late. Something has happened! I need to cry and cry and cry. It feels like the pain is going away as I cry."

Then the sadness follows the pain of rage, hurt, loss, and love yearnings that emerge from her heart. The combination of a capacity to feel the object love, along with the object hunger, and to combine this love with the understanding of object loss and of the remorse of regret, results in the deep grief sadness emerging: "I feel really sad, like someone really died. I never went through such sadness in my life. It's hard to believe that nothing happened on the outside. It feels like both my parents died. This sadness and heaviness seems endless, like there are endless layers on the inside of me, really endless. It's such a difficult thing to go through, psychoanalysis. I don't know where I'll end up. It gets deeper and deeper. Maybe there's something psychotic and then what is it? Who is this other person inside of me? That's what it feels like, like there's another person coming out, a person inside sitting with face in her hands, sitting with such sadness, sadness. I cannot lift my head and look at the world. It seems like endless, like penance. I guess I want to break everything in myself. I never know when I came here what I will talk about; what will come up. I really don't know who I am anymore. It's related to all those sadnesses I never felt before in my whole life. My heart says, `Why don't you talk about the things you feel right now, rather than drifting?'"

And now June's object-related curiosity is aroused as her new self opens up through her sad grieving within the overall mourning. Instead of assuming she knew things about me as she did before when she was creating me in her image, she now asks me a question. As she continues in her sadness of grief she becomes conscious of the crying itself, the crying that has been her royal road to both psychic independence and psychic connection with others. In the midst of her grief, June asks: "I wonder how long I'll need to cry?"

"You'll cry as long as you need to. The crying is possible now, because the feelings within it become tolerable with me as your companion and witness. You're very lucky, June, that you can cry so readily. There are many other people who can't cry. They're blocked," I respond.[1]

June then surrenders to an even deeper level of crying and of emotional release. "Today is my son's birthday," June says.

"Are you crying for that?" I ask.

"I don't know. I feel a bit for him and then anger comes. I feel the fear of his attacks on me, and the guilt related to them. I guess I'm crying for all the people I used to be close to, like my family, crying and crying, that I cannot reach out to. At least I really feel like I'm inside of myself now. It's a very distinct feeling of being inside as opposed to outside. When I cry, I feel the inside. There's an image of myself sitting with my face in my hands crying. You see this is the real me, crying and crying. There are two different places, two different worlds. One world is the world of images, a stage world."

"Like a hall of mirrors!" I tell her.

"Yea! It's like on the outside I'm saying, 'Look how great I am', when living for the mirror and images, but inside it's so different!" June then speaks of a spiritual world opening to her, and she connects it with her discovery of the internal world, and of new whole and true self: "There's a strange low key depth in the internal world. Do you think I'm connected today?" she asks me.

"Why do you ask when you feel it from the inside?"

"I want to test you. I want to know if you can feel it. Before, I didn't know the difference between the inside and outside. Maybe my asking is bringing two images of myself together. On the positive side it feels like an ocean cave today. I really like getting into these places. It feels like the source of something. It feels so connected – my God!" June declares.

"I think you're saying that there is a way of experiencing things now that is like experiencing God," I suggest.

"I think that's true. It's like experiencing an energy – very wonderful! It makes me feel very safe in happiness and sadness. I don't know how this whole thing happened. I feel the shift today. But when the reconnection happens, all of a sudden it's getting connected to a greater source, a channel. When this happens I don't know how I can become more aware, and able to control my sense of being able to go there when I want to."

June begins to speak about the sense of a new self emerging. We speak of this new self being baptized through her tears. June says: "I've been changed, like before my energy and frequency was so low and now everything is tingling, like sparks or something I'm feeling, like joyful! This is amazing. Divine!"

As soon as she says this she has a brief backlash reaction as her old self, the antilibidinal ego self, joined with the negative rejecting object's contempt (father) and envy (mother) momentarily makes her distrust the validity of her evolving and new self-experience. "Maybe I just want to be special so I'm faking all this." But quickly she returns to her inward sense of grief and emerging selfhood through internal object connection (not split off, but now located in the central ego): "I guess I'm crying for my family and son. I wish I could have these feelings I have with you with my son."

I tell her that I feel a peaceful feeling coming from within her now. She responds: "Yeah. That's true." But then again comes the backlash of an antilibidinal attack against her (stabbing). She thinks of an attack she has made on another, punishing herself at this time of pleasure, but also sensing some true pain of regret.

"What was the thought behind the pain?" I ask her.

"I want to have an impact on others, but I can walk away and cut people off," she responds.

I pick up on her visceral cues. "I feel something in your stomach now."

"Fear!" she cries.

"I can feel that!" I say.

"I hope I didn't demolish anyone in my class at school. I'm afraid I'll antagonize everyone against me, when I speak up. It was safer to be mute like before," she says. This fear comes up along with a wish to have exclusive importance to me as she shares her inner life and thinks of wishing to be more special to me than anyone else. She fears the retaliation of others who represent the envious mother again. She fears retaliation from those that she is genuinely walking away from wanting to exclude them from the realm of specialness she has with me. In a parallel situation in her life (used by her unconscious as a displacement), June fears retaliation from those classmates she wishes to exclude from the specialness she has with a teacher. As she continues in the process, June shows the forward and backward movements of the separation process, with its continuing backlash of separation trauma from the past. Part of the process is her attacks on herself (aligned with the antilibidinal ego from within) for her progress, and for her wish to shine as an individual with a sense of specialness of her own.

"I'm really out there. I'm really out there and I feel I'm going to die. It just feels like I can't go on, crying and crying, I want to get away from the feeling. I'm doing something wrong, crying and sobbing."

"You're crying because you feel like a bad child for coming out on your own," I say.

"I just feel like I want you to be my mom and I will be the child, I'd like to hug and kiss you like I hugged and kissed my mother when I loved her," she confesses.

June is able to articulate her object longings and wishes now, directly, within the transference, without displacing her reactions and acting out like she once did. She seeks safety in the positive maternal transference, when she feels her bad objects attacking her again from within, in her backlash reactions. In one moment she faces her existential guilt and remorse, and she doesn't need to seek safety in a haven with me. In the next moment, she faces the old internal attack, and the return of the old self-feeling, then she does need to seek safety with me. I interpret her wishes and she increasingly becomes an interpreting subject (Ogden 1986) who can interpret her own wishes. She is operating much more fully on a symbolic level now than formerly. She doesn't have to somatize her child wishes in her body now, or act out with compulsive and addictive behaviors. I respond to her wish: "If I were your mom and you were my child, you might feel like nothing could hurt you. When you take these steps forward you want to run back to me for safety." I also interpret the defense behind her wish in terms of her general form of psychic change as her new self-parts emerge. She is the agent of her own backlash, as she returns to the punishment of the old parent objects, to cling to the parents of the past, who can still operate within her. She cries as I say this, and then reports a dream, which relates to her new view of me as a separate person beyond the transference sphere of being her mom.

"I dreamed I was with this girl who was in this low-key state, while I was flamboyant. As I stayed with her I became more low key." June associates to the dream and says: "Maybe that was you in the dream. Maybe that's how you truly are, on the inside, low key and spiritual. When I first came into treatment with you I dreamed of Tibet. Now I'm getting hot inside, like a spiritual heat. Now I feel energy, like a sun energy inside. I feel the flow of energy throughout, It's on my face, burning, burning. Do you feel it? I know you feel the sadness and grief, but this is unusual, like a whirl of energies, Yeah, like sunlight, like the sun's on my body and I'm getting a suntan. I think of you looking at me now and I'm probably red! It's such a joyful feeling. I feel like anything is possible now. In the next few months, before your vacation, I feel something really important is going to happen!"

June feels floating and light, the opposite of how she felt in the beginning of treatment. With this spiritual opening comes the deep grieving for the loss of her family, remembering how she left them when she left Australia: "I think this is a painful issue for me to deal with. What happened back there, when I was so numbed out that I could have left my son and family?" She continues to face her dark side, and the critical question that haunted her when she entered treatment.

Each new step in facing her grief, her existential guilt and her existential mourning, beyond the separation mourning of object loss brings a growing awareness of a dialectic, between her old and new self structures. This dialectic has grown out of the deep affect experience of the developmental mourning process. Formerly, parts of her were split off and dissociated, and her self-parts felt like oscillating and oppositional parts when they first become conscious. As she feels her selves coming together and describes visualizing images of roundness and wholeness inside of her, she relates increasingly to a dialectical relation between her inner selves, old and new, healthy and pathological: "I feel this flowing feeling, a lot of joy inside now. This is the kind of flowing feeling I've been feeling here for the first time in my life, and it feels like this feeling can happen now in other places as well."

June then articulates her experience of mourning in relation to her evolution into new self-states and new modes of object connection, in a newly integrated self: "The old me comes back once in a while, but most of the time it is a new way of thinking, feeling, and a new way of relating to people, it's like my life was given back to me somehow. It happened gradually, but it really happened. It's hard to hold in my mind a whole clinical perspective like you. I hope I can learn it. I know what it takes to learn a second language. You really have to immerse yourself in it. Amazing things can happen. Imagine that I could take the action of seeing my son after all these years. Things can turn around! It's so joyful with my son . . . How precious life is! I think I have learned that from you. It seems like I'll be fine this time during your vacation. I know you'll go away and then you'll come back. Before, I thought you'd be in a plane crash and not come back. When I get this flowing feeling I think it comes from you, but I think it must come from me as well."

JUNE'S SEXUALITY

When June first came into treatment, her sexuality was partly repressed and partly imprisoned by the splitting off of self-parts. Her conscious thoughts about sex were mostly negative. She spoke of sex as a humiliating and repulsive experience, in which women had to do things that seemed disgusting to her. They had to "spread their legs and lie on their knees." As she spoke of this, June had feelings of wanting to vomit. All her repressed sexual desires were experienced as repulsive intrusions from a demonic form of father lover.

In time, her associations revealed a childhood memory in which she overheard her father saying to her mother behind closed doors "Spread your legs!" in a cold and assaultive manner. She surmised from this memory that her father was probably in a drunken state. June was chilled and horrified by this memory. Along with her memories of her father's cold assaultive emotional attacks on her, this memory formed the crystallization of a primal scene in which the male engaging in sexual intercourse was a haunting Nazi, dressed in a military uniform, as her father had been in his younger days. The woman becomes a victim, since June's mother was perceived as totally alienated from sex, not being able to speak to June about the topic, and sounding in this remembered scene, in which her father demanded "spread your legs," like a tortured and humiliated being.

Given all this, June denied sexual interest in her current relationship, which became a marriage. She had thoughts in her head of an obsessive nature, when she married, in which her antilibidinal part spoke from its position of contempt, telling her on a repeated basis that it was disgusting for a man and woman to be together as a couple in any form. When she had sex with her fiancé in the early days of her treatment, she said she just thought of getting it over with and didn't feel a conscious attraction to her fiancé at that time. She felt indifferent. The alternative at that time seemed to be to feel humiliated.

However, June had been highly aroused by a past lover, who like her father was both seductive and emotionally unavailable. This lover fitted the blueprint of her internal demon lover. Looking back at her affair with this man, June was conscious of having felt an intense involvement that must have been as close to passion as she thought she could get. Nevertheless, the intensity of her passion seemed to be based more on split off erotic modes of arousal than on any full object relations engagement with this man, which I have referred to as "manic-erotic intensity." Her erotic love object remained the exciting and rejecting object, rather than becoming a whole-object other. His emotional unavailability, in part, was due to an addiction to cocaine and to his erratic presence in her life. Not being able to really have him, June was able to feel emotionally aroused as her insatiable cravings, sometimes focused on food or clothes, could become conscious. The frustration of the cravings helped to bring them to consciousness. When she did not have this type of body arousal with a man who was available and committed to her, she mistakenly thought the problem was in the man himself. She didn't yet understand that it was the very availability of the man that prevented him from meshing with her internal demon lover father object or internal world blueprint. She thought there was no chemistry, or he just didn't turn her on during this early time. Her capacities for intimacy and sustained emotional involvement only opened up with her treatment, and particularly with the combination of object relations mourning and psychoanalytic transference interpretation.

Chapter 7

The case of June, Part 2

A mournful and spiritual journey: spiritual and sexual evolution

"You know, it always feels like I'm dealing with two people inside of me. One is cold, angry and indifferent, and feels shut off, and the other can really feel and imagine how another person feels, and can really feel for the other's pain," June cries as she feels this dialectical dichotomy quite intensely. "I'm grateful I have another chance to deal with this thing I ran from twenty years ago, leaving my son and family. But this other side, this cold angry side wants to kill me for facing my guilt and wishes to repair things." She cries, as she feels the antilibidinal side threaten her in a murderous way, as a personified form replicated from the cold and envious attack of her internal parents. June's newly developing observing ego then responds back to the backlash of the old self with new concern and moral conscience. "I guess I'm going to see for myself what kind of person I am now that I've been able to arrange for my son to visit after all these years."

Then there is the sadomasochistic reaction[1] of the internal attack, reflecting a retaliatory aggression in which June punishes herself until she can realize and articulate her guilt and give it the symbolic value of concern.

"I feel nauseous and feel a stabbing pain in my heart," June says. Instead of the old reactive neurotic guilt, she now feels a realistic concern and compassion for herself – and responds from the new caring side of her: "All these years I've collected so much garbage inside of myself. I was like a dead thing!" As she speaks, she's crying and sobbing out the grief of her guilt.

"Your heart isn't dead any more," I tell her.

"No!" She cries.

"Your new self is evolving through your capacity to feel in your heart now, as you've been facing your grief."

"I feel the things you say right now so vividly today! I see myself right now vividly. I see now my dead part. It almost seems like a mother holding a child."

"You're visualizing things right now."

"It's all of a sudden like having another layer on my eyes now – being able to see some things I could never see before! I'm giving up on controlling things. I think of people in major blow-ups or volcanoes. Now I see myself going to the airport and embracing my son. I saw him in a dream coming down an escalator in the airport. Now I'm visualizing things ahead of time. I never did this before. I had a dream of a cat jumping into feathers. I associated the cat with a new intuitive part of me coming out, just like the woman in a dream with a deep blue dress, which symbolizes intuition. My intuitive part is growing as my new feeling self emerges. I'm overall happy my son is coming. I'm afraid of his attacks, like the accusations in his letters, but I've been thinking of how to deal with it. When he attacks I'll do with him what you do with me. I'll stay calm and listen like you do when I attack," June says.

"Good!" I say.

"I'll just be calm and not get pulled into his guilt and punishments, etc." As June speaks, various aspects of her new and growing capacities to relate to others emerge. Her core and central self connects with the world and with the present now. At first I am a transitional object for her new object relations capacities. As Melanie Klein has written about in her classic paper, "Envy and Gratitude" (1957), gratitude emerges as love modifies hate and its object oriented mode of envious attack. As her analyst I can feel the loving depth in June and her heartfelt gratitude.

"In moments like this I'm so grateful for therapy, for the fact that I've met you. It just feels so precious! Without this I can't imagine going through transformations. I don't think it's possible. There has to be another person. You can't do it by yourself. I guess there has to be another spiritual person in order to go through these transformations," June says.

In a session following this one June feels the backlash of her sadistic side, and expresses her rage towards me in the transference. "I want to smash your face! I'm looking forward to hearing you speak, but it's like I'm speaking! I want to be a person who is giving, loving, and compassionate, but I feel the opposite at the same time. I feel the Mafia, murderous part of me come back. I feel compassionate, but when the other side of me gets activated I feel a sadism!"

As June says this she cries nonstop. She realizes that wanting to smash me is a way of trying to put this aversive rage feeling outside of herself. But she has returned to an envious state, losing touch with her own growth, even as she has come out into the world, finding her voice with others and with speaking in public for the first time. She has regressed to her old position of putting all her talents into me by projection and then envying me. In doing so she feels the rage of the cold sadistic self that opposes her loving and empathic part. However, even in her envy her new growth is clear. She does not project her envy out as a personified external demon as she once did. In earlier sessions she has expressed gratitude for discovering how much this demon exists within, and for being able to understand that she is creating her external battles and dramas. She has expressed intense gratitude for this new awareness, saying how many people remain trapped in the vicious cycle of their own repetitions and reenactments without this knowledge. She has even called the entrance into this knowledge a "loss of innocence and loss of virginity." So now, June is quite aware that the threat of new volcanoes of aggression comes from the sadism inside of her, and she knows that it is not just an envious attack from an internal mother. Now it is her own envy she feels, and she feels it towards another, her analyst, a person who engages with the world through writing books, and giving talks. She uses me as the laboratory to bring her envy into consciousness so that she can face herself and confront her own inner demons. As she acknowledges her own envy the compassionate side of her speaks, in an evolving and progressive developmental dialectic. June tells me a dream about flowers with sweet tulips in the center. She connects the return of her loving side with her crying. Her crying is June's capacity to suffer in a positive way the grief of what is, even if it means feeling the pain of her most sadistic impulses as they emerge vividly into consciousness.

"Whenever I cry here I feel its such a good thing. I always feel better! It never fails! Always the next day is something new for me." She then reports a dream in which she tells her mother that I have told her that it's hatred in the heart that causes problems, not divorce or separation. I am the benign advisor now – a more modified superego than she experienced in the past, not an antilibidinal or primitive superego. June is developing her symbolic level of power in this dream. She uses me symbolically to educate her mother in her dream, the mother who represents her old self. Also, she confronts the mother who creates hate by condemning separation, rather then allowing separation to modify hate.

Again June comments on the dialectic of her old and new selves, as she faces another doubt about herself: "Am I giving to you or stealing from you?" This is a question that comes up around fees with me, and which relates to her changing from wishing to receive money from her husband to wanting to give things to him and to nurture him. As she faces herself in this way, the internal self shift occurs: "I felt shut down and disconnected and then I flipped to the other side. This joyful feeling opened. I'm hearing your voice and listening to what you say and it feels like a melody. I'm taking you in. I'm taking you in. I'm taking you in. I get into this floating, joyful, loving side, and I feel tingling sensations in my body."

Having dealt with her envy towards me she is able to take in a professional presentation of mine that she attends. She does so in a deep way, at the level of her grief, her separation pain and her object longings. "Now I can separate from the basic human feelings of envy and greed. I can trust . . . It started when I listened to your presentation and when I was crying, this part of me, this sexual part started coming up – crying – a joyous part of me. It's a wonderful person in me. I feel like hugging and kissing you," she tells me.

June continues to describe her growth along with her deep body crying and sobbing: "I have really gone though an incredible change with this analysis. I hope I can hold on to this feeling inside for a long period of time. I think this is the greatest gift one person could give another person. It's a kind of joy, a joy like you want to cry. It makes the world so different! Something has dramatically changed. Now I can have vision. Now I can be the source of feelings I thought once only came from you, when I thought I had to be plugged into you to feel. Everything is in this flow. I feel like I have an endless loving stream in me. After going through the feelings of envy and aggression, the light comes out! It almost feels like you have plugged something into me. I want this feeling to be mine."

Increasingly, June feels the feeling of flow and joy is hers, and she begins to see that she can feel it outside of treatment and can share it with others, including her son. Several sessions later she says: "This feeling inside me that you gave me I feel is mine now. I'm radiating! Love is radiating! I feel I'm radiating within myself. You're still my favorite person as far as the evolving of feeling states. I don't think I've met anyone like you."

June then has a backlash into her old empty-self feeling as she suffers the fear of anticipating her son's arrival, a son she hasn't seen for eighteen years. Frightened of how she will stand up to her own moral test, her test of being a mother, she returns to an infant state of being closed off, unreachable, and insatiable. However, she can experience it consciously with me, and articulate it in words. This is a critical change and it helps her grow through the pain as well as to recover into a more advanced sense of self-agency as an adult. She can then face her son in a positive way.

"All of a sudden, I'm an empty shell. One minute everything is fine and then it's like flipping to the other side." June is crying as she speaks. "I don't know what's wrong. I just know I feel sad and angry. It feels like it's on the outside, but I know it isn't. Everyone's trying to help. I've accomplished a lot, but I feel like shit. It's a paranoia. I get people to give me what I want and then I can't take it. You'll get fed up with me too. I need you on the inside! It feels like you're forsaking me! Why do I feel you don't want me?

At the end of the session, I respond to her. "The infant feeling of insatiability you're experiencing again can't be fed. You need to contain it and feel it while you're with me. You need to go through it consciously as you're doing. And then you need to make contact with me at an adult level, which you're doing by articulating the fear in words." After this session, June is still in her fear, but she is also relieved. She goes to meet her son at the airport that weekend, when he comes in from Australia, and she comes into the next session radiant!

"There's joy in being a mother. I can feel it now, because I felt the shame and guilt last session, and removed the blocks to feeling open and the blocks to feeling this new joy. My mother never told me that you receive joy from a child. She always made me feel guilty as if I was just taking and taking from her, which is the same guilt I've felt with you. Now that I can feel this joy again, and the joy of being a mother I feel so relieved."

June's major guilt pain has been faced, and she has made reparations with the object and source of her most profound guilt, her son. "I feel this flowing feeling, a lot of joy inside now. This is the kind of flowing feeling I've been feeling here with you for the first time in my life, and it feels like this feeling can happen now in other places as well."

THE BIRTH OF THE SEXUAL SELF

As already described, when June first came into treatment her sexuality was partly repressed and partly imprisoned by the splitting off of self parts within the sealed off part of her internal world. Her conscious thoughts about sex were mostly of a negative nature. June's sustained emotional involvement during sex only opened up with her treatment, and particularly with the combination of object relations mourning and psychoanalytic transference work in the treatment.

June's first awareness of sexual excitement in her committed relationship came with her willingness to entertain her associations to sadomasochistic phenomena. Although at first repulsed by her husband's occasional perusal of pornographic videos (during their engagement period), when I questioned her reaction of repulsion she was able to see that she might actually be experiencing some form of arousal behind her repulsion. Then she began to notice the bodies and activities on some of these videos, and began to consciously associate to these images. More obvious in terms of her sadomasochistic sexual associations becoming conscious was when she said emphatically to her fiancé, in a fit of anger: "You think you can whip me into shape!" When he replied: "Do you want to be whipped?" she had a strong internal reaction. She liked it when her fiancé spoke to her this way. And she noticed that she also felt some sexual arousal when her fiancé got angry at her and threatened to leave her. He would do this after she would be emotionally withdrawn for some period of time, and she only felt like responding to him when he got frustrated enough to threaten to leave her. Then she would run after him, and try to win him back, opening her seductive efforts through sexual desire aroused by his threatened abandonment. During a session when she realized this, as well as realizing her turned on state in response to her fiancé's questioning, she said that she would like to have a constant fantasy of her fiancé leaving her to sexually arouse her, or a constant fantasy of his emotionally abusing her with insults that were like a slap (her mother's) or a beating. She started having thoughts of being turned on to a man's sadistic or abandoning behavior, and within her own controlled limits she thought she could enjoy sexual pleasure through the lens of this S and M experience. She said to me: "I think I need a man who's hard like a Nazi, dressed in a military uniform. Maybe I should provide props. Maybe physical abuse is too much, but emotional abuse (like her father's contemptuous criticisms and comments) can really turn me on!"

This was the first stage of June's sexuality emerging into consciousness, and it was a stage that took place largely outside the transference. Her other evolutions in the sexual arena would come largely through her psychic engagement in her transference with me, until a full blossoming of her sexuality would emerge, as well as a wonderful capacity for humor and fun. All of June's negative feelings about sexuality, as well as about her body, changed as she fell into a psychoanalytic transference love. Her conscious experience at first was of seeing me as highly and vividly sexual: "There's something Latin about you. You're really out there with your sexuality. You're nothing like other therapists, who seem so drab and dull. The way you dress is so colorful and you really show your legs. Bill [her husband] said you can afford to do that because you've already made it in the field."

One day she reported a dream in which I had a dress up over my head so that my 'sexual parts' were showing, although she amended her first view of the dream by saying: "I'm not sure if it was you, or if it was me, but someone had their dress up over their head." Her reaction to this dream, which occurred early on in her first year of treatment shows June's still undifferentiated state. In this state, personified internal objects of me and of her overlapped in her mind and became part of a Kohutian twinship transference (1971), or merely part of an undifferentiated feminine state as might relate to Mahler's stage prior to differentiation or Winnicott's regression to an undifferentiated state.

However, the regression to a lack of differentiation was clearly not that primitive or amorphous. The figure in the dream was clearly female and had a form specifically related to me or to her in her mind. Furthermore, she or I appeared as part of a couple, the male partner being one of her male teachers, so there was a clear oedipal pattern, or perhaps a negative oedipal pattern, for negative oedipal themes would become vivid in her treatment. But more primal than the oedipal level was that of her early and then later forms of identification with me as a mode for both sexuality and femininity. The dream expressed a fear that sexual things could get out of control, and she had the fear consciously that her sexuality, as well as her hate, could both erupt in uncontrollable and overwhelming forms. But the dream also suggests June's own interest in the female body and its sexual genitalia. Where before she had only shown revulsion for the female body and especially for its sexual organs, increasingly over time, June began to consciously admire the female body as she would associate an interest in the female body with her interest in me. June told me that she was now quite curious about the pictures of females in porno magazines, and that whereas such pictures might once have repulsed her they now aroused her. She said that she was beginning to view female bodies as attractive and to find a beautiful quality in the sexual organs of females. They seemed to her now so much more interesting then the sexual organs of a man. When she went out dancing with her husband, she found herself looking at women more than men, adoring the versatility and movement of their bodies. She also only now felt free to go dancing as she heard my voice in her head saying "Get out there" in such a way that it outshouted the competing and more long-term voice of her mother forbidding her to dance (as experienced profoundly when her mother slapped her after she went to a disco).

June was aware of her attraction to me as well as of her identification with me. Her new curiosities about me opened her up to body arousal. She said that all these women she found attractive probably represented me, but she couldn't think specifically of me as an object of her sexual attraction because "it would be disrespectful." This changed later on. She said that she could enjoy fantasies of sex with women, or of possessing women who appeared in magazine pictures, or possessing women she might see on the street or while dancing. Although June knew these women represented me to some degree it felt safer to think of me through these displacements. However, in reference to her arousal with me directly, which she felt in the moment as she told this to me, she said: "The erotic transference may be the best part of analysis. I was always resisting it, but now I'm looking forward to it." June also showed a pattern of dreaming of kissing male friends or teachers, or of sleeping with male teachers, right after – sessions in which she felt close to me and her love and "in love" feelings were coming up. Being a heterosexual woman it was natural that she should displace her desires for me onto male figures, although she began to have a conscious homoerotic transference as well (in line with Freud's understanding of bisexuality).

Her desires for women led into desires for men, and she told me, following her comments about female bodies, that she was now finding men and male bodies very attractive. She had many dreams of being in bed with male teachers. In part these dreams seemed to operate on a phallic level, where she gained a phallic sense of strength and potency by joining a man's phallic strength in sex. However, the oedipal erotic desires for the father figure were also evident as time in treatment advanced, and such dreams contrasted with earlier imaginings of sleeping in bed with a woman who she associated with me and with her general homosexual desire. We spoke of the linking analogy between this earlier dream with June's getting sleepy in sessions, and of her perhaps wanting to sleep with me. Later in treatment her sleepiness took on a conscious sexual form in her mind, as she spoke of different forms of sleepiness. In one form she felt like a male with an erection ready to make love to me. Another form of sleepiness she described as being like a man with a limp penis after an erection, having finished psychically making love to me in the session.

Even after June moved more distinctly towards a heterosexual orientation in which she was finding many men including her husband desirable, she still had homoerotic wishes that she became increasingly astute at articulating. She said to me one day, during her third year of treatment: "Wouldn't it be great if we were two gay women. Then we could have a special love together that could be even more special than that between a man and a woman. I like to fantasize that my love for you could be made more special if we were together as two gay women." In the fourth year of treatment she had an explicit dream about our bodies coming together in sexual relations, going from the preoedipal love wishes to phallic and oedipal modes of homosexual connection.

In all these ways June psychically made love to me and derived a sense of female desirability and an awareness of sensual pleasure from this psychic mode of lovemaking in the transference. Along with her transference dreams, associations and direct feelings towards me in her treatment sessions came the opening up of her general sense of sexual excitement, as she felt a flow of love and joyous connection emerging between us, and imagined that the wonderful feelings were emerging out of me, and that she plugged into me and then felt the flow through her own body. One day, in her third year of treatment, when she was describing being deeply touched by hearing me speak about object relations theory and treatment at a presentation of mine, she told me afterwards that she cried and felt such joy open up, the kind of joy that made her feel like she had an "endless stream of love flowing inside of her." I asked her if this flow felt sexual and she exclaimed emphatically, without a moment's hesitation: "Oh Yes! Sexual, very sexual. I feel my whole body open up and tingle when I hear you speak."

June experienced a new awareness of her body as she came alive with sexual excitement. This combined with an openness to love and joy, as opposed to being overwhelmed by an internal world closed system that could only manifest as a sadomasochistic sexuality, relating back to June's past reactions to her father and her identifications with him. In this way, June's spiritual side and her sexual side evolved simultaneously. Most importantly, June began to carry this sexual life, lived at first psychically in the transference, into her outside life with her husband, who she also felt more and more loving and nurturing towards. She began now to have "meaningful conversations" with her husband, such as about the nature of integrity, honesty and other issues about life and morality. This contrasted with former conversations that she described as superficial, and with former periods of time when she and her husband would withdraw from each other.

DEPRESSIVE POSITION MOURNING

Pain of regret, and the healing of remorse and reparation

Developmental mourning covers a multitude of psychic phenomena. In June's case the object loss mode of mourning, related to separation and individuation, is particularly distinctive through her psychic integration process. However, there are other aspects of June's developmental mourning that go beyond mourning early object loss as a way of achieving a belated separation. These other aspects are best described in terms of the phenomenological terminology of Melanie Klein's depressive position. June herself commented in the third year of her treatment that she was less and less trapped in the perspective of the paranoid-schizoid position, and much more able to experience the world from a depressive position perspective as she worked through her pain with me. She comments: "I sometimes go back to the paranoid position, but much less. I'm more in the depressive position now."

Klein's depressive position is a psychic perspective with its own constellation of defenses, object relations and self-experience, all of which differ from those of the paranoid-schizoid position. In the depressive position one can feel the pain of the mixture of things. I would interpret June's state of confusion and her inner upheaval in terms of her confronting the pain of the mixture of things: such as her ambivalence over love and hate, of good and bad, good and evil, right and wrong, male and female, giving and receiving, etc. Ambivalence involves paradox and is not easy to accept even as we advance in psychic and spiritual growth. June expressed the anguish of this challenge in a state of grief-stricken tears, feeling the poignancy of the human condition in a churning confusion of love and hate. But more specifically, Klein's depressive position is not just about tolerating mixtures of love and hate. It is about tolerating mixtures of love and hate for the same object, and it's not just about tolerating good and bad, but about tolerating the mixture of both bad and good (or light and dark) in oneself as well as in one's primal internal objects and chosen external objects.

Out of the pain and poignancy of the psychic mixture grows the pain of regret. This is an existential morality and an existential grief, related to hurting the one one loves. No theorist that I know, other than Melanie Klein, is as eloquent on this subject of normal self failings in the face of loving and needing another – an existential dilemma that we live with throughout our lives – although the origins of the dilemma and drama go back beyond the oedipal stage to infancy as Melanie Klein attests. We can't know the psychic form such a dilemma can take in an infant mind, and I don't believe that any infant researcher – no matter how well plotted out by scientific method – can ever fully inform us as to what might be the somatic and visceral affect precursors to this kind of conscious and verbalized existential dilemma. I do think that the adult conscious manifestations of it – those an adult can encounter in a profound regression within psychoanalytic treatment – can give us insights into its origins. There is no way of proving one way or another what the infant experiences, just like there is no way of proving that love or God exists, but we become aware from the inside out. Analysands have a privileged awareness that comes to them by the grace of a unique treatment condition, with its own regimented peculiarities of time and space, and of boundaries and connections, experienced in relation to a trained, and skilled analyst.

Whenever we consciously confront the pain of regret we also confront the deep human hunger to repair the damaged connection with the others towards whom one feels the regret. Nothing could be clearer in June's case, and I would say in the case of all those who successfully mourn with me in treatment. Therefore, Klein's writings on reparation in the depressive position have touched me deeply. In Kleinian thinking there is a profound purgatory of the soul as one confronts oneself in analysis and yields to remorse for one's psychic sins, which I would define as one's offenses to object connection, which essentially are offenses to love. One yields to remorse as one surrenders to Klein's vulnerable position of loving and needing in relation to the analyst. Nothing could be clearer in June's case. Traditional Freudian theory has wrestled with neurotic guilt, and without this struggle and contribution we could never have the luxury of facing the primal human dilemma of existential guilt. Sorting out the mixtures of neurotic and existential guilt is a main part of the work in object relations psychoanalysis. Existential guilt is more aptly named "remorse," particularly in relation to the grieving of the pain of regret in relation to hurting the one you love, whether through indifference, assault, abuse, or just from the limitations of one's own capacity for concern and empathy. Klein sees us all as being born with hostile aggression that promotes continual modes of assault on potential love and on the sustaining object connection. Other theorists, particularly many modern day ones, such as self-psychologists Heinz Kohut (1977) and Frank Lachmann *et al.* (1992), see hostile aggression merely as a reaction to hurt, humiliation and narcissistic injury. They dismiss the primal mode of retaliation emphasized by Klein in her theory of manic triumph and paranoid modes of murderous impulses, and Kernberg's integration of libidinal and aggressive drives with object relations theory, in which he joins Freud's dual instinct theory with Klein's love and hate (envy and gratitude). They dismiss the Jungians who see aggression as a primal force of the collective unconscious with mythic metaphors to describe it in its role of psychic motivation as well as retaliation. Like Winnicott, the Jungians propose the powerful inspirational force in aggression, which requires it to be initiating and not just reactive. Steven Mitchell (1993) has a middle of the road view on these alternatives, acknowledging the innate pressure towards retaliation – calling it prewired in the psyche without any biological reference – and assigning it a reactive role rather than an innately instinctual one. At times I am comfortable with such a mediation of Kohut's innocence and Klein's death instinct, and find it a positive way of viewing the manifest aggression in the world, as well as a way of addressing Freud's second theory, that of dual instinct. However, at other times I am overwhelmed by a need to find a theoretical mode of discourse on human evil and all its vicissitudes. When I read Scott Peck's work on spirituality in relation to psychology, I am reminded of the dangers of denying human evil, and as a Jew I can never forget the holocaust. Otto Kernberg's view on "malignant narcissism," and envy that destroys all good in the other, helps explain evil. Kernberg speaks of the total failure of superego formation in some psychopathic personalities (1998).

Of course, Hitler was the first to declare that he was "reacting" to the aggression of others, a fiction that Stalin and every other dictator abused on a continuous basis. The best that can be said for Hitler's psyche on this point is what Alice Miller (1983) has promulgated in her work. She traces Hitler's actions and attitudes back to a tyrannical father who beat him within an inch of death when he attempt to run away from home, because he could not face living with his father and his father's obvious sadism. In accord with Fairbairn's view of the profound repetition and reenactment of parental crimes on children, by the children themselves, as they grow older and live with the unresolved hate and pain of the early trauma, Miller would sum up Hitler's evil as the worst kind of Fairbairnian reenactment. It can also be seen, however, as a result of a pathological narcissism related to a mother who merged in with his grandiosity and never could allow him to have his own feelings (especially those about his abusive father, as Miller suggests), along with the absence of any paternal or extended family support, with the addition of the father's brutal humiliations. But does any of this answer the question as to why so many followed Hitler? Is this the sum or the cause? What of all those who have similar horrors in their past that express a free will in the direction of reparation and entrance into psychological treatment, or in the direction of spiritual self-reflection that repudiates evil and encourages the confrontation of our dark side? Although I am not comfortable with Klein's death instinct explanation, I cannot relinquish Freud's dual instinct that includes a primal orientation towards aggression. I would agree with Klein that such primal aggression can be modified by a significant depressive position mourning process, with the containment of psychotherapeutic and psychoanalytic treatment, and this involves facing the primal bad objects of one's past as they exist within, and ultimately moving towards forgiveness. A key part of this process is the analysand's capacity to be conscious of retaliatory wishes and impulses, which I would agree, along with Freud and Klein, have an instinctual base. I don't think making the retaliation conscious is enough! The developmental mourning process is essential to reorganize the psychic structure into a more integrated state in which there is enough access to object connection and emotional contact with chosen others in the external world to heal and nurture a sophisticated psychological being. This mourning is required to allow sufficient ongoing processing of internal experience into symbolism so as to understand its relation to interactions in the outside world.

Although some are fortunate to have enough support throughout development to lessen the tendency to seal off the self from contact, or to contain it in a healthy rather than neurotically constricted repression process, most others cannot overcome insatiability and its hostile aggression without a mourning process in a treatment that acknowledges developmental trauma. Also, sadism has a pleasure in itself beyond instability. Satanic cults thrive on the worship of evil and the pleasure of hate. Facing consciousness of one's own retaliatory wishes towards the parents of the past as they have come to inhabit the internal world, in internalized and psychic fantasy, is essential in moving towards forgiveness, as well as towards regret, remorse and reparation (Klein 1975). June's depressive position mourning process, which is in my view part of her overall developmental mourning process, clearly illustrates this mode of psychic progress.

June's Pain of Regret and Reparation

June came into treatment with guilt and only over time did this transform into regret, and into remorseful longings for reparation. This guilt was partly neurotic and partly existential. In the beginning June was quite motivated, and perhaps compelled, to confess her guilt, and to list and describe each and every one of her crimes as she conceptualized them. She had minor childhood misdeeds to report in such a manner, which generally were on the order of sabotaging the colorful writing instruments of an envied schoolmate during her school days. A more self-jeopardizing childhood "crime" was that of swiping an item from a five-and-ten-cent store. Although such crimes were not the chief horrors that June carried in her mind from her past, they blended in with all her later guilt-ridden behavior. The chief grief behind the guilt was not the act of offense itself, but the feeling of hate and the greedy feeling of hunger behind the behavioral offense. June wanted to make a clean slate in her mind, and so she reported everything that haunted her as a symptom of the "criminal Mafia" part of her. One might say that the existential aspect of the actual guilt towards others was minor in these cases, but in June's wish to purge herself in my presence of all her self-conceptualized evil, the burden of her hate was quite weighty. This became vividly apparent when June would consciously identify with an actual murderer, saying that she knew what it was like to be capable of a compulsion towards such a heinous crime. She knew what it felt like to be exploding inside with the flames of rage, or to be frozen in a state of cold numbness, when her empathic capacities were blocked by a "stone in her heart." She feared initially in analysis that an unseen hate towards me would erupt out of control, and her way of defending against this in the past was to withdraw from others. Her fear was compounded by her jealousy of my other patients as well as my male colleagues. In her attempts to be both my only child (she referred to my other patients as siblings), and my lover and mate, she feared provoking others into retaliatory acts, which she also craved to appease her superego that demanded punishment for her crimes. Since I'm a woman, June's wish to possess me exclusively and to get rid of the father figure might be seen as a negative oedipal stage dynamic from a preoedipal Kleinian position. From a preoedipal Kleinian perspective, it might be seen as a wish to return to the dyadic relationship of an infant and mother, but this would not acknowledge the differentiated erotic nature of the wishes. In the case I just mentioned it seemed more like a negative oedipal phenomena. I was her love object. Even when male teachers were seen as the center of her oedipal erotic desires (also serving as psychic displacements for her transference wishes towards me), I was still seen as having certain "exquisite things" that they didn't have, particularly in my attunement to her body sensations and feeling states. So her guilt was expressed more in relation to her open hate for her father figures than in terms of any attacks on me. In fact, when I asked her if she was feeling bad because of her attacks against me in former sessions, she lightheartedly said: "Oh, I don't think you take anything I say to you seriously. I don't feel I have that much power with you. I feel I can expose all my thoughts to you and it's fine. With others I feel exposed, embarrassed and guilty." In this session, following her attacks on a male teacher whom I knew she was still angry with, she felt guilt and began to feel some regret. In her state of guilt, she saw herself as a "leper," with an obvious implication of insatiable hunger and envy behind attacks. June continued, after reporting this image of herself: "Even today I could go after Dr. P, it seems like if I could get rid of him I'd be fine."

As her formerly unconscious hate becomes a conscious anger, with a differentiated object and cause, she feels some relief. Yet, she is struck with the pain of regret, and has a wave of grief come over her, feeling bad about her hatred, no matter how natural it might be for her to wish to possess me in an exclusive love. I could and did interpret some of the neurotic aspect of her guilt here, saying that it might be natural in the stage she was in with me to feel like a child who wants her mother exclusively and therefore wants to get rid of her father. I would also add that she wasn't actually doing anything to hurt her rival. She was only exposing the hate and jealousy she felt in words to me. I would even underline that it is natural to have murderous wishes towards a rival for a transferential mother's affections, encouraging her to make her unconscious childhood feelings conscious. I interpreted her wishes to be special as a natural thing that we all feel, and which we intensely feel as children, questioning why she condemns herself as being grandiose for having such wishes. When June suffers the pain of regret for the murderous wishes that accompany her jealousy it is more natural, a part of mourning, rather than a defensive backlash of rage against herself. As she understands that she was expressing a latent childhood hate in the context of transference, she learns about her neurotic guilt. It is this guilt that has compelled her to accuse herself of being a "leper," just because she expresses feelings and thoughts to me that contain a murderous wish.

Learning that these murderous wishes are a natural part of becoming conscious does not and cannot fully alleviate the existential guilt that we feel along with neurotic guilt. June's regret needs to be expressed because it comes from her heart, and has the pain of self-awareness in it. This existential guilt comes from the Kleinian guilt of hurting the one she loves, in that June's murderous wishes and critical words do kill the psychic image of Dr. P, as she conveys them to me. By exposing the pain of her regret to me, she consciously grasps the full sensation of it, and she is able to turn regret into remorse, so as to prepare herself for an intrapsychic reparation. In the next session, June brings in a dream that seems to express the achievement of reparation with Dr. P, as well as a negative oedipal resolution in which she could have both her mother and father without having to kill off or suffer the loss of either transferential parent. This prepares her to deal with guilt related to her real mother and father. A dream at this time speaks of me inviting her into Dr. P's home, and offering, in a friendly manner, to show her around, essentially to show her the world of men, through the transferential father. I share the apartment with her and when Dr. P comes in "there is plenty of room for all of us." In the dream June is able to make genuine positive comments about the apartment, saying how comfortable and spacious it is.

More directly related to existential guilt is that of June's deep concern – which at first appears as a disconnected entity and a haunting demonic ghost – that she is truly guilty of the crime of maternal abandonment. She had left her son in Australia when he was only 2 years old. Throughout her continuing cries of despair over this, and her need to seek punishment for her "horrors," my sense of her basic integrity was never impaired. I think this was very important for June to face the grievous guilt within her, with its powerful and poignant heart-stabbing pain of regret.

My role has not been to judge June, but to help her understand herself. We all make judgments in our mind, which if rigidly held, become a counter-transference intrusion on treatment. There are many cases, such as that of June, where I have been separate enough not to have that happen. There are other cases in which I find myself struggling on a continuous basis with my negative reactions to the patient (not unprovoked), needing to interpret that which provokes me without becoming stuck in lingering judgments. This latter occurrence happens, for the most part, when I'm injured by a rather narcissistic patient, who focuses with hypervigilance on my faults and failings. With someone like June, however, who despite sessions where her negative transference and criticisms of me as an actual person might be prominent, is able to sustain a genuine appreciation of me in relation to my way of working with her, I am less vulnerable to a sense of injury and reactive hostility in judgments of action. Therefore, with June, I found it easy to be compassionate and objective rather than reactive in my judgments. Although it is not my role to judge, all therapists and analysts are human beings, having judgments about character issues, as well as about psychic structure and psychodynamics.

I know that in relation to June I always believed that she had needed to leave her family and perhaps her entire country for her own psychic survival, and certainly for the development of her psychic health. Prior to leaving her native home, June had seemed incapable of stopping obvious food addictions, and compulsive and destructive behaviors, which were exacerbated by her parents' primitive behavior. While still in her country, June's compulsions were her way of trying to control an enormous amount of anxiety, much of an intensely paranoid nature, which was entirely out of her awareness, whether by repression or by splitting off and dissociating whole parts of herself and her experience. June increasingly became aware of this in treatment, and it is from her own descriptions of her life that I take my views. I also always knew that June's separation from her family and from her mother was critical. She was unable to emotionally separate until she had physically separated by leaving Australia, and then came into psychotherapeutic treatment in the United States. Once June could make this emotional separation, she could make reparations and reconnect with her mother of the present. Her mother eventually joined her.

June's psychic difficulties with remaining in a state of motherhood with her son were tied in with her inadequate separation from her own mother. The initial act of leaving her son seemed a consequence of her need to leave her mother and family. However, had her ex-husband and son come with her initially, things might have been different. As it was, June came to the United States intending to return to her husband of that time and to her son within a year. Yet once she left, she found herself out of touch with her entire family. She became attached to a new boyfriend in the United States after hearing that her husband had proceeded rather quickly to have a love affair. She then derived an excuse to leave her husband and to stay in the United States, where her attachment to shopping for clothes surpassed any conscious attachment she could feel for her family at that time, even for her son. June would come to great grief in her treatment when she confronted the degree of her detachment from any feeling for her family, and especially for her son.

She realized that at the time she left Australia she was in a numb emotional state. "A stone seemed lodged in my heart," she would say. Yet in spite of this June made attempts to visit, speak to, or send gifts to her son. All her attempts to sustain a connection with her son were rebuffed by the child's father and his family, who were determined to blame all on June, and to conveniently use her, as an absent presence without a voice, as their daily scapegoat. So here she was scapegoated by two families, and having her attempts to overcome her former emotional detachment with new maternal offerings being not only rebuffed, but also maligned. What else was she to do but to focus on her new life here? She did this with an amazing sense of commitment given her emotionally depleted state.

June paid an additional emotional price for her severance from her family and country. In her own words, she cut off and denied her past as the "old life," and she gave up interests in history, geography and other subjects that might relate to that old life. She felt she had to make herself anew. She pursued jobs, boyfriends and most passionately of all her new studies in psychology with enormous curiosity and enthusiasm. Her emotional life was blocked, but her intellectual sublimations were at their height.

June's grief over her son became prominent in her treatment. When she first came to treatment she had no idea that there was a chance for reparation. In her own mind it was like the world in Australia didn't exist except for rare and painful visits. Yet, her heart opened through her object relationship with me as an external and transitional object, and her understanding of herself expanded as she understood her transferential and defensive reactions. Sadness in her heart opened the door to communication, where once there had only been alienation. As I indicated earlier, June cried and sobbed out a sense of deep grief that became both compassion and concern. Part of this concern arose from her consciousness of the ambivalent love and hate experience of her son, as they existed in her mind. Consequently, the cold antilibidinal part of June was modified by new connections and internalizations taking place within her central ego, which I have also referred to as an area of libidinal ego connection with her heart center. June became capable of feeling the compassionate part of her come in the foreground of her consciousness more and more.

In a state of vulnerability to her own loving and needing capacities, June cries out the anguish of an empathic identification with her son: "How can any child be without a mother? I can't imagine it, and yet my son has lived without a mother because I left." June's regret becomes more and more conscious, increasingly articulated with time and mourning. She could mourn and so she could love. She could mourn and so her son could live in her mind, where once there were only vampire like entities haunting her with a voracious need and hunger that she feared she could never fill. Now she faced the dark ghost – like the entities of the past: the haunting emotional need of her son for her, plus the feared practical and financial needs she anticipated her son would have if he came to visit her and wished to live with her. Up until the point when her son actually called from Australia, making an unprecedented contact, she only thought of her son as a being far away, forever yearning for a mother who wasn't there. Once he called her, he became a real person who she might meet and actually get to know. To her credit she was able to face the prospect of communication, and she began to hope for some form of reparation. She said that she did not want to excuse herself for her past actions with any cheap justification, even if she had been fighting for her own psychic survival and health. However, she did want to see what realistic reparations and continuing connection could be made with her son. June grew into a capacity to forgive herself, moving from an initial self-blame, self-punishment and self-condemnation to a more objective but also compassionate view of her own limitations and ultimately to a more realistic view of future possibilities to express her reparative intentions.

It is obvious that June had undergone major growth in her observing ego capacities, and in her capacity for concern, for this to happen. Her ability to face her guilt squarely, as well as to face her own anger and the anger of her son towards her (which he expressed for the first time in phone calls and letters), allowed June to integrate herself and to strengthen all her object related and interpersonal capacities. It is interesting to see how this growth, which I don't believe would have been possible without her reaching the deep grief sadness of depressive position anguish, relates also to her reparative process in relation to her parents, the same parents from whom her primal internal objects were first formed. This depressive position anguish can be defined as feeling love for those one also hates. She navigated through this sadness with me, grieving again and again. This grieving allowed June to become the agent of her life. Her capacity to navigate through her sadness with me, and to find the meaning each time, allowed her to yield to forgiveness, drawing on a consciousness of both the wound and the hate inside of her. This was a sadness of the pain of regret, a willingness to feel remorse, and a sadness of opening love and gratitude; and thus, newly found hope for reparative possibilities.

Most outstanding in June's depressive position mourning was her coming to terms with her internal father, and the forming of an opening for reparation, either in reality or in her own mind, despite the enormous hurt and rejection she had experienced from her father. June could not arrive at a place of reparation or forgiveness without first acknowledging both her hate and her hurt openly. She amazed herself by being able to face with me what at first seemed only like an ocean of darkness to her. June recalls her father's sadistic side, as it was felt to knife her again and again. Through evoking memories in treatment, June felt her father's attitude of cold contempt and assaultive cynicism and criticism. Not only did June suffer the direct attacks of a hostile, deriding, and ridiculing contempt, but she had also suffered, during her whole lifetime, her father's abrasive cynicism about being alive, which accompanied his underlying despair and his defensive detachment. At first, imprisoned by an identification with this horrendous coldness in her father, which I have described as her antilibidinal ego side, June could separate from such identification as the frozen stone within her heart melted. Finding love within grief, June was able to consciously remember that which might have been too hurtful to remember before. She began to remember her father's attacks on her femininity and attacks on her attempts to be "out there" in the world. She felt her own hate, now strong and fierce. She now felt retaliatory rage: "He took my libido part and killed it. I now want to kill him in a minute!" She felt then the pain of coming to consciousness of her own hate, a pain that might be all of ours, when we journey into the depressive position state of self-awareness. June's ability to express her retaliatory impulses, her rage, and her wishes towards me was critical, in terms of her becoming conscious of her own identity. When able to speak her retaliatory impulse to another the impulse takes on a validity and reality that can no longer be denied through some nebulous gesture of reconciliation.

The retaliatory wish stands, and it expresses June's symbolized justice and formerly repressed power. Expressing this wish to me in a verbal form articulates the rage intrinsic to June's wound. She expresses, perhaps for all of us, the rage from the hurt committed against our true being – not just a strike against our narcissism which has a naturally injurious effect, but a strike against the very essence of our natural being, a strike against our soul. We strike back. However, to the extent that we can limit this return strike to thoughts, words, and feelings expressed with a neutral witness, as opposed to acting out the retaliatory wish against its object, we survive and transcend the hate that goes with love, particularly with the complex love a child feels towards a parent. No matter how bad the parent is in reality, and Fairbairn knew this more than anyone, the parent is a primal object of attachment that holds us tenaciously in its grip. Going beyond Fairbairn, however, exorcism is rarely possible or helpful. We don't exorcise the parent from our consciousness as an internal object, nor either the old representation of that parent. We must face hate and eventually forgive and repair through the grief pain of mourning. With reparation comes love that goes beyond the old addictive attachment. Even though we may need to leave our parents, or in the most extreme cases, to cut off all relationship with the parents as they exist today, we still can find a way towards a more compassionate forgiveness, and thus towards reparation, within ourselves – even if we cannot carry out the reparation in the external world.

June was able to move to reparation in both her internal and external worlds with her son. With her father, however, the question of external reparation remains open. Nevertheless, June's approach to a question that houses so many psychic possibilities is an amazing feat of human courage in an emotional and psychological dimension. I believe such courage is facilitated by and perhaps is totally dependent on the human capacity to sincerely mourn, and to process the kind of depressive position mourning that engages with guilt as well with grief. This is true even with a guilt that is related to a justly deserved hatred towards a severely abusive or inadequate parent. There is always grief in guilt, and this is because there is always loss of both self-love and object love in guilt.

In the midst of her personal pain, as June recalls her father's assaults on her, she also says: "He certainly provided me with a very intense situation. It was very intense. Maybe he gave me an opening." Here I detect an element of gratitude right in the midst of June's hate. She says: "Men who hate and fear women want to grab the libido part and destroy it." Here is an opening June detects for appreciation of her father, even within a moment of consciousness of the rage she has suffered in reaction to his very real abuse. For now she begins to associate his intensity with passion within her own transformational experience through mourning! Much psychic potential is gained through a grief that brings compassion, for she says at the same time: "Maybe I'm crying for this female who's been castrated by her own father by being subject to situations that can destroy me in a minute." Here she expresses compassion for herself in the midst of her pain. It becomes a pain with less blame as she releases her retaliatory wish: "I feel like killing him in a minute!" and then is able to move on. The compassion for herself can only grow out of a full recognition of her hate and retaliatory wish, as the grief related to this hate is felt. Compassion for herself is related to concern for the other. In a short paper on "The Development of the Capacity for Concern," D.W. Winnicott (1963) speaks of the ability to hold and contain guilt, which needs to come from developmental growth in object relations therapy with those traumatized in the preoedipal years. Once one can contain guilt rather than just reenacting it towards others or towards ourselves in another hostile assault, a true concern for the other can develop.

June is holding her guilt as she openly acknowledges her hate and its source. She speaks her rage and retaliatory thought, and yet stays in a perspective of facing the truth of her own experience. Instead of an action of retaliation then, following her thought and feeling of retaliation, she is free to move on to a reparative wish, in which potential forgiveness lies. In a session following the one I just mentioned, June comes in and says: "I contained my rage today with Bill [her husband] and didn't get caught up in sadomasochism. I analyzed the situation instead. Maybe if I could do this with my father, my father could acknowledge what he's done." Such a hope was a sign of the marvelous survival of the human spirit in spite of the total lack of response from an external father throughout this whole process. In fact, any contact with her father still brings coldness and criticism and a demeaning attitude. Yet, June realizes that her father is fighting to take care of June's legal affairs, related to her still ongoing divorce proceedings in Australia. Despite his hateful attitude, June comes to appreciate her father's devoted and caring actions towards her, without denying how he had hurt her in the past. Her new objectivity, seeing all parts of him in the present, allows June to look behind her father's facade, where June can now perceive a needy child inside her father, as she associates to a dream in which she imagines her father wanting to come live with her. In another dream, her father is a psychic figure, who can set a boundary as well as a barrier against sex. When she brings a man home to her door, she has to tell him to go away because her father is inside sleeping. The parent always stays an active figure in the mind, and June is working out her reparation with her father despite all her injury and rage. She often does this through transference reactions to male teachers. The father is becoming a more separate other in her mind; one who might acknowledge his actions towards her, as she mourns and revises the father within.

REPARATION VERSUS REACTION FORMATION

It is important to distinguish between reparation and reaction formation. If June were to forgive her father too quickly, without facing his true effect on her and her true rage it would be a false forgiveness, and an attempt to protect the image of her parent by "making nice" to him. Since, however, she has faced her rage, as well as her wound and has opened up the pain of the past, which includes an experience of her own retaliatory fantasies, she can move towards true forgiveness, and thus towards a healing reparation within herself.

Similar movement is made by June in relation to repairing her internal and external relations with her mother. Although June had much more contact with her mother and much more ongoing reasons for old negative reactions than with her father, there is a much greater loving side to her childhood relationship with her mother, which June experiences very intensely in her transference experience with me. Thus, she has more love available to her in relation to her mother to help her wish for reparation and reconnection. June has become quite aware of her tendency to push her mother away, and to distance and detach on a continuing basis. In the beginning of her treatment she was openly repulsed by her mother's needs and demands on her. She had much conscious resentment and tended to get silent or mechanical with her mother. However, June's attitude towards her mother significantly transformed as she began the in-depth mourning process and reached the place in her grieving process where the deepest sadness emerged and her old sense of self "cracked open," resulting in a new and more compassionate self developing within her. June began to feel intense grief pain – the pain of regret – whenever she thought of her own cold and distant behavior toward her mother. She knew she really was hurting her mother. On the one hand she wanted to deny her impact, but then she felt frightened that she couldn't have an impact on anyone. On the other hand she could have an extreme view of her impact (aggrandizing her own power) in relation to her lifelong guilt about emotionally separating from her mother against her mother's wishes. Finally, June feels extreme sadness for the very real, but not omnipotent, level of pain she had been causing her mother, and realizes that she is hurting herself as well as her mother.

After her deep level of connection with me, as she mourned, June became aware of her own longing for her mother. She stopped projecting all the object hunger onto her mother, started owning her own part, and then she wasn't as threatened by her mother's overtures. She no longer had to see her mother as a voracious vampire with unending demands on her. She started to sob out the grief of longing for her mother, missing her and wanting to reconnect. As she did this, however, June was overcome by her fear that she could not say the words she felt in her heart. She felt unable to communicate to her mother, unable to say the three simple words "I miss you!" But acknowledging her sense of inadequacy helped her get past it. It was hard for her to change her hard unyielding attitude with her mother, which had become an image. She had to surrender the old image of her mother, and risk exposure as a vulnerable being who had love and needs for her mother still. Her anguish was truly poignant as she wished for reparation: "I hope my mother lives long enough for me to make things better," she cried. Then with a shock of surprise she sobbed: "And my father too!"

DEPRESSIVE POSITION GAINS IN TERMS OF EGO GROWTH

Although at times treatment may require direct intervention in terms of developing and facilitating ego functions, I have found that ego functions develop naturally with the kind of self-integration process that I am describing within the development mourning process. In June's case, she experienced new capacities to both loosen old boundaries and to strengthen her overall sense of boundaries. For the first time in the third year of treatment, she could say "No!" to a demanding co-worker at her job, and could feel confident about her actions: "Even though she was upset, I knew I had done the right thing!" In the first year of treatment she could never have done this. She quaked with fear when this co-worker came after her with unwanted observations and demands. In the first year I had to speak to her about the possibility that she could close a door to be separate from this woman. She feared the prospect was too much for her. In the third year, after her heavy mourning she felt the strength from within to find ways of setting boundaries. Along with the ego function of boundary setting, and the self capacities for concern and empathy I mentioned, June grew in observing ego capacity, communication skills, her ability to understand her own interpretations of the meaning behind her own behavior, and in many other forms of self and ego functioning.

SPIRITUAL EVOLUTIONS

I have found that many of my patients have profound spiritual awakenings during their psychoanalytic treatment when they are open to the developmental mourning process. I assumed that any psychoanalysts would be welcoming of these events, which are so deeply moving in the analyst's own soul (generally experienced through the heart). However, some reading I've done has made me question this assumption, as well as conversations I've had with certain colleagues. I was curious and interested to see that in one of Scott Peck's books, *Further Along the Road Less Traveled* (1993), he emphatically declares how closed many psychotherapists and psychoanalysts have been to a patient's spiritual beliefs and experiences. Indeed, he not only speaks of their lack of involvement in their patient's spiritual experience, even as it occurs within the psychotherapeutic session, but he speaks of their cutting off of the experience, often with theoretical formulations to discount or minimize it. Such attitudes are seen collectively in the field of psychoanalysis as a hangover from the days of Freud's aversion to religion, condemning it entirely as a fantasy or crutch, the opiate of the people.

Freud's attitude has had a damaging effect, but each practicing clinician in the field of psychoanalysis has his/her own responsibility to face themselves and see if they have any spiritual phobias. I believe things are changing somewhat in the field in this regard. I believe spiritual topics are being discussed now for the first time, rather than reducing such phenomena to the realm of psychic fantasy or "merger fantasy." However, such changes take time. Given that I felt some intuitive motivation towards opening to the spiritual side of things when expressed in a natural free association process by a patient, I was interested in Scott Peck's report from many patients he had met who had felt extremely frustrated and deprived of a therapist's willingness to share in the spiritual connections they might be seeking or making. I think it might be helpful to report Peck's own words, given his lifetime of psychiatric experience being attuned to these matters. Peck writes:

A far greater problem, to my mind, has been a vast amount of mistreatment of patients with a correct primary diagnosis by virtue of psychiatry's neglect of and antipathy for spiritual issues. This kind of mistreatment generally falls into one or more of five categories: failure to listen, denigration of the patient's humanity, failure to encourage healthy spirituality, failure to combat unhealthy spirituality or false theology, and failure to comprehend important aspects of the patient's life. The single most common complaint I hear from psychotherapy patients about their therapists (they are just as likely to be secular-minded psychologists and social workers as psychiatrists, but psychiatry has tended to call the tune) has been that they did not or would not listen to the spiritual aspects of their lives. When patients talk about such things as a feeling of calling, consideration of entering monastic life or the ministry, mystical experiences, or even simple belief in God, the prevailing tendency of psychotherapists is to simply shut down until the patients are speaking more mundane matters – or else to actively attempt to divert them to more mundane matters. Many patients have left therapists as a result. Even more common is that the patient, picking up on the therapist's cues, will enter into a kind of unspoken collusion where both agree to avoid spiritual issues. Typically, patients will tell me, "I really like my therapist. He (or she) is a decent person. I feel he is trying to help me, and indeed, he has been of some help. But you wouldn't believe how threatened he gets whenever I mention the spiritual side of my life. So, since I'm getting some help, I've learned to simply hide that side of my life from him and never mention it." I have also heard a significant number of stories of therapists who have actually denigrated their patient's spiritual life. This is not to say that a person's spirituality is always healthy and should never be confronted, but my impression of these cases is that the therapist involved was unable to discern between a healthy and an unhealthy spirituality. (Peck 1993: 246)

In contrast to Peck's description through his patients' words, of the blind eye most psychotherapists have turned towards spiritual matters I have been particularly excited and intrigued by these matters. Those clients looking for a spiritual path within treatment with me often pick this up. The case of June illustrates this, as well as others I haven't written about here. What is so distinctive in the case of June is that she felt from the beginning that she could open the door to spiritual connection through connecting with me. At first she believed this meant "plugging into me," as if, in her fantasy, all the spirituality flowed through me on an ongoing basis, and all she had to do was surrender to plugging in. Over time she realized there was mutuality in our psychic connection that allowed the spiritual channels to open.

From the beginning, June viewed me as having a divine center and an old soul. The first aspect could be assigned to anyone in terms of getting though defense systems, but the second was of peculiar and meaningful interest to me. Although I viewed it, in part, as an aspect of an idealizing transference, I didn't dismiss it as merely that. I intuitively sensed that June's intuition was at work, and that she had a sense of something deep within me that she needed to reach, something that she felt would make her thrive, and something that she had the potential to develop within herself. At the later point in her analysis, when June associated the Dalai Lama to a dream she had and then connected it with me, she also shared with me for the first time that she had dreamed of journeying to Tibet when she first came into treatment with me. Within the treatment process itself she had called me a mystic, a shaman, a dervish and a priest.

If Peck's definition of a mystic can be applied to me in relation to my work with June, I might be able to agree with her. Peck writes: "But certain things can be said about mystics. They are people who have seen a kind of cohesion beneath the surface of things." Now perhaps the same might be said for any perceptive psychoanalyst. Nevertheless, given this definition, I can understand what June was seeking when she said she wanted my vision and my enlightenment. Perhaps she then became a mystic herself when she radiated (her heat) with the joy of experiencing a psychological integration in which "the internal world and the external world come together! It's so powerful and wonderful! Things are so whole and round!" June attributes these flashes to enlightenment, which many would refer to as only psychological. As I see it, this spiritual dimension is related to June's experience of me as an ongoing presence in her mourning and self-awareness process. I think June is correct that she needed me to help her open to new discoveries within herself, but only at first. She was idealizing in believing I had all the secrets within me to be discovered, like Klein's infant who imagines the mother to have the whole world inside of her body. Although I could agree that I have my mystic aspect, I certainly don't live in the area of spiritual truth on an ongoing basis as June might imagine, always "seeing beneath the surface of things." I have glimpses just as she began to have, but nevertheless I receive her view of my spiritual dimension with the utmost seriousness and respect. I would like to share June's spiritual journey in her own words, as she experienced it and is still experiencing it.

With over two years of mourning, June said: "I think you have gone through very intense experiences – like you have experienced the most incredible joy and happiness. Maybe you're able to go into that mystic place. I imagine your role as a priest. You have a cosmic awareness – in some way you're serving others. Bill and I said: 'Thank God for leaders like you with integrity and vision.' Some people only experience one dimension of you – the Clinical Psychologist, but you're much more than that! I have this feeling with you. It's not contrived. It's not manic – of peace and joy. Am I making this up? No! I'm feeling it right now! I want to rise above the negative stuff in others – like the complaints – envy – stabbing – I want to give love because you've given it to me. I want to pass it on. I was where others were before. It's hard to overcome."

Then June comments on her response to what she sees as a spiritual gift from me to her, but she is also aware that she is a very active participant in the process that comes about (mid-third year of treatment, January 30 1997): "I have really gone through an incredible change with this analysis. I hope I can hold on to this feeling inside for a long time to come. I think this is the greatest gift one person could give another person. It's a kind of joy–joy like you want to cry. It makes the world so different! Something has dramatically changed. Now I can have vision. Everything is in this flow–understanding, enlightenment, creativity and love–everything is in it. I keep practicing and practicing. Coming here is a kind of spiritual practicing."

Then she relates to the psychoanalytic process she is in, and then she doubts it all, and regresses to seeing herself plugged into me, forgetting her new sense of vision, which clearly comes and goes: "After going through my feelings of envy and aggression the light comes out! It almost feels like you have plugged something into me. I want this thing to be mine." It is after this that she comes to the conclusion that I have had intense mystic experiences of joy and happiness, and then feels that she has been experiencing the joy of love as a spirit that she wishes to pass on to others.

At moments we even touch on the topic of God. Sometimes this comes with a new sense of self-integration for June, and within this sense is a deep body and being connection, in which a powerful realization of her own interiority is experienced. This is accompanied by a sense of embodiment that she felt her mother lacked. Her "ocean cave" image is the one that captures her new sense of interiority, such a sense brings up her expression "My God!" and I pick up on this. If God is in part residing within us, this sense of interiority provides a critical spiritual connection.

"Inside, it's so different. There's a strange low-key depth in the internal world. Being here feels like an ocean cave today. I like getting into these places. It feels like the source of something. It feels so connected! My God!"

"When you say 'my God!' I think you're saying that there is a way of experiencing things now that is like experiencing God!" I respond to her.

"I think that's true! It's like experiencing an energy – very wonderful! It makes me feel very safe – in happiness and sadness. I don't know how this whole thing happened. I feel the shift today. But when the reconnection happens, all of a sudden it's getting connected to a greater source – a channel . . . This is amazing! Divine!" she exclaims.

After sharing the deepest despair with me a little later in the third year of treatment, which comes as a backlash reaction after risking exposing her ideas in public, she shares her dream of a low-key woman that she associates with me and the Dalai Lama. So vivid in this sequence is June's spiritual connection carrying through her separation mourning, in terms of object loss and depressive pain about her own fate, as she risks an exposure that brings up her exhibitionistic impulses and makes her fear her aggression. Because June is able to share her despair and grief within mourning with me she can totally turn around one hundred and eighty degrees to a heightened spiritual connection, which embodies a sense of "flow" as well as vision. This flow experience might be likened to Wilhelm Reich's original research on unblocking "energies," which he labeled "orgone energy," and which later led to Alexander Lowen's bioenergetic work that focused on opening up this energy flow through a focus on the body and the blocks. It might also be compared to what James Grotstein (1997) has recently written about as "Transformations in O," which he describes as an experience of self-transcendence. In this transcendence, one is temporarily liberated from one's confining psychic structure and internal world imprints. Grotstein is employing Wilfred Bion's theory to discuss this psychic experience and thus refers to Bion's terminology in which "O" is a form of being, as opposed to conceptual knowing. This state of being can have a transcendent dimension.

With this in mind, let's observe a sequence from emotional despair to psychic enlightenment in June, a sequence briefly quoted in another section and other context: "I'm really out there and I feel I'm going to die. It just feels like I can't go on. I just feel like I want you to be my mom and I will be the child."

Then she reports her dream, which answers her wish: "I had a dream that I was with this low-key woman. And being with her, I started to change from being flamboyant to being more low-key. I wonder if this dream has to do with you. Maybe that's the low key you on the inside, deep down, low key. I also think of the Dalai Lama. I had a dream of going to Tibet when I first came to see you."

With the report of this dream, June's initial state totally changes from the darkest and most suicidal sense of despair to an opening to spiritual flow and openness to all possibilities: "I'm now getting hot inside! I feel the flow of energy throughout and in my face – burning, burning. Do you feel it? Like a whirl of energies. Yeah, like sunlight, like sun on my body and I'm getting a suntan. I think of you looking at me. I feel red now. It's such a joyful feeling!"

In this sequence, June reminds me of Emily Dickinson's words, when the poet calls herself "a soul at white heat" (Kavaler-Adler 1993). Dickinson transformed all her sexual energy into such spiritual energy. For June, her sexual heat has been just as present with me as her spiritual heat. But when the sexual heat befalls her she speaks to me of "being in heat," and the animal body level is quite apparent, with me being the hot transferential sexual object.

Another spiritual dimension is June's views of herself as a new kind of woman, one with the intuition of a cat (as she has cats in a dream, when she used to dream of dogs). June now experiences herself as having the body of a beautiful female dancer whose soul is truly dancing within her body. As June tells me "I'm dancing now and loving my body," she also has dreams of a spiritual female emerging. In one dream she sees four women in a rectangle, dancing. Each women is dressed in yellow and orange. June has spoken of me as someone who always dresses in bright colors, whereas she used to dress in black.

With her emotional and spiritual awakening have come a new interest in colors and an interest in dressing in colorful outfits. In this dream, June's Arab women are dressed in bright colors, which may refer both to me as her transferential mother, and to me as a model of femininity as the feminine part of her is developing. To understand this dream we can find an interesting message in the women being smashed. June would generally come into sessions and as she lay down on the couch she would put a tissue over her eyes. This was some compromise between total self-exposure and hiding. Perhaps such a compromise helped June to deal with her shame and ambivalence over her exhibitionistic wishes, which she and I had discussed as her terrors of exposure as she emerged into the world. June had spoken of feeling free to expose all to me as opposed to with others with whom she felt self-conscious. However, she still kept this "tissue mask" between us. Ultimately she relinquished it, but would still close her eyes. June surrendered the tissue mask after dealing with many levels of shame within her.

Another dream brought up June's spiritual side in the striking aspect of female beauty. She dreams of a woman dressed in a deep blue gown coming into a therapy group that she is in with me. "There's a radiant beauty and a golden glow around this woman," she says. In reporting the dream, June explains that she thinks of a blue blouse I wore the week before when she remembers the "person in blue" in her dream. It is a deep blue. Then she also recalls an association to her mother in reference to blue. Her mother was wearing a "light" blue blouse on the day when she abstracted June from a hospital in which she was diagnosed as being fatally sick. It was life or death for June that her mother made the right decision, and chose to bypass the medical authorities and to trust in her own ability as a mother to heal the infant June. On the train, leaving the hospital, June's mother placed the infant June on her lap. June vomited profusely all the way home; all over her mother, who was too depressed – as she reported it to June – to clean it up. What an intimacy there was between June's visceral gut despair and her mother in a blue blouse!

Not so many decades later, June blends her infancy mother with the transferential mother she sees in me, visualizing a woman in her dream in a blue robe that harkens back to two blue blouses. It also strikes me as June tells me this that my deep blue blouse, darker than her mother's, is the color of the biblical lapis lazuli, used in so many Italian religious paintings, particularly those with the Virgin Mary. The Virgin is often dressed in a robe of lapis lazuli blue, perhaps in velvet, with a golden line of decorative motif all around, simulating a halo. The lapis lazuli dress is evident in the scene of the Annunciation, in which an angel from God comes to tell the young teenage virgin that she is going to receive a son from God. She is, in other words, going to give birth to a spiritual being, and perhaps to her own spiritual being, to the masculine side of her that she needs to complete her feminine spirit.

My musings on this now resonate with what June comes up with in her research on blue. She decides that the woman in the dream is a profound spiritual presence, both because of her halo radiant beauty and because of her blue dress or robe. June wants to know more about what the woman in blue might symbolize as a part of herself emerging, and she looks up the color blue she has seen in a mythology with Jungian collective unconscious archetypes. She discovers that deep blue symbolizes the intuitive part of our spiritual being, which June had also been finding in her new dream of cats. She also discovers that the blue color represents a deep and total immersion in one's chosen vocation, and a general enlightenment through this deep immersion in one's chosen work. She relates this deep immersion in work, as a spiritual journey, to both me and to herself. She says that for the first time in her life she feels this kind of total involvement in her work – now that she is studying psychology. For the first time she feels a euphoric excitement as she pursues her studies and the psychological work in her analyses. She also relates such absorption in work to me, saying that it was because I had an overall vision of education in the field of psychoanalysis that I seem so driven – driven to realize the promise and to educate others.

After such speculations, June returns to a backlash terror, fantasizing others destroy what she has because they envy. June's internal mother is envious. She is sobbing as she says: "This kind of energy I got from you. The only way I can help myself is by crying here with you. It's scary. I'm afraid people will destroy this blue person in me, who emerged in my dreams. The better I feel, the worse the other part is. It seems like it's getting deeper. Before I hardly felt anything. It shifts back and forth like I did something bad, something horrible! I see you as having the courage to say whatever you feel and I find that most appealing. On the positive side, I have flowering colors and women dancing. On the negative side, I feel naked and exposed in a humiliating way."

Then later in the year she says: "My criminal impulses come back. I'm feeling the pressure of the drives. I think of things blowing up, like volcanoes and earthquakes. I keep thinking that there is some meaning behind this." It is clear that even at this time when June is most consciously threatened by the impulses within her, impulses which she can no longer dismiss as external entities, she still has faith in the analytic process and its journey towards symbolic meaning. Within this belief is her spiritual quest as well.

June's understanding of both love and creativity gains meaning as she associates both these spheres of psychic spiritual development with me, and then tries to assimilate her experience with me to make the meaning become her own: "Right now it feels like an ocean, sun and beach. It's like you are radiating something. I'm taking it in. I guess it's something good like love. Can you have so much love in you? How can that be? This feeling inside you gave me, I feel is mine now." I do not see June as merely defending against separation and loss with a symbiotic mother reunion fantasy here. Her experience is not just projective or introjective. It is alive. I feel it in the room with her and it has arrived after three years of mourning and grief in which she has repeatedly faced the pain of developmental separation and its object loss feeling.

After June makes her statement about me radiating love on her like a sun (in part an infant level psychic fantasy, but only in part), I let her know that she is touching me emotionally with the meaning in her words, as well as by her feelings. She sobs and cries with joy and delight, with deep body sobs. I respond to her in a way that lets her know she is capable of a deep impact, a deep level of emotional touch. Again, I believe this is like Masterson's communicative matching (1981) after separation has progressed, at rapprochement. But I also see spiritual overtones in the immediate experience and spiritual meaning. I validate what is intersubjective between us: "You're crying now because you touched me," I say.

June experiences my spiritual role with her in relation to creativity, as well as to love. She seems to sense intuitively, as I have, what Klein indicated in her writings, a while ago, that love and creativity came from the same place, and that vision is some combination of both as it transcends to a symbolic level: "You must have visions. Otherwise you couldn't come up with the things you have come up with on creativity. I think you had a mystic experience. I can have it too if I work through my hate, rage, anger, and mourning," she says.

Here we see June's transition from a conscious envy that could turn destructive if repressed or disowned to a more spiritually enlightened state of visualizing how she can grow from the process with me and become like me, although being more of herself, as we work together. I have become an ego ideal for her, as once I was an idealized object. Her ideals for herself grow out of a grandiose side of her, which once had been projected on me. Now she believes she can find her own voice and her own vision. This is apparent in a more spiritual dimension when she sees me as a shaman, one who has been initiated a long time ago, while she is becoming "a new shaman," just initiated. June continually compared herself to me in her spiritual quest, which always involved the element of vision:

"I'd like to have a special experience in analysis, going deep into the unconscious and connecting with the forces inside, seeing the drive inside. You've already had this, but I still [second year of treatment] have all this hate, and part of me is a criminal! I imagine you having a euphoria feeling when things come together, but vision too. The feeling has to go together with it. What will happen to me? In this other world of emotions I have no idea where I'm going to be taken. At the center there's something good, something divine. You have a large soul.[2] People are responding to me differently now. It feels like love is flowing out of me – a sunshine. How were you able to get to this deep place inside of me? It feels like I have a stream inside of me that will never stop flowing. I told a classmate of mine that you have opened me up at my core. This is so transformative!"

[*Later in October*] "I want to be myself, but I can take you in and be like you – like a good musician. Seeing you 'out there' helps me know how to be in public."

Here in this second year, we see a back and forth oscillation between new and old self feeling, as well as between the inadequate self in relation to me being the grandiose self and a new position of transforming into her own spiritual power, with me standing for her future and her ego-ideal (Loewald 1979).

"I seem to be on the surface. I can't touch on the depths of what you get at. It seems like I'm just at the beginning, like feeling the states of mind people reach with LSD. It felt overwhelming to read your book. I felt like – my God – I'll never get there! It seems so far away, like your reflection on theory took years of meditation. One thing I seem to have is the drive, I was afraid it would go away, but it stayed with me. It comes back every time. In the morning, I woke up and the intensity was still there. It comes back all the time. It's like you're almost writing in my mind, and I'm understanding from within. Some internal vision! You can go in and out! Like I think psychotic people go into visions, but they don't have control over it. They come back broken. In your book you're writing about a very mystical thing in clinical language. When I read Klein now it's different. It's kind of mystical. The vision of the whole thing is illuminating. She's describing creation, creation of the internal world. What I really want is that vision! So how does that go on here in the creation process, the most deep concentration. I think I have some of it here – when all of a sudden the internal world connects with the external world, the words take on such an intensity, and the images inside feel so powerful! That's a really beautiful feeling – almost like being high on something. You know, you have a really special gift and people don't know it. People think you know theory, but it's not just that. I read in a book how every mystic has some followers and some relate to another mystic."

June aspires in this second year to be like me in ways that are genuinely connected to her. I'm not just representing a split off grandiose part of her, but rather her true ego ideal, her true aspirations. I let her know that she needs to use me in this manner. I address both the defensive aspect of her use of me and the genuine developmental need for using me as a substitute for her being out in the world. I tell June that she places into me her own capacity for flow and vision, to find herself. I tell her that she experiences flow and vision with me because of our connection. I tell her that she can use me as a transitional person in this way, but that eventually she will feel these things within herself and then with others, as it actually develops clearly by the third year of treatment. I don't want to be reductionistic and speak only of projection, but I do want to make her aware of the degree of idealization that may be involved so that she can begin to see her own potential. The developmental process that accompanies the projection process occurs as soon as she opens from her formerly sealed off self and makes an avenue for connection to me as an external object. In this way, in reference to Fairbairn's view of the internal world, she is emerging into the central self (or ego) area, and joining her former split off libidinal core to me as an outside object in the area of the central self. Fairbairn never developed his ideas on this central self, as he was only dealing with the pathology of having split off self-parts, in a sealed off state, with regressively addictive primal objects. Since he didn't pursue the area of the central self he didn't pursue the self-evolutions into sexuality and spirituality that can be conceptualized to occur within it.

Kleinian theory goes beyond Mahler's separation–individuation phases, with the development of self and other as representational symbols and distinct forms. For Klein, depressive position concern occurs in conscious awareness once Mahler's separation–individuation process has proceeded to a distinct developmental point. One must have a separate self and its unique representation to have a sense of agency that allows for the owning of sadism as a self-initiating impulse and pleasure, and to own the destructiveness of hostile aggression that is often acted out as an unconscious envy. In the depressive position, such unconscious envy, sadism, and object connection destroying aggression can become conscious and be owned. However, when arrested developmentally in the separation phases, consciousness of hostile intent is not possible because the sense of self is shattered by a primitive superego or antilibidinal ego belief in one's own badness (the feeling of being evil). Reaction against such consciousness immediately happens at the visceral, somatic, and unconscious impulse and fantasy level. One retaliates automatically against the knowledge of one's own sadism by splitting off a part of the self, and by simultaneously attacking the libidinal part of the ego. The whole visceral level experience (not yet psychic or spiritual) is dissociated, and it is enacted in further abuse and repetition in the external world of self and other. Then soothing is compulsively sought in dissociated experience in addictions, alcoholism, sexuality and compulsive acquiring, such as food addictions and consumerism. With depressive position growth all this changes. However, first the abandonment depression affects of the separation process must be tolerated. This is only possible in treatment with the emotional and caring presence of the analyst, particularly when one has been traumatized at the early separation period in the second year of development (Masterson 1976, 1981). All this is clear in the case of June. The work of separation and reintegration of self-parts can be illustrated at a psychic structure level by Fairbairn's theory.

Klein's phenomenological focus on the depressive position work is best understood in terms of the central ego area of Fairbairn meeting an external object, without being blockaded by primitive projections. Fairbairn himself didn't delineate this process of healing and movement towards psychic health. His theory is focused primarily on the pathological splitting in infancy that occurs when there is no good enough parent, where only defective parents exist.

The separation process and the depressive position grieving are interactive. They form a dialectic. Both can begin only when the libidinal ego can join the central ego and meet the therapist-analyst, who serves as the transitional external object. Without this contact, the patient remains emotionally split off, with primal splits in self-structure. Once the connection is made, a Freudian form of ego and superego can form. Fairbairn's libidinal ego can be seen as containing a Freudian id or Kleinian id (with a priori psychic fantasy and Jungian archetypes). However, it can also be conceptualized as Fairbairn conceptualizes it, as a child self that hungers for the external object parent to bring it up (psychic structures yearning for interpersonal connection). How this primal self or primitive ego self core is interpreted depends on whether one believes children are born innocent and are totally molded by their experience in this life. Apparently Miller vociferously subscribes to this view, which I find naive. Given all the evidence these days for past life experiences, I think it's naive to think we begin tabula rasa in this life. This would be true even if we were fully molded from experience in interpersonal life and parenting, without a major impact from prebiological instinctual impulse and from Kleinian a priori fantasy, as a psychic aspect of instinct prior to symbolic experience and perhaps prior to all experience.

Fairbairn did anticipate the developmental impact of the internal libidinal ego integrating its affect hunger for object connection with the central ego and joining the external object. However, he did not anticipate the full dimensions of this external connection. He did not anticipate the opening of emotional, spiritual and sexual channels through a heart center, which might be found to reside within

Fairbairn's central ego, or what I prefer to call central self. The heart center of the human being is not in the libidinal ego (which Masterson refers to as a "pure pleasure ego," following Freud), but in the potential self that emerges through the intersubjective connection of the libidinal ego. This intersubjective connection of the libidinal ego can be imagined to be joined to the external object within the realm of the central ego while still retaining an area separate from it. From this synthesis we can then derive the experience of id, ego and superego components.

Although a religious pastor by education, Fairbairn seems to have had a very curtailed vision of the central self-connection and of all the spiritual channels that can follow from this connection. He didn't anticipate the erotic connections and the heartfelt emotional connections that can come from an integrated central ego structure. In the study of June, the spiritual dimensions of this energy are clearly articulated. The case of Laura emphasizes the erotic dimensions, but the symbolization of these erotic connections become increasingly spiritual as well as poetic. Fairbairn never focused on such aspects of psychic health, which are evolutions of what I have called "The Love–Creativity Dialectic" (Kavaler-Adler 1996). Psychoanalytic patients become conscious of the flow of energy as affect, versus the blocking of such feeling. They become aware of the dramas and subtleties of the developmental mourning process, as it unblocks channels for psychic energy to flow. They also become aware of the role of new psychic internalizations, which enhance the flow or block it, as new external object experiences develop, with the analyst in a critical transitional role in this development. There must be such an integrated self formed before Grotstein's (1996) "Transformation in O" can ever occur, in which the self can be transcended for moments in time. Only an integrated self can support, assimilate and symbolize transformations of such transcendence.

June's evolution in later years of treatment

Transformation through mourning in developmental, transference, and life change terms

In the sixth year of June's treatment, the target of her psychic focus significantly changed. She no longer needed to focus on the analyst as an idealized representative of herself. Her developmental mourning process, and all its phases of separation and self-integration had allowed June to transition into a prime psychic focus on her real self, as opposed to on the analyst as an idealized self. Psychotherapeutic work with the defenses and enactments that inhibit mourning process and its parallel process of external object connection and new internalization had allowed June to become her own center of self agency, self subjectivity, and internal world dialectic. Through session after session of mourning process, in which old self and object constellations were loosened, seen with insight, and transformed, June had been gaining a new sense of power that now allowed her to have visions of her own development and life goals.

By this point in treatment, June was able to tolerate severe states of rage and rebellion from her teenage son, and to contain her own rage towards him. As the analysis of her transferences in her treatment progressed, June came to understand the transference towards her mother that was often provoked by her son. Her son completed high school and successfully navigated through college, with a high level of achievement, despite his psychic vulnerabilities from early life trauma. June became increasingly able to communicate with her husband, and began to feel close to him in new ways. She and he now felt like a core family, along with her son. June and her husband learned to work together to confront the manipulative and self-sabotaging behavior of her son. As June became more compassionate towards herself through the understanding that the mourning process could bring, along with the analyst's interpretation of this process, June became less egocentric, and naturally opened then to understanding and compassion towards her husband. She began to see his separate needs and his separate personality, and analyzed reactions of contempt, distancing, and anger that she experienced in relationship to his behavior, successfully differentiating her husband from her father over time. June and her husband began to enjoy each other's company in a large variety of ways, finding new hobbies together, and learning to take pleasure in romance and sexuality.

Such growth in family relations occurred simultaneously with growth in personal and professional areas of her life. June spoke of finding her own voice. She spoke of gradually leaving behind the old self-identity of a mute, silent, inhibited, and frozen figure, who is numb, and unconsciously terrorized by abandonment and annihilation anxieties. In finding her voice, June began to come out into the world through teaching others in her field, through public speaking, through writing personal essays in magazines, and through starting and building a business in public relations.

The transference transformed gradually and continually over a six-year period of treatment. By the sixth year June no longer perceived her own abilities and potentials through her image of the female analyst. Instead, she viewed the analyst as a compassionate, talented, and deeply related person, who had been representing some of her own aspirations. Having experienced the grief of loss, guilt, and shame that comes with a developmental separation process in those who have had trauma in early life separation phases, June became ready to own her individuality and thus to allow the analyst to be a person in her own right. She became capable of objectively seeing the analyst's struggles, foibles, and difficulties, as she could now see others in general as whole persons with strengths, weaknesses, and difficulties in life. She no longer needed to see herself in contrast to the analyst, nor as an extension of the analyst. She could now feel more equal with others, and less excluded from the world as she realized that her difficulties and struggles in life, although unique in some ways, are also common to others in broad terms. She arrived at the sustained capacity for self-motivation in realizing her own goals. She no longer prized a fantasy of living through the analyst.

June had continually experienced progression and regression, with a full range of affect states, and with much more refined affects. June no longer split into two opposing self-states. In her regressions, which still continued at times, June had become familiar with her transference phenomenon of seeing the analyst as a seductive and envious separation phase mother, a mother who could not tolerate her growth, and who feared death without her.

Developing an observing ego through her separation and mourning process, June came to vividly see, in the sixth year, the transference images of the analyst that occur with each new step into individuation through self integration. She came to realize that the transference projection of a mother who will hold her back or die without her, as she progresses towards individually designed goals in her own life, was based on a whole psychic fantasy system. This psychic fantasy system was constituted from early drive wishes and early developmental experience and separation trauma experience. She also came to realize that the figure whom she used to call a demon lover was a conglomeration of a trauma inducing internal mother and a trauma inducing internal father. The negative internal mother wishes her to return to a merged or symbiotic state. She is enraged by any threat of her daughter's individuation. The negative internal father assaults her verbally for moves into adolescent separation and into adolescent feminine development. The split off demon lover figure – which has alternately been projected onto the analyst and onto authorities and mentors in her outside life – is sorted out into its components within the treatment sessions and within the transference work. June continues to have vivid visceral awareness of the changes and degrees to which she could be separate, and thus could experience internal conflict, and have her body and mind feel free, which also comes to mean to June feeling "light" as opposed to heavy.

June visualizes her conflicts and fears of separation in dreams, viewing herself as being poised to make a jump or leap into selfhood or else into death. This fantasy of a life or death challenge suggests June's old terror of losing the mother with separation. In the midst of her fear and desire, June visualizes one crocodile swallowing another. I interpreted this as symbolic of her fears that her own devouring needs for a primal mother will compel her to swallow her mother and to be swallowed by her. However, she also encounters a benign snake in a dream, evoking the phallic power of the real and archetypal father. June now begins to assume this phallic power as her own, using this new power to separate from the internal mother. In the same dream as the snake, the man demonstrates to her how to get out of the dark sewer waters of the unconscious. These dark sewer waters are the murky waters she has been confronted with when daring to separate from a merger with her mother. The man in the dream helps her to believe she can leap to freedom, where a central self, symbolized as containing clear water, awaits her (Fairbairn's potential central ego self).

Concurrent with these dreams in the sixth year (fifth month) of treatment are many new developments in June's new versus old self and the new psychic structure that has formed through the mourning process in treatment. June describes it best in her own words. She articulates her individuation process with refined details of affect change, belief change, idealization and perceptual changes. She also undergoes vivid changes in identity that are characterized by changing her favorite colors, her ways of dressing, her ways of living her daily life, and her ways of conceptualizing her self change process. She has acute visceral awareness in the change process. Also concurrent in this psychic evolution is June's new and ever-improving acuity in perceiving where she agrees and disagrees with the analyst. She is no longer compelled to see things through the analyst's eyes as she would do in the first year or two of treatment. June learns to trust her own judgment, but also is flexible and receptive in her capacity to ask the analyst for feedback, especially when she is aware that she may be distorting reality because of transference wishes and fears. Overall, this allows the analyst to feel a deep sense of her trust, and to know that she can sit back in tranquillity no matter how seriously June is working with difficult and confusing material on the couch. The analyst can help June sort out her own perceptions, feelings, and beliefs. June charts her own individuation and transformation process. The following are June's ways of expressing her emergence into selfhood in her sixth year of treatment.

"I think in the past I had annihilation anxiety all the time. Now I'm aware when I regress to my old self. I was numb in the past. Now I feel the sleepiness and heaviness of regression. It feels like going into a trance state and I can identify it.

When I come out of the sleepy state, I feel light, flowing, energized, refilled with love and creative ideas. The pressure in my head disappears, as I face and feel the pain and conflict in my heart. Then I feel free and light. Space opens up in my mind and in my dreams. I feel like I have talents. When I regress I can start to think all the talents are in you again. I wonder how you can talk at a workshop to twenty-six people in such a related way. I can teach a small class, but cannot imaging speaking to twenty-six people. But when the flow comes back and I feel free and light, I begin to have a vision of how I can do it. The vision allows me to see that the leap into separation and having my own voice doesn't have to be too much. I used to only have visions of your success, and I'd want to be in the shadows watching you do it. Now I see myself out there. It's time for me to put my own things out there, even though I still learn from watching you. I do it at one of my presentations and in teaching. I think I want to move in new directions. I think I want to develop my writing. I don't know how you talk to so many people at once."

"What do you imagine goes on inside of me?" I ask June.

"You get into talking and it flows and happens."

"You've been experiencing that yourself now."

"Yes, I need to have my own voice like with teaching. I need to continue doing it. I need to feel some anger for my separation. I realize now that when I return to perceiving myself as bad, and want to act out being bad so others will reject and exclude me, that I'm just angry, and that it's my guilt about the anger that makes me hate myself and see myself as bad. When I can be conscious of my anger, and know what it's about I'm free. I think I try to recreate a relationship with my mother with you, when I ask you for help. If you help me it's often no good now. I need to find my own way. I really enjoyed teaching. It gave me a lot of satisfaction. I saw myself in a different light. I dreamed about needing to jump from a sewer of water into a middle place where there was clear running water. A man demonstrated how to do it. My being able to contemplate jumping is, I think, related to the internal work I have been doing. I think I have to jump to a new level. I had a dream of taking off veils and exposing myself. I think I've been hidden behind veils, and now I'm more and more ready to emerge."

I respond: "I think you're afraid I'll pull you back, as you felt your mother always did, and as your internal mother always threatens to do with each step forward, pulling you back into sleep and heaviness. But I think you could try to create an external conflict with me over this to avoid your internal conflict. You've defined the internal conflict as a wish and fear of jumping and speaking up in your own voice. You sometimes run from that internal conflict by thinking that I'm holding you back, not the conflict within, between the part of you that is reluctant to separate and the part of you that wants to in order to progress. You and I are defining the conflicts together now so that you can do with or without me, and aren't forced or compelled in either direction."

"I'm coming to a crossroads. If I don't take the leap I'll live a life of sleepiness and boredom, going in circles, and crying 'poor me.' I have worked through so many personal dilemmas, so that new images have opened up. I definitely feel deeper unconscious layers. I'm entering the belly of the whale or the crocodile, the crocodile I saw in my dreams."

June's whole way of speaking about herself has changed as she's become more separate from me. She speaks of her intensity now, instead of mine. She used to imagine herself needing to be plugged into me to come to life. Now she can feel energized by being open to connection with me, and understands the continuing metaphor of experiencing me as pulling her out of infant illness, as her mother once really did. June now experiences her sense of connection to me as a separate person, which is quite a different way of thinking than before when she believed that the very flow of her life fluids depended on being "plugged into" me. June can connect with the deepest places in herself when lying on the couch with me behind her. She can then emerge out of these states, with an overall sense of security, even when she reexperiences a sense of annihilation anxiety as "drowning," "heaviness," "trance," or "going mad." The abandonment terrors have lessened overall. June functions well now in the world, and feels in possession of her intellect and abilities to negotiate different situations in reality, even when she journeys into the depths of sadness, yearnings, grief, and annihilation fears within her sessions.

June is no longer helpless in the tug of developmental conflicts, due to the mother's lack of emotional availability in her separation phases and in her separation strivings. Now, June feels these phenomena as internal psychic conflict, and can create dialogues between the conflicting parts of herself, using my presence and my interpretations to guide her.

June speaks of having an observing ego now that can watch all her fears and conflicts and fantasies, rather than being possessed by them. She still can open to crying to connect to her inner and deeper self, which is now more integrated with her intellect than before. Her crying is softer and less painful now, although to a relative degree. She can also connect to her inner self now without crying most of the time. She sustains all connections better than before. Significantly, June's crying contains the affects of Melanie Klein's depressive position, those of loss, grief, guilt, and intense yearning for connection. When June feels these affects her mourning and separation process moves forward. However, feeling the affects is not enough. She also needs to conceptualize her feelings and her transforming self-states, as she opens a whole developmental continuum of self-experience. All this is best expressed in June's own words.

"This time I'm really facing it. It feels different. I don't want to be in the old chaotic state as far as my financial papers, debts, and bills go anymore. I don't want to create that anymore. Those dreams I had last week seem to indicate that I'm resolving something. I'm working very hard. I didn't get into acting anything out. There are shifts in identity. There have been shifts in my unconscious. It takes a lot of energy to focus on it and stay still, to not spit it all out (oral dynamics of original infant/mother enactment). It would be wonderful to have a clear folder on my desk, where everything is sorted out, and where I know what's there and what's not. You know, owning one's own mess is not an easy thing. It really feels at some level like I'm taking it back. Maybe it hurts to take back the feelings, to feel the feelings. There's no one to blame. It's all me! [*Crying softly.*] Facing things is changing things. I haven't had compulsions this year. I haven't had compulsions to spend money. I was in a state that was largely unconscious before. Now, I'm looking at it, looking at it, feeling it and not acting it out! [*Crying.*] It's true that it's all inside because I haven't been acting out with anything since this summer, since the vacation [*crying*]."

June experiences a combination of loss and deep internal connection as bit by bit she leaves the old self and the old psychic self and part object structure behind. June has a sense of her old self, of her old narcissistic ego dying (defenses dissolving). So June thinks of sorting out her papers as preparing for a death, which would be an entrance into a peaceful state of mind. It is her ego dying, so her real spontaneous, true (soul) self can be born. June is alive fully as this transition takes place. She has to work through the constant impulses of running back into hiding, which she does by yearning to close her eyes and to go back to sleep. Then she has a dream of taking off her veils, of rejoining a split off self that has been covered in a blanket (portrayed in a dream), and of reintegrating to go out in the world and be seen. She has profound feelings of lightening up and opening up into psychic and potential space as she does this. Her son becomes free from her in this way, and progresses. Her husband can communicate with her better, share more of his interests with her, and can move on with his life, with her support. June can now have a new vision of herself, whereas in the early years of treatment she could only have visions of me – as her idealized self-object extension – moving to success.

Now, June sees herself having a free dialectic between her self as a subjective "I" and as an objective object "me." She is coming to life and new images go beyond fantasy to reality. The most profound metaphor for the ultimate arrival of her reality consciousness is that of sorting out her business and financial papers. Now, June can travel in her unconscious to deep fantasy and deep emotional states, and can still come back to being grounded in reality. Her conflict had been about whether she could stand to live in reality. Before it was too painful. With in-depth mourning of the pain, however, she can now face all realities, as symbolized by facing her bills, papers, and finances.

"Maybe I could see myself as a person with everything sorted out on the desk, with spaces on the desk opening, if I do it gradually every week [*crying–the pain of being connected, grounded and of working hard*]. I've created such a tension, such a conflict. It's unbelievable. So at least I know I've internally created it, and externally I'm paying the bills. It was monumental for me not to get into this paralyzed pain state Wednesday when I faced the bills. It was monumental to know consciously I wasn't going back into it, not to go into that old painful state, where I was just paralyzed! All the things I put off for years, as far as paperwork and everything, now I want to take care of it. It hurts! It feels very painful, like some people may feel before dying. They want to sort out everything. That's what it feels like I'm doing. That's what I'm facing up to. It's like the time has come for me – like the time has run out. I want to take care of the things most avoided before. It's like the end of something."

Following these sessions, June expressed great relief and surprise to find out that she was reported to be in perfect health by a medical doctor who gave her a thorough physical examination. All her life she had suffered from somatic conversions of her psychic stress and of her unconscious psychic conflicts and unconscious psychic trauma. When she was in her early twenties and a young mother, her medical reports read that she was anemic. Now, all her somatic and hysterical conversion symptoms were resolved. She could now feel her psychic pain in a conscious way and could work through her pain. The most intense pain she faced had healed, and she came to understand these pains as she relived her separation trauma with each new aspect of psychic growth and success in the world. From this courageous perspective, June could understand her new state of mental and physical health. She told me as her analyst that she gave object relations psychoanalysis the credit for her growth because through analysis she learned to understand the essential process of her own developmental mourning.

In these later sessions, June also responded with new insight to the analyst's declining to increase her individual psychoanalytic sessions to five, as she had once had, from her four sessions per week in this later year of treatment. When the analyst declined, in part because the analyst was using the specific time she asked for her own recreational swimming, June remarked that she found the analyst's setting of this boundary in order to allow for her own health needs and time of pleasure to be relieving. She articulated that her mother would never have been able to set such a boundary, particularly to reserve time for her own health and pleasure. June could now understand the analyst's separate needs from the perspective of someone who has successfully navigated through the separation–individuation process. Her mourning and individuation process had allowed her to operate psychologically from Klein's depressive position, as opposed to from the paranoid-schizoid position, which dominated her when she first came to treatment carrying so much early trauma and preoedipal arrest symptomatology with her. I revealed this rather than encouraging a transference reaction because of June's developmental need to identify with a woman who could experience separation and pleasure.

June herself describes the intrapsychic experience of conflict related to the original developmental trauma around separation–individuation. External events still trigger the conflict, but now she is aware of the conflict occurring within her even when not prompted by external events. This is particularly vivid in the transference, and in relation to me as a real new object to go through her conflict with, unencumbered by her mother's degree of pathology around separation–individuation events. I serve as a more benign object because I tolerate the conflict in her, without significantly imposing my own conflicts around separation. Furthermore, I help her articulate and understand the oscillations within herself around the conflict. Increasingly, with her further individuation she can define the internal events without my interpretations, but it is the holding environment of the clinical situation that allows her to express these internal phenomena without interruption, and with another hearing and understanding her, so that she attains a form of psychic confirmation.

June's dreams reveal to her those struggles around separation that were being repeated with the analyst. She expressed this clearly: "I suppose the dreams mean, on one level, that I am separating from you and also finding myself slipping back into a kind of merger feeling, a feeling of wanting to be back together with you. After I create that I start feeling angry. It was a very important part of my treatment to reown that part of my infant self who needs to merge with mother. Throughout the years here I got that part of me back – very important – but now in analysis I also need to separate. Experiencing that merger was important for me to feel present in listening to music or in reading. I needed to go back and forth from merger to a separate identity. Now, I'm dreaming of needing a man. I think the man represents a symbolic function, a symbolic order, where I can have the merger experience through symbols. This is the 'me opening to sexuality with my husband, fearing less a sexual merger with him and the separation from my mother'."

Sometimes June's potential relationship with her husband is represented by the analyst in the transference, where she can experience intense sexual desire. The analyst may also appear in dreams as a man, symbolic of her husband.

Aware of the transference, and no longer concretizing it as solely a response to me, June says: "What I've begun to see is I'm expecting jealousy from the mother. If I go out there in the world, and have my own projects, the mother will try to pull me back into a merger. What I'm not addressing here is being able to picture the things I want for myself, independent of my mother, what I want in this life. I need to be able to merge, not only with mother, but with a man, my husband – not only to go back and forth. This week, when I got angry with my husband I felt like running back to you, and then I began to feel like I'm merging with you. I need to have the experiences simultaneously with you and my husband. The only way you'll respect me as a human being is for you to respect me with my own creativity, my work, my own projects. I don't fully express myself, because I fear retaliation for my independent plans. That's what I have to do here. Things I resist saying I have to say, even if I'm afraid I'll lose my mother and a merger with her. I have to think of independent things. I must think of my family. I've been with my husband ten years. He has supported me. Even though I paid for my treatment, my husband paid other bills so I could afford treatment. Now Bill and I want a new place to live, a bigger place. This is not so impossible. If Bill continues to do well at work and in the stock market, we can do it. I'd like to start taking it seriously because up till now I haven't."

June goes on to list other goals for her future, like getting a PhD. She says that she has no regrets about how much time and money she has given to her analysis, but she is now thinking naturally of other things for her life and her future.

"As far as the outside, I'm feeling that in my own community and my own profession I could be very successful. I never felt this way before. Now this feeling is continuing more than ever. Also as far as writing I've been reevaluating this as well. It's been a year since I've been in your writing group. I think as far as what I've received from the group it's the feeling that I can write. Before I had the feeling I couldn't write. Due to the group, the belief that I couldn't do it is gone!

I'd like to move to the next stage, where it's more action oriented, where I have written work done to bring into the group all the time. Hopefully I can do that. I still want to rewrite that story I wrote, and the academic paper I wrote. Yesterday I read one of your recent papers. I could stay with reading the paper and feel the flow of it. I thought, if I sit down I could write a paper and be close to your way of writing. The reading was smoother than in the past. That makes me feel I could write smoother."

June's individuation process was forging forward in this sixth year of treatment, having followed and interacted with her.

Chapter 9

The case of Phillip, Part I
Seven generations of grief

Just as the other patients reported in this book, Phillip stands out as one of the most vibrant examples of the human capacity for developmental mourning, with its positive form of suffering. The therapeutic object relations journey in this chapter is one of opening up the avenue to deep grieving for the longed for muse parent, which for Phillip had differentiated father and mother components. Phillip's capacity to suffer in the positive sense of developmental mourning has been both palpable and profound. His capacity to sob through his grief, as well as his capacity to simultaneously conceptualize the process – along with my guidance as a psychoanalyst – is vivid and evocative. Such capacity on Phillip's part displays the healthy psyche that is capable of psychic dialectic: the dialectic of cognition and affect, the dialectic of self and other, the dialectic of monologue and dialogue, the dialectic of symbol and symbolized, the dialectic of love and creativity (Kavaler-Adler 1996), and the dialectic of subjective need and empathy for the subjectivity of the other.

Phillip describes his own drama as one of doing grief work for "seven generations of ancestors." He experiences a conflicted communication with these ancestors as internal objects, whom he feels pressing him forward towards his own psychic and spiritual journey through mourning – a journey that he must volunteer to take both on his own behalf and on behalf of those he has descended from (in what he calls his "DNA line"), who have failed to surrender themselves to such a journey. His grieving becomes their release, for his failure to grieve results in compulsive reenactments that keep the suffocating blocks to love alive, blocks that have haunting internal demons possessing his entire family, through the generations. Driven by a collective force from within, like the artist driven by a demanding muse, Phillip is inspired and launched upon a wrenching and healing journey.

Looking back to the beginning of his treatment with me, Phillip recalls how closed off and shut down he had been, and how frightened of trusting others. Prior to coming to seek my help, he had been in therapy with a man, who had remained a benign father figure in his memory. My impression was that this former therapy had a rather cognitive focus, perhaps challenging Phillip's ego skills, but not engaging Phillip's deeper self core, which had remained in a sealed off state, consequently inducing the subjective experience in Phillip of being "shut down."

According to Phillip, when he initially came to see me he had been carrying a "motherload of grief." As he lay down on a psychoanalyst's couch for the first time, he seemed primed and ready, like a duck taking to water. He seemed ready to unburden himself, while displaying considerable anxiety about how much need he felt. He was also fearful about whether I could tolerate his need. He feared he might have to continue to burden himself by protecting me, as he was compelled to protect all others, particularly his father. Somewhere within there was a child and potential adult who needed to emerge into its full spontaneous nature. Although demonstrating a surface compliance, Phillip's underlying aggression occasionally was revealed, although it was generally expressed in self-deprecating terms. Phillip was afraid he would be too much for anybody, and this was generally played out with women as they became too much for him. Meanwhile his family, and in particular his father, pressured him with disguised and provocative needs, which he prevented Phillip from ever directly responding to. Simultaneously, his father pushed him away with attitudes of negative judgement, while screaming out into the dark with his own sealed off emotional needs. Phillip's extreme sensitivity made him intensely vulnerable to these disguised and hidden cries from within his father, although he continually got emotionally wounded by his father's verbal attacks against him, castrating attacks that derided his manhood, and made him suffer in a masochistic manner as he strangled and turned inward his impulses to retaliate. His psychic solution was, in part, to incubate his father within him in a form of introjective identification, where his father's sealed off child self lived within Phillip, substituting for a consciousness of his own child self and his own emotional needs.

In the beginning of treatment, Phillip's own needs and longings were largely repressed, and they got compulsively played out in the form of sexual fantasy, which was enhanced through self-sabotaging activities, such as drinking, mild marijuana use, sexual promiscuity and the occasional employment of call girls. As Phillip severely condemned himself for his compulsive fantasizing and its related compulsive and impulsive activities, he mirrored and repeated his father's form of derision, playing it out against himself. He protected his image of his father, and developed an antilibidinal psychic structure within himself, where his father's demonic side could be harbored and used self punitively against himself. In this way he held on to the father of his childhood, protected the external father of his current adulthood, and controlled his retaliatory aggression. However, these defensive strategies only succeeded in making Phillip feel imprisoned and depleted of energy that he wished he could employ for creative activities. Also, as he tended to repeat his self-sabotaging defense mode with all others in his life, and particularly with the women he became intimate with, he continually suffered from a form of distancing that failed to allow him the sustained emotional contact and connection that he needed. Ultimately he pushed women away as he started to feel a genuine emotional need for them, or picked women (such as his girlfriend during his first stage of treatment), who did the same to him. He was left in a conti- nuous state of frustration. All this would emerge in the transference relationship in treatment, but the primary opening up to contact that was necessary for defense analysis to lead to transference analysis, and for the exploration of his fears, fantasies, and traumas was to come through a profound and ongoing mourning process in his treatment. Ultimately the mourning process allowed him bit by bit to separate from his internal demon and demon lover father, who he longed for with tremendous passion during the first half or more of his treatment.

Phillip was overwhelmed with the grief of his frustrated longings for a father who fits the psychic mold of Ronald Fairbairn's "exciting and rejecting object," and who also fits my description of the demon lover, as one who arouses desire for an ecstatic merger, while actually being unavailable for the emotional contact, connection, tenderness or emotional touch. The continual disappointment of Phillip's longings resulted in heartache, object loss, and narcissistic mortification and injury, not to mention the pain of a defensive, self-blaming guilt and the pain of true regret about self sabotage that resulted in ongoing self loss. All aspects of this psychic loss needed to be mourned, and Phillip entered treatment with me in a state of readiness for the task (as Hamlet says, "The readiness is all!"). The many phases, levels and qualitative shades of this mourning allowed Phillip to move forward in treatment to the analysis of an erotic transference. The mourning process also allowed him to face primal fears and longings in relation to his mother, who had her own demon lover aspect in his fantasy life, while providing a model for oedipal object desirability and a model for preoedipal infant and toddler yearnings.

The layers of the treatment unfolded naturally, and as an analyst I never attempted to control or direct such a natural process, which made this psychological mode of treatment unique for Phillip. In retrospect, it is clear that Phillip's inner life had a roadmap of its own, which is to some extent a parallel process to that of Mr. M, who I wrote about in "Mourning and Erotic Transference" (1992). For both men, an initial mourning process allowed the full emergence of the erotic transference in treatment, and the mourning process contained the use of the erotic transference to understand the formerly repressed unconscious oedipal longings that caused so much guilt and self sabotage in their repressed form. Also for both men, the erotic transference served as a transitional stage of treatment, with the analyst as a transitional object, to help them move into a full and committed romantic relationship with a new available woman in their lives, leading in both cases to marriage. And with both men, grief about the disillusionment of oedipal erotic love, and grief about infantile wishes for merger with the analyst could be mourned along with separation loss and grief. However, some difference also stands out between the two cases. For Mr. M, the loss of an adolescent homosexual love stood for a preoedipal love object that needed to be mourned before oedipal erotic wishes could be felt consciously in the transference. For Phillip, the initial mourning was for his father, and this was then the avenue for consciousness of erotic oedipal longings, as well as their preoedipal origins, with the mother in the transference. It was very clear, however, that in both cases the initial mourning was related to severe psychic trauma, as well as to disillusionment of child wishes and fantasies. Trauma was less evident in the oedipal stage erotic transference for both

Phillip and Mr. M. The primary holding mother of childhood was intact in the internal world of both men too, so that as the female analyst I could embody the therapeutic holding environment for each man, which could make possible the fulfillment of mourning and its positive mode of grief suffering.

During several years of lying on my couch, Phillip readily begins to yield to what eventually will become a full surrender to both me as a real therapeutic object and to what he called "seven generations" of grief. This allows him to open to conscious awareness of yearnings within him that had been perpetually pressuring him in the form of compulsions, obsessions and mild perversions. In the course of doing so, he progresses in all areas of his life, with major advances in love relations and in his spiritual growth and spiritual beliefs.

CORE MEMORY

There is one core memory that Phillip returned to repeatedly in his mourning process. This memory arose in between all other memories, associations and fantasies that would come up with his depressive, rageful and grief-stricken feeling states. In this memory, he is 2 years old, nestled in the comforting arms of his mother. His forehead is placed against her cheek or forehead and he feels soothed in a fundamental way. He feels her warmth, tenderness and nurturing love, and feels that he and she fit together snuggly almost as one. He feels a sense of security that he may never fully capture again, and will always yearn for. Then suddenly this paradise of material enchantment and embrace is harshly disrupted. His father enters the scene as an archetype of intrusion. Coldly, abruptly, the serpent enters the Garden of Eden. The father as serpent, becomes a negative, rigid, unyielding phallic force that punctures his semi-womblike existence. His father grabs him out of the arms of his mother, and reprimands him, screaming at him, for being a baby. His father speaks disapprovingly to his mother, implying that she is emasculating their son with her tenderness. How will he grow up to be a man? The father's false masculine pride dominates the scene, leaving a traumatic incision in the harmonious state of madonna and child. His reaction seems overblown, outraged, envious, hungry and like the cry of the excluded one. Perhaps the father's own unconscious oedipal jealousy (and preoedipal envy) flare up.

The 2-year-old Phillip is bewildered, but more than that is left crying and bereft, feeling his father's hold on him as brutal rather than tender, in sharp contrast to his mother's, and feeling a kind of narcissistic mortification that could later be interpreted by him as castration. His view of his manhood has been damaged. He is suddenly and so early being told with all the wrath of belligerent accusation that he is falling short of some mysterious requirement to be a "man." Suddenly his very maleness is a threat, because it seems to be separating him from his soft, warm and all encompassing mother. He is wounded in a center of male pride that he is yet to know consciously. Yet he will know this center's many manifestations, as they haunt him in his behavior and in the compulsive disruptions he keeps imposing on his paths to love. He will know this wound in his many compulsions to act out self-degradation and to relive humiliation and shame. Phillip associates many times and in many different ways to this memory. He is aware of always being frightened of an attack from behind, expecting his father to intrude on him.

He is less aware that he might actually bring his father in to disrupt a union with his mother that engendered intrapsychic fears of its own. However, he is very interested in this latter idea when I suggest it. When we reached the stage of analyzing his sexual wishes in the erotic transference, he discovers the primal fears behind these wishes, which indicate that his fantasy of Garden of Eden safety might have a terror in it even more fearful than his father's trespass, and that from this other perspective his father's intrusion could actually be experienced as a scene of rescue. But despite the threat of a primal mother, the fear related to his father, and the not insignificant rage that accompanies it is not just related to fantasy, but had a real experiential base in his father's traumatic intrusion. Whatever threat the oedipal father might have in fantasy, due to Phillip's natural oedipal longings for his mother, which emerge in memory prompted by his erotic transference with me, his father's actual castrating behavior haunts him as a punishment – as a retaliation for oedipal wishes, and as the even more threatening punishment for preoedipal merger wishes. Thus, both preoedipal and oedipal level yearnings become colored by the father's rageful intrusion. Later memories of the father's castrating attacks blended with this core memory and evoked a full range of symbolic associations.

As Phillip revealed this core memory to me, his pain erupted in sobs that pulsated with visceral profundity from the couch. I could feel and hear his sobs. They had an energetic current of their own, but spoke with organic, body-based penetration. To me, this full body surrender to sobbing is the essence of a truly psychically transforming mourning process. Those who have lived through this on my couch have seemed to transform their lives and to reach levels of fulfillment related to a capacity for deep levels of contact, and for in-depth engagement with the process of life, and its modes of expressing interpersonal love and creative self-expression: love and creativity. This memory was one of many that evoked this central self-depth of feeling in Phillip, but it arose again and again, bringing many connected memories in its wake. Love and gratitude towards me could also organically emerge, without blocks of envy and fear, due to the context of deep grief evoked by contacting the yearning behind this memory.

Phillip recalled his father's recent attacks on him in the wake of this memory. During his first year of treatment he had a dream about me that reflected a father transference element connected to these attacks. This dream comes after he has said to me: "When I open myself up to you, I don't want you to act that way. I want you to act differently than my dad." He wants to put all his problems into me: "I can put it all in you. You can take it. Therefore, I won't have to be the one, for once, who has to protect everybody. So I can let go of this horrible burden of having to protect everybody. So I can let go of this horrible burden of having to protect the guy who I feel is committing this holocaust."

I respond: "You're speaking to me more directly about this. I'm feeling it and it's becoming clearer and clearer." My acknowledgement of feeling his struggle with him, helps encourage Phillip's associations, and helps him to continue the mourning process in which he faces the burden and rage he feels in relation to protecting his father, even while his father keeps hurting him and distancing from him. In this dream of the father transference element, you can see that he is attached to the castrating and wounding father, which he fears he might find in me, as he projects his father into me. In the dream, he is placed in a mental hospital and I am a doctor. I'm dressed in a white robe, like a medical doctor, and I'm ordering electroshock.

In his associations to the dream, Phillip speaks of shock treatment as related to his father's castrating "put downs" that feel like "shocks" to his very sense of being, as he responds to his father's nonverbal pleas for emotional contact and closeness. Just as he responds to the mute cry from his father, sensing the hurt and neglected child in his father that is craving contact in its sealed off state, he gets bludgeoned by his father's sadistic verbal assaults, coming in the form of derision. For example, before he goes on a camping trip, his father snidely comments, in front of the entire family (mother and three siblings): "He won't make the mountain climb. He's gotten flabby and out of shape!" The entire meaning of the mountain climb and camping trip is ignored by his father or not received at all by him. The father turns a very meaningful experience of his son (one which has begun to have spiritual implications) into a joke. Phillip is furious, and feels impotent and humiliated. In his dream, he makes himself even more impotent, matching his psychic level of impotence in the face of his father, by giving himself the role of a patient in the mental hospital. I become the phallic woman doctor, or the sadistic father, attacking him with shocks, from on high. I'm distant and officious in the dream, so any sense of warm or empathic connection between us is frozen off. He has lost his holding mother, whom he consciously experiences in the room with me and is left with an alienated and castrating father figure.

Discussing this dream in treatment allows Phillip to question his distrust with me. He has always consciously yearned to trust me. He desperately feels the need to unburden himself and surrender to me, yet his internal bad object (the split off castrating father's sadism) colors the situation at an unconscious level. His dream brings his bad object projection into consciousness. As he consciously faces this inner demon and differentiates it from me, he sighs with relief. Often in mourning loss or disappointment deep body sighs open up. As he opens to a fuller mode of breathing he begins to clear the channels to his heart.

SEPARATING AND POSITIVE SUFFERING

The dream shows that Phillip has an unconscious wish that is in contradiction to his conscious wish for me to be different than his father. Unconsciously he has wished to recreate the intensity of his connection to the internal bad object, which on the higher symbolic level exists as an introject, an introject of the intrusive father of the past and the belittling father of the present. But now that Phillip's wish has been made conscious through the dream, he is able to relinquish some of his attachment to the bad object differentiating from my bad object role in the dream. His sigh reflects a letting go as do his tears, as he reencounters the pain of being trapped in this masochistic submission to his father's sadism. In feeling the pain consciously in the room with me, my presence helps to create a sense of a holding environment in which it is safe for him to open his anger towards his father. He also begins to distinguish surrendering to feeling pain, which invites compassion from myself and eventually from Phillip himself towards himself, from a masochistic state of submission that recreates a position of castration. Also he is ready to see how his guilt towards his father influences his relations with women, who become displacements for his father, just as I become at times.

Phillip had been pushing women away at points of intimacy, causing a self-punitive submission. As he faces his guilt, Phillip begins to set limits on the time he spends with his father, and he stands up to his father when his father insults his current girlfriend. However, he then returns to a backlash of grief, feeling intense regret in relation to his father, always wishing he could get close to him, rather than working so hard to separate from him. Each backlash into grief and loss after separation requires mourning. He mourns both his own loss and that of his father, feeling a depressive position concern, growing out of his former unconscious guilt, a guilt that can now be confronted, transforming from a personified internal demon into a conglomeration of feelings and thoughts. His paranoid position state of mind transforms into a depressive position mentality.

THE CHILD WITHIN

Throughout progressive states of mourning in treatment, Phillip encounters dream images, fantasies, and memories of himself as a child at various stages in his life. Through this journey, he is able to rediscover a spontaneous self in his interior world that had been numbed out and buried. However, before this child within could be discovered Phillip had to disengage himself from a projective and introjective identification defense that he sublimely engaged in when confronted with his father. Before Phillip could connect with conscious feeling with his child self, he had to experience how much he had projected his own child self into his father and into the image of his father, while he introjected the father's sealed off child self into himself. New encounters with his father brought this up. He would report these encounters to me from the couch, with an increasing sense of emotional agony as he conveyed this information to me. The sense of trust he was feeling in relation to me seemed to help him open to the anguish of these encounters. The projective and introjective operations of his psyche were being reinforced by his agonized longing to bypass the barriers between himself and his father, and to finally reach a place of closeness that could be sustained. This was never to happen, but moments of portended contact kept arousing his desire, a desire which had passionate longing endowed within it.

Phillip was passionately striving to reach his father. But unable to do so, he attempted to rescue his father from himself, taking the burden of responsibility into himself that consciously he knew was his father's. He protected his father from any retaliatory comment when his father attacked him. He protected his father from any open confrontations of his father's hostility. And beyond this protection, which may have also been a protection from any of his own unconscious assaults on his oedipal rival, he also attempted to rescue his father from himself. In colloquial, pop psychology terminology, this might be called "enabling" or "co-dependency." Phillip repeatedly suffered the pain of the disconnection between both he and his father, and within himself, while his father was taken off the hook. He felt the grief of the disconnection, above and beyond his father's active attacks. In his anger he would see his father as pathetic. Such conscious anger would help him in his mourning process, since unconscious anger had blocked the process. But for a long while he also stayed trapped in his longings to make it different between himself and his father. Although he would protest that he couldn't rescue his father from himself, because his father had to take responsibility for himself, Phillip continued to attempt to rescue, protect, and take care of his father. He wanted to control what he couldn't control, and despite his awareness of this, and how he got stuck in his own attempts at control, he would break down in agonies of despair and grief when sensing the neglected and lonely child within his father. He would rationalize away his anger by saying: "How can I be angry at him? He's just a child!" And he would continue to get hurt.

However, increasingly, his father appeared to him as a spiteful child, who was running away from contact out of a profound fear. Gradually, Phillip saw his father less as a threatening power of paternal castration, and increasingly as a small boy who is attacking out of impotence and fear. In his first year of treatment, he recalls a memory of his father trying to make a toast to a relative at a birthday or anniversary party. Distinctly etched in his memory is a scene of continual assaultive interruptions by his grandmother – his father's mother – who mocked, jeered and undermined her son in his efforts to make a toast, to the point that her son, Phillip's father, stopped dead in his tracks and with an air of impotence, defeat, and suppressed rage cut off his own attempts to speak positive words of reverence and respect. Phillip observed his father withdraw bitterly into silence. Phillip was never to forget this memory, which highlights his father as the victim rather than the active perpetrator of castration. His heart sobbed out his grief as he recalled this defeated attempt to love in his father. His empathy and compassion massaged the wounded soul of his father in his mind. Recalling this memory allowed him to be on the side of his father, while also allowing him to understand the source of his father's own pain. He could see vividly from this historical scene that his father had been attacked by his mother in the same manner as his father compulsively attacked Phillip.

This memory allowed Phillip to comprehend that his father's behavior was a compulsive reenactment and not just a free choice. Thus, he could feel some forgiveness while not denying the pain his father had always caused him. He realized that his father stayed in a victimized position with his compulsions – never seeking help or facing his own behavior and its effects. The grief over the pain in the memory, which he sobbed out with compassion for both his father and himself, also allowed him to see that his father had a child within him suffering in a masochistic state, never freeing itself to suffer the mournful pain of loss from the trauma itself – always remaining a soul imprisoned in compulsive reenactment. Knowing this helped Phillip to disentangle his own child self from that of his father. Such a separating act, in which he partially took back the projected child self within himself, which he formerly had mentally placed in his father, was supported by his willingness to share the anguished memory with me. The act of sharing allowed an observing ego perspective to be mobilized. Separation proceeded within as Phillip relinquished the introjected child of his father, which had been more psychically incorporated as a visceral and dynamic psychic presence than fully symbolized as a cognitively contained internalization within himself. By viewing his father as the other in the memory he released him to be himself. He could empathize and identify with his father, but he no longer had to become his father or have his father become him. His inner child self, with all its true self-spontaneity and evolving potential, could begin to be free.

MEMORIES OF THE CHILD WITHIN

During the second year of treatment, as Phillip lets go of his neurotic attempts to control things between himself and his father and takes care of the child within himself, he feels a conscious anger towards his father that is part of a mourning and separation process: "Did I say I'm not angry? I'm fucking pissed! I want my life back." He realizes how much of his life he has spent protecting his father. Along with the anger is an open yearning. Yet he openly faces both anger and disillusionment, as prompted when remembering his father's sadistic demands on him to perform beyond his limits as a child. He recalls that once he fell down a ski slope and injured his leg because his father brought him to a mountain slope that far surpassed his ability at age 7 to ski. As he faces these painful feelings of hurt and rage that accompanied disillusionment, Phillip can bring the yearning behind the disillusionment into his more current adult relationships, with his new girlfriend and with me.

Having ended several relationships with women during treatment, he is now in a relationship with a woman to whom he surrenders more fully. He lets go of the self-torture of asking: "Is this the right woman?" As he sustains the relationship he deepens his involvement and finds he can communicate with this woman at a deeper emotional and spiritual level. For the first time, he says he feels what it is like to truly make love, to feel deep yearnings from his heart during lovemaking, without holding back and keeping part of himself in reserve. This opening to love through a sexual relationship with a woman emerges in parallel with his emotional surrender to me in treatment (after earlier anger within a negative transference). I interpret this as his talking to his father and he sobs out more grief and love for his father: "I love him tenderly and vehemently!" After opening to love for his father, he can mourn. Just before opening up his child self, he says: "The deeper I get in understanding and feeling this stuff, the more I need you." He is sobbing and crying and sobbing as he says these words to me, the same level of longing and love and grief that he formerly expressed about his frustrated yearnings for his father. Expressing this loving bond with me directly after expressing rage, accusation and hurt in the negative transference, allows him to face his "pissed," conscious feeling of anger at his father, now having a bond with me and with his girlfriend that can allow more steps towards separation from his father. This separation allows Phillip's own child self to emerge and to separate from the child inside of his father.

His first image of himself as a child emerges as an association to a picture of himself at 3 years old. "I was pure me, pure personality! I wasn't hiding then." He says this as he feels free for the first time to choose his state of mind: "I can be myself at work." Phillip used to feel enslaved to the bosses at work, who psychically served as father displacements. But in this third year of treatment, he feels he can choose to be himself. He has mourned and separated from his father "bosses." He has mourned and separated from his father. Just after this memory of himself as a 3 year old, in the same session (the same session as when he acknowledges his anger towards his father), he shares a dream of a 4-year-old child. The dream is simply: "I was holding the hand of a 4 or 5 year old."

The memory of this dream connects with a deep sadness within him, the kind of grief sadness that he has cried out in his expressions of love, gratitude, and need for me. Perhaps it is the 4- or 5-year-old spontaneous self in him that was able to emerge from the release of this sadness and release of the internal father connected to this emotional depth of grief and love.

After these steps towards separation through mourning Phillip has a backlash into his fears, just as he has a backlash after closeness with his new girlfriend, with whom he has just moved into a new house. He fears that if his past is revealed to his girlfriend, his inner shame will be exposed and will "mess up" his new relationship. He fears he will lose all his girlfriends and will return to a position that has in the past compelled him to call a prostitute and ask her to urinate on him. Phillip's wishes to be dirty become conscious, and he realizes he connects being dirty with sin. He is endlessly seeking redemption for his dirtiness. Instead he expects punishment for sin, since he is identified with dirt and messing up.

At this time he reports a secretly guarded terror, a terror that he will lose his lover, his job, me, and everything, and ultimately end up homeless, rooting around in a garbage can. When someone is "let go" at work he projects his sense of worthlessness onto this stranger and imagines himself being fired. However, it is not yet clear why he fears he will lose my love, and this is to come out in the erotic transference work, in which his guilt over incestuous desires is expressed. (This guilt appears when such desires are expressed in compulsive behaviors with prostitutes, looking at women on the street, engaging in frequent sexual fantasy of a masturbatory nature – all of which make him feel full of shame in relation to his girlfriend.)

Once Phillip expresses these fears he can go further in mourning again. He reaches significant depressive stage feelings of a capacity to feel and understand regret about hurting the one he has loved in the past, guilt about seducing them with promises and then abandoning and leaving them. In a dream he takes gasoline, pumps it into a garbage can, and creates a potential explosion, which results in a fire destroying a house that has been abandoned. He associates to the dream in terms of his past misdeeds: smoking, drinking, smoking marijuana, and enjoying erotic fantasy play with call girls. In the dream, he sees himself as disowning responsibility as he moves ahead with his life, and leaves the resulting destruction from his past behavior behind, only to blow up in the face of those women he has left behind. Consciously, this comes after he has contacted a former girlfriend to say "goodbye" and realizes he has caused her "a lot of heartache!" He had told her he loved her when with her because he felt alone and needed her, but then he left her because he concluded he wasn't "in love" with her. "It wasn't right," he says. He calls her to say he is moving in with his new girlfriend and leaving the neighborhood where this former girlfriend lives. He sobs and cries out the grief of his regret, feeling the depressive pain so poetically spoken of by Melanie Klein when writing about depressive position grief as hurting the loved one. He feels the guilt of hurting a woman who has given him love, particularly since unconsciously she represents the primal parent imagined to be forsaken by growing up and separating (Loewald 1979).

Through surrendering to grief, as well as to new possibilities for love, Phillip opens new childhood memories. Formerly in a pathological mourning state, memories were blocked from consciousness. However, as Phillip successfully mourns in treatment memories open up. The repressed wishes behind the memories open up. He recalls himself at 7: being himself, but being too good in class – being the golden boy" as he plays to his parents' narcissistic images for approval. Then he recalls himself at 10, when the burying of his spontaneous true self became severe. In May 1997, he says: "I see myself in a memory. I see myself in uniform on the Little League playing field, naturally cutting off my feelings at this time. I see myself choking back tears, suppressing my need to cry, I feel strangled at the throat, the block in the energy field of the body beginning to happen there in my throat."

EROTIC TRANSFERENCE

The erotic transference evolves in stages, revealing oedipal level erotic desires, which tell a story about Phillip's longings for the oedipal mother as well as the fears of her. Earlier fantasies about the preoedipal mother have already been discussed and the preoedipal fears interact with the oedipal. All this emerges increasingly as the once all-encompassing father is increasingly mourned. There is no clear ending of one transference and the emergence of another, and no clear ending of one object's mourning and then the beginning of mourning for another. They all overlap! However, there are shades of developmental progression, as the character structure of Phillip's personality unravels. Earlier memories of the preoedipal mother holding Phillip in her arms, while he was seated in his mother's lap, with his cheek and forehead pressed blissfully against her face, also bring frightening associations.

Although the most manifest memory is of the pain and rage of Phillip's father's intrusion on his idyllic Garden of Eden scene with his mother, when I interpreted the father's intrusion as a possible protection from what might become, in his mind, an overstimulating and overwhelming merger with his mother, the following fantasy is evoked. Phillip pictures himself as a 2 year old, pinned to the ceiling because his mother's emotional needs balloon out and expand to occupy the whole room which he and she share in his 2-year-old memory and fantasy. He realizes when he has this fantasy that his fears extended beyond his father, who has always been most manifest in his adult thoughts, and extend to a primal fear of his preoedipal mother as having emotional needs that he can never fulfill. Without his father's rescuing intrusion, Phillip fears he might end up in a life-threatening situation of paralysis and helplessness with his small 2-year-old self, pinned to the ceiling by his mother's ballooning emotional needs.

Such preoedipal fears in relation to his mother move into the background again as his frustrated yearnings for his father return. His rage also emerges towards the sadistic side of his father who, like the "demon lover," neglected to touch him with tenderness and instead touched him with the pain of punishment. He recalls his father spanking him with his hand and with a belt, as he tested his father's limits at 5 years old. He cries with a deep sobbing anguish as he recalls his father hurting and humiliating him, while never touching him tenderly or holding him tenderly. Such memories interacted with memories of his father's neglectful placement of him on a ski slope at 7, when his father encouraged him to do what was way beyond his capacities at that young age. He weeps, but feels rage as well. He believes that his father has a false idea of manhood that continually tortured him, leading to his own masochistic character mode of self-torture. He had fallen on the ski slope and broke his leg at the knee, causing intense pain physically, but even more emotionally. He feels overwhelmed with humiliation again – as in his spanking memories.

Interspersed with renewed mourning of his father, through such memories, are erotic transference episodes with me, which begin to reveal more about Phillip's mother's character. Phillip imagines seeing me behind a doorway with my legs crossed. Associations to this fantasy lead back to a memory of seeing his mother sitting in a swimsuit by a swimming pool, where he can see her crotch showing through her crossed legs. Then he fantasizes seeing me in a red dress, and peeing on me as he has done with a prostitute. He associates the erupting fire in the wastebasket in his dream with sexual guilt. According to Phillip, he had enacted this fantasy with a prostitute to "break a taboo," an incest taboo. He ends up feeling guilt if he acts out the fantasy. In Kleinian terms, when he spoils his internal father and internal mother he spoils himself. When he then has an outbreak of herpes he imagines it is a sign of sin, the sin of killing off his father by having sex with his mother, as he sees both myself in his fantasy, and the prostitute as mother displacements.

Phillip describes the enactment of the prostitute peeing on him, which he wishes to act out with me as a way of enacting his "worthlessness." But his sense of worthlessness is also a self-imposed punishment to avoid consciousness of destructive wishes towards the father and his own violence in "breaking the incest taboo" as he fantasies having sex with an all-powerful phallic mother. Eros can lead to death, as he is captured by the sirens of the mother as phallic demon lover. His herpes leads to thoughts of AIDS, a fantasy of a deserved punishment for his "dark" oedipal wishes, as he kills his father with the fantasy and enacts breaking the incest taboo.

Phillip also had desires to exhibit his erotic fantasies about me to others. While having a phone session, he imagines I am using a wireless phone, where others could listen in, and has thoughts of sharing his erotic wishes towards me in a therapy group he has been in with me.

It is after he expresses his wish to make love to me in the same position as he had recently done with his fiancée ("pinching my nipples as he lay behind me and inside of me"), he reports the dream of leaving behind an exploding fire in a garbage can, with the result of others being annihilated in its wake. His terror of punishment for his erotic transference wishes is also at the level of annihilation anxiety or abandonment anxiety, as he imagines destroying and abandoning others (his parents) to be with his fiancée, who represents the desired mother. The sequence in the garbage can fire dream seems to reflect his guilt reaction and displaced punishment for his erotic wishes. He has trouble having compassion for himself, saying that he has felt worthless deep down; perhaps another punishment fantasy for his oedipal wishes. He mentally lacerates himself with his internal father (superego) saying to him, as he lies on my couch: "Real men don't lie on a couch sobbing." Essentially he castrates himself as he is melting into a deep level of emotional surrender with me, bringing his father into the room between us (acting out the role of the father) as in the fantasy-memory of his father interrupting as his mother holds him in her arms with much tenderness, at 2 years old.

After the dream of the trashcan exploding in the third year of treatment (April 1997), he says: "Someone will find out about these places in me that I don't find acceptable [shame side of exhibitionistic wish]. Then my house will be on fire. I'll lose everything. I'll be deeply unworthy of anybody's love."

"That's a terrifying thought," I respond.

"I'm afraid I'll ruin things with Linda [his fiancée]. My fantasies will take hold and I'll stare too many times at other women."

Phillip is overly condemning of himself, as when he berates himself for having been able to cleverly manage positive associations with both adults and with the forbidden fast crowd during adolescence, as if he was merely guilty of deception. He masochistically indulges in superego assaults that prolong his sadomasochistic relationship with his internal father. The erotic charge appears in a libidinal suffering, which differs but can interact with his developmentally healthy mournful suffering. I interpret the distinction between the two modes of suffering in treatment. The masochistic suffering is related to an enactment from the closed system part of his psyche, while the mournful suffering is from the open part of his psyche, a place of "transitional space." The masochistic suffering is a form of pathological mourning.

Phillip continues his masochistic involvement with his superego by condemning himself for the natural male pastime of watching women – as the song goes, "Standing on the corner, watching all the girls go by." A majority of men do it, but Phillip condemns himself for it even if he doesn't do it in front of his girlfriend. He expresses fears that his girlfriend won't love him anymore (as he has feared I won't love him anymore) if she finds out about his erotic past and about his erotic fantasy life. Yet in reality his fiancée (now his wife) had been very accepting of his fantasy life, especially when he can share it with her in their sexual relationship.

"I'll be entirely transparent to her. She won't love me any more. I don't know if I fear that with you any more." He seems to trust me now as he has risked sharing his "dirtiest" fantasies and memories. I've become safe, but he fears being abandoned for erotic desires that are there in the transference on an unconscious level. This transference emerges in the fantasy that if he is not an infant suckling at my breast, but rather has sexual desires for me. He fears I will turn into a dragon's head (Medusa) and become very dangerous (the primitive maternal superego).

Erotic wishes are dangerous because they involve the threat of betraying the other with another love. Also, however, they involve murderous wishes towards his father. Phillip tells me that his girlfriend (Linda) is reprieving him with love, after he has had his heart frozen by his former sexual exploits. The fire explosion dream represents his destructiveness towards the women in his past, but he is able to open up to love again, as Linda, his fiancée, touches him deeply with a poetic and loving birthday card. He feels unworthy, but in spite of this is open enough to take in her love. He believes this is possible because of his mourning process on the couch, and he articulates this connection to me. When his fiancée gives him the birthday card, he sobs and opens his heart, just as he has sobbed and opened himself on my couch. His capacity to mourn has enabled him to quickly melt from a frozen state when he is touched with love. He allows himself to be touched. He can open his heart. He no longer is compelled to distance through character defense.

For the first time Phillip tells me he is able to feel loved for his true self – because he has been able to expose his whole self to me and has still been accepted by me in the "therapeutic object relationship" (Grunes 1984). Phillip conveys to me that this trusting experience with me allows him to accept the love of his girlfriend in full, rather than pushing her away, as he has pushed others away in the past, which has contributed to him feeling unworthy. He begins to understand that the exposing of his guilt-ridden fantasies has allowed him to feel more acceptable. It is through the grief expression in the mourning process that these guilt-ridden wishes have emerged and become conscious. When in contact with grief affects, he has been able to articulate and symbolize these wishes. His unconscious guilt has become conscious in part through his discoveries within the dream of the garbage can explosion. In sobbing out his grief to me I have become a transitional object on the route to an in-depth love relationship with his girlfriend, who becomes his wife by the fourth year of treatment. His erotic desires for me allow him to understand his depressive guilt towards lovers of the past and the oedipal guilt related to his internal parents.

NEGATIVE TRANSFERENCE AND EROTIC TRANSFERENCE

Phillip's negative transference appeared in intricate relationship to his erotic transference. It is reflective of the father's devaluing judgements that have become internalized and have become part of his superego. During the second year of treatment, Phillip had wrestled with extreme self-doubts that emerged then along with erotic transference wishes; wishes which cast him in the role of an inadequate and unappreciated love object. Tied in with his erotic desires are wishes for rescue.

One day during the second year of treatment, Phillip comes into a session, lies on the couch, and begins to express a feeling of anger. Phillip seems to be feeling the surface of a deep sense of rage, which has unconsciously been with him for a lifetime. The transferential nature of his anger becomes clear both to Phillip and myself. The degree of vulnerability tied in with this transference has been a key factor in allowing Phillip to move further into the evolution of his developmental mourning process.

Phillip enters the session proclaiming an injured sense of resentment. He has called me over the weekend to verify our appointment times for that week, since his business traveling for work disrupted any fixed session schedule. I verified the times for that week and then, apparently, suggested for the future that Phillip might write down the times for himself. When he comes into the next psychoanalytic session he was furious with me for my comment, which reminds him to note down the session times. Phillip says that he is hesitating to bring up how angry he is because he expects I will give him some rational explanation for my behavior, which would not satisfy him at all; some explanation like that I was very busy too and had many patients to deal with, and could not always be calling him to remind him of his times. Despite his articulated fear of expressing his anger and getting a brush off, he launches into what the experience had felt like for him. He is angry that I should imply in any way that he is not holding up his end of things. Didn't I realize how much of a commitment he had made to me? Why didn't I appreciate him, and appreciate the amount of time and money he was investing in his analysis? Underneath this accusation addressed towards me there is a deep sense of doubt in Phillip about his capacity to commit to anyone, a doubt, which he tries to disavow by turning it into an accusation against me. He says that I doubt him, which is an obvious projection of his own self-doubt that is becoming increasingly conscious.

The self-doubt opens up clearly as the session continued. Phillip tells me that he had just pulled back from a relationship with a woman – the second relationship he had since the beginning of treatment) – which was a familiar place for him. He uses the word "of course" to describe his behavior that obviously disappointed him: "Of course I couldn't sustain it," he said, with a tone of sarcastic self-depreciation – a form of self-torture and self-punishment he knew well. He had decided to only see this woman on weekends, instead of more often as he had formerly done. He called this a compromise. He had been unsure of his love for this woman all along, but a sense of gratitude towards her for a form of counseling she had given him had led him to date her, and to find temporarily, through her, a way of running from his fears of being worthless and unlovable. Now, he couldn't sustain the level of contact he had initiated. During this period Phillip had been continually preoccupied with fantasies of seducing other women. He chooses the word "seduce" with deliberate determination as he speaks of this, and even says that he needs to mispronounce the word "seduces" in terms of gender, calling himself a "seductress," "because it had a more electromagnetic sound."

Phillip calls himself a "Casanova." He says that he is returning to another familiar pattern of wanting to lure women into his trap to be soothed with sex, which he does particularly when he is feeling bad about himself and fears he is unlovable. He would invite a woman (one at a time) over to dinner, cook for her, say flattering things to her, and then seduce her into a sexual encounter, during which he would perform further by showing off his artful skills as a lover. All along he would "turn on the charm," and become the golden child that he has performed for his parents (who never appreciated him enough).

After relating this compulsive self narrative to me, Phillip then confesses that he has entertained other thoughts about me, thoughts which give us a clue as to the nature of his rage, and his sense of self-injury, in the beginning of this session. In the midst of his Casanova "seductress" fantasies, he had the insistent thought that if I, "Susan," would just give him what he needs he wouldn't have to go through these elaborate seduction scenes with other women. His thoughts declare that if I would just give him what he needs his persistent sense of insatiable "craving" (both sexual and emotional) would cease. He says that I hold the key to his hunger and desire in my hands. He reports (maintaining an observing ego and therapeutic alliance) that only I would become his real lover, all would be right with the world. He has shared frequent fantasies with me of coming to the session and undressing in front of me. He informs me that he often focuses self-consciously, in his own mind, on the kind of underwear he would wear when he comes to an analytic session, playing with the thought in his mind that he would be revealing his underwear to me when he comes to see me. Interlaced with such thoughts are others concerning himself being the size of a 3 or 4 year old, peeking at me from behind a screen as I uncross and open my legs and then recross them again. He would then become adult size in his fantasy, and would be aroused to come over and make love to me. He associates from this fantasy to a memory of being about 8 years old, and it is then that he sees his mother by the swimming pool, playing bridge with her friends. Her legs are spread apart, while wearing a bathing suit, and as an 8-year-old boy he could see his mother's pubic hair. His conscious memory is of feeling revulsion at this sight, not having wanted to see his mother as sexual. Yet, he can't get the scene out of his mind, and it comes up repeatedly in transference fantasies in relation to me.

It is accompanied by another memory of seeing his mother naked when he is about 7. Generally his parents had kept their bedroom door closed, unless it was all right for him and his sisters to enter. But one day he runs into his parents' bedroom, excited to tell his parents something, and the door is open. He enters through a door that had been left open, and all of a sudden his mother is screaming at him. His mother had been standing naked, while his father poked his finger into her stomach in a gesture indicating his disapproval of her having put on weight. The parents' mutual antagonism may have distracted them from noticing that their bedroom door was open. Perhaps, however, there was some unconscious wish for exhibitionism on the parents' part. In any case, Phillip remembers feeling deeply hurt, terrified and injured by his mother's assaultive and accusatory screams. He may have felt that his secret incest wishes, as manifested in thoughts about her at the poolside or in his fantasies of peeking at her legs from behind a screen, were being harshly rebuked by his mother's scream. Although his mother could not realistically know of his thoughts and fantasies, his unconscious was not rational, and the tone of accusation in the maternal scream felt condemning. He fled the scene, running into a corner in the basement to cry, with all his confusion about his sexual wishes and his shattered beliefs with his own omnipotence churning frantically inside of him. The reliving of such scenes reemerged in the transference with me. For example, in terms of his sexual voyeurism and arousal, and also in terms of the fantasy of the feared phallic (monster) mother, I was often perceived as potentially turning into a dragon's head the minute he would have sexual thoughts about me. His incest guilt is evident in this fear and his mother's screams still lived on in him as a severe accusation of his crime. The tone of accusation in the mother's scream would also be reenacted by Phillip. Her tone would become his when he was in a state of emotional blackmail, in which he attempts to provoke guilt in me for not rescuing him from his life. At this time of treatment (second year), I was seen as guilty of not rescuing him from his insecurities by having the fantasized magic sex with him, the sex that would soothe and cure him.

According to Phillip's memories, after running from his parents' bedroom at 7 years old, he ran downstairs to a corner of the basement to cry. As he did this, he was conscious that his mother would come after him to comfort him, which she did. Swiftly, with only the time it took her to cloak herself in a robe, his mother descended the stairs to the basement, took him into her arms, held him, and soothed his forehead. She also apologized to him for screaming at him when she had been at fault in leaving the door open. In this way, hurt, anger, and accusation could become associated, for Phillip, with warmth, comfort and security in relation

to his mother's comforting body. But sex and naked bodies would remain dangerous, as they were associated with many scary times, including an early memory of
being one and a half, when he remained in a room with his parents making love.
This primal scene memory made Phillip cry and feel miserable as he remembered
it. Such an upsetting memory became joined with the 7-year-old memory of
his mother screaming at him in her bedroom, and then with the swimming pool
memory of seeing his mother's pubic hair at 8 years old.

So today, in the erotic transference of his analytic treatment, he would yearn for
my naked, soft and comforting body to soothe away all his cares. However, his
superego's reaction to the incest threat manifests as an antilibidinal demon lover
theme, that of sexual seduction and arousal leading to possession, entrapment,
sadistic assault, and unknown dangers. I became his transferential mother who can
turn threateningly into a dragon's head. Perhaps my visage turning to that of a
dragonhead is precisely one that captures the self-deflating effect of his mother's
intense scream when in a state of shock. As such it returns to his thoughts repeatedly and is projected onto me as a potential form that I might take if he crosses
some boundary and taboo and should become too sexual in his relationship to me.
As the memory from which the fantasy is derived returns through associations,
Phillip is, for the first time, in a position to mourn the grief of the overwhelming
experience of that childhood time with his mother. Then the split in the maternal
image can be healed, the split in which the warm comforting good mother might
turn, at any moment, into a monster dragon mother (since his sexual wishes in the
transference can appear at any moment).

Further, as Phillip reveals his wishes to enter my body through sex to find the
warm good mother, he begins to experience, in the present moment, his intense
and formerly unconscious yearning to reach beyond my vaginal doorway into the
land of my uterus or womb. He imagines being safely nestled inside a soft warm
womb that he would find within me. The combination and intermingling of his
oedipal and preoedipal wishes, as they manifest in the transference, become
evident. Phillip had no problem acknowledging such wishes, which would become
another avenue to his mourning process, as the fantasy captured the secure good
object he held within, and its holding environment atmosphere. Only through
contact with this good internal object, which could live vividly in the present
through his contact with me in an analytic session, could he find the psychic
warmth and love needed to allow grief affect and memory to be felt intensely while
being contained and tolerable. Thus, a memory of being emotionally overwhelmed
and overstimulated did not have to become sealed off in the psyche as a trauma.
Consequently, the mourning process can unfold, and Phillip does not need to
become the captive of the trap of pathological mourning. The normal splitting of
the mother image can be captured at a symbolic level (the holding mother and
the dragon mother), rather than remaining at a visceral level as a dynamic and
intrusive internal object. The demon lover mother theme need not become a demon
lover complex.

Phillip's tendency is to arrest his consciousness after expressing his wish, but as

I asked him to associate to his wish to have sexual intercourse with me so as to enter my womb, we discover that I change in his mind from a nurturing and all-encompassing womb to a railway tunnel. Then he becomes conscious of the terror of being entrapped inside of me, as if entering an endless labyrinth. Since Phillip also had told me that he pictured himself as half a man and half a beast when he had these bestial fantasies of having sex with me, my own associations then led to the mythic archetype of the man who fights the half man and half-beast Minotaur in the labyrinth of the Greek myth. Would Phillip have to fight the bestial part of him as a rite of passage into mature manhood, in order to separate from his internal and transferential mother and to navigate past the jealous beast father, who also represents a highly instinctual part of himself? Perhaps his capacity to symbolize all that he does in relation to this unconscious (and perhaps collective unconscious) range of experience is the critical separation process that can allow him to live out the flight in fantasy, as he lives out the incestuous sex in fantasy, through the deep grief affects of the mourning process. Throughout all these memories and associations Phillip sobs out his grief upon my couch. (James Grotstein 1996 has written about the half-man and half-beast experience.)

Throughout the session in which the hurt scene of injury is expressed through a negative transference accusation, Phillip experiences the manifest conflicts that would lead to later insight into the unconscious fears and wishes behind these conflicts. In this particular session, I interpret the surface frustration that Phillip creates and recreates time and again as he wishes to reach an emotional surrender with a woman (as well as with his father); a surrender in which closeness and passion could both be contained, tolerated and reciprocated. Yet, he has continually failed to be able to commit himself to the women who existed in flesh, not just fantasy. Many fears had held him back and made him pull away, which provoked the despair and self-criticism he expressed in this second year treatment session. The most conscious fears he related to his relationship with his father, where he felt he was always tantalized with the promise of love and intimacy, which always turned demonically into its opposite: a sadistic attack on his self-esteem or a hostile, cold and rigid withdrawal. His father had played the part of the demon lover in Phillip's mind for a long time, fulfilling the traumatizing character of an "exciting and rejecting object," as Ronald Fairbairn (1952) might see him. But behind this conscious drama, in the theater of his mind (McDougall 1980), is a more deeply buried image that gradually awakens through the erotic and negative transference, where the oedipal and preoedipal fantasy mothers appeared: both part and whole object mothers. In this session with the negative transference accusation, I could speak to Phillip of his backlash fear reaction to closeness in terms of how he had been pulling back from commitment, rather than sharing the hurt and vulnerable place in him from which his state of rage and accusation came. With me he has been able to share the hurt, a hurt with its deep sense of narcissistic injury – the injury of being too small to satisfy mommy, leading to his transference accusation against me that I'm not giving him what he wants and needs.

He calls himself worthless for his defensive and compulsive sexualized behaviors: such as acting out sexual fantasies with call girls, or inviting women to dinner in order to play a Casanova who seduces women into sex without any intention to get to know them or to develop a full and committed relationship. Drinking and smoking pot have been avenues to creating the level of sexual fantasy that aroused and encouraged such behavior. Phillip condemns himself for these acts, which involve treating women as part objects or fantasies, rather than as whole persons. He realizes that his behavior with women reproduced his father's behavior with him. After all he had felt like his father's toy (or part object/self object), an extension of his father's wishes for an idealized "golden child," or an extension of his father's neurotic need for sadomasochism in his role of the castrated child or whipping boy. He had played to his father's images and taken his father's insults. In order to avoid repeating his father's form of aggression, he would often get into a masochistic position with women where he would be subjected to insults from them. Failing to defend himself, because of his fears of his own aggression, he would withdraw from women, and then suffer the guilt of that form of betrayal. In his mourning process, he enters the moral order through his ability to consciously suffer (Miller 1989). It is a positive form of suffering in that he is consciously facing and owning the hurt he causes others.

Phillip pulls back from one woman from whom he had sought comfort, only to find she isn't the right woman for him, after he has proclaimed love to her: "I thought I loved her. I just wasn't in love with her!" He then suffers the agony of his depressive position pain: "I've caused her a lot of heartache!" But before he can feel that much for her he has to feel the hurt and misery of his own vulnerability, as he did in the negative transference in treatment in relation to me as his analyst. In a state of open needing, there seems to be no adequate object of love that could fulfill him, especially, he thought, if his female analyst remained his analyst and didn't become his lover. As he shares some of his wounded pride and self-contempt, he begins to expose and share the shame areas in himself that he had hidden from others by withdrawing from them, leaving them bewildered as to why he would abruptly pull back from them and aborts a relationship in which he has seemed so loving. He exposes this wound in himself to me – this area of shame and frustrated need, which could erupt in rage and accusation. He begins to come out of hiding. He begins to relax the rigid and reflexive defense maneuvers that he had used to ward off exposure to others in the past. Being in emotional contact with me in that area of shame and hurt that he had formerly kept sealed off from contact, he now has the chance to move his depressive position grieving process forward – now mourning the loss of self–as well as of object connection. Thus he opens to new capacities to love, reaching a depth of openness in love, which would become increasingly fulfilling. Finally he reached the point in his next intimate relationship with a woman where he could engage such a deep level that he could say in ecstasy: "I finally know what it feels like to really make love!"

The bonus of this journey into fulfilling love and sustained intimacy turned out to be a whole dimension of spiritual journey and enlightenment that is to accompany and flow out of his psychological journey. In this critical session

Phillip was able to own his aggression. This makes it possible for him to surrender to a position of loving and needing–without consciousness of the aggression one can neither repair nor surrender.

Chapter 10

The case of Phillip, Part 2
The spiritual evolution

Half a year prior to his wedding, during the later third year of treatment, Phillip begins to enter a new spiritual terrain that emerges along with his erotic transference and its analysis. First, he confesses his castration and mutilation fears in relation to a fantasy of entering me sexually and finding I have sharp genitals, which could cause him intense pain. He then shares with me the vision of a clairvoyant who had seen two dark spots on his heart. It is there in the wound of his heart that he senses the root of his "motherload of grief." It is there that he locates the psychophysical source of critical losses from his past, and from that which he believes to have been losses in past lives. Phillip tells me: "I have to make the losses manifest and release from inside of me. I think you saw my wounded state when I came to see you and was shut down. I think you saw my need to grieve and release the generations of pain. I'm trying to do it with you. When I came to you I think I was shut down around my emotions. It seemed it would be the end of me to let it out. But bit by bit I have been letting it out and finding it's safe!"

In this way, Phillip recounted to me his emotional task, which becomes a spiritual task as well. He declares: "So that's the task as I see it, to keep letting it out, and if my parents won't go along with me I guess that's how it has to be – lucky for me I have you. [*During a period of mournful disillusionment with his parents.*] It's lucky for me the world is a loving place. Everyone who sees the world as a cold, unfriendly place has just got it all wrong." Phillip's worldview transformed as he reconnected with an internal good object connection through mourning and transference work.

As Phillip mourns he has been giving up the idea of perfect communication. He comes to accept his parents' limitations. He develops an extreme sensitivity to blocks or obstacles in connection, for example, "clearing" several hours of emotional heaviness with his girlfriend when he neglects to call all day during a business trip. He speaks about his regret with her, apologizes, and in owning the depressive position pain of hurting the one he loves, he clears the blocked emotional communication between him and girlfriend. This sensitivity to interpersonal blocks is experienced in his body: "The other day there was a heaviness around my heart space. This rock, this weight, this heaviness feels like I have a need to make everything OK;" in this case to communicate with his girlfriend about the pain he caused her by not calling from abroad. He relates the body and interpersonal blocks to his psychic character defenses and maneuvers. He picks up his own neurotic denial: "On a subconscious level I'm pretending I don't have so much emotionally on the line."

A month earlier he had commented: "My subconscious will take the premise that I'm not worthy of love at face value, will take that premise and create conditions to attain that. Then it just becomes this vicious circle. I'm trying to break out of it. I feel deep down I'm not worthy of being loved by her. I have trouble staying connected, because disconnecting is a way of controlling my fear that I'll be rejected. I think that's a core belief in my belief system that's been passed down in my family for generations, and that's the one I'm here to heal."

Phillip feared that a compulsion to break away from sealed off areas of rage, hate and trauma would take over. Even to fantasize about women on the street becomes an expression of distractions that constantly threatened to pull him away from being present in his current relationships, particularly with his girlfriend and with me. He experiences it as a powerful drive within him to have fantasies of having sex with me, rather than being able to be emotionally present with me. From a spiritual and energetic perspective he declares that he has to give up his distracting compulsions toward masturbatory erotic fantasy to reach a "higher level of vibration."

Experiencing Phillip's fear, grief and compulsion, I tell him that he can't just discipline himself to give up fantasizing. It is serving a defensive purpose – warding off pain from the past – and his fantasies have meaning that need to be understood. From the perspective of compulsive fantasy as reenacted trauma, as well as the compulsion to release rage from that trauma in a symbolized form, it can be seen that Phillip suffered from a pathological mourning state, which perpetuated psychic conflict. Such a state was based on holding onto painful attachments from his past in which he eroticized both his love and his hate. These past relations had become internal object systems within the closed off areas of his psyche.[1] Phillip now felt extremely sensitive to being pulled away from being present in his life, or from intimacy with me from his work, or from his girlfriend by his compulsive modes of fantasy. Such fantasy was not free and spontaneous, but enacted a self-punitive drama through an obsessive preoccupation. This seemed to be a way of recreating his past and of closing off external relations as well as internal ones, with both their pleasurable and painful components. When he employed a call girl to pee on him in a red dress, and then fantasized about me doing this to him in a session, he was living out a formerly repressed oedipal drama, which had increasingly conscious preoedipal dimensions. Even lusting after women in the street through having erotic fantasies about them became a threat to his presence in the world and to his further development in intimacy with others, as well as with his own spiritual self, which now he could sense as being in relationship with God, when formerly he was not a "believer."

In the course of coming upon his soul and its spiritual journey, he encountered certain "past life" experiences, which had been largely responsible, in his opinion, for his current state of fear in relationship and for what I would describe as his internal state of pathological mourning. He shared such experience with me, at first hesitant as he projected a negative father transference onto me, and feared I would devalue his internal experience. Once I interpreted the father transference, which he was very much ready to realize himself, then he opened his "heart center" again and again.

Now he more fully surrenders to both me and to his girlfriend, and shares that which he had formerly feared to confide: "I'm scared if I tell you about a past life regression you'll try to fit it into a psychoanalytic framework – like a fantasy, delusion or escapism. I guess I fear these things or I wouldn't imagine you as making judgments like that."

I interpret that he may be speaking to his father, and he relaxes from this differentiating interpretation that allows him to separate me out in his mind from his father and from his father's fears and prejudices, as well as from his own. Then he proceeds to recount the journey of an early life spiritual experience of leaving his body. Following this he tells me of the past life regression experience that he had discovered under controlled conditions with a "past life regression" therapist. For my part, I was curious, open and somewhat excited to hear about any experience that had such an emotional impact on him, and I certainly did not wish to place blocks in the path of my own reception. Furthermore, I would never in any case have reduced extreme trauma to a mere unconscious fantasy manifestation, whether its emotional impact was felt to have stemmed from this life or any other one. And to see it as escapism or defense would have defeated the whole purpose of my being a conduit for his processing of mournful suffering due to pain, loss, and regret. As Phillip told me his experience I listened attentively, and there was no need for me to declare a belief or disbelief in the theory of past life regression. The main point is that he had experienced something that was vividly and profoundly real in an emotional sense. He was now making critical connections between overwhelming trauma related to severe object loss and the current load of grief he had been carrying around with him, until his gradual expression of it in his object relations psychoanalysis.

What Phillip discovered with his past life regression therapist was that he had lost a wife and child at a young age, the age of thirty, in a life that he lived two centuries ago. The pain of this loss had never been mourned, understood or released. He had closed down in a state of bitter despair, seriously disillusioned, terrified of ever loving or trusting again, until he died at about age fifty. This was the most primal shock to his being, a kind of inner earthquake that he discovered in his past life regression, although he said he also was aware of other lives he had lived. He described the recovery of the past life memory as similar to viewing a "movie" and seeing his past life self as a main character in that movie. Phillip added to this account: "I know about five other lives as well, but the one in which I lost my wife and child at thirty seems to have closed down my heart space. The energy field needs to be cleared and healed." He tells me this in between wrenching sobs as he releases more of his pain.

"It feels like I'm tearing out part of myself, leaving it behind." He's crying as he does generally at this point during sessions, and it's a true mournful crying, not a sealed off masochistic crying or a hysterical release. "What wisdom is it that I'm supposed to wake up to?" he asks. "Is it that it can just be enough? The way to find that out is to keep going. I guess it just makes so much sense that suffering and joy would be tied together."[2] He continues: "I know that's what this tightening in the throat is. I know we'll be talking! It feels like a lot. I want to thank you for your being there for me – for your constancy and strength, and for all your help."

I can feel this deeply felt expression of gratitude from Phillip, and know that it is a sign of depressive position capacity for love, and for dialogue with another, related to a capacity for psychic dialectic. Phillip sobs and cries as he says these words of gratitude to me. He adds: "I'm just going to stay open moment to moment. I guess it's amazing it can happen at all. When I came here I wasn't a believer. It's a blessing." He speaks of becoming a believer as he makes this journey of positive suffering through the mourning process. His capacity to believe in general has opened up. He can trust more as shown by his ability to share with me the formerly hidden and shame-ridden aspects of himself. He believes in love now in a way he never could before, and speaks of a deepening in the contact between himself and his new girlfriend (who became his girlfriend during his second year of treatment), as they make love, and he finds he can bring his sexual fantasies into an interpersonally shared arena in this relationship. Consequently, he is no longer as pulled apart by a lust that takes him into dissociated trance-like states, away from the person who is there to be loved in the present. He finds many levels of belief – a new belief in his physical being and in his body's capacity to channel the deepest passions, the deepest tenderness and the deepest grief, when blocks, such as those in his throat, are opened up.

He studies the Hindu diagrams of chakras (energy points) in the bodies, and the work of a physicist, Barbara Brennan, also a clairvoyant, who enlightens him about the interplay between body and mind in her writings. He comes to believe that he is capable of commitment and asks his girlfriend, who he has been living with for a year and a half, to marry him. But intermingled with and yet perhaps transcendent to all these levels and avenues of belief is his new and growing belief in spiritual power and in God. In fact, he begins to encounter images of Jesus Christ in a poignant way; images that spiritually appear in his life, as he travels and explores nature in the Southern and Western areas of the United States. He begins to feel a connection with these images and to find meaningful messages in them. He tells me that he was never religious and never had opened himself before his therapeutic journey to any of the religious dogma of his family background. Only now, with mourning and the positive suffering of facing his soul in grief and regret does he open at a powerfully deep "heart center" level to these spiritual beliefs that reflect a vision of God. The phase "heart center" is his phrase. He speaks of this core area of connection where physical, emotional and spiritual energy merge and complete one another. It is a place of electrical vibrations and currents that can vibrate at various frequencies.

In his own words, he describes certain aspects of his spiritual journey to me, a journey that increases in depth and intensity as he heals his internal blocks through mourning. His romantic and spiritual yearnings flourish – both growing in parallel. Both yearnings are captured by his description of his fiancée as he sees her across the room at a party: "I have the fear she's going to be taken away. I just see her at this party, across the room. I know her so well. I feel connected to the very core of her. She's so beautiful to me for I just feel so tenderly towards her. It just feels perfect in a lot of ways. It just feels under grace."

His sense of spiritual dimensions beyond this world is a matter that concerns him in its effect upon him in this world, in his current life. He recalls being a child in bed, and feelings of a force pulling him out to another dimension, away from his bed, his father, his family. He reports having been terrified at that time, but concludes: "I have visions of me lying in bed terrified . . . and yet every experience I have of opening up to this unseen world, or to the world that's unseen to the ordinary eye has been totally supportive, healthy and good for me. It has been soul expanding, as opposed to visiting a prostitute, which couldn't be more soul contracting." In the midst of this expression of his newly growing faith he feels the fear again, which brings up the father transference. "I don't trust enough," he says. "I have fears I'm going to lose you by saying something that you won't accept or approve of. I'll lose your love, your acceptance and all the care you're giving me."

I respond by interpreting that I think he's speaking to his father. He begins to cry and sob: "Yeah," he exclaims. I feel a powerful wave of release coming from him as he lets go of the pain that speaks of his yearnings for his father. He faces that his self-doubts are related to his internal father. He faces that his negative judgments seem related to breaking his father's taboos with sexual behavior, which makes him feel unworthy of love. Yet as his transference feelings and projections open up the intensity of his grief in the moment, he faces his disappointment and anger at his father. He regains himself and is able to differentiate himself from his father. His spiritual journey is a threat to his internal father, who he projects onto me in the transference. As he mourns he can reclaim his own spiritual path. He reclaims his identity. The differentiation comes through an opening to his capacity to love, which has come with his positive suffering and his entrance into consciousness: "I love you so much," he says to me as he feels the anguish and pain of letting go of his father, and feels the joy of feeling his grief in my presence.

He continues: "My father isn't the one I could go to with the 7-year-old self in me. I was never allowed to let go of all the love I feel! So I had to change! I couldn't be the way I am. So now I bring in the block with my father (projected as a negative judgment in the transference), and continue to stop myself from being the way I am. I'm terrified I'll lose you, lose him or lose Linda." He brings in the negative judgments of his father to hold on to the old mode of self-castrating but erotic torture that he always experienced in relation to his passion for his father. But he has to let go of this to free himself to be his true self and to open to a love that is possible in the present. As he sobs out the grief of losing his old familiar negative father, who has become a symbolized introject that he projects onto me, and sometimes a protosymbolic visceral internal object that he feels in his throat, he has a new insight: "You know it's coming to the fore because I'm pushing it. I'm going for it. I'm acknowledging how I feel about Linda. I'm opening to it. It's wonderful! I'm going to get more of it. I've made up my mind. I let myself go out to meet her now. I see her specialness and then allow my backlash emotional reactions afterwards. I'm not freaking out!"

Phillip shared with me his awareness again of his family's ancestry once having communicated to him their need for his grieving process to open the channels to a revered and spiritual flow of life energy within his family. He tells me: "I told you I had intuitive knowledge and factual knowledge of my being the holder of grief for my DNA line, passed on from generation to generation. I have caught on to my soul's lineage, that this life is a receptacle for karma from past lives as well as a receptacle for emotional life from my DNA line, and that these two interact with each other: the soul lineage and the DNA line."

Sometimes, during the beginning of the third year of treatment, Phillip would have experiences of sexual ecstasy while in sessions with me. I never reduced these to psychoanalytic fantasy states through interpretations, even though much could be said about phallic pride exploding with a flourishing erotic transference and an expanding outside love life. When I listened to him I felt a communion with Phillip's spirit, particularly at times of vivid self and spiritual articulation. The grief of mourning always accompanied these states of ecstasy and vision.

One day Phillip said, when struggling with his growth beyond his father in an ongoing separation process (not just an oedipal triumph): "I'm worried that my energy will become so big that I'll expand outward. I see myself glowing and expanding in brightness – a light that consumes my father until he ceases to be present."

"Your father?" I ask.

He is crying and sobbing as he responds to my question: "I know I was saying 'you,' but I'm looking straight at him. That light is my birthright. That is what my destiny in this life is. I was thinking of the corner bistro and wondering if I would go there after the session, and move away from all these fears and spiritual feelings by drinking a beer and closing off. I know if I go there I'll be turning away – to not have to be present with all these fears I have. I can be open in this way, admitting the glowing light, having the heart space open, or can I do all those things I do so that the heart space isn't open and the light can't get out. It's a trust issue, trusting that all those fears are just fears, not real, like a nightmare, that's what these fears are. I need to wake up. It's trusting enough to let these fears go. If I wake up I won't be trying to control these fears. This is the process." Underlying all his fears of annihilating his father as he expands spiritually is a basic fear of loss, which he thinks he and his father share. "It's my choice when I get into a neurotic dance with him because of my fears of loss."

Five months later, he moves from an erotic transference wish into a surrender to love and gratitude, which contrasts with the former frustrated anger he felt accompanying his erotic wishes towards me. Connecting to the love and sustaining such connection, without a backlash of anger, allows him to open to recalling recent spiritual visions. He readily shares these visions with me now, without his former distrust and hesitation.

In the beginning of the session he speaks of dressing after a shower, and thinking of what underwear he would wear in relation to seeing me and in relation to his fantasies of having sex with me. From there he is able to interpret the repetition of these incestuous transference wishes as an age-old neurotic pattern that can take him away from life – and from a real present connection with me. He has more fully become his own "interpreting subject" (Ogden 1986), and is able to understand the meaning of his fantasies as ways of entering his mother's body to keep him safe from his fears. He then relates to me in our real analytic mode of relationship. He expresses gratitude for my help: "Everyone resists getting clear of those age-old reactions. That's why we met, you and me. It's to do some of these things. I think it's really fabulous that you're here and that you help all these people. I think it's a great love thing. I feel so much gratitude to you." He is crying as he says this, sobbing with a heartfelt gratitude. He continues: "I'm waking up from age-old patterns, waking up from it. The whole world is fixed in that trance. It's very powerful! I know I resist a lot. I doubt still. I don't trust. I could see that in speaking to my higher self, my spirit guide. I get stuck in all that old stuff, in primitive patterns and conflicts that are fed from stuff from past lives and from the generational stuff that I have chosen to be born into."

He goes on to tell me of spiritual visions he has had during meditation: "A couple of times in intense meditation I have had visions of Christ. I had visions of energy fields, of flames coming out of me, as if hot coals were in my body. I saw him really clearly. I never had a relationship with a Christian church, or Christ. He's been coming through really strongly in meditation–visual mystic images . . . I've been aware of a lot of stuff psychically for the last six months. It keeps getting stronger and stronger. It's really beautiful. It's really changing me. So I've been spending time in the mornings speaking with guidance, or you can call it channeling. I can see him quite clearly in my mind's eyes. I could go to a couple of particular places, such as in the Sierra Alter desert and in South Colorado and find Jesus any time. I found this painting in oil of Christ. I began asking questions to his presence in this painting. I saw his heart filled with bleeding wounds and yet whole. One can suffer and stay whole, suffer one's own wounds and stay open and keep channels for connections open."

PAST LIFE, PRESENT LIFE, AND SPIRITUAL GROWTH THROUGH DISILLUSIONMENT

Phillip's spiritual life awakens as part of a mourning process that evolves further into areas of developmental disillusionment as he reevaluates parents and parental figures; and he experiences transferential wishes and longings with passionate intensity. Phillip also struggles with his own self-disillusionment, feeling the struggle to accept his rage and his vulnerability, both of which he experiences as in conflict with his idealized self, the "perfect baby," and the perfect golden male achiever. Phillip experiences conflicts around wishes for narcissistic perfection and around his wish to "control outcomes" when he can only release himself into full life in the present moment through relinquishing such control. He articulates to me the maternal transference wishes that he wants to be able to have control over in relation to me, realizing he is holding himself back by holding on to such wishes. Articulating the wishes becomes part of his mourning process as such symbolization and sharing allows him to release himself by relinquishing control and accepting the loss of his child fantasies, such as the fantasy of making love to me and getting to live inside of me, as his transference mother. At every turn his struggle with psychic conflict is a struggle with relinquishing the past through opening to the grief pain of past disappointment and trauma. Increasingly through the acceptance of such grief, he reconnects with dissociated parts of himself that he has disconnected from in the past to avoid profound pain, and profound rage. According to Phillip, facing the pain opens the doors to a full and passionate life in the present, where much love is awaiting him.

New transitional space is opened through the mourning process. It is a space for play. It is analytic space. Through mourning, Phillip has more spontaneous thought and feeling, and thus free associating is more fluid. Phillip also has a fluidity of self-states now as the potential and transitional space between reality and fantasy (Winnicott 1974) is more fully opened. True to Winnicott's area of overlap between reality and fantasy, Phillip experiences a fluid transition between psychic states that are in part fantasy self states and in part memory. He has dialogues with the vision of his 9-year-old self, who he perceives as having begun to defend against feelings and to close off to life. He experiences an "adrenalized" physical feeling in his stomach, like butterflies in his stomach, when he feels he is sealing off again in the manner of his 9-year-old self. His memory tells him that at 9 he sealed off his heart to protect himself from the humiliating attacks of his father, and from his own conflict over intensely loving and hating his father. Phillip also speaks to an infant self, one who feels intense vulnerability and helplessness, which can instantly spark into lightning bolts of rage, with the primitive impulse of retaliatory aggression against the mother upon whom he is so utterly dependent.

At times Phillip reaches beyond this life and relives states of self-experience that he has felt as "past life regressions" with the aid of a past life regression therapist. At first it is one particular life that most predominantly haunts him; that life in which he lost a wife and a young female child, when quite young, only thirty. He recalls becoming bitter in attitude, closing off in a state of blocked and pathological grief. From the time of his loss, Phillip recalls living as if in a living death until he too died at a fairly young age, all his faith and hope desecrated and destroyed.

Phillip is capable of finding symbolic meaning in this past life insight. In this way he learns from that which is intensely and emotionally real, and from that whose effects on his present reality have a cause-and-effect logic to them. This is true for him despite whatever degree subjectively constructed narrative and historical truth converge due to the layering of emotional experience over time. He relives the trauma of that other life in order to learn about himself through this emotional knowledge. He reconnects with the heart that had been sealed off by reconnecting with the earlier man he was in that former life. Phillip realizes from this encounter how much he pushes others away, most particularly those he loves and needs the most, in this life, because of continuing fears from a tragic and devastating loss that still haunts him. He must feel the overwhelming grief he suffered in that earlier life in order to not be continually in a state of defense to ward off the pain of the unmourned trauma. In a state of defense, he disconnects from essential parts of himself that he needs to feel his core heart center, and from all the object relations connections that reside in his heart, integrated through loving affect. To not relive the pain of this man who he may have been in another life, he has been carrying the burden of that man's suffering as an undigested part of his own psyche, a draining alter-ego, dissociated and yet unconsciously pressuring him as an undigested other within (Bion 1963). Now he can intuitively sense the former "unthought known" (Bollas 1989; Winnicott 1954) of that man's trauma. Only by reconnecting to this man can he make the unthought known consciously known so as to separate from the terrors from that other man's life that have unconsciously haunted him, compelling him to push away and reject his present potential.

As we continue our work, and Phillip's mourning process, Phillip recalls two other lives from the past of his psyche. He speaks eloquently of how these lives have each left their stamp of terror, with specific fears derived from each life that can speak in a chorus at times, warning him against opening up in his present life.

Aside from the life of a man with early losses of loved ones, there is the man who had too much wisdom for his time, and whose wisdom was so much of a threat that he was violently accosted and hung from a tree. There is also the life of a woman in his past, a young and beautiful woman, whose illusions of having control over men lead her to a tragic death. Promiscuous and taunting of men, she takes on a rather vicious male character, who not only rapes her, but then takes out a knife and sticks it into her breast, ripping her apart by pulling the knife up to her neck. Just before she dies, she has a flash of insight about her provocative behavior and the narcissistic illusions of omnipotence that she is living in. But then it is too late! She dies in a state of shock. Her legacy of self-illusion becomes a lesson for Phillip.

When plagued with the chorus from his past lives Phillip hears: "You can't be present in your life, because if you are terrible things will happen! If you open up you will have terrible losses. You'll be hung up by the neck, and a knife will be put in your breastbone and be pulled up to your neck." Through the emotional avenue opened up through his mourning process, Phillip is able to hear this voice loud and clear, so that he can now, for the first time, separate from it, and decipher the meaning in its message. Once symbolizing the message he is free to use the knowledge of his past life traumas to understand what had compelled him time and time again to disrupt his relationships and to disrupt his presence in the moment in this life, extending to pushing love and life away, rather than embracing it. The more he rediscovers the psychic sources of his fear, the more he can free himself from the terror of their grip. He can now distinguish past traumas, whether in this or other lives, as living in psychic fantasy states within him, causing him to react against what he needed in this life. He can conceptualize for himself that these psychic fantasy states, born from past trauma, are part of a pathological mourning state, just as is the infant in a rage, lying on a bed alone, waiting helplessly for his mother to return from the next room; or the 9-year-old Little League baseball player standing, with a stomachache, in a detached and depressed state, on the playing field. As he contacts these other selves on the route of psychic fantasy, while feeling the safety of the psychoanalytic holding environment, he is able to contact the sealed off pain that blocked him from the core of himself, from what he explicitly called his "heart center." Phillip tells me that he is discovering that the pain is the door to reconnection and to enlightenment through that reconnection. When he can face the pain, and sob out his grief in a deep and all releasing manner in his sessions with me, he also becomes aware of what triggers his rage in the present, and he becomes aware of the poignant longings for paternal support and maternal care that lie behind his pain and its rage.

Phillip begins to experience psychic fantasies of rage and grief that he can call upon to visualize and feel these states, freeing him from dissociating from himself, as he did in the past to block the effects of these affect states. His fantasy of rage is of having the fire sparks of lightning bolts leap out of him. His fantasy of grief is of floating in an ocean, rolling around in the sea, with the sea being the tears from his own sobbing released in his grief. Unlike other patients who might fear drowning in the ocean of their tears, and who therefore resist even the beginning of crying, Phillip imagines himself able to float, floating around in his own ocean of tears. He interacts with his tears now, rather than warding them off, as he did at 9 years old.

Once Phillip can face the internal world experience of his fears, as derived from the past, he is able to articulate the fears and therefore to separate from them. In this way, he no longer reacts impulsively and compulsively to the unknown fears. He can distinguish his present life from his past and take the risk of being in the present. His fears have been both symbolized and articulated.

THE WEDDING

During the third year of treatment, Phillip marries a woman who he has come to love deeply. He had lived with her for a year, and had moved with her from New York to a West Coast state. He continues his sessions each week with me over the telephone. The day of the wedding, and the whole weekend surrounding it, was a time when Phillip was able to feel the full expansion of himself in the present. He felt full of love, and was able to reach out to relatives and friends through his love. They responded back, and there was a full wave of dialogue and mutuality in loving. Phillip felt his "heart center" expand, and felt an intense richness of the many flavors of feeling experience. He felt the spiritual connections strongly. Given the strength he gathered by being so powerfully present, both within himself and with others, he was able to keep himself separate from the neurotic "dramas" that his parents enacted and sought to impose on him. He could feel loving moments with his father. When his parents behaved like "pathetic children," who wanted all his attention, and who showed their resentment for not being the center of his attention by "giving him the silent treatment," he was able to maintain his equilibrium, and to give them his attention when the wedding guests had departed.

Days after the wedding, Phillip felt a physical reaction to the lessening of the expansion of his heart, as things returned to their normal pace. Yet, in this winding down transition, he had a fascinating psychic experience of a metaphysical nature, showing him the role of his own choice in allowing a positive experience of separation with those he loved. It was in a session with the past life regression and chakra therapist (based on the work of a physicist with clairvoyant powers) that Phillip experienced his body become a birth canal for the psychic departure of his friends and relatives from his own body, which had internalized them. He gives birth to these internal presences (objects) after the weekend's union, springing them free again to enter the world. This experience began with Phillip first seeing white light emanating from his body, after his internalization of intense love over the weekend of the wedding. Then he experiences these figures leaving his body, with his psychic disposition in his body needing to be an open one, in a certain body posture, to maintain the aspect of a birth canal. Phillip found that if he failed to keep this posture, and began to push to help these figures leave his body, his energy would get denser and the figures would get stuck. He actually visualized the spirit of his brother trying to emerge and leave his body. When he tensed up by pushing him out, his brother's "foot got stuck," and he couldn't move through the boundary of Phillip's body to an outside place of separation.

Phillip also discovered that on the right side of his body was a whole dense area, where he was bound up with constrained and defended aggression. He associated the area of blocked aggression with the inheritance of aggression he had experienced unloaded upon him in his father's "out of the blue" attacks. He was conscious of not wanting to express retaliatory impulses. He did not want to hurt anyone like he had been hurt. He did not want to be forced to identify with the aggressor, and to be compelled to reenact the aggression on others (often, he had turned it in upon himself).

Therefore, his muscles held on to the tension of the aggression within. Phillip wanted to be free of the tension, and to be free of the denseness of energy that blocked him in this area. He received a vision during the night, coming through the image of Jesus Christ. It was a message informing him that he could transform his aggressive energy, and would not have to use it in hurtful attacks, like the ones he was subject to from his father. He was extremely relieved to believe that he would not have to become the aggressor in order to give up the part of being the victim. He realized that his retaliatory impulses could be processed psychically in a symbolic form that often spoke in his psychoanalytic session with me.

Following this psychic experience, Phillip was able to contact the anger at his mother that had lain dormant behind the hurt and rage in relation to his father. He also processed a new and acute experience of disillusionment in relation to a father figure, his boss at work. He consciously faces his own hurt and injury without denial, and without idealizing the father figure, and is able to repair the image of the father figure without retaliating, and without denying his rage and injury. In other words, he seeks reparation, and does not wall off to protect the image of the father figure with reaction formation. Although attacked at a meeting by his boss, in an idiosyncratic and inappropriate manner, he retains his voice and his sense of self, and is able to assert himself without counterattack, and without withdrawing in shame as he might have in the past. He simply says to his boss after the attack: "I don't think that is a fair comment." He is aware that he does not lose his voice as he had done in the past, when attacked. He has less shame, even though he is still human and vulnerable to attack. After the attack he speaks up at the meeting, and he witnesses the fear and weakness of his boss who fails to engage with him when he is assertive. Later, he reflects on the incident of being attacked in the meeting by his boss, and is able to share the experience with his wife. He is able to take in her help, and share together in analyzing the boss's defensive attack. He comes to understand that he has been a narcissistic mirror for his boss, who would like him to remain in the role of bachelor, who continually drinks and parties.

Both his father and his boss are threatened by Phillip's being able to commit to love and to a woman. He can no longer serve as the self-extension for his father or boss. When they cannot face their own feelings in love and marriage, they attack Phillip. Understanding his boss allows Phillip to separate from the threat of attack. He then can bypass retaliatory impulses, and regain a sense of love for his boss. He retains a positive view of his boss and of his boss's overall love for him, feeling his own tenderness towards his father and towards this boss as father figure, even while fully confronting his own disillusionment about his boss as he views him in his weakness and insecurity, and in his aggressive impulsivity.

Phillip repairs the boss's image within his own mind, and uses his disappointment as a positive developmental step in disillusionment, allowing him to transform retaliatory aggression into some tolerable grief. He is not caught in a pathological mourning state, where he must cling to an idealized image of his boss, or of his father. Yet he is able to maintain a "good enough" image of the father and father figure, as he retains his own separate voice, and doesn't, in his own words, "get pulled into the drama."

Phillip's working through of his anger and disappointment with his mother is somewhat more complex, and takes him to an earlier level of psychic experience. His transference with me serves to trigger his memories, fantasies, and association to his relationship with his mother, back through different points in time, until he immerses himself in an infant state.

Again he is able to separate from the mother in the present by understanding his anger at her loss in terms of a whole pattern from his past. His grieving of the loss he feels for the infant state allows him to open to the rage he also felt in that state, which had been unconscious until recently. His own words vividly describe his mourning and working through process, in relation to his mother. His psychic fantasy and memory is prompted by his longings towards me felt within ongoing psychoanalytic sessions. First he imagines me dressed in a black bra and black slip, standing in his mother's bedroom, as I am experienced, with a consciousness of metaphor, as his mother. He leaps off from this image into a scene of much psychic conflict and much infant vulnerability, encountering rage as a phantom, and fear as a profound terror of infant death.

In his words: "I see myself in a room as an infant. I see you in the room also. You're my mother. You're standing there in a black bra and black slip, holding me. You put me down on the double bed, where I can't roll off. Then you leave the room to go into the next room to get whatever dress you're going to put on. I'm lying on the bed, and I don't know if you're going to come back or not. I can't tell if you're going to walk back into the room twenty seconds later or whether you'll walk out and I'll never see you again. Maybe you'll be dead. I am lying on the bed staring at the ceiling, and my neck doesn't even lift my head to see what's happening. My legs are these useless pieces of toy flesh. I can't move about on them. I want to speak and all that comes out is this inarticulate wail. I've got no power at all to take care of myself [*he's crying*] – no power to feed myself – no power to say what I want and need – no power to move myself. I'm just like utterly and completely dependent on you. I don't want to feel all this stuff. You know I don't want to feel this vulnerable, needy, this powerlessness. I don't want to feel so dependent on someone who clearly doesn't have the judgment or love for me to not walk out of the room all the time. I can't take care of myself. I can't even walk. I don't speak. I can't even lift my head. I just feel this amazement seeing that all that is true – seeing that I'm completely powerless and dependent in that way. And you would walk out of this room, knowing what the implications are, and it fills me with this rage towards you – this feeling I could just crush you or strangle you – for failing me so acutely and so insensitively, as I see this force coming out of my little infant self, a force of rage leaving my heart and body, like in a third dimension – going off to accomplish its intent. I see it leaving me and going out the door you went out of, finding you wherever you are, and destroying you! And then the rage is gone, and this phantom that's left my body is gone. It's accomplished its mission and dissolved. What's left in its place is my knowledge that I've created the very thing I most feared. I truly am alone. There's nobody coming back for me.

"All of a sudden I'm aware of birds singing, the breeze blowing, the curtains and the sunlight coming into the room. I realize I'm utterly alone! All of a sudden I woke up to the present moment, to the beauty of what's around me. It's wild! I was expecting that this phantom would go out and destroy you and I would be alone. This was what I had feared. Instead, all of sudden I'm gurgling happily with birds singing. I'm alive to the moment – having released my rage and my fear. What do you know? OK, so now I'm on the bed, alive to that moment – a happy baby gurgling on the bed. You walk back into the room with a dress on a hanger. You say something affectionate. Everything's OK again. Then we start a new cycle. You put the dress on and then leave the room again, and once more I think, wait! Hold on! My legs don't work, and you're leaving me alone!

"It's the way I feel about mom now. She left – checked out, not entirely, but compared to what she could be – is – one twentieth is in evidence. I see myself taking care of her when my parents visited me and Linda – although in a new way – of taking care. She wants the old way so badly. I think she does anyway. So I see myself taking care of her when she was here, and I see myself taking more care of her in the future, when she gets older. I see the reaction in myself, like that infant's reaction. Wait a minute! It's not supposed to be like this. I'm the needy one. You're my mother; the one who meets my needs and sees what they are, without me having to do any more than cry. Whatever I lack, whatever nourishment for my fears, my stomach needs, you give them to me. That's your role. That's how it's set up. You're not allowed to change how it's set up. You're not allowed to change the rules. The rules are that I'm the needing one, the powerless one, and you're the provider for what I lack. Those are the rules! I didn't make them up. I just work here. I don't own the place! I'm not God.

"Now, all of a sudden my mom is the one lying on her back, as if she were a big fat baby. Only this baby is pretending that she's powerless. Except she feeds herself food – no problem doing that. She lives for that. It's her number one compulsive pleasure. Drinking is right up there too. But she refuses to allow herself any emotional sustenance at all! She pleads for it – constantly, of course! She's desperate to get it, of course! But she can't take it in in a way that does her any good. The more she can't take it in, the more desperate she gets, and the more she needs. She's lying there like a big fat baby, saying, 'Phillip, you're walking out of the room on me. You're getting married! You're moving away and leading your own life! Can't you see I need you so desperately, and you could give it to me if ever you would?' Now it's me feeling this rage again at her: 'You're not a baby, except that you make yourself so out of fear and to manipulate me!' It's like I hold her down on the bed, the same bed I was on as a baby. She's lying there as an adult, pretending to be an infant! I'm yelling at her, strangling her and then I stop and the anger clears!

"As I thaw out in my mind's eye, she's there dead, sure enough! She's dead! I killed her. I look at the curtains in the room. The shades are pulled down, even though it's daylight. It's over! She's dead! We're still in the same room, but on the left side the shades are down. On the right side of the room the shades are up, the windows are open, the curtains are blowing and the sun is coming in. Then I'm lying on the bed again, on the sunny side of the room. I'm an adult with the shades pulled down. I'm an adult hanging my head in shame and grief, grief that she's gone, and guilt that I've killed her and guilt that I feel so much relief that she's finally dead! But then I feel all the grief because I don't have her anymore. She's supposed to take care of me. I said: 'she' *that it was her I was strangling and not you.* I don't know where in the description I switched from you to her, when I was describing my experience of her during the wedding. I'm questioning how the transference is working here. Do I feel this rage towards you? That same need of comfort and security, the feeling of comfort and that I crave. I feel that you give that to me. I'm remembering back to my last session. You asked me a question near the end of it. Then just as I was answering it, your call waiting checked in. You had to answer it, and I was on this telephone limbo space. I was crying! I was having sobs pass through me and I was thinking that it is the same thing, as my mother leaving the room. It was like you left the room at that moment of need! So I'm wondering if there's rage and anger towards you, of course. I don't feel it. I'm not in touch with it. I don't know if I'm not in touch with it and I'm scared of it, of if it's not there.

"I'm seeing you in my mother's bedroom in that long black slip and black bra, going out for the night, going out to a party. She has a dress on with black under-wear, and is going to some party! So it seems like you know if I'm seeing you leave the room that when that phantom leaves my body to go do its aggressive violence, it would follow it could be you it would land on. All this is out of my head now. I don't feel it! The rage is at my mother. She's my actual mother, and she's the one I'm having this actual struggle with, about who gets to be the baby! I say: 'No, you're my mother. I'm the baby!' Or I really don't want to be a baby any more. It doesn't work for me. For her own sake, I forget me. I'm not wanting to play that role with her! I'm not wanting to be the baby myself. But she thinks herself helpless! At an unconscious level she has all the power and that's what she's defending against. She's scared of her power. You and I do not have that going on. You're not trying to be a baby and be dependent on me.

"It does piss me off that at the time of our wedding, which is about me, about my new wife, and about us coming together, about lifting us up to a new level of vow-ing and of joy – that at that time she should be so selfishly infantile, demanding throughout the weekend that she requires all this attention, whenever I saw her. Because she was freaking! I do have some anger about that. It's there. I don't really want to be a baby! I want us to have love between us. On one occasion that I told you about, my mother was all of a sudden there. That's what I recall. Maybe I want to talk to her like I talk to you. Maybe I want to be this open with her. Maybe I want to cry in front of her, and have that be OK – just like I can be open with you and you don't panic. You don't fear about our safety. You're the same. You're steady and all right, even if I go all the way back to an emotional place of being an infant. You are your independent self. I can be me and I don't have to protect you. I want to be who I am with my mom, and have her be OK. I don't have to be what she wants, to be her drama. But I'm still not able to be with her like I am with you. She's not there for me like that. Maybe I'm not there too in that way. It takes two to tango! I could let go of her. I have to let go of the old way of being with her . . . I have to release to gain. I have to release the old way to get what I want in a new way."

MORE PHASES OF SEPARATION THROUGH MOURNING

In sharing his fantasy of the infant whose mother walks out of the room, Phillip claims his own abandonment terror and annihilation anxiety. He also claims the primal rage that his homicidal fantasies expressed at a symbolic level. This rage was felt by Phillip as omnipotent, and as a defensive reaction to feeling extremely helpless and vulnerable.

In the latter phases of treatment, Phillip faces his intense vulnerability and the infant longings behind his later defensive reactions. In doing so, he faces his depressive pain and then converts paranoid externalization into depressive position working through of psychic conflict. To do so, he must reown parts of himself that he has before seen in his parents. He differentiates his parents' problems, vulnerabilities, and defenses from his own. Phillip finds himself relinquishing a fantasy of an ideal parent, the fantasy parent who would provide for his every need, even when his own inner self is sealed off from expressing its need. He must mourn the idealized womb parent and face the difficulties, responsibilities and rewards of being an adult man.

Increasingly, Phillip defines his own mourning process, even while in it. He speaks of his own resistances to self-integration, and he speaks of how it feels when he disconnects from his heart and is left with a nauseous and adrenaline-like feeling in his solar plexus.

Phillip faces the parents of his childhood who have become internal objects, from whom he can only separate by emotionally contacting core memories and grieving, the old self enmeshed with the longings of the childhood parents. He also faces the parents of today, and in doing so he faces the authority figures in his current life, such as male superiors at work who need to be seen objectively and held accountable for their actions, rather than being neurotically protected by him from his own rage and judgements, as he had done in relation to his father in the past. Phillip reviews the past consequences of the former neurotic protection of the father, with its defensive self and other idealization. He remembers the subjective sense of feeling hollowed out inside, with a continuous internal tirade of self-attack, sometimes felt as castrating and even as suicidal, as in a fantasy of falling on his sword and committing hara-kiri.

As Phillip experiences his childhood through memories, he also experiences alive connections with his child self, at various stages of development, as they exist within his internal world. He has dialogues with self-representations, self-fantasies, and the sensory experience of himself as partly memory and partly internal object. He feels his 2-year-old self, his 9-year-old self, or his 14-year-old self, as well as his infant self, as live and dynamic figures. These dynamic internal selves are subjectively alive, as in the sense of the British object relations theorists' internal objects, Melanie Klein and Ronald Fairbairn, in contrast to the conceptual notion of mere mental representations of an object as theorized by the American object relations theorists, such as Edith Jacobson and Margaret Mahler.

He speaks to the 2 year old within who feels full of light and love, and who suffers the pain of not being able to have his mother receive him through the light of his love. As he glows radiant, playing in the kitchen with his blocks, in the presence of his mother, but with his mother's back to him, he suffers the unconscious loss of his mother, who he remembers as being fully preoccupied with the vegetables she is cleaning in the sink. Speaking to me of this, he creates me into a better mother by voicing the opinion that I would be able to receive his love if he could surrender it to me as he had to his mother at 2, but also fears such surrender due to the mentally imbedded memory of his mother's lack of response to him.

In saying so, he does surrender, as he does at many moments with me, expressing his gratitude and his love as appreciation of the process he experiences flowing with me and with my alive presence. He tells me that he had been in despair about himself when he first came to see me for psychotherapeutic treatment. He tells me that he remembers telling me that he thought he was too undeserving of help, because of all his "dirty" addictive habits – drinking, taking some drugs, and promiscuous sex. He recalled telling me that he was convinced that the therapy process wouldn't work for him. Phillip continues, telling me that he recalls that when I questioned why he had such a belief he had felt hope for the first time, after having reached a point where he had felt suicidal, and felt like jumping off a roof. He says that he began to surrender by suspending his disbelief, and allowed himself to sob out all the pain of his childhood that had become the burden of a "motherload of grief" and the obligation to mourn for seven generations. He tells me in his fourth year of treatment that he began to believe in the process, with the real belief in it developing gradually over time. But as he tells me this, he is grateful for my belief and for my "consistent presence" and accepting attitude. He can be poetic in his expression of gratitude, and moments of gratitude allow for an openness within him to new positive internalizations created from the communion between us in his moment of openly expressing gratitude. Psychic space expands within him and between us. A dialectic between him and I then develops about his mourning process. This mirrors a growing dialectic between his adult self (Fairbairn's central ego) and the internal objects and self-states within his internal world, all derived from his childhood experience mixed in with fantasy and memory.

Phillip comments that his 2-year-old self is quite reluctant to leave me, as his transferential mother, when he has thoughts of his treatment progressing far enough for him to be more on his own. Although he decides for realistic reasons to stay in treatment for now, as I still contain and galvanize his deepest grief experience, he also experiences the 2-year-old child in him protesting against ever leaving. The 2-year-old Phillip wishes to cling to my neck. He experiences the threat of separation at first from a paranoid stance of reliving his father pulling him out of his mother's arms. However, as he clings to me he also realizes that he will need to walk on his own and try out his growing capacities for autonomy, and for ultimate independence from me as an external other. In a vision of a water tower from my office window (in one of the rare in-person sessions in a treatment that in the fourth year is carried on by telephone from halfway across the country, lying on a couch with a speaker phone), he imagines the water tower as a wonderfully adequate container for emotion and consciousness, as it contains water (tears of grief), and as I have contained his grief and allowed him to internalize a more adequate internal container than he had internalized previously from his original mother. However, such realization is in conflict with the 2 year old that wishes to cling to me, and he articulates a conflict between independence and dependence increasing.

The 2 year old is also the psyche of grandiose pride in his "perfect infant" self offering itself to his mother, seen with her back turned. He must relinquish this sense of perfection, which gets tied in with expectations to perform in roles to meet the idealized images of his parents in relation to him. His wish to be perfect becomes a powerful neurotic obligation that emerges in him and makes him pull away from intimacy with women later on, when he can't keep up the image.

He has spoken to his 9-year-old self even more often, the guy who knocks himself as his father knocks him, by calling this child self, "Mr. Nine-Year Old." He is the withdrawn and self-inhibiting latency age child, who hardens himself against his own pain, needs, and tears. He stands on a hockey field, in a competitive sport that pleases his father, feeling nauseous within and full of depressed misery. He is already giving up his true emotional self to protect his father from disappointment, and to withhold emotionally from himself as his father withheld from him. Then he contacts a memory of himself at 20, sitting at his parents' dinner table, looking at his father. His father looks like he wishes to appear powerful and clever, but his inner self reveals itself in a way that feels traumatic for Phillip. He sees in his father the child within, who is full of neediness and despair, miserable in his sealed off state, never believing his need can be responded to. Phillip sees his father as a mirror of himself at that moment, aware of a needy child within himself who is also in despair. He may be locked in a paralyzing state of projective and introjective identification with his father – and so in a sense he is frozen. Yet, in his old state he experiences the agony of wishing to protect his father, then unaware of his unconscious rage, but aware of his inability to rescue his father; or to gratify him, he turns against himself in his own mind. He sees himself knifing himself, ripping himself to shreds inside with self-taunts and self-attacks, modeled on his father's attacks on him. He imagines himself committing hara-kiri. In fantasy, he is suicidally stabbing at the internal self that he experiences as undeserving, and as "unworthy" in a Japanese sense. He feels the sensation viscerally, of being hollowed out. His inner emptiness accompanies his despair and his unconscious rage turned against him. In Fairbairn's sense he is in a moral defense, blaming himself to protect the parent upon whom he would like to depend. But his longings go beyond such defense. In a more Kleinian sense, he protects his father out of a depressive position stance of loving the hated parent, of wishing to suffer the pain of depressive despair, to avoid hurting the one he loves (Winnicott's "capacity for concern").

Phillip goes beyond a spurious guilt to a pained compassion, but he is neurotically locked into a closed system of protecting his father from his rage. His compassion is not free, although beginning to emerge as a fantasy. He must mourn and grieve in treatment to free his compassion from the neurotic and masochistic defense that keeps him locked into a pathological identification with his father.

Then he fantasizes kicking his father to free himself. But kicking him with boots turns to kicking him with baby feet and getting under his skin. Being inside his father in fantasy, he longs to enter a maternal womb, but shockingly feels his father as barren. There is no maternal womb in his father. He must turn back to himself for an internal form of containment.

GUILT IN GRIEF AND GRIEF AS DIFFERENTIATED FROM GUILT

Phillip learns in this latter phase of mourning about the nature of his guilt, both in its preoedipal and oedipal dimensions. He speaks up at work in a situation requiring him to voice an opinion that threatens two male superiors, one his primary boss. Although he is applauded for doing so by the corporate managers that are reviewing and evaluating these male supervisors, he still reacts with an immediate unconscious backlash. He becomes flooded with punishment fantasies. On the day when the evaluation committee is to meet with his boss, he suddenly has fantasies that he himself will be fired, ending up out on the streets without resources. As the fantasy continues further, his wife is imagined leaving him because he now doesn't have a professional job, or money. He imagines himself "rooting around in a dumpster," an old man without teeth, all alone in the world. All these fantasies of self-annihilation and loss, as well as of humiliating castration, are familiar to him, but now they are all urgently mobilized in an unconscious reaction to his speaking the truth at work, rather than protecting his boss, who plays the role in his mind of a father figure (father displacement). Consequently he believes he must be punished for murdering his father.

Although it is his boss who is being called on the carpet for irresponsible and incompetent behavior, and even though Phillip is needed by both colleagues, and by the corporate firm itself, to speak the truth about his boss's sabotaging behavior towards the committee, his unconscious guilt propels him into a retaliatory assault on himself (Fairbairn's antilibidinal ego attack). It is his boss and the committee chair who may have invited disciplinary reaction by the evaluators of the firm he is employed by. Their behavior has created such a disruption of the committee Phillip works on that discharge of the committee's chairman has become necessary for the committee to function at all. Phillip sees this, and his healthy conscience guides him to speak the truth about the behavior of his boss and of his committee chairperson. Yet his unconscious superego retaliates. The retaliation repeats the internal world drama of his lifelong mode of engagement with his father. The trauma is repeated in his mind with his punishment fantasies. He tells the evaluators whom he must speak to a painful truth about his superiors, making sure to let them know that "I take no pleasure in saying this!" Is this just a negative of some unconscious oedipal rage impulse towards his father figures or father displacements, which he turns against himself in a superego attack, retaliating against himself with punishment fantasies? From a Freudian structural model perspective (id, ego, superego), it might appear this way. Internal psychic conflict of an oedipal nature might be seen to explain this self attack from a Freudian structural model perspective. But the essence of Phillip's internal world agony would not be seen through such a lens, and the grief and mourning of his depressive position despair would not be seen through this lens.

I propose that it is more helpful to see the reenactment trauma being played out by Phillip here, and the developmental mourning that is necessary to help him let go of reenacting the trauma. I suggest that Phillip's identification with his father figure, in the expectation of that father figure's punishment, speaks more about the conflict between separation and love for his father than about expectations of a paternal retaliation for unconscious murderous wishes that he might harbor towards the father in relation to oedipal phase motivations. It is his love for his father that makes him consciously grieve the loss of the father ideal and grieve the very real loss of feeling empathically for his father, when his father is faced with a truth about himself that Phillip realizes he can no longer protect his father from. Phillip's grief-laden anguish is the healthy part of his psyche speaking. It is the neurotic part of his psyche that speaks through punishment fantasies related to a neurotic form of guilt, as opposed to an existential or depressive position (Klein) form of guilt.

Phillip's grief is the pain of loving an imperfect father, who in many ways has never grown up. Phillip himself is growing into a maturity that far exceeds that of either his real father or his male father figure bosses at work. So his grief is in part the grief of the child growing up and leaving the parent behind (Loewald 1988). It is the grief of separation; not only the pain of his own feeling of separation, but also the pain of separating from a father who still longs to use him as an extension of himself, as a defense and protector, and as a way of avoiding humiliating truths about himself. Through introjective identification he feels the loss of his father in the separation as his own loss. He feels his father's fate as his own. He punishes himself with fantasies of failing that are really mirror image reflections of his father's mode of failure, for his father had failed in the business world. In addition, his father figure displacements at work are bringing on their own failure.

What is so important in working with Philip at this point is helping him to distinguish his grief over his father loss in the process of separation and his neurotic guilt. Phillip is quick to rally himself to conceptualizing this distinction along with me, as he sobs out the pain of how it hurts him to speak the truth and to expose his father to the pain of the reality consequences of his behavior. From this grief perspective, which is a core experience of developmental mourning and of Klein's existential depressive position concern, his comment to the business firm's evaluators that he "takes no pleasure" in reporting the sabotaging behavior of his bosses, can be taken quite seriously, rather than being seen as a negation of his own aggressive impulses towards his father. For indeed Phillip has deep and profound grief that he suffers in his sessions as he tells the sad tale to me, conveying the burden of his sense of responsibility as a mature man. He suffers the anguish of entering the moral order, as related to the existential suffering of growth and separation. He doesn't want the truth to be what it is. Yet confronting his own past denial, and his former neurotic wishes to rescue his father from what is, in order to merge with him in an idealized and unreal love, he must face the truth and begin to speak it. Only by speaking a truth that unfortunately implicates his father figure, Larry, for Larry's own real failings, can Phillip liberate himself and his co-workers from a tyrannical aspect of these father figures' paternalistic mentality, and from the exploitation of him and his fellow co-workers due to the narcissistic defense operations of the father.

Finding his own voice in this man's world of son and father work relations is as profoundly necessary for his own growth as it is for any woman poet or artist that I have written about. Not only is his own growth and freedom at stake, but also his capacity to mourn the past that has confined him in an internal closed psychic system, and has compelled him to reenact self-sabotage to save his father from his rage; a rage not only precipitated by psychic fantasies and oedipal rivalries, but by the trauma of living with a deeply flawed father, whom he loves and whom at times he has loved more than himself. This is his grief, and it is part and parcel of his liberation, and also sharply distinct from his imprisoning neurotic guilt. He does not merely cling to a wish to protect his father for the purpose of defending in some Freudian reaction formation mode against his innate aggression. Neither does he cling to the wish to protect his father from truth and reality as merely a Fairbairnian moral defense; one in which he must rationalize his father's faults to keep his father as an omnipotent protector, without which the world would seem too threatening for psychic survival. He does not just think of self-punishment to keep his father's image untarnished. His wish to protect his father through his own neurotic denial and defense is an act of child love that must be relinquished, not a mere denial of hate (Freud) or of terror (Fairbairn) of having no objects or no protective security without a benign parent.

His wish to deny truth and reality to protect his father can be best understood from a Kleinian perspective that subordinates oedipal dynamics to the depressive position pain of hurting the one one loves, and of separating from the primal mother. Klein's phenomenology enables us to see love as primary in this stage of Phillip's responses and conflicts. It is Phillip's conscious suffering of grief that allows him to bear the love for his father without being coopted into a neurotic relationship to his father in order to protect his father. It is Phillip's grief that helps him bear his love, and to not collapse it into a neurotic mode of symbiotic alliance with a flawed and sometimes destructive father figure. Hate and fear are secondary here to love. For even in the yearning for object connection the primal object is less powerful, and certainly less omnipotent after grief and separation than the love itself that allows for truth and free speech, a speech coming from an integrated consensus of heart and head. The mature love for his father that grows out of

Phillip's art of free speech and separation is love that allows him to love himself. It is in contradiction to this emerging self-love that can align itself with compassion for the other, while not being a co-dependent enabler, that Phillip feels compelled to attack himself and torture himself with self-punishment fantasies. Here is the limit of grief in the instant and the line drawn into a reactive neurotic guilt. For his self-punishing attacks are his old reenactment of hara-kiri against himself, as he speaks of in a fantasy of how he internally pictures suicide when viewing his father across the dining room table, with his father's sealed off feeling self appearing behind a grandiose façade as a miserable, needy and unloved child. If he pictures himself as the punished one, he gets his father off the hook, even though the truth tells him that the fault is indeed his father's. He cannot help the unconscious backlash that throws him into a turmoil of self-torment. He wants to hold on to his father by being his father's whipping boy. He will sacrifice himself again.

Phillip doesn't see the links between punishment fantasies and his guilt towards his father, and his wish to cling to an old reaction of merger with his father, until I intervene with interpretations. Then, in a moment, he sees the whole picture. His capacity to grieve and then to symbolize makes his conceptual abilities immediate and sharp. Phillip immediately has the vision of his neurotic reaction, beating himself to excuse his father, and to cling to the idea of still being a child with a fantasy father whom he could admire and look up to. He is not retaliating against himself for wishing to murder his father and win success for himself (not that he hasn't brought to consciousness his murderous fantasies, feeling freed of his rage by imagining the specifics of strangling his father. But this murderous rage is not necessarily his competition, but rage in reaction to being traumatized).

Now Phillip is accepting his own success only as he grieves and faces the truth of his willingness to be responsible enough to have this success. His father and father figures have failed in this way. He must live in this truth and grieve it. He mourns and sobs in each session with me, putting all the linking together between past and present, between father and father figures and between preoedipal and oedipal wishes towards his father. He wants a preoedipal merger with a fantasized maternal father, who would have a womb. He wants security in this paternal womb. For such fantasized security he has been willing to relinquish his own growth and to imprison himself in a compulsion to provide a false security for his father. He also wants an oedipal father whom he can revere as a mature man of conscience, but now in speaking the truth he is free to face the lack of it. Only through grieving can he travel past despair in grief to renewed love in grief. Then he can accept a father with flaws who may now change and allow himself to have flaws, and yet to grow beyond his father in morality and responsibility as he is doing, he can love a flawed father and now love a flawed but more deeply enlightened self. His aggression is contained in self-attack. In seeing its neurotic guilt origins, however, he can let go of it and embrace his own struggle to love both himself and his father with compassion. He showed his capacity to suffer the truth of what is the essence of Melanie Klein's depressive position and its entrance into an adult moral order. His success at work and life is born in the moment of mournful regret, not in the moment of murderous oedipal rage. And now the defensive motive of his father's rage can be seen objectively as it appears before him in a dream.

The fantasized milk and honey, associated with his parents, is now seen as "poison" for him.[3] Joining in his parents' neurotic dance becomes toxic for him. He must see this again and again, repeatedly and painfully feeling the external parents and their internal residues as beings to separate from. Each time he realizes the toxic bad object aspect of his relationship with his parents, he sobs out the cry of grief. His anguish is continuous through our sessions, as he frees himself more and more.[4] He frees himself, not only from the past, which compels reenactment without memory and connection, but also from the internal bad object situation once based on a regressive sadomasochistic symbiosis with his parents. It is not just the past that we are compelled to repeat, as Freud noted, but it is the past as it is preserved in this internal world situation. The internal parent relations became frozen in time and compulsive reenactment through projective and introjective identifications occurs, which must be relinquished through grief so that we are no longer compelled to constantly repeat it. This is the journey of anguish, a journey of love being released through grief that Phillip is increasingly capable of navigating. His heart connections expand with each new episode of grief, and he offers his heart to me as the good enough companion on his journey. I need no longer be seen, to such a large degree, as a parent. But I can feel his own struggles to rediscover a parent's love in my own heart. Being with him is often enough, but differentiating interpretations are also important to help free him from the stereotypic reactions of his old closed off internal object system. As he reenacts these scenes with father displacements, and formerly with mother displacements in romantic love relationships, he can now experience the compulsion in the reenactment, and can feel the level of grief sadness that allows him to relinquish that reenactment. The affect journey in the mourning process is critical, as Melanie Klein first discovered in 1940.

Chapter 11

The case of Laura, Part I

Mourning as the poetry of female eroticism: homoerotic evolutions of a homosexual woman within developmental mourning

Laura was deeply and traumatically disappointed each time she fell in love. During her adolescence and young adulthood, Laura was assaulted by repeated cycles of traumatic disappointment, as she would become infatuated with, or fall in love with, women unattainable to her, both gay and straight. She would begin by idealizing and idolizing these alluring and "exciting object" women, and then after the disappointment in their rejection and unavailability she would devalue them, already being engaged in adoring another. The cycle would repeat itself again and again. Prior to analysis it seemed that the cycle would never end, and that she would constantly be torn away from her life and her real relationships by overwhelming longings for an unavailable mother-lover, the artist mother goddess of her dreams. She feared she would perpetually suffer the search to refind a lost love object, which was based on an internal object fantasy of her mother, in both her preoedipal and oedipal level dimensions.

With the adolescent development of a homosexual eroticism, Laura sought out artistic women who to her were both goddesses and muses. She searched for the holding or symbiotic mother she had lost repeatedly throughout her childhood, the loss becoming a painful source of wounding, making her feel her love was bad, soiled and tainted, and most certainly that it was unrequited. Falling in love with me in the transference was inevitably to result in the repetition of this painful theme of unrequited love, as Laura had to experience her erotic desires as a one-way street, without reciprocation, although they were received, felt and understood by me, generally in a loving and caring manner. Since Laura was able to relive her pain in a less traumatic manner than in her life, while being psychically held by me within the holding environment, she was able to tolerate a conscious remembering that emerged along with fantasy themes of erotic lovemaking with me. Laura remembered a series of overtures of homoerotic love to heterosexual women who rejected her, and the rejection of one bisexual woman, an artist who had been the object of love and adoration in high school and college, who devastated her most of all in a torturous erotic encounter when in her late twenties. With her object relations psychoanalysis, Laura's recall began to extend beyond such memories. She became able to recall, with increasing clarity over time, the primal rejections with her mother that led to the later rejections with female displacement figures.

In toddlerhood, Laura had the first threats of abandonment from a mother who was always threatening to leave the family. At 3 years old, Laura remembers her mother as "putting on her red lipstick," while declaring she was leaving her husband, which included leaving Laura. Laura became hysterical and had a tantrum. When the mother ended up staying and giving Laura a coke to calm her stomach because she began throwing up, Laura believed it was her tantrum that convinced her mother to stay. This event is quite poignant in terms of Laura's psychic splitting, because it came in the same era as Laura's most loving memories of her mother.

Laura cherished one particular memory of her mother, one that played a big role in helping her to trust that there was goodness in the world, although she could lose this trust when retraumatized by a separation that felt like an abandonment or by a rejection of love that felt like both abandonment and annihilating humiliation. In this memory, Laura was tenderly undressed by her mother in a warm room, and a warm house, after being brought home, in a chilled state, wet from hours of walking in the snow and singing Christmas carols with older children. Laura recalled with exquisite detail how her mother gave Laura her undivided and total attention at this time. She recalled her mother's loving attitude as she undressed and cherished Laura. Such attention would become increasingly rare with a mother who became more and more depressed and bitter with the passing of the years, after having felt compelled to relinquish her former career as a painter for her role as mother, which she experienced as a martyrdom of the highest order. The sacrifice of the mother's career, which the mother seems to have experienced as a reluctant submission, was viewed by Laura as coloring her mother's views of her children so that Laura retained a feeling of being "damaged goods" in her mother's eyes.

Once Laura reported that her mother said: "If I knew you and your sister would have inherited your father's congenital health problem I wouldn't have had children!" Laura explained in response: "But then I wouldn't have been born!" Her mother's disregard for Laura as a valuable being in her own right (separate from just serving the role of her mother's self object) was not lost on Laura; nor was the mother's disregard for Laura's feelings in saying this to her. Her mother's indifferent lack of responsiveness at times could be seen increasingly clearly by Laura as a result of her mother's internal narcissistic preoccupation. This cold non-responsiveness and indifference alternated with her mother's paralyzing extreme of intensity in matters of Laura's performance as a student, artist, and potential bride to a successful man, treating Laura as an extension of herself. As an adult, Laura began to distinguish her mother's narcissistic preoccupations from her artistic devotions. Her mother focused obsessively on her own inner life, and particularly on her own pain; the same pain that Laura tried desperately to become a part of, in her desperate longing to have, and help her mother by becoming a part of her. Being separate – as with attendance at school – was a torment. Laura was continuously threatened that her mother would leave home while she was away in school living her own life. Laura would jump out of her seat in class, as the hours progressed and the school day drew to a close. At the sound of the school bell at three o'clock, she was driven into a manic frenzy of anxiety to run home and discover if her mother was still there or had left the nest, a nest she clearly viewed along with her mother as the mother's prison. Awakening often in the middle of the night, Laura would look through the banister at her mother below, painting alone downstairs in the middle of the night.

During Laura's early childhood, she tried to hold on to the early good mother by becoming part of her mother. She gave to her mother the kind of undivided attention that her mother had once given her, as encapsulated in the 3-year-old memory of being undressed with tenderness, love, caring concern and warmth, following her exploits in the snow. The mother's behavior at that early time would become quite the exception as Laura grew, and yet it was the image of that poignant moment that stayed with Laura and allowed her in many ways to become her mother's mother, and her mother's self as she became continuously engaged in trying to recreate that image of love and warmth through joining in with her mother. She became her mother's mirror and self-extension, and her mother's confidante, as she wooed her mother back to her, day in and day out. Her definition of love became that of joining in the pain of the other, for that is what she had done with her mother. And on those dark days when "the sun never came out!" because her mother lay morbidly still and frozen in her bed, failing to rise, it was Laura who was summoned (as the parentified child) by her helpless father. She would sit for endless hours on her vigil and mission, as she struggled inwardly, beyond all power or reason, to find a way of reaching her mother. Her mother's withdrawal could be icy, primitive and all too complete, but the moment it yielded to tears or words Laura would be there to serve her. When the tables were turned, however, and Laura expressed the normal distress, frustration and longing of a child in her own tears, her mother's hostile dismissal was immediate, giving Laura the sense that "it was the most humiliating thing in the world to be a child."

Her mother's overt aggression was as cold and cutting as her withdrawals. When Laura sat down on the floor and cried in protest – following observing a baby sister receive her mother's tender ministrations after crying quite loudly – her mother rebuffed her, rather than caressing and comforting her. In fact, her mother assaulted her with a punitive attitude: "If you don't stop crying, I'll give you something to cry about!" and struck her. This left Laura puzzled as to why her mother could cry and she could not. Such harsh intrusions on Laura's internal fantasy and psychic structure constellation of mother–child love, became split off and dissociated in a negative mother–self constellation that can be described in psychic structure terms as Fairbairn's antilibidinal ego, with its rejecting object part or internal saboteur. This was the constellation imbued with the affect of hostile aggression or object related hate, and it had to be dissociated from the loving mother constellation that Laura wished to cling to consciously for basic psychic survival. Laura's hate threatened the mother–child bond that had never met with an adequate separation. Later in treatment Laura would discover, through the work of the transference, how both her hate and her longings for her mother existed simultaneously. Her mind had always had to keep them divided from each other so that her perceptions of mother displacements were at first untarnished by the hating mother constellation that was imbued with her own split off rage. Within time, however, a new disappointment caused the object to turn from the exciting object mother muse into the rejecting object mother demon. Repeated traumas with mother's retaliatory acts became split off after the rage and pain was repressed or denied.

Contributing also to the "bad self and object," or hate side of her psychic structure were other distinct events that became prolonged and compounded. Laura was assaulted for crying, when she had by contrast responded to her mother's pain with nurturance, mirroring and empathy. Laura also remained perplexed as to why adults could cry, and her mother in particular could, when children were severely punished for doing so. At 14 years Laura is affronted by her mother's bitter reaction to a letter sent by the director of a camp where Laura spent her summer. The letter was a prosecuting report, naming Laura as the deviant culprit of homoerotic love. Basically, the mother was informed without any discussion or consultation with Laura that her daughter was infatuated with various female camp counselors, and the mother was asked to take action. Again, without any discussion with Laura, her mother bought the camp director's pejorative view and judgment of Laura's infatuation, just as she had always swallowed, "hook, line and sinker," according to Laura, early condemning reports by babysitters, which had led to an ongoing chain of mortifying punishments for Laura. Laura's mother responded to the camp director's account with a mixture of hysteria and cold contempt, which seems to have been her main manic defenses against her own unmourned grief. Laura's mother took the camp director's report as a foreboding view of sexual aberration in her daughter, and being herself alienated from sex, let alone homoerotic sexual desire, reacted with a vicious hostility. Her mother telephoned her, and when Laura tried to speak about her reaction, her mother hung up on her. This severed all emotional connection and affection that had sustained Laura. Laura therefore felt not only abandonment, but self-annihilation.

To Laura, her mother's withdrawal from her at this point left her all alone in the world. For those new females onto whom she had projected her mother's image and idealization, along with investing in them her newfound adolescent sexual passions, had all denied her the special friendships she had desired. Each in turn had spurned her, and her reaction of acute object loss, felt subjectively as unrequited love, seemed to Laura to occur without explanation. It was not till years later that Laura realized that she was chasing the essence of unavailability, as she expressed her love for women repeatedly through many adolescent and adult years, to straight girls and straight women. Spurned at every turn, at 14 years old Laura felt she was losing the light in her mother's eyes as well! Her subjective experience at this time with her mother would emerge into conscious clarity through her transference lens, with me as her analyst. Laura's continuing terror that she would lose the light of approval, warmth and love in my eyes, when she expected me to be angry, hurt or disappointed in relation to her, revealed with amazing vividness what Laura must have suffered at this traumatic time in her adolescence – compounded by all the earlier annihilating rejections by her mother. When Laura returned from camp at 14, her mother's appearance as matriarch and hostess at the dining room table was to transform into the visage of Medusa. Iced over with disapproval and condemning contempt towards the daughter she experienced not just as the son she never had, but now as the prodigal son, Laura's mother was poised to serve the family members at her table with the granite stone attitude of a love frozen into the deepest hate. To Laura, her mother's sharp facial features took on a diabolical and stark radiance, as her artist muse mother – (the mother of former emotional and creative inspiration) – turned vapid with psychic death.

In response to the witch hunt at camp concerning her homosexual infatuations, and in response to her mother's acute and unforgiving rejection – all at 14 – Laura went into hiding. She desperately sought to suppress and disguise any hint of homoerotic longings, fearing the rejection of her school friends, sisters, and especially Laura's best friend, Sharon. Later in analysis, Laura associated to the image of a guillotine, as the knife blade of her mother's castrating and annihilating rejection. Just like a guillotine, the maternal rejection severed her head from her body. She was not allowed to connect to her body and all the love, need, and sexuality within it. Her mother had told her to not love men, implying they were all to be mistrusted, as her mother mistrusted her father. Laura thought this meant it would be okay to love women, but at 14 her mother's frigid view of her as an outcast gave her the message that she couldn't love women either. The powerful and magnificent feelings she felt in her body had to be severed from her mind by repression. She became overly intellectual and compulsively driven in intellectual work, trying to compensate for her loss, without any support or avenue to mourning it. Laura even tried to hide consciousness of her homoerotic longings from herself, fantasizing that she really only wanted to be these female camp counselors' special friend, not wanting to believe that her love was "queer" and "deranged" as her mother seemed to think. However, this self-deception was always challenged by the very real physical responses and eroticism she felt for some of her friends and acquaintances, for she couldn't fully cut off and guillotine her body out of existence. When Laura returned from camp at fourteen, she and her childhood friend had a "sleepover" reunion in her mother's house. As in early childhood, these 14-year-olds shared the same bed. They talked of their respective summer experiences. Her friend, Sharon, talked of her first experience with kissing a boy. Laura was terrified because for the first time in their long friendship Laura felt she could not share with her best friend the actual nightmare of that summer, in which she felt most strongly her homoerotic feelings, and was universally rejected for them. Instead she talked of her involvement with the camp theater group, never revealing what had happened, and feeling for the first time in her close friendship a gulf of distance and silence between her and Sharon, which caused her acute pain, again like the annihilating knife blade of the guillotine.

At the age of 16, Laura's mother sounded the death knell on her relationship with Sharon by accusing her friend's sister of being a call girl, and saying that Laura's association with Sharon would hurt her social and marital opportunities. She also convinced Laura that her friend had "betrayed" her by neglecting to tell her about some summer courses she was taking to help her get into a good college. Believing her mother's accusations, and feeling outraged and wounded, Laura called her best friend and broke off her friendship without any explanation. And so this gulf between Laura and her friend at 14 became unbreachable at 16, due to her mother's jealous interference. Laura was not allowed to have her beloved friend, because her mother would not allow her to love another woman above herself. When the later anguish for this loss opened within Laura's analysis, the poignancy of her grief was palpable. Yet for thirty years Laura was to suffer the pathological mourning state in self-sabotaging reenactments that could never bring her friend back, nor the earlier mother that she so yearned for in her perpetual infatuations with women.

The visage of Medusa appeared in Laura's perception and psychic fantasy as chiseled in gray granite, not even in marble. The gulf and barrier between her and her mother seemed infinitely wide, wide as the "Grand Canyon." Separation from me, her analyst, during the summer, would later take on such a black attitude – an attitude of an endless void. At 14 years, unlike earlier times of maternal rejection, Laura would retaliate with her own cold and abandoning rage. For the first time in her fourteenth year of life she would totally dissociate from her internal good and loving mother constellation, in relation to her external mother. She was compelled to cast out the loving self and mother constellation onto other women who psychically served as mother displacements. This is why a psychotherapist who had worked with Laura for a dozen years prior to entering psychoanalysis with me would come to view her as "a hamster on a wheel,' endlessly searching for the childhood mother love, and mother, muse, artist outside her main interpersonal relationships, always tiring into exhaustion from the psychically Sisyphean task.

From the age of 15 into her adulthood, Laura would cut off from her former role as her mother's confidante and as the empathetic mirror of her mother's pain. Her mother later expressed a naive puzzlement about "what had happened." At 16, Laura's withdrawal was broken by a conscious eruption of overt rage towards her mother. When she pursued her mother to express it, her mother slapped her once, and then once again across the face as Laura challenged her again. At this point, assuming herself an adult, Laura began to pack to leave her parents' home. She was confronted then with her father's forbidding posture. She was forced to stay by her father, in what might seem like a perverse alliance with the wife whom he himself had to leave many times in his own way. Laura's father obviously wanted Laura to stay. Laura was touched and overwhelmed by her father's power and his love at this time.

THE FATHER'S ROLE IN THE INTERNAL PSYCHIC STRUCTURE

Laura's internal psychic structure could be conceptually understood in relation to her internalization of her highly intense, erotic and divisive experience with her mother, as it split itself into alternate self and object part constellations, probably from the time of her toddlerhood. Yet her father's influence on her as both a separate object and as an object fused in with the mother, needs to be understood as well. In some ways he may have been fused in with the alternately loving and hating attitudes of the mother. However, more obvious is the role he played as a separate object for identification, providing an alternative to the identification with the volatile, frigid and contrived femininity of the mother.

In the beginning Laura's father seems to have been very much a love object. Remembering back as early as the age of 3, Laura recalls the excitement with which she experienced her father's daily homecomings, after a long day at his legal practice. She was told later that she would get so excited when he returned home from work that her little trousers would fall down as she took out toy guns from a holster she wore around her waist and said "stick'em up!" Of course, this memory has much meaning, not only in terms of highlighting the normal little girl erotic excitement during the oedipal period, but it also reveals interesting facts about the gender identity cultivated by Laura and by her parents for herself. It was not a little girl playing with dolls that greeted her father, nor a little girl in a dress. Her role as surrogate son was supported and perhaps highly promulgated.

From this memory alone we can see in Laura's history the combination of self-object choice and gender identity focused on one and the same object, as opposed to being neatly divided between the parents. Laura's female and oedipal attraction to her father indicates Laura's predisposition towards men as sex objects, but the masculine part of her identity was likely to cause conflict with such an orientation. In addition, as her mother and other women became highly longed for love objects, the pull towards a masculine identification might become particularly convenient, particularly when her father represented an aliveness that her mother insufficiently provided: a core body aliveness with an eroticism highlighted in sexual activity. Laura's identification with her father's earthy, embodied and vividly sensual longings proved to be profound. Although intelligent and intellectual, Laura's father did not sublimate his eroticism into a symbolic art. He acted it out on a carnal fashion that extended to a buoyant and salacious sense of humor, both inside and outside of his marriage. He was, in Laura's assessment, an incessant flirt, brought to vital and vivid life the moment any young woman entered a room in which he himself resided. He also loved to protect, care for, and bring women to spontaneous life. He might overwhelm them with his often off-color humor, but he was also highly entertaining and cherished the novelty of each woman who entered his sights. How sad then that he should be dismayed by a bevy of daughters, always considering them second rate to a son. Nevertheless, he did entertain his two daughters, as well as other women with his sense of humor. But his sense of humor also disclosed a subtle strain of contempt in the form of chauvinism that affected his daughter as well. His stories were often of male authority figures humiliating young women for their more self-advancing and perhaps feminist intentions. There was an uneasy mixture in him that Laura found troubling to sort out: on the one hand, his worship of women as the objects of desire, and on the other hand, the derision of them as possible competitors.

Nevertheless, this paternal mixture was easier for Laura to stomach in some ways than that polarized mixture she often collided into where her mother was concerned. Some of Laura's fantasy life highlighted this mixture, which unlike the mixture within her internal mother, was not so much a mixture of love and hate, as much as of submission and love. One chief erotic fantasy that Laura with her poetic sensuality was able to take much pleasure in was that of a submission to anal penetration by a group of male father figures at the end of which Laura opens up to a deep and tender love that she had been up until then withholding. The group of men in this fantasy had a loving aspect, although their forceful penetration was sometimes conceptualized as rape by Laura. They took pleasure in Laura's pleasure, once she surrendered to a desire within that met up with her submission to their coercion. They delighted in her orgasms from this forceful engagement, and they were thrilled by her blissful discovery of tender love commingled with erotic release at the end of the anal sex scene. In the transference, I, as a woman analyst, was mingled with this crowd, either as one of them, or sitting by as an observer. But I apparently took on a benign role in the fantasy, even though I was there as part of a father transference that had sadomasochistic eroticism highlighted within it.

The father in this fantasy, despite being a conglomerate, is overall a ravishing lover as opposed to a malicious rapist. But this does not obviate whipping with belts or forced penetration. The paternal males are willing to use their power to compel an emergence of a loving self, where once it was sealed off and imprisoned behind withholding and oppositional defenses. Her fantasies were not initially so explicit about her sexual desires for men. But as Laura's homoerotic transference became increasingly conscious and understood, her sexual fantasies of men became more frequent. They also changed from an exclusively sadomasochistic nature to more of a deeply loving and penetrating sexual intercourse.

Another view of Laura, in relation to the male figure, is that presented in a poem that Laura recited to me about strong-limbed young men and their romantic female partners. Laura's sexuality was often expressed in a highly poetic and rather spiritual manner, and in this case she expressed it through a poem. Of course, even such a poem might not be as poetic as her own personally related desires, particularly as she expressed them within the context of the erotic transference in treatment. Nevertheless, this poem had serious import for Laura, and when she told it to me she was recalling a period in her life when her heterosexual desires had been more prominent than her homosexual ones. This was not immediately clear to me. I questioned Laura as to whether she identified more with the young men or young women in relation to this poem about the romantic idylls of spring. Incensed by my question, she blasted me with criticism for my "failure" to not heed her accentuation of her heterosexual desires at the time, when she was remembering her life in relation to the poem. However, after her anger, she reflected and came back to me with an apology, appreciating that I might have been indicating something important to her. She said that after some reflection she realized that when she first discovered the poem she had indeed identified with the "strong limbed" young men, longing for pretty girls, although later she was much more swayed by desiring these young men in the role of a female. She told me this particular poem during a period when she was mourning the loss of her heterosexual orientation, and her loss of men as romantic mates. Therefore, my question was not in line with her psychic locus at that time. However, there had been so many sexual fantasies in which Laura would picture herself in the role of the men that my question was understandable and ended up hitting pay dirt (this existed side by side with Laura's fantasies of being a woman making love to another woman).

When Laura identified with men in her fantasies, they were usually lusty, sensual, earthy and erotic men with a markedly healthy sexual appetite. She also could see herself as "the cock of the walk" amongst a group of feminine women. Her identification with her father in this case was clear. She consciously thought of him as playing the "cock of the walk" role of seductive lover and flirt whenever women were around.

Where does all this leave us in relation to the father's coloration of Laura's internal psychic structure? I believe that the father's chauvinistic side, which evidenced an air of contempt and manic defense, would have been internalized as part of the overall aggressive, negative, and certainly contemptuous mother object. The more warm and accepting side of her father could have been internalized as part of the mother's more tender side, split off from its polarized aggressive constellation. However, I also believe that the father's erotic aspect was internalized as a separate entity, differentiated from that of a preoedipal maternal love. I believe it became a part of a more central ego identification and a more libidinal aspect of the conscious central ego form. This is in contradistinction to being split off as an exciting object tantalizing an infant libidinal self, or as a rejecting object – constructed from the undigestible and unsymbolizable part of the mother. Throughout Laura's life, her healthy and highly conscious erotic core would serve her well in helping psychically to survive. This was true even in the midst of the inner devastation related to her mother's repeated emotional abandonments.

Laura did lose her libidinal central self at times, under the stress of abandonment trauma or severe narcissistic mortification, but this part of her was quick to recover (along with her admirable intellect), once the traumatic decompensation was contained by the therapeutic relationship. When Laura could securely express this libidinal part of herself within the psychic container of a masculine and symbolic identification, she had an important self-center to rely on. It is for this reason that despite Laura's many acute disappointments with her father as she grew up – particularly in relation to his erratic and failing ability to protect her from her mother's rages and threats, and his even more hostile role in forcing her through guilt into a caretaking role towards her – Laura always retained and sustained a good deal of gratitude for her father, and much admiration. She was able to identify with what was probably for her father his most life preserving quality: the ability to come to life and live in his body when around women.

UNREQUITED LOVE AND THE GROWING NECESSITY FOR FUTURE MOURNING

After her traumatic experience in camp at the age of 14, Laura decided to never again let any of her feelings for women be known. However, she did fall in love with a woman in her senior year of high school who went to the same college with her. Unknown to Laura, this woman was having an overt affair with another female friend and distanced from Laura. Laura felt deeply rejected at that time, hoping only for this woman's friendship, despite the pressure of her deep attraction to her schoolmate. The rejection of her love resonated with her earlier rejections at age 14 by the female counselors, the director of the camp, and by her mother.

Laura was totally devastated. In anger and despair she turned to men. There were men in college who pursued Laura. They were attracted to her and she was attracted to them. Laura was bitter and tired of pursuing women who seemed always to reject her. She went on to marry a man who initially seemed sensitive and desirable. They had a 14-year marriage in which both grew professionally. But she was riddled with longings for women, which she kept hidden partly due to the horror of her past rejections by them and due to the stigmatized nature of homosexuality. Also contributing to Laura's incognito existence was her lack of knowledge of the burgeoning gay and lesbian movement, and of women that would embrace her and rejoice in her lesbian feelings. In the tenth year of the marriage, the woman whom she had loved in high school and college contacted her. This woman was now divorced, and confided to Laura her feelings for women and an affair she was having with another woman and another man. Laura was transfixed and tantalized! Laura confided to me that she had loved this woman deeply, and still did. She continues to tell me that she and this woman planned and experienced a weekend together of lovemaking, which ended tragically for Laura.

After the severe humiliation and disappointment sustained by her at age 27 with her cold college friend turned demon lover, Laura fell into a deep depression. As she emerged from this depression, she became immersed in lesbian feminist literature, which appeared overtly in the early 1970s. Through such lesbian literature, as well as through bits and pieces in the media about the gay community, Laura was able to discover the lesbian and gay community. This ended her isolation from others who expressed and felt the same homoerotic longings. She was then able to leave an unhappy marriage of fourteen years, and to live independently, as a lesbian woman. For the first time, Laura felt pride in her homoerotic longings and pursuits. The silence of her adolescent and young adult years was broken at last. Laura felt a deep love and gratitude to the lesbian and gay community for their support and love.

Yet Laura's longings for an omnipotent form of muse mother would compel her to repeat the demon lover theme in her life, in which she longed for unavailable women, who would reject and humiliate her. The unmourned losses, grief, and humiliations of the past haunted her. She would need to come to psychoanalysis to mourn the split ideal and demonic sides of her primal mother that led her into a compulsive repetition. The erotic transference in treatment with me would become the ultimate vehicle to this.

MOURNING AND EROTIC TRANSFERENCE

The memories I have been recounting emerged through an intense mourning process, during the first three years of object relations psychoanalysis. This developmental mourning process consisted of grief for actual object loss as well as grief related to the wounds of narcissistic injury, the grief of unrequited love and loss of love, the mourning of grief due to transversing developmental impasses within separation–individuation, the grief of existential limits and life choices, and the depressive position grief related to hurting the one you love. All these aspects of the developmental mourning process were woven into the fabric of transference phenomena, with a prominent role of erotic transference in this psychoanalytic treatment.

Although traditionally the erotic transference has been seen, ever since Freud's first article on it, as a defense against remembering, I believe that from an object relations perspective it is essential to see its phenomenological role in providing a transitional object experience for the patient, and in providing both a view of the internal world as it exists in relation to the deepest unconscious desires. Erotic transference also provides a road to memory, as well as opposing memory with a screen against feeling the links to differentiated memories. The most intense erotic desires are always illustrative of early infant experience, as well of all levels of preoedipal and oedipal experience, and all that experience derived from both the preoedipal and oedipal levels that continues into adolescence and beyond. As Louise Kaplan (1996) has illustrated in *Female Perversions*, oedipal level experience effects the reworking in the internal world (or preconscious) of preoedipal experience, along with preoedipal experience having effects on oedipal experience. Therefore, preoedipal trauma that gets retriggered in the oedipal period intensifies this phenomenon. The erotic transference often reformulates early infant and toddler experience in oedipal terms. This can be seen quite vividly in this story of Laura.

Laura's erotic transference was prominent from the outset of her treatment, and Laura herself was aware that I had become an object of desire in her fantasy life from the very beginning. She was also aware that I might help her understand herself through understanding these fantasies, because she had read an article of mine prior to entering treatment.

From the beginning, Laura experienced me as her artist muse and feared I would become her "demon lover." She expected me to attract her and repel her at once, just as her mother had. I was the displacement oedipal fantasy mother, just as many women had been for her, particularly women writers or artists who she had fantasized having affairs with. She agonized over her sinful betrayal of mind in relation to her steady live-in lover and partner of fourteen years, who "she loved more than life itself." Thus, Laura, trod her course like the hamster on the wheel, always turning her head towards the new female attraction, having left men behind as lovers a while back. When I turned her head, I was giving a public presentation, which she attended as a professor of sociology, seeking to dabble in psychology after a long course of personal psychotherapy. Drawn to me, and repelled at once, she later described her initial view of me as "hating my stockinged legs and too high heels" (not the lesbian ideal surely!), and simultaneously being drawn into an "ocean of longing" in her attraction to me. She also said that she was intensely turned on, not only by my body, but by my "brilliant mind" as experienced through one of my presentations, a theoretical paper with a clinical case. I fit into the category of artist for Laura as I had, according to Laura, an "erotic intellect," and a flamboyant style and language. I also fit into the category of artist, her mother's category, which consequently made me a muse, because I had written books about women artists, which she had somehow heard of in her academic environment as a professor of sociology in a small private college. So I was ripe as a target for her projections of the muse goddess artist-mother.

I also was ripe for the dark side of that role, as the erotic demon lover, similar to Fairbairn's exciting and rejecting objects. One of Laura's first fantasies about me, while on the couch, was that I would stab her with a knife in her vagina. I certainly was the phallic mother for her at first, and this was reflected in her initial fears of my interpretations. It was also reflected in an early dream in which I appeared as the idealized goddess muse, but with a penis. I was seen in the dream as myself, undisguised, with long flowing hair, dressed in long silk gowns, and yet with a penis. I was seen in the dream as floating down to Laura from above, within a theater of stage dramas. I hovered above Laura's bed, in the dream, and was surrounded by light, like a religious icon. My erect penis brought Laura to associate to a combined mother/father object, who she experienced as having the omnipotence and seductive tantalization of a demon lover figure, as she had understood that figure in writings of mine (Kavaler-Adler 1993) that she had already read prior to her interest in entering into treatment with me. During Laura's treatment the unfolding of her erotic transference fantasies moved from Laura making love to me as a man and/or woman in an active phallic position, while I was in a passive receptive position, to another stage of sexual fantasies. In the new fantasies I was experienced as a phallic woman with an erect penis, making love to Laura from an active position, with her in the passive receptive place. Laura associated this new phallic woman in her fantasies with her father and her father transference, following a phase in which I was the feminine mother. As the oedipal follows the preoedipal, she then had a phase of erotic transference fantasies in which we were both part of a triangle, and the sex had triadic, but yet whole object themes. She could be either man or woman in this fluid oedipal scenario. She was sometimes a man penetrating me along with another man, and at other times she was a woman who shared the lovemaking with me from a passive receptive position. In this latter fantasy, a man, whom she believed both she and I were attracted to, penetrated us both. At other times I was the phallic woman penetrating her along with the man.

Laura would come to realize that all this related to wanting both her mother and father sexually. As she traveled through different developmental eras in her erotic fantasies in treatment, she mourned more and more deeply. She had always had fantasies of a group of men anally penetrating her, resonating back to early enemas she had painfully endured at summer camp. Through the mourning process, she was able to modify the nature of her anal sex fantasies with what she associated to be a group of father figures. The orgasm fantasies changed from anal rape and humiliation to love opening up in her through the anal penetration, and later to a more mutually satisfying intercourse with men that shed its sadomasochistic themes. Laura could later envision a gratifying and loving intercourse with a man, or with many men, without needing a theme of humiliation to excite her and bring her to orgasm. However, the nature of the erotic transference themes and their interaction with a developmental mourning process will be more fully explicated later. In speaking of the beginning of treatment it is necessary to speak of how frightened Laura was of me at the initial time when she asked to work with me and to enter an object relations psychoanalysis. An initial dream speaks of the kind of primal terror that she experienced at our first psychoanalytic consultations.

Dream

Laura recalled her first dream in a highly visceral way as she told it to me. She was being suffocated as all the air was pumped out of a series of subterranean chambers that she was forced to enter. She found herself running to escape death, as steel doors between the chambers slammed shut behind her. She barely made it through each door before it slammed, just a breath away from annihilation in the suffocation of the chamber that she was running from.

Then there was a change of scene to a cameo of a woman and man, both anonymous, sitting at a small coffee table, split off from any other atmosphere of a café. The woman at the table unzips her chest, and gives her heart to the man. In describing this Laura has fears and a foreboding of a psychic death in her new analysis, seeing herself as the woman and me as the man. She associates to fears of a repetition of unrequited love, and of my trying to "make her straight," as a fantasized therapeutic goal. Laura made clear to me that many lesbians had such a fear, and therefore sought to avoid analysis with a heterosexual analyst. Nevertheless, she plunged in, believing in spite of her fears that I could help her, risking both the love of her heart and her erotic desires in an attempt to learn about the compulsions that were attached to her feelings and passions.

Laura was threatened from the beginning by the intensity of her feelings for me, and it actually took Laura several years of ambivalence before she approached me for treatment. Laura told me that she would feel a rush of intense emotion whenever in the consultation room with me, which she described as an overwhelming "ocean of longings." I felt the power of her affect in highly visceral sensations, especially when she was too apprehensive in the beginning to share her feelings, which would later become explicit and differentiated erotic fantasies. Without this symbolic communication, Laura felt drowned in the ocean of longing. She often conveyed this to me, as a sense of awe and reverence, revealing more of the idealization within her erotic love lust than the demonic side. Yet, she was quite clear that she had "paranoid thoughts" about me. Her general sense of mistrust was put under the headline of another horrible agony of "unrequited love." In referring to this apprehension, Laura would describe the adult trauma of the first time she had fallen in love with a woman who was bisexual and not straight. She had hoped (in her late twenties) that this would be different than her acute disappointments, when falling in love with straight women in her past. Having discovered a woman who had lived at least partly as a lesbian, she had hoped that her desperate wish for mutuality in love would finally find its fulfillment. To Laura, her new starlet of artistic and erotic arousal was perhaps the only living creature who she might find satisfaction with. She had yet to discover that there was a gay and lesbian community.

Therefore, it was a knife in her heart, vagina, and womb that she experienced all at once when her vulnerable state allowed the axe of unrequited love to fall. The weekend she had hoped to be a paradise of ecstasy and harmony, turned into a nightmare. The snow fell outside and ice of past hurt and hatred moved in around her heart. Soon her chosen lover sarcastically dismissed her and spoke of another female lover, after Laura laid herself open at her feet. Laura's new target of passionate desire certainly became the tantalizing and rejecting object. Laura nearly imploded with her unrequited longings and their intense affect.

Many times, but with different details, Laura had confided to me the tragedy of this infamous weekend. Thinking that she had been rejected by the only available woman alive, and one with the proper credentials of artistic self-absorption as well as the dual-edged sword of warmth and ice, Laura's despair knew no bounds when the weekend failed. It was clear that Laura feared that her encounter with me in treatment would lead to the same kind of descent into hell and horror. She had given her heart and soul to this woman, and in the end had been viewed with a kind of nauseous disdain. None of Laura's actual positive personality traits had been perceived by this woman, and Laura was cynically and distastefully dismissed, with a rather wry comment by her love object: "Oh I thought you would be very different, but I guess I was wrong!"

In spite of her terror at our first meetings, Laura gradually began to find some trust for me. This trust allowed her to share her first erotic transference fantasies. She would share these fantasies with me as they arose, along with intense feelings within her body, as she lay on the couch in my office. She was a brave soul from the beginning, and her courage extended to an acute intellectual curiosity about her internal life. One example of Laura's symbolized erotic fantasies was of having an affair with me at my office, where she would spread my legs, take my "pearl" in her mouth, "drown in my come," "wrap me in a blanket" afterwards, and then feed me (as she placed her own infant self into me and proceeded to nurture it). This fantasy also included a negative oedipal triangle, which revealed itself in an addendum of free associations.

Laura imagined meeting my husband, who would be in an enraged state as he banged on my door and entered my office. She imagined having an open skirmish with him as he was jealously "defending his territory." Another frequent fantasy with a multitude of versions was of being in an audience while a man – sometimes my husband – made love to me, and she would cheer me on towards my orgasms as my male lover forced me into a state of submission by beating me, which she imagined I would love, or merely penetrated me, as I surrendered to him in a state of passionate and hungry lust, from a passive receptive position. She could also imagine herself as the male lover, in a ménage-à-trois with a male lover who appealed to us both and provided us both with pleasure. Laura imagined me with other men as well, sometimes with a man she had been attracted to, and one whom she believed to be respectful of me, and whom she imagined to be an adequate peer and competitive opponent for me. However, when she couldn't identify with my male lover, she would be powerfully jealous and competitive with him. ("The thought of him putting his penis into you drives me crazy.") Each of these fantasies shows psychodynamic constellations that relate to Laura's developmental mourning process as it unfolded.

When Laura expressed her erotic transference fantasies, she might be defending against both memory and powerful feelings that would come up at other times. Yet, within the context of the fantasies were the disguised memories and the hidden yearnings behind them. On the surface she would identify with the phallic penetrating other in the fantasies, whether she appeared as herself as in the fantasy of having an affair with me at my office, or as an alter ego of my husband, who she imagined was beating me and then penetrating me. These phallic fantasies would occur frequently to Laura, because they allowed her to assume a lusty hunger for sexuality and for phallic power, both of which she had originally experienced through her father. Her identifications with me in the fantasies were more latent and less manifest, but they were the key to understanding the split off feminine and infant longings that Laura was both defending against and moving towards in the compromise formation of the erotic transference fantasies. When her lovemaking fantasies were particularly tender, her own nurturance might prevail over the actual phallic penetration of my inner being, and then the longings of the infant within her would be more overt.

In that particular fantasy, Laura speaks of spreading my legs and of "taking my pearl," and she doesn't neglect to speak of her wish to drown in my come, after she penetrates me and gives me an orgasm. The whole description is highly poetic, and it very quickly moves into her wishes to wrap me up in a blanket, to feed me, hold me and make me smile with contentment. In this fantasy I play the role of the receptive female figure, which speaks for Laura's latent feminine wishes. I allow my legs to be spread and I can yield to penetration in Laura's fantasy in a way that Laura yearns to do, and when this becomes more conscious in treatment, she comes to mourn for the loss of men, and of male penetration for herself. Through this mourning, Laura is able to yield increasingly to offering her inner being to me in the treatment relationship, so that she might reconnect with formerly sealed off levels of herself, parts of herself that she had buried. But when she does yield to this feminine side of her, surrender comes with much rage, and with many memories of her mother's punitive humiliations. However, it also brings her capacity to open and yield more fully to both emotional love in friendships and to emotional and sexual love within her real life love relationship. This particular tender fantasy of Laura making love to me also discloses a deep infant part of her that resides within the more mature feminine part of her. When Laura wraps me up in a blanket, in the fantasy, one can almost touch the tender baby feeling, as her maternal side yields to the infant within her. Her wish to hold me after making love, and after wrapping me up in a blanket, is easily converted into a scene of a mommy cuddling her baby. No wonder that Laura feared being overwhelmed by an "ocean of longings" each time she risked the actual feeling expression of her erotic longings for me, as they come up in her body in the moment.

It was often after Laura had been disillusioned by the frustration of experiencing her yearnings for me as a recreation of her earlier experiences of unrequited love that she would travel emotionally from rage to loss, along with the developmental correlates implied. Once Laura could open to the grief feelings in the mourning of this loss, she could then reawaken memories of earlier loss. This would lead to renewals of Laura's loving capacity, highlighted in the "eternal now" moment with me.

Laura repairs her angry accusatory attacks on me with her love and concern. At such points, Laura might feel such powerful feelings of love for me that she would risk sharing her body sensations and feelings, those which would become split off as somatic and obsessional blocks to connection if not expressed. On such an occasion, Laura has spoken of her intense passion as a throbbing and opening in her vagina, and sometimes has trouble breathing from the intensity of the heartfelt cries that eventually emerge from within as tears. When receiving these feelings, as well as the erotic fantasies that both screen them and deliver them in disguise, I have felt a need to breathe deeply to allow Laura the transitional space between us – which is also analytic space and psychic space – to provide a container for her penetrating me with her words and feelings. Although sometimes my role might be a more interpretive one, it has been essential to provide this avenue for Laura to express her internal erotic life in the transitional space of the analytic session. As she expresses her fantasies and feelings directly to me, in the moment, our transitional analytic bond and space provide a critical avenue of converting the defensive function of the erotic transference into the curative function of integrating her internal life with an external object relationship. Gradually over time Laura has seen how the sharing of her fantasies allows her to get to the raw body sensations and emotional feelings behind the fantasies. Such sharing helps Laura come out of a sealed off state in her mind, where her fantasies have been masturbatory, often distancing her from being present in her life and with the woman she loves. As she shares her fantasies of me with me, and opens her heart and vagina in a concert of object desires, Laura gains access to an external object relationship with me. Consequently, she can become increasingly present in the external world with me. Then she can become increasingly present with others, and most particularly with her female lover, with whom she has a deep and abiding friendship along with erotic love.

However, with each new opening to such overt communication and object contact, Laura has her backlash resistance, as she fears just the opposite will happen. Sharing with me brings up Laura's oedipal level guilt and jealousies. Therefore, she imagines she is betraying her lover in opening up to me and in having me in her mind at all, especially as a prime object of her erotic passions. A combination of the frustration within the realistic unrequited love aspect of the analytic situation, and of her fears of committing an adulterous betrayal of her lover with me, causes her to turn cold and cynical: "What are we doing here!" All this disguises and inflames her oedipal guilt. In her core Laura feels she is committing incest by making love to her mother. In this light she is betraying her father. But she also experiences her betrayal of her real life lover as a mother figure she is betraying to go to her father, as if she is opening the door to her parents' home, allowing her father to enter, when her mother is trying to lock him out. This actually happened to Laura at 3 years old. Her mother had locked out her father, because of one of his adulterous affairs coming to light. Laura stood on the stair-case of her home watching her father banging on the door with his fists, ordering Laura to let him in, something she was incapable of at 3 years old. Her father yelled at Laura that he would kill her if she didn't let him in from the bottom of the stairs. At the same time, Laura's mother shrieked from above that she would kill Laura if she let her father in. This put Laura in an unresolvable bind, causing her to ascribe her desires for both men and women as love objects to be forbidden. Throughout most of her life, Laura carried an early prohibition against love for any other, whether the target of that love were a man or a woman. She faced the ongoing internal threat that she would be annihilated by both her parents for whatever love choices she would make.

THE NEED FOR THE HEALTHY PARENTAL COUPLE

The division between Laura's parents was a torment for her, despite the fact that it gave her a certain position of power in relation to playing the part of the mediator between her parents. In her fantasy life, Laura sought to repair her parents, as they existed within her. When she had erotic transference fantasies, such as the one of my husband beating me and making love to me in Italy, she was constructing a new parental couple, which included the sadomasochistic element between her parents, but in a benign form of sexual play, where it could spice up the eroticism of a healthy and loving couple. Other fantasies of my husband making love to me emphasized both the phallic and tender aspects of lovemaking, possibly excluding the overt sadomasochistic element. Laura would think of my husband sexually penetrating me, and would feel both an excitement and a jealousy. However, beyond either of these reactions was Laura's yearning to unite my husband and myself as a couple, although she always entertained the alternative scenario of being in my husband's place or joining me as a woman with another man making love to both of us. There were times when Laura's desire to have the united parental couple was particularly strong, and such fantasies of tender lovemaking between my husband and myself could be accompanied by mournful thoughts about how Laura's own parents had very rarely appeared happy in each other's presence. One day during her third year in treatment, Laura said that she imagined my husband's joy in being with me, his ecstasy in watching me shop and in participating in putting beautiful outfits on me. She imagined the thrill within him, in my presence, as if he wanted to leap across the room to kiss me, especially when I would smile at him and praise him. She loved to luxuriate in her mind's scenario, in which both love and admiration would flow between myself and my husband, bringing us both an open joy. She imagined feeling safe, warm and secure in such an atmosphere, when she added herself into the scene. She would feel protected in a way she had never felt with her actual parents: "My mother would never have been present enough with my father to make him feel such overt love!"

OEDIPAL ROMANCE, PREOEDIPAL YEARNINGS, AND EROTIC MOMENTS

The split off feminine receptive self and its vulnerable infant self-core were generally projected outward in Laura's fantasies. I was seen as the receptacle of her infant and feminine selves, and the beating fantasy reflected the same belief as the anal rape fantasy in relation to father figures, the belief that a woman had to be forced into opening up to love. Such a belief can clearly be traced to Laura's mother, who Laura saw as immured in a frozen frigid state, walled off against love, particularly when it was offered in a sexual form. Laura preferred to see herself in the role of the phallic and penetrating love partner, with me playing the role of the feminine and receptive self, although her anal rape fantasies were an exception to this. Nevertheless, Laura's yearnings for offering and receiving love needed to come out in the open through her own firsthand feeling experience, to help her to discover the infant self at the core of her being. Her fantasies both shielded her from the direct expression of the need within her, residing at the infant self-core, and they also led the way into the necessary contact with her infant core. Each time Laura suffered any disappointment in her wish for reciprocal and requited love, she opened to feelings of loss and to memories that helped her to contact the vulnerability within her. Each memory of loss through unrequited love led to a new piece of mourning. As she opened to her mourning she also opened to love with me in the moment. She felt this love through intense and passionate body feelings. With increasing self-integration through developmental mourning, however, she also was able to fantasize the yearnings of the infant and child selves that lay behind the adult erotic longings.

FROM PROTOSYMBOLISM TO SYMBOLISM IN THE GIVING OF THE ROMANTIC GIFT

In the beginning Laura attempted to enact a love affair with me through sending me beautiful long-stem red roses. She had talked about doing this many times, which was how she would respond to falling in love with a woman in her past. Despite discussing the impulse to do this and the desire behind it, she felt compelled at times to actually do it. She wanted the beauty of the flowers to speak their own symbolism, telling me that after I received the flowers she imagined them opening to me with such a full color, smell and redolence, that they could represent the way she felt her heart, mind, and body opening to me. So again, as in her fantasies, Laura was able to play both a masculine and feminine role here. She was the man in taking the courting role of sending me the flowers, and she was the female in symbolizing her body opening to me through the opening of the blooming roses. Laura would say that she regressed to an early place in doing this as well, a child place where words could never be adequate to express feelings. Only an image or symbolic gift could.

It was through the mourning process that Laura was able to go beyond the enactment of wooing her muse mother-lover through sending flowers, and beyond using the flowers as a protosymbolic expression of her own feelings. Increasingly she could speak her flowering feelings through words as she felt the feelings in the room with me. She would open to longings, and offer them to me by saying things like "I want you so much right now" or "I'm feeling this throbbing feeling in my vagina, wanting you." Sometimes the feelings would rush up so powerfully she found it hard to speak, and she could feel suffocated with them or dizzy.

Yet, it was in these moments that Laura began to reveal the deeper longings that had differentiated out of a diffuse ocean within her. It was in such moments that Laura revealed the heartfelt expression of yearnings that had formerly been split off and projected onto the "other." She was able to own and articulate wishes to sit on my lap, and to have me stroke her hair, wishes to be held and comforted at my breast as an infant might be. Such moments of courage spoke volumes from the tender voice of the child within, but also revealed a dark side to such wishes, a dark side resonating back to the most primal terrors of the muse mother turned demonic. One day, when Laura announced her core wish to inhabit a special place in my vagina through phallic penetration, which would result in her inhabiting the interior side of my womb, the underbelly of her fantasy flipped dramatically into consciousness. She reported a black swirling terror coming forth, the black vortex of my imagined infinity of darkness, and the impinging threat of being suffocated and lost within my womb, as it turned into an infinite black hole within her mind.

Subtle and not so subtle observations of my appearance, as a very real and corporal being, might lead Laura into associations to such wishes and longings. She might remark that a certain pair of high heels I wore made my pelvis tilt in my dress in an enchanting attitude. Such amorous comments had their own poetry, and were spoken from the adult erotic being in her. However, at moments of intense vulnerability such comments might take on the aspect of her profound internal need. For instance, she would envision being nestled against my body. In her wish to fill me up with happiness, she would swell with praise for both my mind and body! If she commented on my thinking, for instance, she was eloquent. She demonstrated a deep capacity to receive my thinking and to integrate it within her. If she spoke about my body, she was equally eloquent, but was also seductive, tantalizing in her own way.

When I interpreted the defensive aspect of her overtures to me, Laura was hurt. Nevertheless, she was capable of suffering the grief of the hurt, and therefore could use my interpretation as an opportunity to open to the deeper places within her where the wounding of the past resided. For instance, when she spoke to me of how my appearance in a particular dress must devastate those around me, she wished for a friendly or perhaps even "devastated" response to her praise. As I stayed quiet to allow us to discover her motivation at that moment, she felt overwhelmed with rage and then grief. Her first response was to think I was offended. My interpretation was that "If I don't respond as an aroused lover, I become a cold mother offended by sexuality, one who withdraws her love." Laura felt the interpretation, and perhaps the act of interpreting itself, at first as a mortal blow. I was exposing her wish to arouse me, and her acute vulnerability to a feeling of unrequited love that was based on the close engagement she maintained to a cold and angry side of her mother, as it existed personified within her. Such moments brought the disillusionment of transference wishes, such as wishes for me to exist as an ideal lover and love object, or wishes for me to represent her own feminine side at its most attractive zenith. I was not playing out her well-plotted internal scenario as the one reciprocating her instinctual love with an instinctual response. I was not actively supporting the primal love between women that she cherished by the enactment of an oedipal romance in relation to a woman. It was a crushing disappointment for her, as it would be for any analysand at the peak of oedipal erotic desire. Such moments of disillusionment tested my survival as a real object from whom Laura could seek connection and support. I had to be intensely sensitive to the pain in her vulnerability at these moments, even if it first exploded forth as cold sarcastic rage and an incipient anger. If I could be there sufficiently in a deep emotional sense we could navigate the impasse into a fullblown process of mourning, which would bring memories, dreams, and rich core self fantasies and longings, both oedipal and preoedipal, which lay latent beneath her overture to me.

My survival in the sense of Winnicott's (1974) notion of object survival would involve a sustaining of emotional availability without retaliation or abandonment.

A broader view of this survival would also involve a sensitivity of attunement at these vulnerable points, as well as an understanding of where Laura's own angry assaults and accusations might be coming from at a poignant moment of self-exposure. Given that I could be there in such a way, to a "good enough" degree, the psychoanalytic rewards were forthcoming. It was rarely easy. I might try my best not to retaliate when she criticized me and questioned why I was "changing the rules on her," since I now had declined to always actively empathize with her wishes and to reflect them back to her with words and feelings. Yet, my momentary silence had felt like an abrupt disruption of her former expectations, both transferential expectations and human expectations, particularly in the light of an earlier therapeutic attitude of response I might have assumed.

All this had to be discussed, and part of what came about was the extreme disillusionment of the belief that we could be one, as mother and infant, as oedipal child and parental erotic love object, as child and couple, or as the adult lover and beloved. The gap of separation, which had emerged into the analytic space between us, was emerging again. Through its experience, Laura became increasingly free from her own interpretation that our new mode of engagement, on a less symbiotic and more separate level, would dictate the inevitable impasse of unrequited love and its implications, meaning to Laura that she was inadequate, a failure, and thus unlovable. This new freedom came from Laura mourning the sense of loss that would open up along with her powerful but disappointing experience. At one time, in an earlier state of such disillusionment, during the first year of treatment Laura had said: "You were the only one who had come into the abyss with me, but I had to think again after you fell asleep during my intimate description of lesbian lovemaking. (*Well, not quite! I thought.*) You certainly will not win the lesbian of the year award! Again I'm confronted with the difference between us and it hurts!"

Two years later, in the third year of treatment, Laura responded to my momentary silence, and to the forthcoming interpretation of her wish and fear, and of her good and bad mothers, as that same divide between us. Then she demanded an apology from me for answering the phone (which I never usually do) during her session and interrupting her at a point of deep emotional grief. I almost cut her off five minutes before the end of the session, as I misread the time. She was filled with cold accusatory rage as I failed to submit to what felt to me like a coercive demand. Upon reflection, Laura realized that she had catastrophized the five minutes of session time lost, even though I had made a momentary mistake. She also realized that she was reading into my behavior all of her mother's emotional abandonments, along with all her mother's threats of actual abandonment. Ultimately she understood as well that she had been in the grip of a cold, controlling and punitive attitude within her own rage, which mirrored that of her mother's punitive coldness, and that in the grip of that identification and its reenactments, which was pathological in its compulsion – indeed was coercive towards me – she had demanded an apology from me that I could not give freely from within.

A mutuality and dialectic of response grew out of this transference disillusionment as memories and feelings of the past, those being projected onto the moment and onto me. When this was understood the traumatic loss contained in the memories could be mourned. Laura mourned the ideal mother she wished for. She also remembered the pain she felt in response to the cold and abandoning side of her mother. Through this mourning and its remembrance, and through the opening of psychic space that comes about as grief allow the yielding of defenses, Laura could open into communication with me as the presence of the external other. Since she had projected the internal object onto me, the internal object could become symbolized and thus differentiated and detoxified. The intersubjective and interpersonal dialectic emerges.

The dialectic did emerge between Laura and myself. Laura told me that she had to remember that I had rarely been cold to her, although she saw me that way whenever she became overwhelmed both with anger and with a desperate wish to repair the bond between us. She also acknowledged her own coldness at these times, which came as quite a shock to her, because in her own words, "It's not part of my self-concept." She had encountered a dissociated part of herself that had become overt in her behavior within the analytic transference situation. I, in turn, acknowledged that I may have had an angry expression on my face when she was being coercive with me, and when I was trying to get through to her. I apologized for any degree of rejecting behavior I had expressed. She responded that she thought I must have felt she was very ungrateful for all I had done for her, especially when she accused me of such emotional abandonment. I, in turn, responded that I believed that she carried this fear within her, as part of a whole scene with her mother. I said that I was mainly concerned with how to speak to her at the point when she was being so accusatory and coercive. Her goodness, her gratitude, the deep loving part of her certainly had not been forgotten by me, I told her. Yet, the fear she carried of losing my love touched off the deepest pain in her since with her mother there had been hatred that had come between them (at fourteen). This hatred had truly wiped out Laura's consciousness of an intense love between them for most of her life. No wonder Laura might see a flash of anger in my eyes. She believed that flash of anger was a growing hatred that might freeze all love for her out of my heart forever, as she had felt happened with her mother after the break between them when she was fourteen.

Such was the reparative dialogue that could follow Laura's mourning of object loss as well as her loss of her mother's love. She felt both each time there was an impasse between us. After a reparation of this sort, Laura had expressed her wish that I could hug her. I responded with an interpretation that it was a mother's hug she wanted. Laura had attempted to avoid the vulnerability of her wish for me to repair all the hurts of the past with a special mother's hug by playing the phallic lover role. Yet, it was the bottom line of her wishes towards me, and she began to accept some of the truth in it. Her reflexive tendency might still be to project her need and wishes onto me, but she was increasingly reowning these projections. During the second year of treatment she had said to me: "I know that deep down you must long for a relationship with a woman, which can give a special kind of closeness, different than with a man." Although Laura might assign such a primal wish to all women, during her third year of treatment Laura was able to become less focused on providing me with something essential that was missing for me. She was able to become more focused on her own frustrated longings, as they expressed themselves within the transference with me. As Laura owned and expressed these wishes more, she became increasingly present with her real life lover. Also, certain formerly repressed aspects of her, such as her femininity, began to emerge more into consciousness.

DREAMS

With the abundant richness of Laura's internal life, she was able to bring dreams into treatment on an ongoing basis. Several dreams stand out in terms of the dynamic struggles within her internal world, and in terms of the process of her developmental mourning as it transpired.

An early dream of an elephant running, thundering down a beach, captures both Laura's sensuality as well as her self-concept as someone who is as instinctual as an animal. It also captures Laura's unconscious heaviness with the weight of her own needs; needs which she saw as grotesque and huge as an elephant. Such a dream has been recalled by her at different times, for it gives a flash of the self-concept she had at the initiation of treatment.

Many of Laura's other dreams were overtly transferential in nature. Her associations brought the transference to light. A dream during her second year of treatment included slippery eels that surrounded and engulfed her, and sleeping sharks that threatened to awake and attack.

Sharks and eels dream

"I am in my bedroom, only it is not my bedroom. There is a king-sized bed, which I am lying on face down. Suspended from the ceiling by ropes are sleeping sharks. I am afraid to move lest they awaken and devour me in a hideous feeding frenzy. I had been masturbating after my partner had fallen asleep, and was afraid my movements and vibrations [orgasm] would awaken her and I would be embarrassed."

In the dream Laura is desperately trying to throw eels back into the water as they leapt out at her. Laura's first associations to this dream were of the sleeping shark being her female lover, who was asleep while she lay in bed masturbating, and whose temporary waking startled and embarrassed her. Then she said that the eels seemed to represent my needs, which she feared would overwhelm and engulf her. I thought the sleeping shark was much more than her present-day lover or myself as a real object, but was at a latent level the mother from the past who would punish others by withdrawing to her bed as if asleep, when the mother was full of rage, which was manifested as a paralyzing cold depression. The sleeping shark could also represent the biting rage that Laura had repressed, and which had awakened in the transference with me.

Laura and I then focused on the other image in the dream, the image of the eels. I suggest to Laura, in response to her association to the eels being my needs that they might also represent her needs. Laura's first responses to this suggestion was quite antagonistic, although she was generally amenable to me associating to her dreams and interpreting them along with her. She was almost shocked, as if hit by some intrusion that touched an unconscious layer in her that she was not so willing to meet. My words seemed to evoke shame in her. Yet Laura reflected deeply on my interpretation over time, and replied over a series of several sessions.

Laura did not find it pleasant to think of herself as the one with overwhelming needs that might be as slippery, erotic, and body based as wet eels were. She was used to thinking of her mother's needs as being the burden of her life. After all, wasn't it Laura's task as a child to be her mother's confidante, to commiserate with her when she was upset by her husband? And wasn't it Laura's job to try and wake her out of her semi-catatonic state when her mother became the "sleeping shark," withdrawing into a position of anger and depression that threatened to erupt into rage? Laura's father had reinforced such a parentified child's role for her. He had dragged Laura home from school with guilt-provoking comments such as: "What did you do to upset your mother?" Yet, Laura's cooperation with such a role became a highly defensive posture for her, as well as a way of enabling her mother's defense. When Laura fitted into her mother in this fashion she had not been required to feel her own needs. All her needs and feelings could be projected onto her mother, who became the needy elephant that Laura had to carry on her back. When overwhelmed, Laura sought to evade her mother's needs as well as her own projected needs. This is seen in the dream of throwing the eels back into the water. In the dream, Laura tries to get away from the eels. She puts them back into the water, which might in part represent her mother's body as well as her own unconscious. But the task of doing so was a futile task, just as was that of trying to comply with her mother's needs. Meanwhile her own needs were repressed, and pressured her from within in an unbearable fashion, promoting projections that could now be sorted out in the transference.

When Laura thought about my interpretation of the eels being her own needs, which she feared would overwhelm her (and perhaps me), she was stirred at a very deep level. She was stirred up at the level in which her inner child self resided with its dissociated and disguised libidinal hungers. Following this awakening, Laura proves grateful and expresses her gratitude in an emphatic manner. She tells me, with a great deal of feeling, that she is appreciative of having such a compatible analytic partner in me, one who she now experienced as acutely attuned to her. After Laura was able to engage in a dialogue with me about my interpretation of the slippery eels being her own unconscious needs, I was experienced by her as sensitive to her needs and to her diversions from them, as we worked on this dream together.

But what of Laura's overall defense against consciousness of her needs and desires that was woven into the fabric of her personality? When Laura had a dream of a dance, which she called a manic dance representing the psychic state of pathological mourning, we both could share such a symbolized vision of that overall personality defense.

Laura reports a dream in which a man and a woman are dancing round and round, waltzing to a popular tune that she cannot erase from her mind. The tune is derived from a song whose chorus reads as follows: "He married the girl with the strawberry curl and the band played on."

Laura identifies with the man in the dream, who is dancing with the blonde woman. Her mother had blonde hair, and her mother represents both her oedipal love object (alternatively to her father, who was also an oedipal love object for her, but not the only one) and her own feminine side, which was swept up in a dance that would never end. The man is drinking as well as dancing, and the line of the song that goes: "His head was so loaded it nearly exploded," Laura relates to her own overwhelmed state of unconscious psychic pressure, including the pressure to yield to her profound homoerotic wishes that she had tried to bury during the first part of her adult life. Laura's dream associations recognize the dance as manic. The dance goes on and on, as does the repetition of defensive behaviors in the repetition compulsion, when the pain of grief and its remembrance of the past must be warded off. It is a state of pathological mourning for the same reason as manic defenses reinforce the warding off of true mourning, and then mimic the true mourning with a surface dance of hectic and frustrated emotion. This is accompanied by an inebriated state of mind of being in a trance, unconsciously reenacting the past rather than being present and merely recalling the past from a position of reflective thought, achieved through separation and self-integration.

Glass bowl dream

A more recent dream in the third year of treatment is that of Laura appearing as herself in a dream. She is sick and frail. She has a tiny body that she describes as my body, and she is waiting for me to come and visit her. She is also wearing a brocade robe, like the one her mother would wear when she withdrew to her bed. In addition, Laura is holding a glass bowl in the dream. When I come by to see her in this dream, I don't stay, although she wishes me to. Instead, I leave, and I take her golden glass bowl with me.

Among Laura's associations to this dream is one main one that she focuses on. According to her, not only had I not stayed with her in the dream, leaving her alone and longing for me in a highly vulnerable state, but I also took her glass bowl with me, which she associated to as a symbol of femininity. Consequently when I left her, I took the essence of her potential femininity with me, a femininity lying latent in a fragile form that might be represented by glass. Further associations revealed that Laura consciously viewed me as representing her feminine self. She told me that she loved watching feminine women, although she never felt like one of them. During a period in her life when she became deeply involved with a male lover, her budding feminine side ended up feeling like a failure when her male lover rejected her. Rather than seeing that she was externalizing her need for validation, her solution was to identify with other feminine women, who she would watch and enjoy. However, she did so from the perspective of the "cock of the walk," joking and flirting with them as her father had done with women. I said that her use of me as her feminine self seemed more like a problem than a solution, for if she could only experience her feminine part of herself vicariously, through another, she would lose that part of herself when that other – in this case, me – was not around. The dream illustrated the dilemma brilliantly. She was left not holding the bowl, as it were, and thus she was left in a sick, debilitated, and lonely state, without the feminine part of herself.

Another dream may have been a similar comment on her severing herself from her feminine side. In the dream, she was performing a surgical operation on another woman, in which she would remove the woman's uterus. The operation was a painful one, and it was a difficult one. The operation symbolized the unmourned pain of sacrificing, perhaps too much, her own personal femininity, like the sacrifice symbolized in her earlier dream of the glass bowl that is taken from her. Following this dream, Laura had other associations to her feminine self. She began to feel a painful grief about not feeling she could fit in with feminine women as one of them. She felt the pain of being excluded following one group experience with women. This acute pain brought back to Laura the sense of exclusion she had felt when standing outside her parents' bedroom as they had sex. As a child, she couldn't understand why they would let her into their bedroom when they were fighting, but not when they were having sex. When she was a teenager, one day she did open the door by mistake, and was more aware of what was going on. Her parents were the negligent ones, who had failed to lock the door, failing to maintain the necessary exclusion that reinforced the incest taboo and the maintenance of boundaries. They actually may have unconsciously wished to exhibit themselves, but Laura also wished to join them by a voyeuristic act, although her conscious oversight of opening their bedroom door was embarrassing to her. After this rift in boundaries, Laura's parents came down to the family table for breakfast and everyone sat in cold silence. Nobody dared discuss what had just happened.

So both exclusion and its attached broken taboo have continued to haunt Laura. The pain of feeling excluded from a group of feminine women, except as she might engage them from a masculine attitude, left Laura with the wound of "not fitting in," not being one of them. Performing a medical operation to excise the female uterus (the womb) that branded her still as a woman, and thus prevented her from denying her womanhood, was a painful psychic truth to bring to consciousness. Giving birth to such consciousness, without a safe womb from which to emerge, is always traumatic. Although Laura wished to enter my womb, she had found the dark side of that wish too threatening. She was left a woman without a womb, as evidenced by the dream's image of a glass bowl. The bowl signified the roundness of a feminine womb as well as the roundness of a vaginal core. Laura's dream symbolized the archetypical feminine forms in this manner; forms that Laura was extremely ambivalent about accepting as part of her own anatomy.

As the pain behind this dream emerges, Laura begins to live through a new stage of mourning that brings her feminine wishes more to consciousness. As a result, perhaps, she began at times to wear a string of pearls, given to her by her mother, with her usual blazers and slacks. She is amazed by some reactions to this, and takes careful note of them. A waiter in a restaurant she frequented daily for years begins to notice her in a manner different than prior to that day. Laura says that he suddenly becomes exceedingly attentive to her, falling over his feet to please her and cater to her needs. Laura attributed this sudden change in the waiter's behavior towards her to the fact that she was wearing pearls for the first time; obviously attuned to the dynamics of her own symbols of gender with their personal and archetypical dimensions. The same day as this incident with the waiter someone else says to her: "You're all dolled up today!" Laura reflects on these two reactions to her appearance with the feminine addition of pearls, and concludes that if such a minor addition of a feminine element to her wardrobe draws such a dramatic response, who knows what changing a whole article of clothing might precipitate? She jokes about this, and months later decides to wear some cosmetics to a party.

At an earlier point she feels desirous, for the first time in at least a decade, to buy a dress for herself. At the time when she buys it she feels very strongly about it, perhaps appreciating the new symbolism she might draw power from in her style of dress. However, she modifies what she considers too radical a change by putting the dress aside and choosing to actually wear a pants suit with a more soft and delicate fabric than she might usually wear, adding a piece of jewelry. But then, a year or two later, Laura makes a firm decision to start wearing dresses, and modifies her appearance in other ways that allow her feminine beauty to come out in the open, to come out of hiding. She then begins to feel a link with her mother that she formerly rejected. Laura is increasingly owning her feminine self, rather than settling for the symbolic role of her mother's "son." Actually, she had felt like a second-rate son, since she had been seeing herself as a woman in disguise. The deeper nature of Laura's womanhood is becoming less threatening to her as she mourns and separates from the internal mother, the mother of the past, who had so desperately wanted a son.

Laura's capacity to discover her recessed and repressed feminine side, and to open up a dialectic of gender identity and sex object choice desires within her, where once that dialectic was foreclosed, can be seen as developing in parallel with the integration of formerly split psychic structure within her internal world. The primal self and mother/other objects within her had at first been part objects, split into idealized and devalued parts, or good and bad. Through her mourning process, with the continuing reliving of her early experience in the transference, she was able to integrate the part selves and part objects increasingly, as well as differentiating and separating the self and object components. She had a vital subjective experience of this psychic structure integration process, experienced in relation to her internal mother as she encountered her in the transference with me.

Chapter 12

The case of Laura, Part 2

Strands and cycles of mourning and unrequited love: modes of mourning

Many different forms of mourning have contributed to the increasing self-integration that is evolving in Laura. Developmental mourning includes the processing of all the affects of grief as they occur in relation to both object loss, and the related self loss that occurs along with the loss of the object as its ideal fantasy form is surrendered. Disillusionment with the object may be part of repairing self-image and self-experience. Such disillusionment is part of developmental mourning, and it may be experienced along with other forms of mourning. The forms of mourning are interwoven within the fabric of an ongoing psychoanalytic process. One form of mourning that evolved for Laura was that of loss related to fantasies of abandonment, in which she lived traumatic separations that had haunted her since childhood. Laura also experienced the mourning of her real external parents, as they died during her adult life, and as her mother died during the years of her psychoanalytic treatment. Her sense of loss from the past could lead to the sense of loss in the present and vice versa. Often Laura's love for me, in the psychoanalytic object relationship called "therapeutic object relationship" (Grunes 1984) became associated with love for the good parent objects, particularly the good mother, and could lead to the sadness of grief over the loss of her actual parents. Laura relived with much regret the illness and deaths of her parents. For example, during one session Laura explained that as she had looked into my eyes at the end of the prior session, she experienced me as having eyes that were "so soft, warm and tender." I could interpret this as her projection onto me of a good mother image, after a reparative session in which she resolved a feeling of anger towards me, which involved her transference. During that last session, Laura had projected her mother's phallocentric orientation towards men onto me, seeing me as always taking the side of men against her, prompted by my making a positive and supportive comment about a man she disliked and onto whom she projected a powerful negative judgment of herself. When her associations to this reaction, led her to open to the mournful grief following her anger, she distinctly recalled a memory of her mother's preferential attitude towards men. She realized that she had just viewed me, as prizing my male friends as "stallions," and consequently felt the loss of the fantasy ideal mother who she had fantasized to place her at the center of her attention at all times! Touching base with this persistent psychic fantasy, Laura then reconnected with me through the differentiation of the mother of the past from me in the present. In doing so she felt a powerful feeling of love that allowed her to see me in a loving aspect, seeing me as having tender eyes towards her: soft, warm and loving. Perhaps what she saw in my eyes was not only the refinding of a good mother, after sorting out the projection of the disappointing mother (the one who only prized men), but she projected her own present feeling of aliveness, creating a good object as well as reexperiencing one. She also felt the actual love I could feel for her, particularly when we had both just shared a significant moment of analytic work. This present loving experience in the therapeutic object relationship allowed a form of forgiveness to develop within Laura towards her internal and formerly internalized parents. In taking in my love, and joining me in the mutuality of experience of the analytic work, and in the give and take of love between us, she was softening and modifying the view of her parents, and of her mother in particular.

Laura could increasingly see beyond particularly painful memories now to allow a fuller view of her mother and of her mother's motivations. A natural sense of forgiveness developed within Laura, as opposed to the artificial kind that she might have formerly expressed in a defensive manner of reaction formation and moral defense. Laura's anger was a key link in the chain of mourning as grief for the loss of the ideal (as opposed to good) mother, as expressed frequently in the negative transference.

But further than mourning the ideal mother, and experiencing a disillusionment that could allow anger, sadness and a renewal of love, Laura also saw a loving look in my eyes that she could take in because she was more present with me after this piece of mourning. Seeing this loving look in my eyes, Laura remembered a warm look on a statue of a woman that her mother had left to her as a legacy when she died. While the statue still resided in her mother's home, she remembered it as being massive, imperious, and imperial, the Gorgon head. After several years of psychoanalysis and receipt of the statue as a gift, she was shocked to realize it was the bust of a shy gypsy girl who appeared tender and modest, as opposed to hard, unyielding and bigger than life. Her earlier perception of the statue was seen through the transference projections of her demon-muse mother.

Laura mourned the ideal mother whom she only had in fantasy. She was able to let go of the old ideal mother and its demonic dark side through finding a good enough mother in the image of our work. In addition, she was able to mourn the very real loss of her external mother who had been dying. Thus, the process of mourning within the psychoanalytic frame of transference, and the analysand's object relations capacity to take in the analyst as a real object evolved simultaneously.

Abandonment depression mourning, separation mourning, the mourning of the death of the external other, and the mourning of the ideal parent disillusionment are important aspects of the developmental mourning process, which I have been addressing in this case. However, there are also other aspects of mourning that can be illustrated in the process of Laura's treatment. Laura discovered the mourning of life's existential limits, as she faced choices in her life, and reconsidered them as she faced these choices with fuller awareness in the course of her analysis. Laura has also lived through the mourning of narcissistic injuries that involves self-loss and self-healing. These narcissistic "wounds" interact with the disillusionment of the parental ideal, involving the experience of the mournful loss of a fantasy object. Laura has also experienced the depressive position mourning of hurting the one she loves. Further, she has felt the anguished mourning of self-disillusionment.

All these aspects of mourning involve the surrendering of old self-images and the integration into her self-concept of dissociated self-parts that had formerly been alien to her sense of self. Consequently, there is the surrendering of old psychic structures, and the reformation of new psychic structures. There is simultaneously the integrating of split good mother/bad mother, love/hate psychic structure that evolves through the abandonment depression mourning process. This occurs as the mourning process is both lived out in the transference relationship with the analyst and is repaired in the "therapeutic object relationship" with the analyst.

In the latter part of the third year of treatment, Laura declared that she was aware for the first time that she could be angry at me while also being in love with me. She tells me that she understands now how she could have both hated her mother so intensely during her childhood and adolescence, and also have longed for her so intensely! However, when in a state of hate, she had not realized that she also had the dissociated state of longing operating within her simultaneously. Laura becomes conscious of the two formerly dissociated self-states, through her deeply emotional experience in the transference with me. Therefore, Laura is able to mourn the loss reactive to separation breaks between her and her mother sufficiently to repair the links between these two feeling reactions to her two mother internalizations. Thus she could perceive a new mother who was tender and present with her and the one who was angry, cold, emotionally withdrawn, and threatening abandonment. All the forms of mourning involved the reparation of object loss, and related self-loss. This allowed Laura to integrate the two divided self-states, with their polarized primal mother object images, and with elements of the father blended in with these images. Through mourning, Laura also is able to integrate the formerly dissociated grandiose self, bringing it together with the needing self.

MOURNING AND NARCISSISTIC INJURY

Laura had frequently suffered the effects of emotional and physical attacks by her mother. Laura reexperienced critical aspects of her narcissistic injuries, felt at the time of such attacks, through associations and memories that she felt being triggered by transference longings and disappointments. One memory arising in such a manner was of Laura's mother cutting her down in a truly castrating manner, expressing the phallic mother as a sleeping shark that had awakened. It was after Laura exhibited some paintings as a young girl that her mother dramatically exclaimed, in an acerbic and ridiculing manner, showing off to her own friends, "Too much brush!" Laura's reaction was to feel devastated, and it was basically at this precise point that she resolved to give up her painting. Now it was necessary for her to mourn the self-ideal that she was giving up, as she decided both not to paint, and not to be an artist of any kind. However, Laura could never process her mourning at this earlier time because she was too alone with her experience. So the blocked mourning rankled in her as wound that ached, but yet was repressed out of consciousness. Not having mourned her ideal self-image, Laura then was compelled to project the ideal self onto another. This other always became the muse godmother, who flipped to the demon side of the demon lover, when a combination of erotic arousal and injured narcissism occurred again. Not feeling the pain of injury that was repressed each time with the renewal of the hurt and disappointment, Laura could only begin to do the necessary mourning needed to heal herself and her self-concept at the time when she had the support of my presence and compassion.

Laura's mourning of narcissistic injury allowed the memory of other injuries to emerge and to be mourned. Some of these included her mother's slapping her if she cried, and her mother's distrust of her. This attitude from her mother exacerbated Laura's defensive tendencies to believe that she was bad or inadequate in line with the reports of others, such as babysitters and camp directors. She recalled traumatically frustrating times, such as when her mother and father joined in forcing her to lie face down on a bed as a punishment for crying and getting upset. Lying on the couch, Laura reexperienced the terror of this time. She was able to bring it to consciousness, with the anguish and agony of a child helplessly forced into the paralyzing grip of her own rage. She also reexperienced the trauma of her mother's threats to leave her, which began when she was only 3 years old, despite her own child wish to never leave her mother, even when her mother would enter the unknown land of death. At the beginning of a session, following her mother's funeral, Laura reported that she felt like she was lying in a coffin while on the couch. I interpreted that she wanted to jump into her mother's grave and lie down there with her mother, reflecting her childhood wish to die when her mother would die, because life without her mother would be an intolerable separation.

Another incident of maternal narcissistic injury occurred when Laura was in her late teens, at the point when Laura was scheduled to graduate from a prestigious college but found out that she still had some summer courses to take, which would postpone the date of her graduation until the fall. Her mother's response to this summer delay in Laura's graduation was to viciously accuse Laura of "plunging a knife into her father's heart." It was a terrible accusation, and an interesting image, since early on in her treatment, Laura had feared that I would stick a knife in her vagina (the knife of unrequited love). When Laura actually spoke with her father about her delayed graduation, her father said: "So what's the big deal!" Laura's father was obviously not the problem. The damage, however, had been done by the mother who was probably projecting a situation of her own past in relation to her own father. Laura's mother had been unable to complete college. To Laura, it was the spearhead of the phallic mother that she felt stabbing her in her heart.

THE DREAM OF A SELF BEING REBORN, A SPIRITUAL BIRTH

One particular dream of Laura's offers testimony as to the success of Laura's mourning of self and object loss as it is felt in response to narcissistic injury.

In the dream, Laura sees some young, beautiful and naked women running together, through the waves of the ocean, as if emerging from the water below. They have colorful streamers flying out from behind their backs, something like the image of the runners in the film *Chariots of Fire*. They invite Laura to join them, but she must remove her clothing and even her glasses. She is struck with the terror that she would not be able to see. However, the women insist, and she yields to their request. She joins them, and feels a sense of intense liberation, as well as a sense of being part of something grand and beautiful.

Laura's first associations to this dream concern the intense vulnerability she feels without her glasses. Also, she speaks of the grandeur and beauty of these women in their state of nakedness, symbolizing liberation. She also associates to the flying streamers as celebration of womanhood and womanhood in the raw.

I have chosen this dream as evidence of Laura recovering from narcissistic injury, in part because it evolved after her suffering the rage and grief of such injuries, which she often felt at first in the transference with me. Also, I chose it because it shows the emergence of a primal, whole, infant, and feminine self. In Heinz Kohut's terms, it might be seen as the emergence of a dissociated and latent grandiose self from behind a diffident "closet narcissist" kind of inadequate self. Heinz Kohut uses the term grandiose self as a core and potentially healthy part of the self that must be connected with the central and conscious self in order to bring the whole self to life. This is quite different than Kernberg's use of the term "grandiose self," which is a pathological construction of merged idealized self and idealized object components in a defensive and rigid constellation, which wards off the needy part of the self, and its inadequate self-feeling. Kohut is speaking of a true self-kernel (like Fairbairn's libidinal ego or self), which can be reunited with the central ego (or central self). It first emerges into consciousness in a grand form because it is coming from an infant level of experience. This Kohutian true self-core must emerge initially in this grandiose manner, because its psychic structure was originally split off and dissociated (by traumatic narcissistic injury). It must rise up out of its dissociated state, as if out of the ocean, or out of the ocean of the unconscious (a combination of dissociation and repression perhaps in this case).

The infant aspect of the emerging grandiose self can be seen in this dream's primal vision. It is a vision of primal unity of women, and thus of an archetypical mother and a primal female infant, as opposed to a mother with a pseudo or second-rate self, which relates more to Laura's false self. The nakedness of the women attests to the infant experience of raw, nude experience, and to the fact that Laura feels infinitely more nude without her glasses, which could reflect how an infant feels when it has a fuzzy focus in its optical vision, as it does at birth and in its earliest life. Without glasses, Laura's vision can be blurry and she can therefore merge into her sister figures without any clear differentiation between them (Wright 1991). They blend together in a diffuse mixture akin to Michael Balint's primal return to a preoedipally traumatized self, to a state of an "interpenetrating mix-up." So the diffuse, naked and glorious excitement of the infant state in birth is captured in the dream. And Laura's first associations to the dream characterizes the water that the women are running within, as if emerging from a womb in the moment of birth. Laura further associates to the womb being my womb, and I have already discussed how she then also gets in touch with the dark side of this image (as a vagina or vortex that sucks her into a black, dark and possibly suffocating womb). But in this dream, the brilliantly light side is seen, the glory of god-like spiritual celebration in birth – the commentary of spirit in the still undifferentiated soul. The streamers of red and blue, yellow, and other bright colors flying out from the women's backs are also evidence of the glory of birth, and the glory of potential love in this world, beginning with the mutual love of infant and mother.

Of course, the naked women can be seen as adult women as well as infants, despite their naked form. On a more manifest level, Laura can be creating an image of the glory of adult lesbian love. However, the diffuse quality of the figures and the lack of a clear and differentiated vision in the female figures make this explanation more manifest and acceptable to the consciousness of an adult woman. The second interpretation can be seen as a vision of a group of infant female figures, who are merging with each other, as Laura may have experienced merging with her mother. This infant merger then gets compounded with oedipal and adolescent eroticism. However, both views of the dream make up an ambiguous paradox and dialectic. One can see the genital and oedipal eros imposed upon the blueprint of an earlier era, rather than vice versa (Kaplan 1996). I view this core and primal self-emergence through the lens of developmental theory rather than through the lens of pathology. The healing of self-injury can lead to the emergence of a primal part of the self, which was formerly dissociated; and thus, did have to be enacted in disguised ways.

In Laura's case she could not own her more grandiose and exhibitionistic side, let alone her homosexual side, as long as she remained attached to her mother. Her mother's narcissism would not permit it. Laura had always been compelled to mirror her mother, rather than receiving mirroring and confirmation from her mother for her true nature. Consequently, Laura was forced to mold herself into a diffident attitude, acting as the mother's self-extension, never daring to compete with her mother for attention of her own. This could be seen in Laura's diffidence in relation to me in the transference, where Laura never placed herself on an equal level with me. Laura never yet viewed herself as my equal and certainly not as my competitor. This obviously defensive perspective had to be questioned, and analyzed. It clearly related to her relationship with her mother, where in order to be separate from the mother, rather than existing as a mere self-extension, she had to guarantee she would not threaten the mother. In its extreme form, Laura had to be a failure to defend against challenging her mother and her mother's fragile narcissism. This sense of herself as a failure was built into Laura's self-concept. It was reflected on an ongoing basis in her diffident manner (when not enraged or angry) and her modest demeanor in relation to me, particularly as the transference mother.

MOURNING OF EXISTENTIAL LIMITS

A part of developmental mourning is the mourning of the limits related to the human condition (such as forming an identity as a man or woman), as well as the limits of our own choices as human beings who possess free will. Within Melanie Klein's theory such mourning would fall within the domain and dynamic of the depressive position. However Klein does not highlight this aspect of the depressive position, which has a developmental thrust more prominent than the working through of depressive despair about the human vulnerability to hurting the one one loves.

Laura's choice to commit herself to both a homosexual marriage, and to a homosexual community and lifestyle, is a choice that has its own form of limits, and its own price to pay. But we all have to come to terms with the limits of both our sex object choice and our gender role identity choices, given that we all have bisexual tendencies. Two of the natural narcissistic injuries of growing up relate to the necessity to relinquish omnipotent and narcissistic fantasies that (a) we can be two genders at once, with two different sets of genitals; and (b) the fantasy that there is no difference between children and adults so that we could give our opposite sex parent the same pleasure as our same sex parent (Kaplan 1996). We also generally grow into a certain sexual object choice. That choice comes after periods in our childhood where homosexual connections are powerful, even though we might not feel them as consciously erotic. However, for someone such as Laura, who has lived through oscillations back and forth between extremely conscious erotic and explicitly genital longings for both sexes, the commitment to a sexual orientation is definitely one of accepting limits. At times this is felt as a sacrifice and a sadness. It becomes a cause for heartfelt grief. Furthermore, the sex object choice for Laura is not free of complications in the realm of gender role identity choice. Although sex object and gender identity are different choices, they overlap and affect one another, particularly when, as in the case of Laura, she has tended to play the more masculine role in the homosexual couple that she is a part of. Coming to terms with the losses of overt feminine self-expression, and its emphasis on emotional receptivity in the sexual area, is not easy. The degree of loss can be modulated, however, if the psychic truth of mourning is faced.

Laura is still choosing her degree of femininity, and her degree of feminine receptivity in sexual matters, and in interpersonal relations. On a purely emotional level (if there is such a thing) apart from explicit sexual relations, Laura is extremely well developed as a receptive person, who can listen and even take in the "melody" of the other as she has spoken of taking me in as a "melody" at times. Laura has bumped up against the limits of her fifteen-year marriage to her lover. Although she might protest she is left with the reality of her grief, yet this grief is balanced out by the great depth of her love for her partner, and her partner's love for her. As far as her gender role orientation in the world, Laura has had some more latitude here. She can choose to navigate the gray areas of androgyny, and perhaps to benefit by the richness of a bi-gender mixture in matters of dress and social manner. Nevertheless, the cost of not fitting in with a group of feminine women as truly one of them, particularly when certain topics are brought up, is felt keenly by Laura. She has worked hard to forge social relationships in the lesbian and gay community, where she can feel much more at home than anywhere else. Yet, with the mourning of the pain she feels concerning the sense of exclusion with other women, she has also become more flexible and more adaptable in the modes in which she can connect with other heterosexual women who have feminine orientations. The depth of her connection with those outside the lesbian world has definitely increased with her mourning process.

More poignant is Laura's struggle over the limits imposed on her by her sexual object choice. She might wish that she would not have to make such a choice. Yet reality demands that she does make the choice. She made the choice many years prior to coming into psychoanalysis with me, and has felt threatened that her choice would be disrupted at times when she contacts the pain of losing men as both social and sexual companions. At such moments of realization and possible regret, Laura fears that if she allows her yearnings for men to become conscious again she could disrupt her life by disrupting the most secure and loving relationship she has ever had. At those moments Laura might wish to repress her feelings again, but she also realizes that this is equivalent to chopping off a part of herself, and would truly be a self-castration. Laura's only choice is to face her loss consciously, and to grieve the loss. This mourning, facilitated by the treatment environment and relationship, can hopefully free her to more fully commit herself to the homosexual choice she has made and to commit herself to the person and to the lesbian community she has chosen, as well as to the other communities she exists in as an intellectual and professional person. This road of grief is not an easy one and we all tread on it when we make life's choices, especially that most central one of choosing one partner as an exclusive and monogamous sex partner. For some a professional choice can also be a grievous one, as other talents and professional avenues need to be surrendered when we make a commitment to one profession. Hopefully, in both these areas of choice we find that the very act of commitment will allow the deepest parts of us to become engaged so that the fulfillment is ultimately much more than we could ever have by spreading ourselves around. Nevertheless, in my opinion, the loss of exploring and trying out other options needs to be accepted at some point in order for such deep engagement and self-fulfillment to happen.

So we all need to grieve our losses when we commit our deeper selves (heart and soul) to love and work. When our commitments allow us to feel fulfillment we feel reprieved from feelings of loss, and from the hunger of wanting what is on the other side of the fence. But such reprieve is never continuous, although it may be more than temporary. We all have times of longing for something that our own chosen commitments exclude us from. For example, my own choice to be a psychologist and psychoanalyst has precluded the possibilities that I be a dancer or a full-time writer. Every summer when I have more time to write, I feel the same old yearnings to be doing my writing full time, even though when I actually return to my psychotherapeutic and psychoanalytic practice I feel a renewed depth of engagement, along with feeling that I have missed such work, and feel a joy in reconnecting with patients whom I deeply care about. Still, the next summer I will fantasize being a full-time writer again.

This existential struggle to accept life's limits, which is an essential aspect of Melanie Klein's depressive position state of mind, is one that is highlighted in the lesbian experience of needing to mourn and relinquish poignant aspects of heterosexual life in order to commit in depth to a homoerotic relationship. Without such commitment the deeper fulfillment of life cannot be felt, although some of the intensity of preoedipal omnipotence must be relinquished to find a less intense, but perhaps equally passionate level of engagement, in which contact and object connection override an addictive instinctual intensity. All possibilities are not open. The lesbian life is an existential choice that involves limiting aspects that heterosexuals experience as well when they give up the oedipal love object, and resign it to fantasy, so that they can move on to real relationships with non-incestuous love objects. For the choice to take place in the lesbian – a choice towards commitment in love relationship – the dream of bisexual self-dimensionality must be relinquished as an enacted reality, and be cherished perhaps as a creative resource for psychic fantasy. For Laura bisexuality existed in many modes of fantasy, extending from her first thoughts of making love to me as one woman to another, to then transforming into both myself as the man in the lovemaking, and herself as the man. At later times we operated sexually as a ménage-à-trois in Laura's mind. Such fantasy ultimately turned into heterosexual fantasies of mutual rather than sadomasochistic lovemaking with men that could operate in a conscious dialectic with earlier forms of fantasy in which I or she is a woman making love to another woman, with or without an actual penis.

Laura came to realize through her analysis that her transference fantasy of me as a phallic mother had the benign side of me as a woman with a penis, who could lovingly penetrate her. The bisexuality in this fantasy also became apparent to Laura in terms of us understanding together her father transference within the fantasy. When she gave me a penis she endowed me with her father's longed for phallic prowess, and for his earthy "cocksure" lust that her mother had so defended herself against. Through my being in the fantasy, Laura enjoyed her father's phallic lust, as she also enjoyed my femininity. How Laura actually endowed herself with this masculine phallic pride and lust became the subject of analysis as well. How could she deal with the yin and yang of psychic femininity and psychic masculinity, while still mourning and accepting the limits that life's relationship and gender identity choices offered her? Could she own this as a creative endeavor of depressive position self-integration, rather than being oppressed by a paranoid position fear of limits operating as constrictions that demand the splitting off of self-parts and/or a paralyzing mode of repression? Laura's mother had been significantly repressed in sexuality and her father had operated in a life where he had to split off the lusty sexual parts of himself from his marriage commitment, to a large degree. How could Laura use her newfound consciousness of the feminine as well as of the masculine parts of her psyche to make creative choices, while still tolerating the limits of a monogamous lesbian relationship choice? In order to explore all this openly, Laura needed to know that I, as her analyst, could be open to viewing her commitment as a choice and not as a pathological constriction. She needed to know that I could be in a depressive position state of mind with her, and not in a predominantly paranoid state of mind, and she needed to know from the beginning that psychoanalysis as a clinical practice and profession did not limit me in this attitude.

PSYCHIC DETERMINATION VERSUS A VIEW OF PATHOLOGY

As is generally well known today, it is only recently that psychoanalysts have become less prejudiced towards both homosexuality and women. Although I have the greatest respect for Freud's contributions and for his ingenious discovery of unconscious motivation and of all the phenomena in the disciplined practice of psychoanalysis, when it comes to the topic of treatment of those with homosexual sex object commitment choices, I am glad I am not a Freudian! I am liberated by being primarily an object relations psychoanalyst and theorist, when it comes to this matter, although I would be only half an analyst without a deep understanding of Kleinian, as well as Freudian instinctual life, and of the psychic fantasy related to this instinct life. Nevertheless, the followers of Freud who have been biased against homosexuality are being untrue to Freud on two counts. They are being untrue to his discovery of bisexuality existing within all of us at an unconscious level. Also, they are being untrue to his mandate that psychoanalysts should be neutral (from a psychic structure standpoint mediating between id, ego and super-ego). That is, they should not seek to judge their analysands, but to understand all these conflicting motivations, and to help make all their motivations conscious so that any one analysand can use this knowledge to make decisions on their own about how to live their own lives. This is easier said than done (and Freud didn't do it in practice, as opposed to in theory), but it is an ideal to be striven for, and one which I am increasingly taking to heart.

This ideal had been thrown out the window by Freudian analysts when they began to work with homosexual personalities, while holding the bias that homosexuality was abnormal, pathological or just unnatural. It is a hard distinction to make, but a necessary one that homosexuality may be unconsciously determined in every single case (aside from genetic predispositions, which have yet to be studied), but that does not mean that it is something dysfunctional that needs to be corrected. Everything is unconsciously determined! We are all the results of the repressed and of the unconscious experiences of our childhoods, as they live on in us through powerful identifications and reenactments. Some of this can be changed through psychoanalysis, but only if the person being psychoanalyzed wants it to be changed once they are conscious enough of the unconscious roots of their motivations to make such a choice. Psychoanalysts are putting the cart before the horse if we in any way attempt to direct that choice.

When I first met with Laura for a consultation concerning her psychoanalysis, we discussed this issue immediately! Laura asked me if I believed homosexuality was pathological, and rather than explore her reasons for asking such a question, by gathering her associations to it, in the usual psychoanalytic manner, I answered her question. I answered her question because I was more concerned with not starting out with an unspoken impasse between us, manufactured by the tradition of psychoanalysis, than with being a psychoanalytic purist about technique. My answer was simple and I believe has provided a kernel of mutuality and rapport that could be developed into a trusting relationship in treatment. I told Laura precisely what I have been articulating here, that I believe homosexuality is unconsciously determined, but that does not imply the conclusion that it is pathological. Laura not only accepted this as an answer, but she agreed that she also believed that homosexuality is unconsciously determined. She also acknowledged that she would be interested in finding out about the unconscious factors that determine who she is, including who she is in terms of her choice to live as a lesbian, which had been a hard won decision over many years of her adult life.

There was never any doubt that Laura was deeply committed to her lesbian marriage and to her lesbian community. However, her capacity to sustain a relative state of fulfillment and intimacy within a monogamous arrangement was mentally threatened by her transferential longings for her mother-muse goddess/demon lovers. This threat would have existed for her even if she was committed to a heterosexual marriage. In fact, when she was married to a man in the past (for many years), she was drawn towards affairs with women, and ultimately such affairs allowed her to leave a very unsatisfactory marriage.

When Laura entered treatment she was well established in her homosexual object choice, and in her specific object choice of living with the woman she loved. At the time when she experienced grief over the loss of men as lovers and sex partners, with a specific sense of loss of male penetration, Laura would become temporarily alarmed that she would be forced to reconsider her life. She felt the power of her suppressed yearnings emerging into consciousness again. At these times, she might want to stop the whole analysis, because she feared the poignant suffering of the male object loss. Not only did she feel it in relation to specific sexual and love relations, but she felt it in relation to the loss of the kind of male attention that she might receive if she had possessed the appearance and manner of a more feminine woman. When her feminine side was engaged, she could long for the kind of attention and affection from men that she saw other women receiving, the kind of attention that she had received when she was younger and had been dressing in a more feminine way and had been more openly expressing her deep affection for men as mentors, father figures, and romantic partners. However, she had also been scared of such attention when she had received it. In fact, Laura's current masculine mode of dressing was seen by her, in part, as a disguise or protection. In her thinking, if men did not respond to her then she wouldn't have the opportunity to be seductive with them in return. This would protect her from being overwhelmed by a need to deal with the consequences of that mental attraction to men, and with its feared threat to her long-term relationship with her partner. Despite such rationalization, however, Laura has felt life impinging on her, and has been forced to consciously suffer the loss of men flirting with her and the attention of male sexual engagement. It has been hard for her to accept the experience of mourning such loss in relation to men, without immediately cutting off her feelings to stop both the pain of the memories and thoughts, and the shame of having them. It is also hard for Laura to experience the mourning without fearing that she would be compelled to react to the loss by changing her life.

Laura's thinking reflected her fear of facing the loss of men that might extend back to early childhood loss. To avoid the difficult mourning of such pain, she would rationalize that she shouldn't feel a loss because she is in a relationship with a woman she adores as a friend, confidante and erotic partner. Why deal with her sense of loss of men being more actively in her life when she had so much, she would ask herself? The answer she discovered was that her love partner cannot save her from her internal life. Gradually, Laura is coming to believe that she can tolerate at least some of this form of mourning without having to do anything to change her life or love object choice, as far as a committed love relationship is concerned. She has begun to view the mourning of the loss of men in romantic or social relations (aside from her good relations with male friends and colleagues) as one of the "necessary losses" that are a result of her homosexual choice. She has come to view her choice as establishing certain existential limits and consequences that need to be faced consciously, and accepted as the work of mourning is done. Laura wishes for her female friends to understand her feelings more empathically, to understand that she can be attracted to and love both men and women. She wishes they would accept this, because she feels left out without their awareness, if not acceptance, of her love for men. She adjusts to her discontent with these female friends with humor, at times. She jokes, quoting a prominent lesbian writer, that being gay is the only minority you can join overnight, in the twinkling of an eye. Yet Laura fears her female friends are threatened by her, and by her wish for their acceptance. This apprehension on her part harkens back to her mother's brutal lack of acceptance of her bisexual longings. Laura feels more alone with these feelings than she would like to be. Yet she knows she isn't all alone with the feelings, because she can share them with me in analysis and can feel the support of my presence when she is in pain.

Laura also feels it is necessary to state to me that she does not necessarily represent all lesbians, saying that she believes many lesbians lack the yearnings for male companionship and male penetration that she is quite in touch with. In my own experience as an analyst I have worked with quite a few lesbians and I have often found them to miss and yearn for male romantic partners and explicitly for male penetration at times. This is not true in all cases, and when not so it can only remain an open question as to whether such yearnings remain unconscious or are truly absent or undeveloped. Unfortunately, such questions are often exploited for political purposes rather than left to psychoanalytic exploration over time.

THE DEPRESSIVE POSITION MOURNING OF REGRET

There is a particular form of developmental mourning that is not adequately described in terms of object loss related to death, separation, or abandonment. This form of mourning relates to the loss of love, but it also is about one's own agency in that loss of love, and one's own role in disrupting loving object connections through one's own aggression. This form of mourning is about the pain of hurting the person one loves. It is about one's own more fine-tuned sense of guilt, as it turns to grief affect related to remorse and regret. This is not about neurotic guilt, but about existential guilt, the guilt of truly hurting the other by one's own aggression, and not merely the kind of aggression needed to separate from a symbiotic mother, who won't let go. This form of mourning is best described by Klein as the pain, grief and despair of the depressive position. The fantasies and anxieties of this position involve visions of damaging the heart, body and mind of the other, who on an unconscious level can always be associated with the primal mother object.

How does the transference expose the painful regret highlighted in Melanie Klein's theory, of hurting the one you love? Laura speaks to me through this aspect of her transference: "It was so heartbreaking after I left that other session, when I got so cold. I felt like all the warmth in the world was gone, like those days when my mother withdrew to her bed and it felt like the sun never would come out. That's why I had to call you afterwards!" Laura is exploring why she had called me after a session in which she was angry and accusatory towards me, just following my leaving for summer vacation. She had been terrified that I would leave without her being able to make reparations to me. She had tried to coerce me into apologizing to her, during that session, for something from the preceding session. After she left she realized that she had catastrophized the situation. She became concerned that she had hurt me. Although Laura had never seen herself as cold and accusatory, because that had been primarily her experience of mother whenever her mother was angry – each time Laura experiences the pain of her regret after becoming angry at me – she increasingly realizes that she can get cold, sarcastic and accusatory, just like her mother. Her realization of this is partly prompted by my comments on her behavior, as I have attempted to respond to her without submitting to her coercion. It is extremely hard for Laura to perceive her own coldness, because, as she says, it hasn't been part of her "self-concept." Laura finds it painful to realize that she could be cold like her mother. Yet, she does know that she felt she had hurt me, and once she is hit by the pain of that, her sense of regret, as well as her fear of abandonment, compels her to repair her connection with me as quickly as she can with an apology of her own. She imagines then that I must have felt bitterly disappointed in her, and personally hurt, because after all I had done for her she is proving to be so ungrateful! She couldn't wait to tell me this and to see my face again and hear my voice. She is terrified that she has killed off all the warmth between us, and all the warmth in me. She tells me that she is afraid that I would never show approval of her again and that she would never see again the warmth in my eyes again, nor the warmth of my smile. In fact she fears that I would never smile again. She fears I would freeze up and turn into the Gorgon head, the head of Medusa that was the image of the cold stone-faced mother that she had seen at the dinner table, when she was 14 years old, coming home from camp after her mother had withdrawn from her because of her attraction to female camp counselors. Laura associated back to this memory, and visualized her mother's face as a cold stone granite and as the head of Medusa. She imagines the snake dagger attacks of the cold and silent mother. At that teenage point in her life all relationship between her and her mother had been extinguished. Her mother had been enraged that her daughter could be so unlike the way she had wished her daughter to be. Her shame and rage united in a frigid glare that seemed like stones in her mother's eyes to Laura, stones where the eyes should have been. The assault of her mother's alienation made Laura remember all the former times when her mother had threatened to cut her off in order to walk out on her father and the family. The threatened abandonment had left its mark, but her mother had always returned to her warmer self after a few days.

When Laura turned 14, however, the rage was on both sides, between her and her mother. Laura was hurt deeper than ever by her mother's rejection of her, and by her mother's unwillingness to even listen to her side of the story. The cold war was a bitter war indeed, and Laura went into an internal state of despair, fearing that she would never get her warm mother back. It was over forever! Although she was angry, she also had terrible guilt at seeing her mother's accusatory stare. She believed that she had stabbed her mother. But this was all mixed up with her mother having stabbed her, and perhaps she experienced the stab in her vagina as well as her heart, because when she entered treatment with me she would fear that I would stab her in her vagina.

When I answered the phone in a session (which I never usually do) it became an incident of me stabbing her, abandoning her, not giving her the time that I give others. She came into the next session ready to defend herself. However, when Laura became aware of her cold and accusatory manner, and her coercive insistence on receiving an apology from me, which cut off communication and contact, rather than facilitating it, she became bereft, bereft with the depressive despair Melanie Klein speaks of, bereft with the pain of regret.

She couldn't wait to speak with me. She felt she'd die if she couldn't repair things. She remembered back to age 14, when she had had thoughts of killing herself. At that time, all the warmth had gone out of the world for Laura. When she started to feel responsible for it, she started to grieve. All her grief hit her like a powerful weight and she felt a sadness that felt infinitely thick and heavy. The sadness was a symptom of her love and of her need for the transferential mother, and for the real analyst she had hurt. Sometimes in such a state she became overly apologetic, and I needed to explain that I had not lost a sense of her warm, giving and grateful side. I just had found it difficult to speak to her when she was trying to force me, through guilt accusations, designed to induce guilt. Together, we then sought out her real offense and the exaggerated fantasy of annihilating all love in me that went with it. As she remembered her mother, when 14, she began to see how she was living out the past with me, because she had never fully mourned her grief over the loss of her relationship with her mother from that summer. But Laura's sense of regret over attacking me in the present was real as well. She felt better when she was able to cry deep tears of sadness while with me, feeling regret and remorse, and rebuilding the loving connection with me inside of herself, as I stayed present and empathized with her pain.

Laura had not hurt me the way she had fantasized, but she had frustrated me and left me in a cold manner as I was leaving for the summer. She needed to repair her connection to me, so that she could mourn this loss with me. As she apologized, she needed to understand that her fantasy of keenly and deeply hurting me was, in part, a projection onto me of her mother's very real hurt when Laura was 14. All this sorting out of the past and present, of me as separate from her mother, and of hurting in a state of feeling hurt, was part of Laura's mourning process. Her mourning involved processing the depressive pain and its fantasies, of hurting the one she loved, both in relation to me and in relation to the internal mother (lodged within her from the past), who I represented, in addition to representing a new external object for an alive relationship in the present. Laura's mother seemed to come alive in the room with us again as Laura mourned the loss of love that her anger created; a realization that could only be felt after her own hurt was felt and mourned – the hurt of disappointment in relation to both me (the external object) and her mother (the internal object).

Within this time of mourning there was also a dialectic created in which I was able to freely apologize for an angry moment in which I seemed cold to her. My apology helped Laura to reconsider how I appeared to her at that moment. She exclaimed that she had to remember that I never really got cold with her even though she expected me to be when she felt cold with her own anger. Prior to my apology she had attacked herself for her coldness toward me, not only mentally, but somatically as well. After my apology Laura was able to associate to her somatic symptom. She could then realize that her own anger turned inward, against herself, played a part in creating the symptom. She said: "I couldn't forgive myself for getting cold towards you." I interpreted her somatic attack as a punishment for her rage, as she feared she had not sufficiently repaired her hurtful attack on me. Her anxiety that she had not repaired her attack on me was exaggerated by the internal mother she carried around with her from the age of 14, who never forgave her, and who retaliated with coldness and later slaps across her face. I chose to apologize to Laura for a moment in which I thought I had spoken to her with some anger. However, the content of what I had been saying at that moment was important. I spoke of her projection of her cold mother introject onto me at any time when I wasn't feeling her pain as mine, because of her wish that I be completely inside her pain with her. My apology for the element of annoyance in my attitude as I interpreted her projection and the powerful longing for intimacy behind it, allowed Laura to receive me psychically through my reparative gesture, and to show more reflective understanding of my interpretation than she might have otherwise. This reception of my reparation also allowed her to forgive herself, but the intervening emotional step was of mourning the loss of love that she had felt as she opened herself to receiving my apology. She yielded to a deep sadness, combined with the sense of her own hurt and the renewal of loving feeling with me. I knew as she cried in response to my apology that she was receiving me and my apology as a whole constellation, which could be sustained as a psychic reparative element within her.

Laura's reception of my apology, combined with the pain of her own regret over attacking me, allowed Laura to move from the protosymbolic level of somatic and interpersonal enactment to that of interpersonal communication. It allowed her to understand my interpretation of her coldness as a reaction to her disappointed fantasy that I would be fully inside her pain with her, not just being empathic to her pain from a separate position. She could understand the symbolic communication in this interpretation now, and could associate to it on a symbolic level. Consequently, she realized more about her lifelong belief that love was defined as being in the other's pain, since she had merged into her mother's pain. She recalled how she sat in her mother's bedroom and watched her mother display a frozen look on her face – a mixture of contempt and pain, while her mother withdrew into a frozen paralyzed position, controlling all those around her, while simultaneously losing all sense of her own agency.

REPARATIVE MOURNING IN LAURA'S CASE OF UNREQUITED LOVE FOR THE HOMOEROTIC DEMON LOVER

The repetition of unrequited love in Laura's life with women seems to have followed a cycle of an abandonment depression mode of trauma, whose reenactment depends on an internal split psychic structure. In fact, with this psychic structure the demon lover theme of reenactment is inevitable, and the saga of a traumatic rupture in the love object connection plays out its malignant theme. The muse turns into a demon with the life/death sense of disappointment and the demon turns into the visage of death. In Laura's mind, the visage of death appears as Medusa. The Medusa-mother appears as a head that freezes Laura into a cold primitive rage that eviscerates her and threatens to exclude her from the life force altogether, in as much as she experiences her basic life force as emanating from her mother. Laura had said: "I believed, as a child and adolescent, that everything I had I had derived from my mother. If my mother ever died, I did not want to live." When her warm symbiotic mother turned into the cold Medusa she felt her own sense of self being annihilated.

The inevitable turn of the muse into the demon lover, following the Fairbairnian mode of the exciting internal object turning into the rejecting part object, was a cycle built on the split of the early primal object into two extreme idealized and demonic objects. These split object forms (part objects) were accompanied by visceral overtones, and by the psychic impact of compulsion towards reenactment in behavior or obsessive mental activity. The split primal object, when disrupted into split parts through traumatic separation early in life, is more than a symbolic image or introject. It operates on a protosymbolic, rather than a symbolic level.

OPENING TRANSITIONAL AND POTENTIAL SPACE IN TREATMENT

The road to symbolism

There was a gradual transition from the protosymbolic experience of the erotic transference in Laura's treatment to that of the symbolic experience and containment of it. On her own, in the fourth year of a three times a week treatment, Laura decides she feels sad about "giving up being my lover" in her own mind. Leading up to that point is Laura's relinquishment of her protosymbolic activity of sending me roses and calling me on the phone.

I also changed my approach in her treatment to working with the erotic transference, in conjunction with Laura's growing psychic readiness to move towards a more developmentally mature symbolic level. I changed my behavior in sessions from receiving her feelings, wishes and desires, while containing the excitement and tenderness in my own body, towards interpreting the symbolic meaning of Laura's erotic transference fantasies.

An example of this new approach is of a more active interpreting. Laura speaks of frequent fantasies of a male penis being on the point of penetrating me, and adds that she imagines the same penis penetrating her. Through her associations to this fantasy, which come more easily on the new plane of symbolism she is inhabiting after much mourning, I am able to interpret that she is wishing for her mother, as seen in me through transference displacement, to receive sexual pleasure and to finally have sexual fulfillment and enjoyment. Laura pictures both her mother and I as yearning for the penetration of a penis. But this becomes her yearning. She wants to be penetrated side by side with her mother, in a threesome that blends her love with her mother through a wonderful mixture of sexual pleasures and passion, ignited by the abstract penis. As we discuss this, Laura associates the abstract penis to the more differentiated male figures of her father's crowd of professional cronies, those who would sit around and make sexual jokes with her father within a male club setting. We analyze together, as the mutuality in the sessions grow, that the penis she wishes to penetrate me and her with me as an alter ego in relation to her mother, is that of her father in a multiple sense, a father represented by many male colleagues who in their joking form of verbal sexual play shared the act of sex with women.

As we talk, Laura experienced a sense of "play" in our session. She had not been up to this in the past, when she had resisted symbolizing her feelings and sexual wishes with me into defined levels of conscious psychic fantasy. She comments on the play element in the next session, believing that I had changed in engaging with her in the mutuality of play. However, I point out to Laura that although I may have changed with her that she had changed in being able to play with interpretations with this new degree of mutuality and dialogue, showing the degree to which this capacity for dialectic was enhanced through the work of analysis, with the prominent process of mourning. We enjoy a new kind of symbolic play and community between us. Having this rapport with me, allows Laura to further proceed in her developmental journey towards relinquishing the protosymbolic modes of enactment of erotic transference, and to benefit from the symbolic level.

At a later session Laura speaks of arriving at the sad and mournful point of no longer being my lover in her mind. Yet the resistance naturally arises in concert with this progression. In another session in her fourth year of treatments, Laura is possessed by a transference projection of me at the beginning of a session that she fights against relinquishing, and she attempts to coerce me into believing in its reality through the pressure of the protosymbolic level of projective identification. Fortunately, I have become separate enough from her to process this, and the erotic wishes behind the projection emerge into fantasy symbolic form, having their own path of progression in the content of the symbolism. She believes in the inception of the session that seeing my head turned down at one moment means that I am angry and disappointed with her. What she conveys to me about the nature of this projected material, her vision of my anger and disappointment, is an old story in her analysis. I am seen as a mother who is outraged by her seductive overture, which she pinpoints as having occurred at the end of the prior session. Although she herself had wished me to take her doorknob comment as a playful joke, it had turned overnight into a nightmare for her, and she projects a nightmare response – the Medusa head mother – onto me. She believes I was highly insulted, offended and disappointed in her because she joked about meeting me at a hotel. Contrary to her unconscious reaction, after she made her comment and left the session, I did experience her comment as a note of humor, prompted by a sadness of having to depart from me. Therefore, I respond to her conviction that I am offended by saying that she is projecting a feared response related to her own anxiety about her hunger and her aggression, and related to the internal mother she carries around with her.

Laura resists my defense and transference interpretation, and states emphatically that the fact that my head was turned downward as she entered the room was a sure sign that I was really upset and angry with her. I acknowledge that my head may have been turned downward, but I say that in my experience everything else she attributes to my reaction is her projection. Laura gets angry and I interpret her anger as a demand that I engage in acting out this old scene from her old script with her other. I say that 99 per cent of what she is assigning to me is a projection and that her anger at me now seems to be a reaction to my not participating in her script, which could be disappointing a sadomasochistic impulse she is feeling. She then confirms my point by expressing a highly aggressive sexual fantasy, first of throwing me against the wall and fucking me, and then of strapping on a dildo and opening me up to a marvelous experience of pleasure. I comment again on her angry tone as a sign of her being disappointed that I am not enacting this sexual fantasy with her. I ask her why she is so desirous of pleasing me, as she has such a powerful need to open me up sexually and to give me pleasure in her fantasy through a phallic penetration that she thinks I wish for, relinquishing the more sadomasochistic aspect of the fantasy. Laura responds that pleasing me is her way of making sure that she imprints herself as a vital presence in my mind (as opposed to her earlier insistence that my reception of her must be through experiencing my own vaginal desire for the concrete lesbian sex act). As she says this, Laura's feeling state transforms, and Laura is able to tell me that she is feeling a warmth between us now that is bringing up another sexual fantasy. In this new fantasy she is caressing me tenderly as she makes deep, passionate and affectionate love to me. I acknowledge her warmth and say that she has received my question and interpretation in the psychic space of her mind, and is now able to feel tenderness towards me that is a sign of her gratitude, in relation to my work with her in the session. On an object relations level, she is nurtured and gratified by this interpretation, surrendering the instinctual level of gratification she at first demanded in the session.

Following this Laura sustains much tenderness with me, and has fantasies of having me in her home as a guest, sitting in a comfortable chair by the fire. She expresses wishes to soothe away tensions with the warmth of the room, the fire, and her companionship. This follows a new piece of mourning in which Laura tells me she is feeling the sadness of giving up being my lover, even in her mind. With this sadness in relation to me, to our object relationship and to her transference, she also feels deep sadness in relinquishing a relationship with a past lover, who has now decided to more completely withdraw from her life. She also experiences the grief of compassion for her sister, who was feeling ill. The sadness, following her anger, renews tenderness and allows Laura to develop a broader capacity to love – women and men.

With increasing strides towards the processing of both the grief and sadness of the depressive position and the conscious aggressive fantasies of that position, Laura has been expressing more symbolic capacity and more capacity for gratitude.

When responding to a separation between us, after one of my vacations, Laura clearly outlines her feelings in a differentiated symbolic vision, at the oedipal level of erotic desire. She speaks of her vision of us reuniting after my return in genital terms, imagining her entrance into me in a phallic way, with my "beautiful vulva and clitoris opening like a flower, glowing, radiant and receptive."

Although the symbolic fantasy begins with phallic penetration, as if Laura had a literal penis, the affective emphasis in the fantasy shifts to the joy of being with me, reunited with me, not as an infant reentering the body womb of mother, but as an equal, engaging in sexual intercourse. The "reunion fantasy" (Masterson 1976) is at a phallic and genital level, and therefore the ecstasy of reunion has an explicit mutuality, an explicit sexual pleasure, and an explicit sense of psychic inter-penetration that is not compromised by the anatomical poetic license involved, since Laura didn't anatomically possess a penis. The symbolic level of fantasy allowed Laura to experience a psychic penetration of me. The symbolic level of fantasy also allows Laura to experience an interpenetration that transcends, but does not defensively deny, the anatomical or biological realities of her corporal existence. When Laura tells me this erotic reunion fantasy it is relayed with an abundance of loving feeling, and with the mind expanding aspects of Winnicott's capacity to play within transitional and potential psychic space. Unlike earlier times when Laura was overwhelmed by telling me such erotic love feelings – because the potential fantasies were still embedded in somatic and visceral proto-symbolic expression, making Laura feel that she would have to get up from the couch or cut off the feelings – at this later time (in the fourth year of treatment), Laura's capacity to symbolize her fantasy allowed her to contain her own affect. Thus, she becomes much less dependent on the containing functions of our joint "therapeutic object relationship" (Grunes 1984), or the "holding environment" (Modell 1976; Winnicott 1974). She was aware that it was the mourning process, with both its preoedipal and oedipal level conflictual desires and disillusionments that made it possible for her to reach this point with me, her analyst.

It might be argued that Laura's continuing need to fantasize herself as a phallic figure with a penis, in relation to her desire for me would leave her feeling far too vulnerable to castration anxiety, since in fact she possessed no literal penis, and was not her mother's fantasized son. I would respond that Laura's capacity to symbolize now allows her to face her castration fears directly, so that as the mourning process of psychic loss and disillusionment continues to proceed, Laura is more equipped than ever to resolve her castration anxiety, and to therefore decrease her level of psychic injury and vulnerability in relation to phallic level experience of self-annihilation (Hurvich 1997). Following the session in which her erotic reunion fantasy was expressed to me, Laura reacted with grief and a sense of injury when she thought she was not being considered for a professional position. When, in relation to this reaction I interpreted her phallic level experience of the fantasized loss and the sense of injury, in part, as feeling impotent, like she was being castrated, she was very capable of responding to this with fertile analytic associations.

As Laura's symbolic capacities continue to develop she becomes ever more capable of conceptualizing her own developmental process and treatment process. She is quite articulate about her sense of gratitude to me and to the overall analytic treatment process. As Klein (1957) has stated, the capacity for gratitude is an outgrowth of the conscious acceptance and symbolization of oral, anal, and phallic modes of aggression. Containing hate in symbolization, along with the critical factor of mourning the grief related to it (the grief of loss related to hate and its painful guilt), allows love to survive and thrive, and allows object relations connections to grow and deepen – both in external interpersonal intimacy, and within the internal world. This can certainly be seen in Laura's case. Around the same time as Laura's erotic reunion fantasy, she expressed the following feelings of gratitude to me. She said: "Your encouragement has meant a lot to me. I realize also that what you've been doing all this time is exactly what you should have been doing." I ask her to elaborate.

"You've never taken advantage of any analytic opportunity to try to convert me from my lesbianism. You've always wanted me to experience all sides of my psyche, including my sexual yearnings for men, so that I could feel and understand my deepest longings as well as conflicts. You've wanted me to be free, and to have all my psychic energy available. As a result I've become more spontaneous and alive, and can understand the deepest motivations of both myself and of others. You've wanted me to be the best I can be, whether lesbian, heterosexual, or bisexual. Psychoanalysis has been the best possible process for this to happen in. Those who believe that psychoanalysis can't work with lesbians, because of implicit gender bias and stereotype in analytic and Freudian theory are wrong. The main thing is that the analyst be open minded, and be true to the analytic process, rather than to personal prejudices. As you said in your paper [i.e. "Mourning and Erotic Transference"], the erotic transference is a metaphor for all of the deepest desires of the psyche, and it can be symbolized, not just for analysis, but also for communication. Sometimes I've gotten worried about where this analysis is going. I was afraid I'd just end up being enslaved to you erotically, but I realize now that's not the point. I realize that the eroticism and love for you, which I have been able to express in treatment, have enriched my relationship with my partner rather than threatening it. I have felt great satisfaction, but the tensions in the relationship can bring up my fears again, and I need to keep relearning that my feelings for you bring up fantasies about an internal object relationship that I will be compelled to repeat if I don't understand it. Whenever I have a fantasy of enacting the intense incest wish for my mother as artist and muse lover now, I can quickly know and experience that this is just a compulsion for reenactment. That knowledge releases me. Then I can more fully appreciate all I have with my real lover and partner."

The grief of Laura's mourning continues now at a more differentiated oedipal level of experience. Laura's capacities to negotiate the depressive position state of mind allow her to appreciate how her mourning process permits her to expand her capacities for sustained love, and her ever-growing originality and pleasure in intellectual, and self-expressive work. In my own theoretical words, Laura has attained a new level of "love–creativity dialectic," as she has expanded both her capacities for intimacy and for creative work finding great personal meaning in them. Laura has told me that although her deep love and gratitude for her lover were always there, she could only articulate this love through the mourning work in analysis. She can now define her love and offer it through words to her lover in a way that sustains the depth of communication necessary for a long-term relationship to grow. She is also finding that her work as a professor has become much more of a creative process for her as she has learned to listen to others in a whole new and different way, in her words, hearing the "music" as others speak, sensing the inner self of the other behind and through the words. As her capacities for self-articulation have grown, Laura finds new talents for writing, and for teaching, growing and blossoming into fulfillment from within her.

Chapter 13

Mourning and creativity

A journey through a male artist's development

Melanie Klein integrated her conceptualization of mourning process with her primary clinical and phenomenological theory of the paranoid-schizoid and depressive positions. It is within the psychic state of the depressive position that guilt and loss are experienced since attachment to an ambivalently loved object can be tolerated. Once guilt and loss are experienced, related to an amalgamation of love and hate for the object, with the predominance of love over hate, mourning becomes possible. Since mourning is so critical to self and psychic integration in the theory of Klein, the depressive position tolerance for sustaining love, along with the tolerance for conscious aggression for a lost object becomes the fulcrum of psychic growth, change and transformation. This has prompted Caper (1988) to comment that Klein's depressive position should actually be called a mourning position. I would concur with Caper's view. Depression, unlike a psychic state of readiness to mourn, refers to the blocked melancholic state referred to by Freud. Depression is a state of deadness promoted by defensive muscular and psychic control which operate against psychic capacities and strivings that promote grief and grieving. By contrast, Klein's depressive position is a psychic state of conflict and process, not a state of pathological deadness. The depressive position comes in shifts of progressive internal self and object integrations that supersede and alternate with paranoid-schizoid position psychodynamics. Unlike the splitting off and projecting of disowned parts of the self, in the depressive position the painful aspects of the self are contained and psychically processed. Affect experience is the main route to this process, whereas mourning is the overall gestalt of this affective process that involves the resolving and integrating of internal object relations as psychodynamic process.

Mourning is characterized by a sequence of affects that allow the integration of split off object experiences so that whole self-experience, with its characteristic psychic resilience, results. Once we establish that mourning is a fundamental developmental process, it becomes the obvious path to all primary self capacities, including creativity. I propose to illustrate that mourning is the clinical process that transforms creative potential into increasingly integrated forms of creative expression. In the following case, I present a snapshot view of an overall mourning process that leads to developmental advancements in the psychological level of the process of creativity, and its content.

THE CASE OF LARRY

Larry entered psychoanalytic treatment when he was struggling to be an artist, while working at a low-level position in a corporation. He was disturbed at his lack of enthusiasm about his painting and his artistic progress. His inadequate relationships with women were also distressing. He had many women friends, but found it difficult to sustain any romantic relationships. The few sexual relationships he had were not only short-lived, but devoid of the kind of romance he imagined possible. Larry saw his job as a temporary means of making money. Therefore, he put little effort into his job and his work relations. He was constantly dissatisfied with what seemed to him to be a generally empty life.

Indeed, Larry's life did appear empty, and his detachment from me, his analyst, as well as from his own feelings, suggested why his life lacked zest. However, within six years of analysis, during which he moved rapidly from two to three and then to four sessions a week, Larry became an enriched person, who prospered professionally, and romantically, with sustained development that matured out of a newly found aliveness and basic spontaneity. His passive-aggressive neurosis gradually yielded to mourning and interpersonal contact. The emergence of transferential themes related to each parent began to put Larry in touch with the pain of his past and the deprivation of healthy object relations that had shut him down emotionally.

Paintings

Larry's painting was the avenue by which he attempted to communicate the barrier he felt within himself and between himself and other people. Early in the treatment, Larry's paintings were characterized by stiff and basically lifeless male and female figures, who were entrapped in all kinds of geometric obstacles to their contact with each other. Their eyes were also turned away from each other. But an intense yearning for contact could sometimes be observed in the contorted postures of certain male figures. The female figures were generally indifferent to these men who craved contact. Larry would try to describe his internal frustration by describing the visual images in his paintings.

Larry's outside world resembled the internal world represented in his paintings. In treatment, he became aware that he had always been at a distance from people, which was reflected in his early paintings. In analysis, Larry articulated his cravings for emotional contact, and for erotic love with women.

Larry had dated a few women, but most were very distant emotionally. Although some of these women were highly seductive, they could not tolerate emotional intimacy. They would break up with Larry as soon as he began to become important to them. Other women he dated were generally unrelated and uncommunicative. Most of the time, Larry did not have any dating relationships, let alone any sustained romantic involvements. Some of his friendships with women were more sustained. However, these friendships mirrored the images in his paintings. He longed to convert most of his female friends into girlfriends, but they never thought of him as a potential boyfriend. Sometimes they used him as a confidant to talk about other men.

Larry's work life had a similar dullness. Passive-aggressively rebelling against his father's values, Larry kept himself in a low-level position. His father was a corporate executive who had pushed his son to apply for many jobs with executive friends' companies. Larry managed to sabotage all his father's ambitions for him by dressing inappropriately for job interviews and by presenting himself as incoherent and yet grandiose. Eventually, he found a job on his own, but secretly viewed it as beneath him, maintaining his position with as little involvement as possible.

During the course of Larry's analysis, he dreamed and painted. Both his dreams and his paintings relate the story of the change in his internal world. They also demonstrate the changing level of his capacity for creative self-expression as well as the changing dynamics in his personal creative process.

Dreams

Houses appear in Larry's dreams as a theme of evolution. Early in his analysis, Larry dreamed of wandering around lost in a forest. In time he comes upon a slightly cleared area where a small hut is. The hut is dark and hidden by bushes, ivy, and overhanging branches. The windows of the house are shut and boarded up, so that the inside is unseen and seemingly inaccessible. If we look at this house as symbolic of Larry's own self, we can observe the way in which his internal life was sealed off from contact with the world. Over the course of the mourning process that occurred in Larry's treatment, the image of the house was to transform into an open and elegant New England house, reflecting his self-transformation.

The closed down hut of his early dreams also appeared in other dreams as part of his more grandiose self in isolation, represented by a castle in a desert. This dream castle actually recreated a deconstructed hut in the forest of his childhood, in which he and a friend would play during his latency years, imagining that the elements of the hut were actually a castle. The castle in the dream was tall and dark, capturing a dissociated aspect of Larry's self. This isolated and cut off part of Larry yearned to expand and yet was small and underdeveloped while aspiring to grand dimensions. Gradually, over the years, both the small bush-covered hut and the castle were transformed into a more recognizable house of "live-in" dimensions. A porch manifested in front of the house, which had a clear area surrounding it. People were in that area. The patient was no longer alone in his dreams. He had friends with him! They all surveyed the house with curiosity. Now, the windows were no longer boarded, and lights could be seen from within. The door was open for visitors. The frame of the house then expanded into the elegant, but yet modest dimensions of a New England home. Eventually Larry entered the house in his dreams, along with friends, and his friends found furnishings within. Carpets appeared on the floors and pictures appeared on the walls. In one dream,

Larry got trapped in the still dark and empty basement of the house. But in the same dream, he emerged into the light again. Then new dreams showed the house to begin to reflect the colors and textures that spontaneously appeared in his new paintings, bright and vibrant colors and textures that vividly contrasted with the early dark grays, browns, blacks and beige colors in his early paintings.

This evolution reflected the mourning process in treatment that was developing, in which Larry became aware of both his aggression and his feelings of loss. Many memories of lost friendships emerged in Larry's free associative thoughts during treatment, and once he could experience the regret for how his passive aggressive distancing behaviors had pushed friends and potential lovers away, he was able to surrender to the affects of grief. This process was aided by interpretation of transference resistances in which Larry detached and distanced from the analyst while he lay on the couch, indulging in morose complaints about expected rejection by the analyst, while simultaneously pushing her away by repressing his affective responses. One of his feet would signal to both of us how he would be psychophysically pushing against his inner affect experience, as his foot pushed down against the couch. Simultaneously, the analyst felt herself being pushed backwards into a state of sleep. She suspected she was reacting to Larry's repression processes, as he unconsciously fought against consciousness of his feelings of desire for the analyst, feelings of loss of old love objects, and impulses of unconscious retaliatory aggression towards the erotically desired female analyst who he expected to reject him. With interpretation of his resistances to affect experience Larry gradually opened to a whole range of desires, impulses, and affects. His erotic transference became vivid, and served as a transitional stage of relationship in his movement towards an intense romantic relationship with one woman who he would chose to marry. His passive modes of aggression transformed into active expressions of discontent and frustrated desire.

Along with consciousness of erotic and aggressive impulses his capacity for tolerating mournful affects developed, particularly those of guilt and grief-laden sadness. He began to symbolize guilt as conscious experiences of regret, which could be integrated, since they reflected his growing sense of self-agency, as he increasingly owned feelings, fantasies, and impulses. Larry's capacity for tolerating and processing grief affects became simultaneously and increasingly enhanced, confirming Melanie Klein's view of promoting mourning and natural psychological development through integrating aggression into consciousness. Before describing Larry's mourning process more fully, the change in his paintings and dreams promoted in that mourning process will be discussed.

Parallel process of paintings and dreams

Larry's paintings showed a parallel process to that of his dreams. Over time, the stick figures who were bent over themselves in contortions, or who were geometrically trapped in external obstacles, gradually changed. First there were couples, men and women who began to come together. Engaged in transference, Larry began in our sessions to refer to all these figures in terms of transactions between him and myself. For example, he described the figure representing me in one painting as leaning on his chest, pressing down on him bodily, seemingly urging him into an affective response. In the middle phase of his analysis, Larry described many such images in his paintings. His figures were no longer behind barriers, but they engaged awkwardly. Mutuality was still missing. I merely leaned on "him" in his painting. "He" gazed at "me" from various angles.

As Larry's analysis emerged into a full-blown oedipal erotic transference, his paintings changed more dramatically. Men and women began to touch one another, to see each other. They looked at each other now, with mutual gazes. Their formerly stiff bodies became lithe, flexible, and resilient. Humor could now be found in the paintings. Amusing scenes of sublimated aggression were depicted, such as a man looking under the hood of an automobile while another smiling man was about to close the car's hood on top of him. All the subjects in Larry's paintings became more spontaneous, just as he himself did. Joy entered the paintings, then lust.

Textures in the paintings changed. These new, thicker textures echoed the syrupy textures that Larry described. His descriptions related to his paints and to the semen he ejaculated in the excitement of wet dreams. At the same time the drab browns and grays of his early paintings gave way to vibrant reds, greens, and blues. The men and women changed even more! They caressed and held each other. Their faces expressed compassion. Erotic joy seemed to resonate between the figures.

Work–creativity dialectic (part of love–creativity dialectic)

Larry's creative process was also transformed. Formerly, he feared that he could not paint and work full time. But gradually he felt sure enough of his spontaneous creative capacities to trust that he could freely come and go from his painting, without losing touch with it. Larry's relationship to the work he did for a living was also undergoing a metamorphosis. He began to feel some connection to his co-workers. His greater sense of emotional engagement led him to develop his competency and to take on more responsibility. Having worked out his antagonism towards his father, he rose through the ranks to an executive level. As his work in the corporation became more a part of his identity, Larry's enjoyment of his work as an artist grew. His artistic efforts became much less compulsive. Larry did not feel his paintings were all he possessed. He had his analyst. He had found new friends and new colleagues, and ultimately he had a girlfriend who became a fiancée and later his wife. He painted at his leisure. He grew more confident as his painting became richer in texture, color, and story line. He began to share his work more and was accepted into a gallery. Now he had the confidence to rent his own studio, to separate his work as an artist from his home and social life. As he saw himself to be a professional painter, he no longer felt engulfed by an exclusive artistic identity.

Love–creativity Dialectic

Overall, Larry developed a dialectic of mutuality reflected in his life in the world, as capacities for psychic dialectic developed through the mourning process in his object relations analysis. He developed a dialectic of mutuality, not only between himself and others, but between his business work and his artistic work, as well as between his artwork and his social and romantic lives. He could freely go back and forth now: no geometric barricades appeared in his paintings. He could even give up painting during the course of his engagement period so that he might indulge in as much intimacy as possible with his fiancée. He knew he would return to his work when ready. This confidence arose as his internal life, which had formerly eluded him, was at his fingertips. He was spontaneous, alive, flexible, humorous, and romantic, as never before. He could tune into his feelings and reactions, and help his fiancée understand him deeply too.

Free motivation rather than compulsion

Larry became able to connect to a totally different kind of woman. His wife was warm, emotionally alive, tender, sensual and erotic. She encouraged intimacy and closeness, rather than rejecting it as his former girlfriends had. Free of compulsion in his artistic work, Larry conveyed the ecstasy and poetry of his painting to me during our sessions. He spoke poetically of the velvet and sensual light tones that shimmered through his studio windows while he worked. He described the rich seductive colors on his pallet, and the sensual and emotional pleasures of the act of painting.

As his work became more immediate, and less cluttered by preparatory rituals and doubt, and the pleasure of the creative work itself deepened, the freer Larry felt to disengage from his creative work for extended periods of time. Although renting his own studio had been a preciously valued achievement, when the time came to give up this studio so that he might save money for his wedding and move out of town and buy a house afterwards, he made the transition with nostalgia rather than resistance.

Larry's mourning process

Larry went through many phases of mourning within his seven years of treatment. Early in Larry's treatment, his yearning for a preoedipal mother was at first felt by me and by Larry himself, as it appeared in memories and in the transference. One memory of a painful separation from a male friend at latency apparently was a screen memory for early yearnings towards the preoedipal object. The memory was also about a poignant object attachment and object loss in its own right. The scene was a dug-out hole in the Oklahoma wilderness. He and his friend, Dave, used to fantasize that the remains of a building they found in their private wilderness was the foot of a giant castle. This was their land of enchantment. It was a romantic world where friendship and adolescent homosexual love could bloom.

The height of their mutual enthrallment arose one quiet summer afternoon, when they lay side by side, and also half on top of one another, inside their hole. They didn't speak. They were at peace. Perhaps at that moment Larry experienced a sublime feeling of bliss that he had always yearned for, a feeling that he may have never quite achieved in infancy, with another who was full of tension and depression.

In contrast to the soft bliss of this memory with his latency age friend were the memories of his mother as hard. In one dream, Larry banged repeatedly on a tree for a response. It turned out the tree was made of petrified wood. He finally gave up, concluding: "You can't get blood from a stone." Even if earlier at her breast Larry had found a softer mother, the bliss-filled time of feeling his friend so present and so close was not necessarily a screen memory, or at least not simply one. It could be the fulfillment of yearning that had long been aroused and frustrated by his early mother.

Larry's earliest memories of his childhood were of frustrating scenes between himself and his parents. He remembered his parents, and perhaps his mother more often, telling him as soon as he learned to talk that he must stop, hold his breath, and not say anything unless it was really important. Such directives threw Larry, still a toddler, into a tailspin. His urge to speak felt like a gasp that was being pushed back into him. His words got all contorted inside, just like the bodies that appeared in his early paintings. All spontaneous gestures and voice felt arrested. He was stunned and stuck newly dumb. His excitement to convey his feelings was crushed. He felt like he was forced to literally swallow his words. Deep body tensions were established at this time that made withdrawal backward and inward into himself a reflexive reaction.

Because of the tension that revolved around expressing himself in words, it is no wonder that the happiest time Larry remembered was the time of tranquil silence as he lay comfortably in body contact with his best friend. All the more reason that when he was forced away from his friend by the same parents who "forced" his voice away from him, he felt internally desecrated.

His parents were having trouble in their marriage when he was about nine, and with an abrupt attempt at a resolution, they decided to leave town and to move to California. There was no discussion with the children. Before Larry knew what was happening, he was sitting in the back of his family car, peering mournfully out the rear window. He had never even said goodbye.

The last time he and his friend Dave were together they hadn't discussed his departure. Neither said a single word. They got into some ridiculous fight over nothing. Now he might never see him again. Nor would Larry see the other friends he had made in Oklahoma. He felt defeated – dead inside.

Only later in his analysis did Larry mourn the loss of his friend Dave. He also mourned the loss of the kind of quiet contentment that he had so treasured during those few precious moments, those few precious days that occurred as the crystallization of the intimacy with his friend blossomed over a two-year period. As Larry's grief-laden sadness emerged, alternating with the angry protests against his parents that he had never made to them then, his potential tenderness was born.

This tenderness touched Larry and touched the analyst. Larry embroidered his memories with the feeling of tender love felt belatedly now in the present. While on the couch, with his face hidden from my direct view, Larry let me know that tears were in his eyes, tears formerly blocked and suffocated. I felt him in his tender tear-filled sadness and he felt me feeling him, so that a Winnicottian (1971) holding environment was established from which mourning could continue.

Mourning his friend, which galvanized psychic yearnings for a good preoedipal object, was just the beginning of Larry's mourning in treatment. He often mourned for parts of himself, child parts that had been injured and left behind. He remembered shame-filled experiences of paternal castration. One memory of being punished and spanked was especially humiliating. Another memory surfaced of his father going into a rage and slapping him across the face. Both memories brought back to Larry his despair at ever being understood. The spanking episode was the result of his stealing some quarters from their next-door neighbors in California because it was his only way of expressing his misery and his wishes to retaliate against the parents who tore him away from his friend Dave and his other Oklahoma friends. His father was not interested in his explanations. Both parents united in their desire to punish him. They saw him as immoral, as a thief! He was forced to apologize to his neighbors in words his parents made up. He couldn't even use his own language of contrition. He went through what felt like his trial and conviction in a numbed out state – dejected, passively obedient. He saw himself as a piece of shit, as a cast out turd. He waited in his room, as he was commanded to by his father. He waited, feeling the minutes as hours, not knowing what would happen next.

Centuries seemed to pass. Then his father entered his room and ordered him to "drop your pants." His father spanked him on his bare behind, never once looking at him in the face. The boy submitted, his self-hatred drowning out awareness of his hatred for his father. Later he would act this hatred out, doing everything possible to disown his own aggression as he associated his father with aggression. However, unconsciously he identified with his father's detachment. Larry commented on how even at the height of his father's aggression towards him, in the midst of his humiliation, the father seemed detached and uninvolved, seemingly doing what he thought he had to do. Larry felt that he didn't even receive the dignity of his father's personal sense of anger.

Larry had repressed his reactions, unable to tolerate the awareness of how lonely and unimportant he felt during his humiliating castration. In treatment, his hatred towards his parents, especially his father, came alive. So did his shame. He asked out loud the questions that he could never have asked at that time. He made the protests he had been unable to even whisper. His secret superiority emerged as well, his belief that his father was contemptible. But he had always treated himself with contempt, repeating his father's behavior towards him. He had dreams in which another man split off from him, or came inside of him. Sometimes he had dialogues with this other man. He realized that this other man was a part of him, another half. He had his father inside of him (as an unmetabolized object), and there was nothing he could do about it. All he could do was make peace with his father, by understanding his father's pain and grieving now for both of them. His rage at his father spent, his feelings of shame and humiliation beginning to heal with the expression of his internal wounds and the expression of his shit-flawed self-image, he was ready to make amends.

Moving from the paranoid-schizoid to the depressive position, Larry was able to realize how much pain his father must have carried to have been so numbed out himself, so filled with rage, so indifferent to anything his son said or thought.

Forgiveness came to Larry as he felt empathy for his father's loneliness. The whole family emerged now too, one that had eluded him as a child. He could see how his father was emotionally rejected and dictated to by his mother. He saw his mother's pain too, for she was jealous and lonely with a husband who was in love only with his work, a husband who frequently had affairs with his secretaries. The whole picture began to come together in Larry's mind. Larry began to have two whole parents. In this way, he could become whole.

Larry was freed by his capacity to feel the chain of affects from his anger, to the narcissistic hurt within his shame, and to the loss within his sense of loneliness as he separated from his internal bad part-object parents. Grief followed anger and hurt. Only then could he feel his parents' pain within his own pain, without the threat of losing his own separate perspective.

He would never get to communicate to them what he had felt, and his grief was partly for that. There would always be a barrier between them. But as he communicated his pain to me, his analyst, he psychically healed the rift with his parents and grew to empathize with their pain. He grieved the loss of what they could never be to each other. Through grief he allowed a tender sadness to emerge within him that was the pathway to contact with others. He could know and touch others now, and they could know and touch him. It is at this point, when painting became more tactile and colorful that Larry emerged from his despair, as if experiencing rebirth. His dreams showed his sense of self growing whole. His barriers against me were analyzed and resolved, as he could let me feel him and could feel me in return.

Mourning of the oedipal love object

As Larry regained the cut off part of himself, the part of him that had been sealed off and split off in response to abandonment and castration trauma, he became capable of expressing an oedipal level erotic transference. In the beginning of treatment, this erotic transference was latent. Erotic desires were expressed in sadomasochistic fantasies of being tied down by a woman and made to submit to all kinds of sexually arousing tortures. His fantasies echoed his passive submission to women when he entered treatment. Further back, they echoed his "enslaved" position in relation to his mother, which was chiefly characterized by his inability to say "no" to her every evening when she asked him to go into the kitchen and get "my" icecream.

One dream shed light on the deeper level of his humiliation. He dreamt that he was forced to sit naked at the dinner table by his mother. He shivered from the cold, felt mortified as others sat at the table for dinner. When someone gave him a blanket, his mother flew into a rage. His associations revealed that he thought his mother was becoming sexually stimulated by his nakedness. He felt exploited by her and not cared for. This dream appeared early in treatment, prior to his mourning the hurt of his shame and the pain of feeling for both his mother and father.

Larry eroticized his rage. He inverted himself into the role of the victim, and controlled others by being controlled. His sexual fantasies, which he cherished and nurtured during his secret masturbation rituals, were filled with his erotic victimization. Sometimes one woman tied him up, sometimes three did. One dream revealed his transference to me as one of these women who intimidated and even terrified him. The woman in his dream was huge compared to him. He was forced to please her in all kinds of ways that substituted for sexual intercourse, since his penis was too small. The dream showed his secret terror of being erotically seduced and persecuted by a huge female, while he was small and helplessly enthralled and dominated. The huge female is of course a form of fantasy mother displacement from the time when he was a small oedipal child and his mother was much larger and more powerful than he was. By constructing and controlling his sexual fantasies and sex play, he could turn his terror into erotic thrills. In this dream he didn't have that control, and much of his emotional withdrawal from me in the clinical situation could be understood in reference to his terrified inhibition and his hidden erotic longings.

Larry began to emerge from his guilt and shame-ridden cocoon by sharing his masturbation fantasies and dreams. As he did so his physical dimensions became, in his fantasies and associations, more proportionate in relation to mine. His dreams now revealed all sorts of phallic explosions. Often these dreams were wet dreams. In one dream, there was a tidal wave of emotion coming in at both of us from the outside. I appeared as a holding environment mother of safety in this dream, but it was clear that he saw both of us threatened by the breadth of his passion. His emotional longings had to be experienced full force, just as his phallic eruptions, in order that the two could come together. Larry spoke of standing up to the tidal wave and facing the fear. He felt he could face his passion because he had me by his side.

As Larry's tidal wave of passion came out into the open, separating from the ocean of the unconscious, and coming into the light of day, he wooed me fiercely. He constantly thought of "lines" to say to me as he entered my office. He revealed this with some degree of embarrassment, testing the waters. Over time his shame diminished. His awakening sense of humor became more predominant. Also, Larry began to constantly observe what I wore. He would wait to see if I would wear a red dress. If I did, he said that he hoped I wore it especially for him. He found everything I wore exciting. His confessed secret attraction to me, containing his wish for me to wear a red dress, became an ongoing motif in his daily speculations about whether I had dressed that morning with him in mind. This period, when the oedipal desires emerged, during his fifth and sixth year of treatment, brought dreams and fantasies of me lying beside him in bed, or of me suddenly appearing at his doorstep, and coming inside his home to make love to him. He wanted to feel the pressure of my body, our tenderness, our caressing. He imagined us sharing our secret flaws together, bonding through the sharing of our shame, revealing the awkward areas of our bodies, evolving an exquisite attunement to each other's body surfaces.

Then there were Larry's desires for me to yearn as intensely for him as he yearned for me. Once, upon meeting a young woman he was attracted to, he vividly described to me his pursuit of her, painting a scene for me that culminated in a sweet, sensual, and prolonged kiss. Not receiving the reaction he expected, he burst out uncharacteristically (which felt as if it were accompanied by the stamping of a foot): "God damn it, I want you to be jealous!" His mother always had been jealous of any girl that he showed interest in. He resented her behavior as it made him feel overwhelmed with guilt, but now he realized that he wanted this jealous reaction from me.

As I had become so vividly painted as his oedipal love, only disappointment and mourning could bring him to make the transition from it into finding a true love who could be his own. A critical time of growth came during my summer vacation, before his last year of treatment. Larry reported to me that after my departure he had awakened in the mornings with the weight of grief and sadness he had never known before. It caused him to weep. His sadness was the full impact of his realization that I was never going to come to his home, to his bed. I would never be his.

Surrendering to this truth, Larry emerged from his cocoon radically altered. He experienced a newfound determination, a willingness to take risks. He joined a dating service and within three dates he had met the woman who became his bride. As he began to date her and to know her, his painting mirrored his erotic joy. His romantic fantasies were replaced by romantic realities better than any fantasies could have predicted. His courtship with his fiancée was filled with surprises, gifts, and tender concern and caring. On Valentine's Day, Larry canceled one of his analytic sessions (for which he paid) to take his fiancée to the Tavern on the Green, and generally, in his words, "to give her the royal treatment." (Now I was jealous!) It became clear that I had served as a transitional love object who had clearly been relinquished by having been internalized within him. When Larry left treatment, he said: "You will be deep inside of me for the rest of my life!" But he also had said: "You're no longer the focus of my erotic longings." As his treatment drew to a close, his fiancée was the one who empowered his female figures with sensual joy and erotic delight. The colors and shapes danced. His paintings now had lyric, regardless of whether Larry painted on an external canvas or on the canvas within his internal world.

Chapter 14

The divine, the deviant and the diabolical

A journey through a female artist's paintings during her participation in a creative process group

Jane is a female artist who for two years participated in one of my writing and creative process groups. The group has been in existence for fifteen years. Throughout Jane's attendance, the group was comprised of one man and five women. During her second year in the group, Jane also began individual therapy with me. During this second year, Jane's participation was marked by major psychic and personality changes, which are evident in the paintings that she presented to the group.

The relationships Jane developed with her fellow group members helped her to embark on a critical "developmental mourning process," a process reflecting a lifetime of developmental changes, including the traumas, losses, and regrets related to separation–individuation, "abandonment depression," and existential grief. Jane's mourning allowed her self-integration process to evolve and become manifest in her paintings. In addition, the act of painting itself allowed her to carry out the process of mourning at a visceral and symbolic level, while at the same time expressing the affect, memories, and transference related to her grief – first solely within the holding environment of the creative process group, then also within the context of individual treatment.

In this chapter, I attempt to show the correspondence between the developmental process revealed in Jane's paintings over this critical two-year period and her mourning process that occurred within the creative process group. The individual treatment enhanced this mourning process by highlighting the associations, dreams, memories and transference that had already emerged within the creative process group.

It may be useful here to briefly describe the creative process group, which meets weekly. Every other session, each member has a 30-minute period in which to present any creative work in process and to ask for the kind of feedback she/he wants from the group concerning this work. To facilitate this process, group membership is limited to no more than six people. Besides their feelings and conflicts related to the progression or arrest of their creative process, members also share their associations to their artistic work. If they do not actually present a piece of work, they are free to discuss their current struggles with feelings, conflicts, and life situations. Both members and myself then help make connections between

Figure 14.1 Early self-fragmentation

their present associations and their creative process, focusing on where they may be stuck or blocked in their work and where they may be going with it.

EARLY PAINTINGS

The process of progression

Although Jane presented many paintings to the group, I have chosen to discuss only those paintings that especially highlight her developmental and psychological growth. The first paintings Jane brought show an involvement with what might be divine, but they also hide the more diabolical elements of her internal world. They were distinctly different from her later paintings. These first paintings had a motif of handprints and dots (Figure 14.1). Some reminded us of stained glass found in

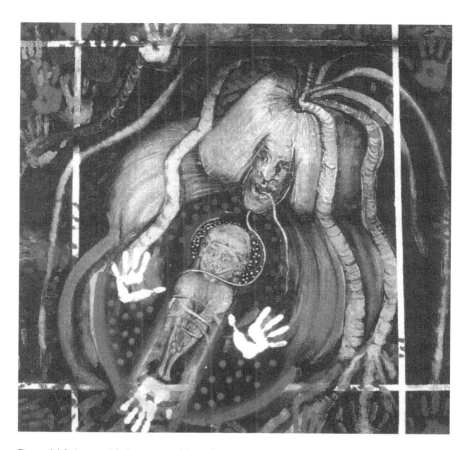

Figure 14.2 Internal father as psychic embryo

cathedrals. Without exception these paintings were painted on a flat plane. There were no complete human body forms. Rather, there were part object forms of hands, which could have been child's handprints, as made when playing with a finger painting set. The childlike imprints of these hands suggested that everything beneath the surface in Jane's psyche was still hidden. The handprints were arranged in designs that gave the paintings a decorative effect rather than one of psychological meaning.

The next set of paintings Jane showed the group had an entirely different texture and quality. Figures began to emerge from a no longer flat surface (Figure 14.2). Although still far from possessing human forms, these early figures had either grand or miniature dimensions. The large androgynous figure emerging from the background of handprints possibly represents Jane's yearning for a god-like divine figure. Because of its nearly three-dimensional quality, this figure transforms the surrounding space, making the space also almost three-dimensional. What a strange creature it is. Snakes swim out of its head, and there is an embryonic creature inside of its midsection. The figure's face is severe and masculine, capped by hair cut in a moderately long pageboy. The hair seems to be made of straw or wheat; as such, rather than flowing femininely, it is stiff. The snakes emerging from this androgynous but still somehow masculine-looking creature are wheat colored like the hair. But although they seem to form a decorative hairpiece, the snakes also take on an animated life of their own. This androgynous creature is also apparently pregnant. A small but not tiny figure rests in a uterine state within its center. This embryo has a mature but enigmatic face, reflecting an androgynous persona, but its hair and braids suggest a female form, as do the red lips and staring eyes. Although the embryonic creature's arms are tied together with a cord wrapped around them like an umbilical cord, it has no lower body. A handprint, however, juts out of its foreshortened and cut off arms. The handprint "substitutes" for this smaller creature's hands, but it is also evocative of some ominous genitalia. The fine finger digits may also be seen as five phallic extensions, complementing the phallic forms of the snakes emerging from its "parent's" headdress. Two handprints on the side of the uterine body container, outside of the small creature's compartment, also complement the phallic design while enhancing to the abstract quality of the body shape. Round red shapes resembling large dots, or berries, underscore the surrealistic quality of the piece, almost making it seem as if this androgynous creature is lost in space, even though the embryo is contained inside a larger form. Indeed, this larger creature holds on to and perhaps even communicates with the small and slightly feminine looking creature, as the end of the embryo's umbilical cord enters the parental chin, continuing up and out through its mouth. Looking down to the smaller embryonic creature, the viewer can see that a piece of this tube is also in its mouth. This set of paintings then shows Jane's strong oral preoccupations.

Jane's free associations to the group permitted her to suggest an overall interpretation. First, in associating to the painting, Jane speaks of a defensive and compensatory identification with her father and of her fantasy of him as a huge phallic figure. Having viewed her mother as a symbol of devalued femininity, Jane does not have conscious identifications with her. In fact, throughout her life she has consciously attempted to be the opposite of her mother; while unconsciously she has tried to find some sense of her own body shape through a "phallic construction" (Jane's own term), related to her image of her father. The painting highlights various ambiguities in Jane's psyche as she attempts to merge with her father as a grandiose god figure while unconsciously experiencing him as quite a miniature (in terms of the emotional support he provides) figure in real life. Jane tells the group about her belief that she was super-special to her father and her subsequent painful disillusionment on realizing this was more a wish than any reality. Her father was actually quite detached not only from her but from the entire family, but his physical holding of her when she was a child caused her to form a bond with him in her own psyche that she held on to. Thus Jane created an image of a strong father who would keep her separate from her mother and from her mother's wishes to merge with her by pressuring Jane to submit to being like her.

The painting I have described captures two sides of what Jane did with her own wishes for merger after she disowned her mother and projected all the shame-ridden and devalued parts of herself onto her mother (a process she later reenacted with her female analyst in the transference). In the painting, the embryonic figure is clearly merged with the larger androgynous figure. We can look at this merger, enacted via the oral feeding tubes and umbilical cords, in two different ways. We may see the larger figure as the fantasy father. As such he reflects the large body proportions of Jane's actual father, the grand dimensions of a preoedipal fantasy father, and the amorphous shape a child might see as she looks at her father from a perspective in which only his head is differentiated and clear. But if we see this larger creature as a projected father image, then the smaller figure can be interpreted as being Jane herself, in the form of an undeveloped figure, totally dependent on her father; her identification with him unconsciously deemed by her necessary for her survival. Jane's unconscious fantasy is that she is alive only as long as the symbiotic connection lasts. (The power of this fantasy is reflected in the painting, where she is clearly not even born.) Although the hair of the smaller figure in the painting suggests some feminine aspect, the genitals are clearly erased, and thus denied. The sexual ambiguity is underscored by the handprint, which although covering her genital area, gives the figure a phallic aspect, with the five fingers pointed downward suggesting five phallic extensions with downward erections extended from the potential lower body.

In her comments to the group on her childhood fantasy of her father, which she no longer felt to be accurate, Jane offered an alternate view of these two figures. In speaking of the loss of the grand image of her father, and her later apprehension of him – particularly on seeing him, as a consequence of old age and illness, as physically frail and weak – Jane began to speak of the psychological weaknesses of her father. She described his vanity, self-preoccupation, and disconnectedness from the family. She told the group of her childhood longings to believe that he wanted her rather than her mother, explaining this as a [typical oedipal) fantasy she clung to in order to disguise her actual lack of importance and distinction to him. Jane also recounted her struggles with the idea of a strong phallic force, which she had imagined as her father's penis attached to a weak man. In one dream that she recounted to the group she imagines her father's penis as being erect and red but extending from a frail, elderly, yet infantile body. When she looked at her father in this new way as his life waned (not from illness but in the general aging process), Jane observed that she felt she must support and resuscitate him to bring him back to life. Her sharing of these associations with the group led her to the following interpretation.

The small embryonic creature in the painting, she felt, could be her father. Perhaps she was the larger creature resuscitating her father, breathing life back into him through a feeding tube, shared mouth to mouth, a cord that "ends up" as an umbilical cord. Perhaps she was the more masculine but androgynous figure herself!

My own interpretation is that the ambiguity is never resolved in the painting, but

Figure 14.3 Born into time

is built into it. Perhaps the snakes emerging from the larger figure's head are meant to be associated with her father, and with a form of phallic power suggestive of evil, which snakes often symbolize in mythology.

EARLY MIDDLE PAINTINGS

Born into life

Jane entitled the next important painting she presented to the group, "Born into time" (Figure 14.3). The birth theme possibly supports what Jane had already disclosed to the creative process group as part of her history– that her mother gave birth to her through a Caesarian section, leaving Jane with the impression that she had not entered the world through a natural birth, and therefore needed to repair the situation by being born from within through her paintings. In this painting, the artist has moved clearly away from symbiosis with a masculinized figure; rather her focus has shifted to birth into a state of independent being. The painting shows three figures, side by side. These figures seem to express three stages of birth in the same being. The figure on the right, constructed of colored and striated snake formations, has a tiny curled up sleeping embryo deeply embedded in its womb. In contrast, the figure on the left is half formed and half awake. Half-human and half apelike, this creature looks like it is just beginning to open its eyes and look out into the world. The expression on its face is dazed, the eyes are half shut, and the head is curled into itself. The creature has no genitals or legs. Although it is emerging from a womb of snake formations, this womb seems more adequately containing for a birth than are the wombs in earlier paintings that seem like penises swirling into snakes. Here the creature comes out from a section of the womb that partly resembles a woven basket opening and partly looks like fingers (with red nail-polished tips) that are opening. This figure has both amorphous and phallic qualities. Masculine phallic and female womb part objects appear merged at the stage of psychic development seen in this painting.

In the center of the painting is a much bolder and dramatically awake figure than the other two figures. In fact, we may view it as an infant who is fully awake and screaming just after birth, because its eyes are wide open and so is its mouth as if in a shout or scream. Two handprints on each side of its torso, flatly but acutely applied, suggest more of a thrust open towards life. As often with babies, the head appears like it may be too big for its body. Yet the overall extension of the figure is what stands out. The striated snake formations of the womb area are reduced to a background motif, suggesting that the womb has been left behind and the figure is fully born into life, as the painting's title reminds us. But some portion of the womb still seems to be encasing the figure in diagonal enclosures, and the womb appears to be in vivo in the process of transforming into a cape, an article of clothing that covers the figure. There is an energetic movement in this figure radiating out to its surroundings that enlivens the entire painting, giving the viewer quite a different impression from that of the static formations of Jane's earlier paintings. A background design at the upper part, consisting of multicolored dots and black lines, suggests the surface veneer of the earlier paintings. But here the design is fuller than previously; the painting has the quality of stained glass, giving a spiritual transcendence to the whole scene of birth.

Yet even the most dynamic figure, the middle figure, inherits the body and psychic disconnection discernible in the earlier paintings. For example, the handprints are disconnected from the body. In addition, although the neck emerging out of the top of a cape has the human figure form, with a head above the neck, and the neck also connected to the torso, the torso has a hole in it, making it appear like a second head has been cut out of the torso. This shadow imprint of a cut off second head reinforces the impression of disconnectedness conveyed by the painting.

Another interesting aspect of this vibrant figure is that the surface of its body, appears as less than human; indeed, it appears more turtle-like. That is, the square indentations on the front of the body resemble an armor-plated turtle shell. As in Jane's earlier paintings, an animal – human anomaly is indicated, and gender issues in human forms are avoided, with the figures being born having no genitals.

Figure 14.4 Unnamed movement towards a feminine self

LATE MIDDLE PAINTINGS

The feminine and the deviant

A strange and ambiguous creature totally dominates the space in the next significant painting that Jane presented (Figure 14.4). In this painting, the breasts and fleshy body parts give the appearance of a female creature. This figure is fuller in form than any in her earlier paintings. The figure has legs, but the artist evades the genital area by balancing the figure on its stomach, with its legs behind the stomach. This painting has a more cohesive appearance than Jane's earlier paintings due to her consolidation of all part figures in one dominating creature. Nevertheless, the creature's birth process still does not resemble any in the natural world. It is giving birth to two heads out of its body, and one of these heads is emerging from a huge hand formation that extends out of the side of a thigh rather than an arm. The other head figure, which is obscure and without distinct features, appears to be a fleshy head that may resemble the head of a baby. Yet this "baby" is not emerging from a female womb or vagina, but rather from the back of an upper thigh of a distorted female form, or possibly out of the back of a creature that is half female (it has breasts and its legs are rather feminine in shape) and half animal. The head emerging from the gross leg–hand formation has more distinct features than the other head and looks like a small male Egyptian idol, possessing painted eyes and a striated gold and red painted headdress.

Although this singular figure has large and pendulous breasts, leading the viewer's eye downward to rolling swells of flesh in the torso and then to human shaped legs, it arms are foreshortened, as are most of the forms in Jane's paintings. But, in a departure from earlier paintings, where arms are generally cut off from body parts and therefore useless, here Jane has carried the arms downward, until they metamorphose into full forms like the front legs of an animal. The legs end as hoofs, rather than lower arms and hands. Yet there is the distinct figure of a hand, enlarged and extending from the left leg of the figure, which cradles and gives birth to the painted Egyptian head creature. In other words, a seemingly masculine figure emerges from a feminine form.

The background of this painting marks another departure from Jane's earlier work. The striated snake formations of the previous paintings have yielded to orange and blue decorative designs in all areas, except for the headdress worn by the figure itself. The background designs have the colors of an Indian blanket, or that of some kind of wallpaper. There is a distinct division in this painting between the flat one- or two-dimensional decorative motifs in the background – reminiscent of Jane's flat designs in her earliest paintings – and the full fleshy and human animal moving towards the viewer as represented by the dynamic three-dimensional figure, created via chiaroscuro and artful perspective. The amorphous boundary between these two areas, of the fleshy figure in front and the background blanket design, occurs in only one place in this painting, in the female figure's headdress. A trace of the merging evident in the earlier paintings remains here in the blending of background and foreground, where the headdress of a pointed phallic striated form (no longer red, but orange) metamorphoses from a distinct cone-like shape on the top of the head to a less contoured horn-like striated shape, emerging from the back of the head, where it merges with the design of the background wallpaper (or blanket).

This strange creature seems to be hairless, but it is also possible that the hair is suppressed and hidden under the headdress and hat form on the top of the head. In either case, the female-like body is not softened by any feminine flow of hair. Without such a feminine flow, the figure appears stark, if not rigid in form, in this way recalling the more masculine figures in earlier paintings. This creature also has a strange, almost estranged, aspect. One eye is wider and more formed than the other. Both eyes glare, their focus overly intense. The face has a stony expression,

Figure 14.5 Full-bodied woman

and the stiffness of the nose and mouth evoke a chiseled in stone quality. The creature's ears are also lopsided and unbalanced, with the left ear foreshortened into a kind of hole that expresses its own deviance from the normal human form.

Despite its strangeness, this figure marks the closest that Jane had come in her art to the world of flesh and blood human and female figures in all their three-dimensional dynamism. The deviance of individual body shapes from realistic human forms suggested to me an interesting dialectic between realistic perception of body forms and body forms molded by internal psychic fantasy.

LATE PAINTINGS

Female at last

Jane's last significant painting represents great growth in its degree of self and body integration (Figure 14.5). Its cohesion lies in the realism of the human form.

The balance between masculine and feminine aspects of the human form, as well as the dialectic between the masculine and feminine symbolism surrounding the central figure is evocative and distinctive. The painting signifies a dramatic culmination of Jane's developmental process within the environment of the creative process group.

This painting marks the first time that I was able to label any figure in Jane's paintings a true woman. This woman looks out at us with eyes apprehensive but focused. Her face is bold and somewhat distinct, but not stony, and her lips, nose, and eyes all have a full and natural form. The distinctly female body has well-shaped and plump breasts that are neither elongated nor exaggerated. Her head, neck, arms, and torso are each appropriately proportioned to the volume of the full figure. For the first time we also see arms that are full and formed, rather than cut off, foreshortened, or transformed into animal hoofs. One arm is cropped at the picture's edge. But the other arm extends into a full hand, with detailed fingers and even nails. This hand, raised in an athletic or militant pose, holds a striated tube form, somewhat like a spear.

The female figure has an overall majesty. Despite the masculine toughness of the torso and the vividness of its muscular development, it remains fully female in character. Interestingly, this female quality does not extend to its lower body dimensions. The figure is cropped at the waist and so there are no genitals or legs. The issue of a womb or vagina is again evaded. Yet despite these significant omissions, in this painting the figure form has finally evolved into the shape of a woman.

The spear represents a very interesting male–female duality. The striated snake forms – so much a part of the background of Jane's earlier paintings – are now contained in distinct shapes, with a thematic relationship indicated between themselves and the painting's figure. The spear is not sharp; moreover, it becomes a tube. In addition, although its surface is covered by striated lines, the spear does not appear to be a snake. Rather, its phallic aspect yields to the feminine form of a tube that might be a fallopian tube opening in the female womb. In fact, out of its forward end a small creature appears to be emerging, as if possibly during the act of birth. This part of the tube is thus "open ended." What emerges from it is unformed and inchoate, leaving a mystery for the viewer to solve – what is the precise nature of event occurring? Still the painting does present an evolving, emerging, and thereby birthlike situation, in which a human womb is suggested, even though this womb is separate from the lower end of the human body, where it might be associated with the female vagina. The disconnection the artist maintains here is that of the female's distinct genital sexuality. The female has an external womb! This phallic womb tube opens its end to what might be an oral cavity, in which there is a tiny being with teeth, or possibly these are tiny fingertips curled up as baby fingers are at birth. Out of this portion of the tube, where these teeth or fingers emerge, extends a long stringlike, snakelike creature. This creature is not composed of striated forms, but of smaller lines and indentations, more like those of a real snake than those in Jane's earlier paintings of the larger phallic forms resembling Egyptian motifs and clothing. The snake in this painting may also be an umbilical cord stretching from the tiny figure in the womb tube.

The female figure in the foreground presents us with another form that appears to be an integrated consolidation of formerly split off parts. I am referring to the headdress neatly and firmly fitting the head of the woman who so forthrightly confronts us in this painting. The headdress has no pointed phallic extensions like those in the headdress in the painting Jane presented us in earlier work. Here the headdress is like a hat, but a hat with more feminine than masculine contours. The part hat extends backward and downward from the band around the head. Both the band, snug fitting like a cap, and the back part, flowing down like hair, are painted in multicolored stripes. These stripes pick up the motif of striation and Egyptian headdress established in Jane's previous paintings, but here they consolidate what in those paintings seem like snakes into a rich fabric motif flattering to the feminine form, rather than opposing it with the masculinely textured phallic erectness in the earlier paintings. The multicolored stripes of the hat complement, rather than mimic, the striated form of the external womb tube. Instead of the stark alternations (and oppositions) of red and white stripes, there is a multicolored flow of blue, red, purple, and gold suggestive of the richness of fabric rather than the animal aspect of a snake. Still, once again, a creature that appears feminine has no hair. The presence of hair is only suggested underneath the flowing fabric. This hint lends a mystery to the feminine form that can be enticing, although it also suggests that the most feminine flowing aspect of the self is hidden, as are the genitals. The muscularity of the woman's body, which allows the viewer to infer a masculine tension in the figure, despite its distinctly drawn breasts, may be consonant with the evasion of direct feminine flow (the absence of freely flowing hair).

The figure in the foreground in this painting is less separated from the background than the figures in Jane's earlier paintings. In addition, the background has circular designs that express more of an organic and perhaps feminine form than the backgrounds in earlier paintings, largely constructed from striated phallic snakes or disconnected handprints and surface dots. There is a much more organic feeling in this painting. Also, circles of wheat seeming to form something like a straw basket that provides another containing womb shape. This shape corresponds to the straw color of the hair in the female and yet still somewhat androgynous figure, in which an embryo is housed. This painting shows a new emphasis on circular flow, as exhibited in the containing figures with their archetypal references to female wombs. The entire background of this painting then takes the viewer into a female world, in which not only part object breasts of full-blooded women are visible, but also in which there are acknowledged maternal functions. The artist is no longer disowning her maternal origins. In accepting that she is born from a maternal womb, she can be fully born into her own female body as the woman born of woman!

But the female womb forms are balanced, in the upper corners, by crosses. These crosses, although novel for the artist, show some continuity with her former work, for they may be seen as abstractions of her earlier snake formations and striations. The crosses also suggest an unconscious spiritual meaning, particularly as they appear at the upper edges of the painting, pointing possibly to heaven.

The dialectic between the masculine and feminine parts of the artist is much more flowing and interactive in this painting, and the achievement of overall integration (in contrast to the polarization of masculine and feminine forms) is more fully realized than in earlier works. However, the artist's discomfort concerning the female genitals is still present, as indicated by the disconnected womb imagery and her evasion of presenting the lower portion of the female body where the genitals would be. The masculine muscularity in the female body is also significant as a defensive armor against feminine softness and female vulnerability. Nevertheless, the female part of the artist's personality is born here into the shape of a fully alive and dynamic woman, whereas formerly this female part was presented either as an androgynous embryo with the disguise of phallic finger extensions for genitals or as a disconnected figure with exaggerated female body parts. Now a full female figure is realized! This is the last painting Jane presented to the creative process group.

MOURNING PROCESS CONCURRENT WITH PAINTINGS

During the period Jane painted these pictures, she was also opening to a beginning developmental mourning process, which allowed her early infant self to emerge. Both the group and her individual analysis with me provided a holding environment for this mourning process to occur. By developmental mourning, I mean the mourning related to childhood traumas and losses, which allowed Jane to move on with a self and psychic development that was formerly arrested. The same self-integration that permitted Jane to assimilate formerly split off and disconnected self parts enabled her to portray this self integration process in her paintings.

The split off parts can generally be described as infant parts of her that Jane needed to own in order to become realized as a female. These parts had been previously locked into split off and projected devaluation of the feminine. As Jane painted, she mourned, but the mourning was opened up more fully through the holding environment in the creative process group and during individual treatment. The analysis of her defenses, projections, and transference opened the way to a mourning process that had developmental progressions. Without the emotional holding in her group and in individual therapy, Jane probably would not have proceeded in this developmental progression within her paintings. Rather, she probably would have continued to reenact early fragmenting processes and self-disconnections, as she warded off internal experience. This, as we have seen, revealed itself in surface design without depth or three-dimensionality in her early paintings.

Significant dreams, fantasies, and memories highlighted Jane's mourning process. As long as these dreams, fantasies and memories were unconscious, Jane was compelled to defensively split off basic parts of herself and thereby avoid the primal affects of rage and grief related to the repressed phenomena. This response, which left her in the disconnected state from her repressed interior life, is depicted in the surface quality and the fragmentation of her first paintings. But as the mourning process proceeded, Jane started to connect with disowned (or split off) parts of herself as she no longer needed to maintain a defensive position of self-sufficiency to seal herself off from her pain. The object relationship with the creative process group, and towards the latter end of the second year in the group, with myself as her therapist, provided the critical connections that helped Jane's mourning proceed.

Two dreams especially revealed Jane's oral level infant self split off from consciousness and appearing as intensely vulnerable creatures. The reowning of this infant self permitted her to weep her way into connection with her sealed off feminine and female potential.

The first of these two dreams is of herself as a 2- or 3-year-old toddler who has been left like a feral wolf outside the family home to fend for herself with tiny animals and other creatures. In this dream, Jane sees herself as a naked or half-naked being, who has been shut out of her family home – and out of her mother's kitchen – possibly left to starve. Through glass doors, she looks into this kitchen and sees her family eating, oblivious to her.

In this dream Jane directly identifies with her own infant self. But in the second dream she encounters a being who appears manifestly dependent on her, but who may also be viewed as a part of herself, split off, yet unconsciously connected through projective identification. In this second dream Jane sees a delicate horse that died of starvation through her own neglect in caretaking. She has forgotten to feed the horse, which may represent a child part of herself. In the session in which Jane recounted this dream, she wept profusely, even more full of the pain of grief and longing than when she recounted the first dream to me. Now she felt this intense regret, which is a significant aspect of grief as Klein has spoken of it within a depressive position mourning state. Jane's relationship to the fantasy horse may have been partly like that of her psychological relationship to her children and students (she is a teacher), and perhaps even to her paintings, and certainly to the creatures within her paintings. On the conscious level, she felt she needed to take care of the dependency needs of these others, as a "good" and nurturing mother, yet fearing disappointment with her own capacity to fill this maternal role. But unconsciously, the dream shows how she had also denied for so long her own dependency needs, and certainly the early infant and toddler preoedipal needs now evoked in the context of the analytic transference, both toward me and the creative process group members. Jane tried to evade the consciousness of her own dependence by always experiencing it through projective identification in relation to others, whether the others were her husband, children, students, friends, or analyst.

In the writing and creative process group there had been another female member whom Jane felt a deep need to nurture. Jane saw this woman as more vulnerable and openly needing than even she was. However, this other woman had over time become increasingly willing to expose to the group her own vulnerability to emotional need, as she mourned and also felt the nurturing support of Jane. Through this other group member's example, Jane began to vicariously experience her own dependent needs without directly confronting them. But over time, as the changes in her paintings showed, she did connect with her split off dependent self.

Yet in this second dream, in which Jane saw herself as responsible for nurturing and sustaining the life of a frail horse, she failed to be the good mother that she consciously wished to be. Rather, she let the horse starve to death, perhaps as she had always fantasized herself to have been starved to death emotionally by her mother, particularly during her frail preoedipal years. She knew that she had been a colicky baby as well as that she had not had a natural birth, but had somewhat artificially entered the world through a Caesarian section. It is no wonder then that Jane may have needed to create a natural psychological birth for herself on a symbolic level, through painting baby creatures being born on canvas.

Jane often described her mother as hard and closed, with a stony face – a woman rigid in her schedules and compulsive organization, unable to yield to contact and connection because of an emptiness inside that even as a child Jane had sensed unconsciously. Being dependent on her mother instilled deep terrors in Jane during her childhood. These terrors took the form of annihilation anxiety that she handled in her later childhood by a defensive stance of self-sufficiency. Possessing good internal resources and talents, Jane was able to seclude herself in her room and there work at her own personal projects, withdrawing into her own world within her mother's house.

But viewing herself through this second dream as a depriving and neglectful "bad mother," Jane glimpsed the shadow side of herself. She witnessed herself playing the very role she had assigned to her mother. In her dream about the horse, she became that which she always feared herself to be – her own bad mother. In facing her dream by telling me about it, she faced too the dark unconscious side of her wish to compensate for her mother's deficiencies by being the mother she believed her mother could never be (both compensatory and competitive). Jane was living her worst nightmare in this dream, that of being the very internal bad mother object that she sought to oppose and counteract. Unconsciously, she identified with the horse "child," and also with the oral level bad mother of infant starvation. The unconscious starved child came to consciousness, but with it Jane had to face the immensity of her grief over her own failings in relation to her exaggerated attempt to be a "good mother."

Jane's mourning process was also about confronting the deepest and darkest terrors of her oral infant period. She brought these terrors to consciousness first through symbolic images and then by connecting words to them. Mourning always includes this essential "naming" process. In one dream early in her individual treatment, and later in her creative process group mourning, Jane saw an image of what she identified as "death barges coming to get me." This image captured her fears at the level of annihilation anxiety terror.

At the anal, as opposed to the oral, level of her developmental mourning process, Jane faced memories of a forbidding anal stage mother, whose rigidities overlapped with a possessiveness that could have blocked separation–individuation strivings for Jane if she did not possess the internal resources that have been mentioned. This was the mother who provoked shame and humiliation more than terror. Jane's memories triggered fantasies of this mother, and she experienced these fantasies in projected form within the psychoanalytic transference. She remembered this mother as so rigidly and obsessively organized that she would attack in fits of narcissistic rage if anyone posed a threat to any of her attempts at omnipotent organization.

In infancy her mother forced Jane to eat on a rigid schedule. Later in high school, she vented her rage by throwing Jane's clothing out of her dresser drawers. When Jane came home from school she found all her belongings dumped out on her bed, the demand being obvious that Jane reorganize all her personal items in immaculate fashion. Jane did not miss the threatening rage behind her mother's gesture, and her conscious and unconscious levels of shame were incited each time she reexperienced this gesture. Jane received the message loud and clear that she was being told that she was "bad" for being messy, which could also be read as her mother's claim that she was "dirty." In discovering this unconscious shame, Jane was freed up by the mourning process. She then began to be able to play, in Winnicott's sense of play and the creativity of everyday life, with the concept of being messy, rather than of masochistically ingesting the accusation of being "bad." Jane told the creative process group at this point that she was just enjoying painting "doodies," as if symbolically playing with her feces was one of the greatest pleasures to now be experienced in adulthood, although the harsh maternal treatment of her during toilet training was marked on her for life. Jane had many dreams of overflowing toilets and obsessions with "bowel movements" in the morning to make herself feel "right" during the day. Perhaps the striated snake forms in Jane's paintings represent some more refined forms of feces in her paintings.

The anal rage mother struck a chord of deep anguish in Jane as she remembered a much later, but startling memory, of her mother's reaction to her father lying down to rest on a bed in their household just before his heart attack. She recalls that her father in grave need of rest pulled back the fastidiously made bedspread to lie down only to be verbally assaulted by his wife for spoiling the bed. This memory not only underscores the mother's pathology, but is enlightening as to Jane's own trauma at her hands.

During this two-year period, Jane described conscious memories from her late teens and early adult life. One memory was of her parents condemning her for leaving the garage door partially open after parking her car in it. She related this scolding to her current habit of waking in the morning and thinking that she was "bad" if she didn't get immediately out of bed to wipe up a drop of water left by her husband on the floor after a shower. By recalling these memories in her analytic therapy sessions, Jane was able to link them to her fantasy of being a bad child or bad person. By becoming aware of how she projected it in the transference, she was also able to see how much she projected her bad mother onto the world. One example occurred when Jane imagined me chaining her to my arm with a diamond bracelet, which I could yank anytime I wished to, demonstrating the omnipotent quality of my control over her.

At 12 years old, Jane decided to stand up to her mother and to tell her what she really thought of her. Having seen herself as too compliant, Jane expressed her anger openly to her mother. For Jane it was an act of separation and self-assertion, which she experienced herself as failing miserably at. This incident left Jane alone with her own accusations and hatred of her mother because her mother didn't survive Jane's opinions and feelings with any understanding that her daughter was attempting to communicate something important for them both. Rather, Jane's mother retaliated with the punitive and the abandoning remark, "Things will never be the same between us!" because her mother had reacted to Jane's open and direct confrontation (and probably to the retaliatory impulse involved) with her own vengeance,

Jane was left with her hatred and her unconscious guilt about this hate as she felt it intermingled with her act of assertion. It was at this point in her life that Jane said that she "gave up on words," committing herself more fully to her visual talents as an artist. The memory of this dramatic exchange between mother and daughter emerged into consciousness through a powerful transference experience in which Jane protested when I asked her to refrain from showing me a painting at one point during her individual psychoanalytic treatment. Jane's initial response was extreme anger, casting me into the role of the bad mother, who she saw as depriving. Then the pain behind this ragefull anger opened up and brought a critical piece of mourning through memory. Jane recalled the confrontation with her mother. This memory was evoked when I asked her why she couldn't tell me her feelings and memories in words rather than through a painting. Jane understood why when her association to my question brought the memory of her confrontation with her mother. Words had failed her at that time. Her mother had not received her words as a communication, but only on the presymbolic level as an attack. From then on, words seemed useless to Jane as a means for expressing her deepest feelings and emotions. When I asked her to surrender her visual communication and to try words, her old rage at her mother – so much of which had to be formerly repressed, thereby demanding reenactment and repetitive compulsion – was thrown at me. Between the time of this negative transference blast and her next session, the critical memory came through unconscious connection into consciousness, and Jane willingly recalled it with me the next day. As she did, she grieved and felt the anguish of her lost hope for love, understanding, and relationship with her mother. I could feel a deeply emotional responsiveness in myself, as I empathized with her pain and helped her through the mourning process of putting it into words.

Jane's conscious rejection of her mother had begun when she was a child. At an early age, she had retaliated against her mother's control by vindictively smashing a present her mother had given her. Her retaliatory impulses were strong and powerful, but at this earlier stage were acted out as opposed to being spoken. They would not be expressed in words until she relived this buried past with her mother in the transference with me. Transference allowed Jane to symbolize her retaliatory rage and to begin to feel vulnerable feelings of love and longing for her mother that she had long ago shut off and displaced onto men, first her father, and later, her husband. When Jane shut those feelings off, she had simultaneously devalued her mother, freezing her image of her mother into that of the "bad mother" in response to this traumatic experience.

One way Jane had of rejecting her mother was to devalue and repel her mother's feminine self and her female identification with her mother. This rejection Jane carried out at a body level through her transference projections onto me of the devalued mother (a split off devalued part of her internal world). Jane told me that she viewed any clothing I wore that was not tailored and tweedy as some horrible feminine display, a display she associated to as being like "smelly vaginas." Jane's smelly vagina fantasy was analytically explored by the two of us. Her associations to this transference vision of me – which she acknowledged was imbued with powerful projections from her internal world, split off as parts of her self from past experience – led her back to another significant memory that she was now capable of deeply mourning. When she was about 10 years old, she had entered her mother's room at night and found her in a nightgown. Jane remembered a faint smell, which she labeled, using a 10-year-old's vocabulary, as "yucky!" Later she surmised that maybe her mother had just had sex.

Seeing the progression of Jane's paintings, it is clear that she had split off infant and female parts of herself that she later reowned and connected to through her developmental mourning process, as it manifested in her paintings. Reviewing Jane's transference associations, and her memories as they emerged in the group and into her individual treatment, reveals the nature of her self-rejection, as it corresponded to her mode of rejection of her mother. The memory process in treatment explains the relationship that led to her particular views of her mother, as they came to reside as fantasies within Jane's internal world.

Another element of Jane's mourning process becomes understandable in light of this internal worldview of her mother. For Jane had attempted to compensate for both early and late losses in relation to her mother by idealizing her father and his external masculine persona and image. She wished to have a penis, as revealed later in her analysis when Jane dreamed that in a state of rage she wanted to fuck an image of buttocks "up the ass." She was shocked in the dream when she realized she did not have a penis!

Jane's sublimated form of identifying with her fantasy of her father's phallic grandeur was to take on what she later called a "constructed identity," as opposed to a true identity. This constructed identity consisted of wearing clothes and sometimes costumes that presented her as a sharply defined phallic, as opposed to, feminine being. In the extreme form of this constructed phallic identity, Jane went to parties dressed in dramatic masculine attire, such as her "Napoleon" outfit. During the course of Jane's mourning process, she began to surrender this constructed phallic identity, which she had used as a compensatory penis. This phase of her recovery may be seen in her paintings when she substituted head-dresses for snakes and overt penises. Jane felt a devastating loss in relinquishing the use of her constructed identity, or what I would call an image presentation or an "image object," or an "image self" or false self. However, the loss was repaired and compensated for by her newfound authentic identity as a full woman, as shown in the evolution of her art.

Chapter 15

Conclusion

Unlike Emily Dickinson, who psychically wed her demon lover as she withdrew increasingly from life, all the clinical subjects in this book enter the world more fully as they mourn and relinquish old object ties. They contact the more vulnerable sides of their personalities. Then they yield to love in relationship. Simultaneously, they yield to spontaneous creative self-expression from contact with their internal worlds.

Through the words and images of the analysands, there is continuing growth in self-agency, self-reflection, interiority, whole object relatedness, and empathy – as separation–individuation and the accompanying integration of split off self parts takes place through developmental phases of mourning. In addition, a spiritual dimension emerges as a transitional phase in treatment, explicitly, in some cases, implicitly in others.

June expresses yearnings for an idealized object that transform into a yearning for God. All this is seen in the transference, as she first dreams of entering psychoanalysis as a point of entry into the spiritual land of Tibet, the home of Zen Buddhism and the Dalai Lama. June's individuation comes through merging in fantasy and then through separating in reality by confronting her grief. June's unique identity and "idiom" develops (Bollas 1999) as she individuates through the rage, love, and grief of mourning within the "therapeutic object relationship" (Grunes 1985), and as she surrenders to her wishes to merge with the analyst within the transference relationship in combined affect states, and in psychic fantasies that constitute idealizing and twinship transferences (Kohut 1971). Such merger transferences (narcissistic or self object transferences) operate side by side with split off bad object transferences that are temporarily displaced outside the treatment and then are later reowned within the transference.

June mourns major losses of her life, as the transference allows June's grief over separation from each parent object in the internal world to emerge. She surrenders to her separation grief and to the grief of an early infant illness that complicated the separation phases with a mother who was already resistant to separation. The analyst, in turn, surrenders to June's wishes to merge affectively, allowing the fantasies of merger to come to consciousness – and allowing split off states of childhood need to be integrated into the central self. The analyst also yields to June's journeys into separation and to her struggle to individuate and find her own unique idiom.

The interpenetrating surrender can be seen to be essential to the continuing flow of the mourning process while grief evolves backward into varying phases of June's life throughout her treatment. This critical surrender, which involves profound contact with June's internal world through grief affect, helps her to feel hate and love for both her parents. Through such profound grief memory, lived in the present, she comes to an understanding of the severe deprivation and emotional abuse that she suffered at the hands of her father, while simultaneously enduring the punitive reactions of her mother to her moves towards separation. Ultimately, June mourns a current separation that allows her increasingly to surrender to letting go, in the face of conscious yearnings to cling to the husband who had become a replacement for both her father and mother on various psychic levels.

The conscious reliving of trauma seen in this case, and in the others in this volume illustrates how an object relations therapy that involves facing the pain of trauma, rather than going around it, is distinctly different from spiritual approaches that try to transcend trauma. The latter discourage rather than encourage the conscious facing of the pain. Only by confronting the psychic pain can the agonizing losses involved with any trauma be mourned.

When transcendence is attempted without the active mourning of trauma, psychic arrest inevitably results; it can feel, in terms of internal object relations, like psychic possession. Ultimately, the trauma is reenacted as in the story of Emily Dickinson, the trauma is re-enacted despite the yearning of healthy parts of the personality to connect with the spiritual realm.

To truly heal trauma, the spiritual dimensions of life need to be contacted through the grounded avenue of body and heart connection. This involves consciously facing the pain that is either sealed off in splitting and (sometimes somaticized) dissociation or repressed into a symbolic unconscious. When Dickinson wrote "To scan a ghost is faint, but grappling conquers," she had the right idea: she tried to use her symbolic capacities to consciously face her pain. But she failed at ultimate reparation because she could not mourn on her own, as did Emily Brontë, Anne Sexton, Virginia Woolf, Edith Sitwell, Sylvia Plath, Katherine Mansfield, Diane Arbus, and so many others. Due to the lack of a good enough object internalization to allow the sustained capacity to tolerate rage and grief affect in order to mourn, Dickinson had to shut down her heart and even, to some extent, her mind as she deteriorated psychologically, rather than progressed.

By contrast, in the foregoing cases of successful mourning, where the holding environment and therapeutic relationship in treatment allowed the process to evolve in natural developmental phases, the core psychic connections opened as the heart was allowed to open through the healing of critical and primal early trauma. Therefore, the transcendence intrinsic to love and intimacy and to creativity and self-expression could emerge.

Experiencing spirituality without a heart connection, however, leads to a radical switch from yearnings to merge with a god-like muse into a state of possession by an internal object, which can be projected out and externalized as a demonic figure. This demonic figure often surfaces as the proverbial demon lover figure so vividly depicted in the poetry, prose, and art of brilliant woman creators with psychic arrest from primal trauma. The demon lover figure is an object relations symptom of a pathological mourning state, which results in the developmental arrest. Only through heart connections, based on more love than hate towards one's internal objects, can the psychic avenues to development be opened. More love than hate is needed to process mourning. More love than hate is needed to revive or build an internal whole object so that external object relationships, based on an internal psychic blueprint, can be sustained and enhanced.

Those who seek transcendence but end up with psychic possession enter a living death in the form of psychic paralysis. The female sculptor, Camille Claudel, is a striking example of this psychic possession enacted concretely. She spent the last thirty years of her life incarcerated in a French mental asylum, where she languished away without any artistic work or artistic interest while maintaining the conviction that her longtime lover Auguste Rodin was literally a demon possessing her. She created her own state of psychic possession by displacing onto her former male muse a denied hatred for her mother who was actually responsible for Claudel's extended incarceration. Claudel, like many others with early trauma, was unable to heal her traumatized self core and move on, in the absence of the forum for mourning provided by object relations treatment.

To reconnect with one's heart, one must relive trauma on an affective level that forms psychic links rather than disrupting them (Bion 1963). Such emotional reliving in the sense of developing consciousness and agency in one's current life always involves pain, coexisting with aggression rooted in abandonment/depression/rage and the terrors of annihilation anxiety.

In the case of Phillip, who deeply wished to love and cure his father, we saw how the latter's utter rejection of Phillip's vulnerable internal self (his true self) caused the son to close off his heart. It remained closed until he could mourn in object relations psychoanalysis. Phillip saw his own wounded and rejected child self metaphorically in the vivid image of Jesus Christ – representing endurance of suffering while sustaining the capacity to love. It was through facing losses from many childhood phases of the past, even those that Phillip associated to past life experiences, that he felt able to connect with his internal wounded self and still psychically survive. Phillip discovered that he could sustain the capacity to love even while remembering the childhood emotional abuse that he was exposed to. This gave him hope and a new faith in life and relationship.

Healing of early trauma is needed for full acceptance, even though real healing (as opposed to manic reparation) is never completed and the vulnerability to new wounding remains. When Dickinson inevitably failed to mourn and heal her early trauma on her own, not having the holding environment of treatment and the expertise of an analyst acquainted with developmental mourning, she tried to psychically compensate through a pronounced masculine identification based on her yearnings to both merge with and identify with her father, who she also saw as a spiritual figure who endowed her with potential symbolic capacities. In her compensatory state of masculine identification, without the balancing identification with an adequate feminine figure (her mother was schizoid and emotionally detached), and without the development of her child self into a vulnerable but powerful feminine form, she became metallic and emotionally withdrew behind rigid and constricting schizoid defenses. This caused Dickinson to write: "I can kill but I cannot die" (1960: 369). She constructed a false self through her masculine identification, one which could kill through aggression but had no feminine yielding (and spiritual) potential to surrender or "die." She became a victim to this false self.

Dickinson understood that the pathological mourning state in which she lived, encased in a false masculine self, is death to the child self that grows up into the vulnerable side of the personality and endows the feminine self with life and energy. In her poetry, Dickinson cried out about her victimization. She broadcast themes of demon lover possession. As I spoke of in the early theoretical chapters, Dickinson wrote of "The metallic god who drills his welcome in" and of the god who let loose one thunderbolt that "scalped" her "naked soul." Her psychic fragility and annihilation anxiety terrors, within a powerful abandonment depression demon lover theme, are clearly articulated in the words, pauses and arrests in her poetry. In fact, the dashes used by the poet express the blankness of the infant's inside, when disconnected from the mother (Wolff 1986).

We see in the case of June how what begins as an empty self that feels as through she has a metallic pipe from her head down to her legs, yields to a fully heart-connected feminine self through mourning within treatment. Phillip too, had an initial empty self feeling that shared some of this metallic quality. Only after entering a grieving process that he characterized as mourning for seven generations of grief did his internal state change and in turn generate profound changes in his external object relations. His psychic merger had been his way of trying both to protect his father from his own rage and to rescue his father's internal wounded child self from its sealed off and injured state. The result was the disowning of his own child self, which left Phillip empty and also at the mercy of his father's continuing abusive attacks on him. Now, however, Phillip reowns a split off self by experiencing his rage and by mourning the loss attendant on merging with his father. To separate meant, for Phillip, experiencing the pain of deep grief and feeling the agony of a frustrated love for his father that could never survive in the face of his father's actuality. When Phillip surrenders to the pain and anguish of this grief he is internally rewarded with being able to tolerate and symbolize his rage so that he recognizes it in relation to other male authority figures. He is also rewarded by having his internal emptiness yield to the softer affect states of sad grief loss and then to a sad but profound love. Ultimately, his life energy is renewed through contacting his continuing capacity to love and thus to also create from the internal loving object core within.

Like June, he feels continuously reborn with each phase of a critical developmental mourning process. Phillip's separation mourning in relation to his father, which later leads to mourning his father's actual death, is followed by and sometimes accompanied by his mourning for the idealized mother that he projects onto the analyst, when he isn't projecting the father transference onto her. The mother whom he wishes to make love to, to marry, to merge with, to be held by again as he was at the age of 2, is also the mother who he experiences as having overwhelming emotional needs that she inappropriately placed upon him.

While mourning his love of an imperfect and insatiably needy mother, who could never protect him from a father whom she too was in fact victimized by, he contacts an image that symbolizes his dilemmas in the world of relationships with women. He psychically enters his mother's womb by picturing sexual entry into his mother's body as he imagines making love to me, his analyst, in the transference. Then he finds himself trapped in a railway tunnel – the archetypal labyrinth and the negative and demonic and engulfing side of the yearned for mother of primal nurturance and fantasized erotic love.

Through deep grieving on the psychoanalytic couch, Phillip encountered the early love for his mother that he had repressed. He also encountered the love for his father that had been so continually frustrated throughout his life, leaving him in a masochistic position with men and often in a sadistic position with women. Facing this love also allowed Phillip's combination of guilt and hate to turn into regret, an important developmental aspect of the mourning process. After analyzing his hate, traumas, losses, and the frustration in relation to his internal parent objects, Phillip was able to open to renewed love, to surrender to the heart connections that would render him capable of adult intimacy. For the first time in most of his adulthood as a grown man Phillip yielded to love during erotic desire in sex, making a profound connection with a woman who is to become his fiancée and then his wife. For the first time he imagines a loving marriage, entirely different from his parents' tortured model, and furthermore imagines fathering a child with the woman he loves. He and his wife both open to spiritual studies together as well.

Mourning has evolved for Phillip, as for June and Laura, as well as for the other analysands in this book, through the conscious feeling of the internal wounds, rather than through sealing off the wounds and trying to transcend them. In retrospect, these phases appear to have been transitional stages in treatment, and in the developmental process of separation that Phillip was navigating through the mourning process. The spiritual beliefs associated with these transitional phases endure in his later psychic evolution, but they become less prominent in his mourning process later on, as he then relates directly to his psychodynamic conflicts in terms of his interpersonal relationships. The spiritual and transitional experiences become less important as literal truths as Phillip's interpersonal world becomes alive with day-to-day intimacy and whole self experience. Yet, the metaphors still stand, and Phillip continues to find them useful. Such transitional phase spiritual dynamics can be seen vividly as well in the case of June. To some extent, this is seen also in the case of Laura, where the emergence of the sealed off infant self, with its awakening feminine self potential can be seen to be a mid phase phenomenon in her developmental mourning process.

In the case of Laura we see how the female self that had been split off and dissociated, leaving a masculine false-self façade, became reborn in a dream of an infant symbiosis with idealized and innocent (without glasses–without insight) female selves. In this dream Laura sought to unite with the nude, innocent, infant and feminine forms in her complicated strivings for selfhood and for individuation. She threw off her false masculine construction, her false self, and was liberated in the psychic fantasy of merger with innate and life-giving female figures. However, to be joined with these figures, Laura had to relinquish insight and conscious knowledge as she had to surrender her glasses in the dream. Through mourning the losses related to childhood trauma, Laura reached a stage where her potential true self with its disowned feminine form could be reowned and then could begin to be assimilated into her psyche. However, first she had to reown the female genitals that she had given away to the analyst in psychic fantasy. She resisted doing so, but her unconscious warns her of the loss, and her analyst confronts her. She awakened from her dream of innocence and accepted the responsibilities and wardrobe (both psychic and concrete) of adult femininity.

Together with this rebirth into a renewed innocence that precludes symbolization and insight (without glasses and naked in her dream) came the grief of facing the choice of giving up the feminine in its potential maternal aspect, as Laura confronted a dream of having her uterus surgically removed. Many forms of mourning and grief contributed to the reintegrating of a feminine self that Laura had split off and put into the analyst through projective identification. The dream of the analyst going off with the very female genitals that Laura had freely given her highlighted the psychic defense of disowning her adult female side. The reintegration of the female genitals and feminine self became the avenue to self-agency and self-reflection and to the related capacities for love and creativity on a symbolic level. The erotic desires became conscious and separate from the incestuous wishes expressed repeatedly in the transference as the heart survives the wounds of mourning and loss.

The manic defense, evidenced in Laura's dream of an alcoholic dance that never stops, also yields to the pain and reality of grief, as well as to Laura's regret for her failure to be there for her parents at the end of their lives as much as she would have liked to have been. By this point she is able to forgive them (and indeed has entered a personal spiritual place), having come to own her retaliatory impulses now that she sees the parental abandonment of her childhood with increasing clarity.

In all the cases illustrated in this book, when the patient can feel the pain of childhood traumas, she or he becomes able to grieve loss and able to understand current anger as having elements of infant and childhood rage experience, as well as having elements of the real and distorted childhood victimization. The deprivations and abuses must be faced without denial to find the true self, but the rage and hate related to them also need to be relinquished as the losses of unrequited love are mourned and forgiven.

In the case of Jane, the female artist whose paintings illustrate the journey of her developmental mourning, the capacity for self-expression in words as well as images is regained. Jane's negative transference leads to a 12-year-old memory of confronting her mother with her anger, and being faced with an emotional abandonment: "Things will never be the same between us!" The artist, forced to remember through the expression of her transferential rage towards the female analyst, has the acute insight that she had unconsciously given up on words when traumatized by her mother's emotionally abandoning hatred. Filled with experiences of annihilation anxiety, felt consciously for the first time during her psychoanalysis, Jane realizes that she had to give up on words to psychically survive her mother's rejection. She splits off her rage into self-fragmenting images in her paintings. However, when challenged to feel and remember in analysis she realizes she has created images of death, "death barges coming to get her," that are harshly resonant with Emily Dickinson's poems on being led to the land of death by a dark and mercurial gentleman, a refined, later life fantasy of Dickinson's demon lover.

The dissociated and repressed rage has created a continuing unconscious threat of self-annihilation that had appeared in numerous symptoms, including the loss of words for self-expression. When Jane regained words as tools for self-expression she was able to use them to gain psychological insight into the developmental mourning process as it unfolded in her object relations psychoanalysis.

Once again, the mourning process negotiates the interplay between the separation–individuation progression described by American object relations theorists (e.g. Margaret Mahler), and the integration of split off self-parts (in Jane's case the feminine self) described by British object relations theorists, stemming back to Melanie Klein. The whole self of the Kleinians can be paralleled to the true self of D.W. Winnicott and also to the separated and individuated self of Margaret Mahler. When we integrate split off parts, along with the affects and part objects attached to them, we are propelling separation–individuation forward. Grief affect, and the insight of memory and differentiation that accompanies it, is needed to further an individuation process that calls for separation, differentiation, and integration of disowned impulses, affects, and self and object constellations that have remained merged since childhood.

In the case of Larry, the male artist, a similar process of self-integration interactive with separation–individuation is seen. His paintings and his dreams tell the tale and they tell a parallel tale. In his paintings, where once there were geometrical constructions that barricaded one part of the self against the others, as they barricaded those in the internal world from one another, there were later people alive and talking to each other – people laughing, smiling and being together. As Larry's mourning process proceeded, the barriers yielded to avenues that could join one element of self and internal world to another. This led into a path of friendship and ultimately into a path of eroticism combined with love. The closed and darkened self, represented in the dreams by a shut-off hut in the wilderness or desert, comes to life, just as the human objects emerge into vital form; likewise, the shut-off shack becomes an elegant New England house, with open windows, curtains, furnishing and a comfortable porch – a home designed for the pleasure of its inhabitants, who now are capable of existing in a state of "being" and of taking in the environment.

As Larry's capacities for tolerating the painful grief affects of mourning developed so did his ability to tolerate consciousness of both erotic and aggressive impulses and to integrate the two. Grief-laden sadness evolved out of frozen anger and repressed rage, as early child yearnings came to consciousness within mourning. Such consciousness brought love and desire to life again. The shame and deprivation experiences that caused the repression of love and desire, and the aggression that empowered them, had been faced, remembered and understood.

With progressive developmental phases of mourning, evidenced in the artwork, Larry was able to open symbolic capacities that had lain dormant. Then, he could symbolize the guilt that unconsciously paralyzed him in the form of a conscious and poignant regret. As he took increasing ownership of his feelings, fantasies and impulses, Larry's interiority and sense of self-agency expanded. His dreams became alive with color and texture, as did his paintings; his sense of humor emerged as the grief of childhood loss and disappointment came to consciousness and was defined. And as Larry became proficient at initiating mourning by tolerating grief affects, he could be seen as confirmation of Melanie Klein's promoting of psychological development through the integration of aggression into consciousness after analysis of the resistances encoded in psychic fantasy formations, and of Fairbairn's integration of a split off libidinal self into the central self area.

In sum, the developmental mourning process, as a paradigm of object relations psychoanalysis, can be seen to offer an integration of American and British object relations theory in its application to clinical work. The theory in this book has been an attempt to define the intricacies of developmental mourning as an alive clinical process that can mediate all aspects of psychic change, as it occurs through the relinquishing of old and pathological internal object ties.

This new metapsychology is a natural outgrowth of psychoanalytic theory, dating back to Freud, as articulated here in the early chapters on the explicit and implicit role of mourning process in Freud and in each of the major British theorists. While the American theorists could not be outlined in the same detail, the major impact of Mahler's separation–individuation theory has been defined throughout the volume, along with references to Thomas Ogden, James Masterson, Sheldon Bach, Jeffrey Seinfeld, etc.

The clinical cases bring the theory to life, providing us with an in-depth process to substantiate the theoretical roadmap. Three of them are particularly illustrative of how developmental mourning unfolds out of the ashes of pathological mourning and psychic arrest. The interplay of the holding environment, the real analyst as interactive, and the transference emerging from internal object projections (dissociated and repressed), all emerge clearly within the evolving context of mourning through developmental stages. And revelation of each analysand's unfolding awareness of her or his mourning process as it is lived in treatment is optimized as each is allowed to articulate her/his own personal understanding of developmental themes and her/his personal vision of the spiritual dimension of psychic experience.

Notes

2 A new metapsychology for clinical phenomenology and psychic health

1 See Kavaler-Adler on "Charlotte Brontë and the feminine self" (1990).
2 See Daniel Stern (1985) on "rigs" of self and other that are internalized since infancy.

3 A phenomenological theory of developmental mourning

1 This psychic suffering is described by Klein as a depressive position ownership of aggression, and as the conscious facing of guilt and loss, through grief affect. Betty Joseph (1989) also writes of suffering the kind of pain that precedes the depressive position connection with the object in mourning (the one lost or the one towards whom one feels guilty). Joseph describes this kind of pain as existing on the border of the psychic and the physical worlds. It is the pain of being psychically born after one's psychic development has been arrested, but it is not yet the pain related to a differentiated object. It is the pain of entering or reentering reality, after living with vital parts of the self, operating in a dissociated form. It is the kind of pain that definitely depends on the presence of another to make it bearable, the other who can be with the person (the patient throughout the process of psychical birth, without prematurely imposing interpretive knowledge on her. It is an emotional state of contact and transformation that, still pre-symbolic, is not yet receptive to cognitive formulations or functions.
2 Another way of conceptualizing this alive heart of libidinal object longings in the self might be in terms of D.W. Winnicott's theory of the "true self" (1974). For the true self to evolve out of its internal psychic potential, an outside other must be present who is willing to surrender her own needs and to serve as a subjective object (related to Heinz Kohut's "self-object"). This would either be the mother during the infant's development, or the analyst during an object relations treatment, in which primal trauma is relived and brought to a symbolic level of understanding. The transitional space between the internal world and the outside subjective object is the free area for potential development of true self-spontaneity, play, and self-initiating gesture.

4 Mourning as explicit and implicit in psychoanalytic theory

1 Here I speak of true affect love in contrast to an idealistic worship of an "image object" (Kavaler-Adler 1996). In idealistic worship, the attachment to an image object is not based on an affective tie to an object with whom one has had emotional and psychic contact and connection, but on the wish to see ourselves as identified with the image represented by the object. This image can sometimes take the form of a conceptual ideal or philosophy.

6 The case of June, Part 1

1 See Balint on the "witnesss" to mourning in *The Basic Fault* 1979.

7 The case of June, Part 2

1 A collapsed dialectic, with no transitional space, in Winnicott's language, or with no third intersubjective area, in Thomas Ogden's terms.
2 At this earlier time, this statement seems to reflect a projection of her large soul. There is less immediate feeling behind this statement than later on when she feels something evolving in her as she is evolving with me.

10 The case of Phillip, Part 2

1 Fairbairn (1952) speaks of these sealed off areas of the psyche as split off parts (libidinal and antilibidinal egos), split off from the "central ego" area of the central self.
2 Bion addresses Phillip's discovery of the suffering of pain as being intimately joined with the capacity to feel joy. He wrote: "People exist who are so intolerant of pain or frustration (or in whom pain or frustration is so intolerable) that they feel the pain but will not suffer it and so cannot be said to discover it. The patient who will not suffer pain fails to 'suffer' pleasure" (Joseph 1989: 9).
3 See Ronald Fairbairn (1952) on the "poison pie" that must be eaten because it is the only food. This is a metaphorical explanation for the forced swallowing of the bad parent as an internal object, since the primal object is the only source of psychic nurturance in the beginning.
4 See George Pollack's many publications on mourning as a psychic liberation process.

References

Bach, S. (1985) *Narcissistic States and the Therapeutic Process*, Newvale: Jason Aronson.

Balint, M. (1965) *Primary Love and Psychoanalytic Technique,* London: Routledge.

—— (1979) T*he Basic Fault,* New York: Brunner Mazel.

Bennet, P. (1990) *My Life a Loaded Gun . . . Dickinson, Plath, Rich and Female Creativity*, Urbana: University of Illinois Press.

Bion, W. (1988) *Attention and Interpretation*, London: Karnac.

—— (1989) *Elements of Psychoanalysis,* London: Karnac.

Bollas, C. (1989) *The Shadow of the Object: Psychoanalysis of the Unthought Known*, New York: Columbia University Press.

—— (1999a) *The Mystery of Things*, New York: Routledge.

—— (1999b) *Hysteria*, New York: Routledge.

Bowlby, J. (1963) 'Pathological mourning and childhood mourning,' in R. Frankiel (ed.) *Essential Papers on Object Loss*, New York: New York University Press.

Brontë, E. (1941) in C.W. Hatfield (ed.) *The Complete Poems of Emily Jane Brontë*, New York: Columbia University Press.

Caper, S. (1988) *Klein*, Newvale: Jason Aronson.

Cody, J. (1971) *After Great Pain: The Inner Life of Emily Dickinson*, Cambridge: Harvard University Press.

Dickinson, E. (1960) in T.H. Johnson (ed.) *The Complete Poems of Emily Dickinson*, Boston: Little, Brown.

Eigen, M. (1996) *Psychic Deadness,* Newvale: Jason Aronson.

Fairbairn, R. (1952) *Psychoanalytic Studies of the Personality*, London: Routledge & Kegan Paul.

Freud, S. (1917) 'Mourning and melancholia,' in *Collected Papers*, 7: 152–73.

—— (1997, 1931) 'Female sexuality,' in *Sexuality and the Psychology of Love*, New York: Touchstone Books.

Greenberg, J. and Mitchell, S. (1983) *Object Relations in Psychoanalytic Theory*, Cambridge: Harvard University Press.

Grosskurth, P. (1986) *Melanie Klein, Her World and Her Work*, New York: Knopf.

—— (1996) 'Transformations in O,' *Journal of Melanie Klein and Object Relations* 14: 109–41.

Grotstein, J. (1993) personal communication.

Grunes, M. (1984) 'The therapeutic object relationship,' *Psychoanalytic Review* 71: 123–43.

Guntrip, H. (1976) *Schizoid Phenomena, Object Relations and the Self,* Madison: International Universities Press.

Hurvich, M. (1997) personal communication, New York.

Jacobson, E. (1964) *The Self and the Object World,* Madison: International Universities Press.

Johnson, T.H. (ed.) (1960) *The Complete Poems of Emily Dickinson,* Boston: Little, Brown.

Joseph, B. (1989) *Psychic Equilibrium and Psychic Change: Selected Papers of Betty Joseph,* New Library of Psychoanalysis, 9, New York: Routledge.

Kaplan, L. (1996) *Female Perversions,* Newvale: Jason Aronson.

Kavaler-Adler, S. (1985) 'Mirror mirror on the wall,' *Journal of Comprehensive Psychotherapy* 5: 1–38.

——(1988) 'Diane Arbus and the demon lover,' *American Journal of Psychoanalysis* 48, 4: 366–70.

——(1990) 'Charlotte Bronte and the feminine self,' *American Journal of Psychoanalysis,* 50, 1: 37–43.

——(1992) 'Mourning and erotic transference,' *International Journal of Psycho-Analysis* 73, 3: 527–39.

——(1993) 'Object relations issues in the treatment of the preoedipal character,' *American Journal of Psychoanalysis,* 53, 1: 19–34.

——(1993) *The Compulsion to Create: A Pyschoanalytic Study of Woman Artists,* New York: Routledge. Republished as *The Compulsion to Create: Women Writers and their Demon Lovers* by OtherPress (2000).

——(1995) 'Opening up blocked mourning in the preoedipal character,' *American Journal of Psychoanalysis* 55, 2: 145–68.

——(1996) *The Creative Mystique,* New York: Routledge.

——(1998) 'Vaginal core or vampire mouth: visceral manifestation of envy in women: the protosymbolic politics of object relations,' in N. Burke (ed.) *Gender & Envy,* New York: Routledge.

——(2000) *The Compulsion to Create,* New York: OtherPress .

Kelley Von Buren, A. (1971) *The Novels of Virginia Woolf, Fact and Vision,* Chicago: University of Chicago Press.

Kernberg, O. (1985) *Borderline Conditions and Pathological Narcissism* (Master Work Series), Newvale: Jason Aronson.

——(1998) '*Perversions*', Division 39 Annual Conference, American Psychological Association, Boston.

Khan, M. (1974) *The Privacy of the Self,* Madison: International Universities Press.

Klein, M. (1940) 'Mourning and its relation to manic depressive states' in *Love, Guilt and Reparation and Other Works 1921–1945,* London: Hogarth.

——(1975, 1940) *Love, Guilt and Reparation and Other Works 1921–1945,* London: Hogarth.

——(1980, 1946) 'Notes on some schizoid mechanisms,' in *Envy and Gratitude and Other Works 1946–1963,* London: Hogarth.

——(1980, 1957) 'Envy and gratitude', in *Envy and Gratitude and Other Works 1946–1963,* London: Hogarth.

Kohut, H. (1971) *The Analysis of the Self,* Madison: International Universities Press.

——(1977) *Restoration of the Self,* Madison: International Universities Press.

Kubie, L. (1958) *The Neurotic Distortion of the Creative Process,* New York: Farrar, Straus & Giroux.

Lachmann, F. M., Lichtenberg, J.D. and Fosshage, J.L. (1992) *Self and Motivational Systems,* Hillsdale: Analytic Press.

Loewald, H. (1979) 'The waning of the Oedipus complex,' in *Papers on Psychoanalysis,* New Haven: Yale University Press.

Lorenz, K. (1974) *On Aggression*, New York: Harvest Books.

McDougall, J. (1980) *A Plea for a Measure of Abnormality*, Madison: International Universities Press.

—— (1995) *The Many Faces of Eros: A Psychoanalytic Exploration of Human Sexuality*, New York: W.W. Norton.

Mahler, M., Pine, F. and Bergman, A. (1975) *The Psychological Birth of The Human Infant*, Newvale: Jason Aronson.

Masterson, J. (1976) *Psychotherapy of the Borderline Personality: A Developmental Approach*, New York: Brunner Mazel.

—— (1981) *The Narcissistic and Borderline Disorders*, New York: Brunner Mazel.

—— (1985) *The Real Self*, New York: Brunner Mazel.

—— (1996) personal communication.

Miller, A. (1983) *For Your Own Good*, New York: Farrar, Straus and Giroux.

—— (1986) *Prisoners of Childhood*, New York: Basic Books.

Miller, J. (1989) *The Way of Suffering: A Geography of Crisis*, New York: Georgetown University Press.

Mitchell, S. (1993) *Hope and Dread in Psychoanalysis*, New York: Basic Books.

Modell, A. (1976) 'The holding environment and the therapeutic action of psychoanalysis,' *Journal of the American Psychoanalytic Association*, 24: 285–308.

Morgan, R. (1986) *Demon Lover: On the Sexuality of Terrorism*, New York: W.W. Norton.

Ogden, T. (1986) *Matrix of the Mind*, Newvale: Jason Aronson.

—— (1994) *Subjects of Analysis*, Newvale: Jason Aronson.

Peck, M.S. (1978) *The Road Less Traveled and Beyond*, New York: Simon & Schuster.

—— (1993) *Further Along the Road Less Traveled*, New York: Simon & Schuster.

Plath, S. (1961) *Ariel*, New York: Harcourt Brace Jovanovich.

Seinfeld, J. (1990) *The Bad Object*, Newvale: Jason Aronson.

—— (1993) *Interpreting and Holding*, Newvale: Jason Aronson.

Sewall, R. (1974) *The Life of Emily Dickinson*, New York: Farrar, Straus & Giroux.

Steiner, J. (1993) *Psychic Retreats*, New York: Routledge.

Stern, D. (1985) *The Interpersonal World of the Infant*, Newvale: Jason Aronson.

Sutherland, J.D. (1989) *Fairbairn's Journey into the Interior*, New York: Free Association Books.

Winnicott, D.W. (1965, 1963) 'The capacity to be alone', in D.W. Winnicott *Maturational Processes and the Facilitating Environment*, Madison, CT: International Universities Press.

—— (1965, 1963) 'The development of the capacity for concern,' in D.W. Winnicott *Maturational Processes and the Facilitating Environment*, Madison, CT: International Universities Press.

—— (1971, 1969) 'The use of an object and relating through identifications,' in D.W. Winnicott *Playing and Reality*, Harmondsworth: Penguin.

—— (1971) *Playing and Reality*, Harmondsworth: Penguin.

—— (1974) 'Fear of Breakdown,' *International Review of Psychoanalysis* 1: 103–7.

—— (1975) 'Hate in the counter transference,' in D.W. Winnicott *Through Paediatrics to Psycho-Analysis: Collected Papers*, New York: Basic Books.

—— (1982, 1963) 'On communicating and not communicating: leading to a study of certain opposites', in D.W. Winnicott *Maturational Processes and the Facilitating Environment*, Madison, CT: International Universities Press.

—— (1982) 'Transitional objects and transitional phenomena', in D.W. Winnicott *Playing and Reality*, New York: Routledge.

Wolff, C. G. (1986) Emily Dickinson, New York: Knopf.
Wright, K. (1991) *Vision and Separation,* Newvale: Jason Aronson.

Index

abandonment vii–viii, 75; demon lover 67; June's case 141; Laura's case 194, 196, 201, 213, 220, 277; Phillip's case 185; reliving of trauma 274

abandonment depression: communicative matching 102; developmental mourning 2; Dickinson 100, 275; Jane's case 253; June's case 85–6, 92, 93, 99, 103–4; Laura's case 221, 222, 235; Masterson 2, 28, 37, 85–6, 100; separation 37, 138

abused children 64–6

addiction objects 80

addictive behaviors 81, 84, 107, 123, 138, 186

adult models 20

aggression 7, 13, 14, 118–19; antilibidinal ego 30; Bowlby 68–9; capacity for gratitude 240; demon lover 4, 45; depressive position 138; existential guilt 232; hostile 8, 15, 17–18, 66, 69, 75, 93, 195; inward 54; June's case 91, 100–1, 110; Klein 56, 57–9, 61, 68–9, 118, 119; Larry's case 245, 246, 249, 279; Laura's case 195, 201; the melancholic 49, 50, 52, 53, 55, 59; nightmares 22; ownership of 23; parents 52, 93; persecutory 8; Phillip's case 150, 168, 169, 180–1, 190; reliving of trauma 274; sadomasochistic 12, 66; self-attack 50; split off 9, 22, 55, 61; unblocking 32; Winnicott 37, 74, 75, 76, 79; see also anger; hostility; passive-aggressive behavior; rage

alcoholism 92, 138

alpha elements 9, 38, 45, 65

ambivalence 39, 45, 47, 50, 117

anal stage mother 268

anger: Bowlby 69–70; June's case 143; Larry's case 279; Laura's case 232, 233, 234; Phillip's case 156, 157, 163, 181; see also aggression; rage

annihilation anxiety 21, 75, 274; Dickinson 275; inside world 31; Jane's case 278; June's case 141, 142, 144; Larry's case 267; Phillip's case 161, 185; see also self-annihilation

antilibidinal ego 26, 27, 30, 31, 66, 92; attack on the self 15, 23, 51–2, 53; belief in one's own badness 138; emotional connection 33; internal objects 62; as internal saboteur 4, 36, 60; June's case 83, 93, 95, 96, 106, 108, 125; Laura's case 195; Masterson 93; object representation 97; Phillip's case 188; psychic conflict 35

anxiety: aggression 18; inside world 31; June's case 88, 123; see also annihilation anxiety

Arbus, Diane 273

archetypes 14–15, 56, 138

arousal: June's case 109, 114, 115; Laura's case 223; Phillip's case 164, 166

assimilation 9, 25, 26, 28, 265; see also self-integration

attachment theory 68

attuned reception 1

avoidance 28

Bach, Sheldon 43, 279

bad objects 2, 4, 7, 9–10; externalized 76; Fairbairn 9, 25–6, 36, 53, 55, 62–6, 97; Freud 47; inside world 32; June's case 106–7, 272; Masterson 93; parent idealization 53; Phillip's case 154–5, 192; split off from self 23–4

Balint, Michael vii, 70–4, 86, 282n; internalization 48; preoedipal stage 61, 225

Balanchine, George 11

beast metaphor 21

benign regression 71, 72, 73

Bennet, P. 91

beta elements 9, 38, 45, 51, 55, 65

29665940R00173

Printed in Great Britain
by Amazon